D0944418

MASTERPLOTS II

POETRY SERIES

MASTERPLOTS II

POETRY SERIES

5

Pro-Ten

Edited by

FRANK N. MAGILL

SALEM PRESS
Pasadena, California   Englewood Cliffs, New Jersey

Library of Congress Cataloging-in-Publication Data
Masterplots II: Poetry series/edited by Frank N. Magill
    p. cm.
    Includes bibliographical references and index.
       1. Poetry—Themes, motives. I. Magill, Frank
    Northen, 1907-   .
PN1110.5.M37   1992   91-44341
809.1—dc20   CIP
ISBN 0-89356-584-9 (set)
ISBN 0-89356-589-x (volume 5)

LIST OF TITLES IN VOLUME 5

MASTERPLOTS II

Poetry Series

PRO FEMINA

Author: Carolyn Kizer (1925-   )
Type of poem: Lyric
First published: 1963; collected in *Knock Upon Silence*, 1965

The Poem

The words *pro femina* are Latin, meaning "for the woman," and the opening line is an imperative sentence: "From Sappho to myself, consider the fate of women." This announcement of the topic is immediately followed by the exclamation in the second line, "How unwomanly to discuss it!" The implication is clear. Women are not to speak of their own history of oppression — or even to recognize it — for to do so might lead to a demand for change. That is precisely what the poem does demand: a change that will end patriarchal control of women's lives.

Forging unity among women to create this change is central to Carolyn Kizer's thesis, and throughout the poem she uses the plural "we" for the narrative speaking voice. "We" thus bonds the speaker and her audience ("real women, like *you* and like *me*") as parts of a whole: women, who together can change the world. The poem develops the thesis through numerous references to traditional societal attitudes about women's "place."

Part 1 addresses the narrator's anger at the way women have been treated. Women are entitled to the same freedom that men take for granted, but women who "howl" for "free will" are scorned and accused of being "cod-piece coveters." Ignore such epithets, says the narrator. Men have denounced women for their vices, but in fact such vices were caused by women being set apart as inferior. Women have traditionally forgiven men or acquiesced and "worshiped God as a man."

Now women are "freed in fact, not in custom," and they can begin to change the customs and lead the world in a new direction. As mothers, they have developed respect for life and place life above abstractions such as "national honor." If women are allowed to speak out and to be more than simply wives and mothers, they can teach society to adopt this attitude of caring; then "we might save the race." Meanwhile, if given the chance, women will change, develop, and grow as they struggle for liberation.

Part 2 addresses the problems that have arisen from man's treatment of women. The poet announces her theme here as the "Independent Woman" (non male-identified). Women have been "maimed" in their efforts to expand the roles alloted to them, for men disdain their unladylike behavior and choose instead the "full-time beauties" (as defined by men). Both women and men need "well-treatment," but men pretend that only women are dependent and use that as the excuse to keep women out of "the meeting," the decision-making.

Women are fitted into roles designed for them by men, thus masking women's true selves and their true participation in humanity. The superficial obsession with women's physical appearance, with all the cosmetics and restrictive clothing (including "shoes with fool heels"), keeps women occupied with trivial vanity while men, in functional "uniform drabness," conduct the business of the world. If a woman refuses to play her male-assigned role, if she uses her mind instead of her looks, men reject her. If she acts out the role of posturing, ravishing sex object, she will not develop her talent and intellect. Women must escape this double-bind; the independent woman will have to create herself.

Part 3 specifically addresses the problems that male dominance has caused for women writers. The narrator refuses to accept a continuation of this dominance and declares: "I will speak about women of letters, for I'm in the racket." The successes, she says, have been single women; the failures have been women who married for security, gave in to self-pity, played helpless to win men's favor, or disparaged other women "to stay in good with the men." Some are "traitors" who say with men that women should remain passive.

Women's writing should not be some "prettily-packaged commodity" but should speak the truth, for women "are the custodians of the world's best-kept secret:/ Merely the private lives of one-half of humanity." Men ignore or patronize women who speak this truth, and some women respond by aping the ways of men. Others use the positions they attain to "flog men for fun, and kick women to maim competition."

Change is underway, however; there is hope of ending the old roles that warped and bound women. If women work hard, join together to stand up for their rights, speak and write the truth they know, and take pride in their freely chosen lives, nothing can stop them. Men and children will share in the luck of living in a world with such women; all humanity will benefit.

Forms and Devices

Like much contemporary poetry in the second half of the twentieth century, "Pro Femina" is written in free verse. There are no syllabics or rhyme to use as a defense between the author and the material. As in any lyric poem, there is a clear sense of the author speaking through the narrative voice to express her own thoughts and feelings.

Kizer assumes an educated reader (audience) familiar with her allusions and references. She assumes, for example, that the opening mention of Sappho, the sixth century B.C. lyric poet, will suggest to the reader the long history of women writers and will also suggest their "fate"; Sappho's works were deliberately and systematically destroyed by men who equated "Sapphism" with lesbianism. The numerous references throughout the poem resonate with meanings and connotations that do not lend themselves to easy synopsis. They provide a compressed rhetoric that gives the poem its force and wit. The individuality of Kizer's writing style exemplifies her central argument that women have a right—a responsibility—to create their own works and their own lives.

Central to the thesis is the use of the first-person-plural pronoun "we." It is a shifting referent, variously meaning we feminists, we women writers, we women in general, but always in the sense of seeing women as the half of humanity whose emerging voices must be heard.

The tone is one of acerbic irony. Mixing the colloquial with suavely elegant phrases, the narrative voice is both tough and insistent. The word choices reveal the problems that rigid gender roles have caused: women maimed, scorned, neutered, turned into "cabbageheads"; women made into scabs (like the scabs who betray striking workers by taking their jobs) who "kick" other women "to stay in good with the men"; women whose lives and writings have been denigrated, denied, and destroyed.

Women have developed qualities that men should adopt: respect for life, caring for others, and "keeping our heads and our pride." Women are asserting the need for new attitudes, and if they "defect to the typewriter" and honestly tell their "secret," all humanity will benefit.

Alliteration, a caustic wit, and punning wordplay (paronomasia) add zest to the argument throughout. "So primp, preen, prink, pluck and prize your flesh,/ All posturings!" says the narrator, scornful of such superficial goals. She speaks of the "toast-and-teasdales," making alliterative and punning reference to Sara Teasdale, the American poet who wrote slight, "sensitive" verses expected of female writers. "But the role of pastoral heroine/ Is not permanent, Jack. We want to get back to the meeting," laughs the narrator warningly. When she says, "even with masculine dominance, we mares and mistresses/ Produced some sleek saboteuses," she at one stroke succinctly suggests that much more could be accomplished if women were given full opportunity, alludes to men's view of women as either wives or mistresses, carries out the image of horses and mistresses as sleek, objects to derogatory feminine endings (such as poetess) by coining the word saboteuse for saboteur, and makes fun of men who cannot even recognize when their beliefs are being attacked.

The poet uses vivid images throughout, as in the three stanzas which critically summarize the way women of the time were expected to dress. Lines such as "Strapped into our girdles, held down, yet uplifted by man's/ Ingenious constructions, holding coiffures in a breeze/ Hobbled and swathed in whimsey, tripping on feminine/ Shoes with fool heels" catalog literal restrictions and lead to the conclusion that such emphasis on appearance keeps women "in thrall" to their own surfaces and trivializes their lives.

The poem uses satire to show the cost exacted from women who insist on more than superficial beauty: "So, Sister, forget yourself a few times and see where it gets you:/ Up the creek, alone with your talent, sans everything else./ You can wait for the menopause, and catch up on your reading." Here as throughout the poem the elliptical allusions (being up a creek without a paddle, or waiting for menopause, when supposedly men would not choose you even if you tried to be a beauty) combine with the sharp and outspoken wit to give a rich texture that implies more than the words first seem to say.

The time to insist upon more is here, Kizer says. It is time to "stand up and be hated" if that is what it takes to break the cycle of devouring and being devoured.

Themes and Meanings

The poem is a feminist manifesto for change. The first-person narrator creates a feminist analysis of the history of women, focusing on women writers, which shows the ways women have been warped by trying to fit into the script that patriarchy has written for them and the challenges that continue to face women as they insist on equality, autonomy, and "free will." The liberation of women is a vital cause whose goal is nothing less than to save the human race. Women make up "one-half of humanity," and their new stories must be lived, spoken, and heard. Society as a whole will gain from this fuller definition of humanity. As Kizer says, "Relax, and let us absorb you. You can learn temperance/ In a more temperate climate."

Kizer is one of the generation of American women poets who were the first group to dismantle existing views of women and speak for a revolution against patriarchal control. Kizer and other poets such as Denise Levertov, Maxine Kumin, Anne Sexton, Adrienne Rich, and Sylvia Plath lifted the constraints on women writing the truth about their lives. They both refused to accept the place society had assigned women and refused to "write like a man." Above all, these poets and others who have followed them think of women as "we." They recognize the need for unity and love among women in the common cause of ending sexism. Carolyn Kizer and her sister poets, like all the most enduring writers, question their society and insist on the creation of a better world.

There have always been exceptional women who recognized and spoke against male dominance. In a 1984 author's note in *Mermaids in the Basement: Poems for Women* Kizer thanks the earlier French writer Simone de Beauvoir for inspiring "Pro Femina." Such thanks could extend back through the nineteenth century women who struggled for suffrage and women's rights, to Mary Wollstonecraft's *A Vindication of the Rights of Woman* in 1792, or back farther than male-dominated history has allowed women to see. Never, however, have so many women writers spoken out at the same time and gained such a wide and receptive audience as in the last third of the twentieth century. "Pro Femina" was published in 1963, half a dozen years before the contemporary women's movement gained widespread momentum or public attention.

Kizer's poetry was in the forefront of that movement; it served as a prototype of what subsequently became a rising tide of women's consciousness. "Pro Femina" is indeed "for the woman" in all senses of that phrase. Its message is for (directed toward) women; for women in the sense of seeing women as a category for discussion; for women in urging women to become fully functioning independent beings. It speaks for women, telling women's story with a directness that shocks and enlightens, and it urges women to tell their own stories. The message of the poem is female, political, and revolutionary.

In *Mermaids in the Basement*, the poem "Fanny," from Kizer's book *Yin* (1984), appears in sequence as "Four: Fanny" in the section entitled "Pro Femina." While not following the form of parts 1, 2, and 3, it can be said to present a specific example of the theme. Fanny, the narrator, took care of Robert Louis Stevenson in his last years of life on the island of Samoa. While Stevenson writes, Fanny endlessly plants trees and crops and vegetable gardens to sustain them. She tries to keep a journal, but finds that Stevenson is marking out passages and making changes. She starts censoring herself, then abandons the journal entirely. She is one of the "mutes," unable to write the truth of her life, like the "millions/ Of mutes for every Saint Joan or sainted Jane Austen" mentioned in part 1. Kizer re-creates Fanny's life through this poem and lets Fanny speak. The poem ends with Fanny's proclamation that now that Stevenson has died, she will "leave here" and "never again succumb."

Lois A. Marchino

PROLOGUE

Author: Yevgeny Yevtushenko (1933-   )
Type of poem: Dramatic monologue
First published: 1957, as "Prolog," in *Obeshchaniye*; collected in *The Poetry of Yevgeny Yevtushenko, 1953-1965*, 1965

The Poem

"Prologue" is a poem in free verse, its sixty-six lines divided into six stanzas of uneven length. Written in 1953, shortly after the beginning of Yevgeny Yevtushenko's career, the poem can be seen in retrospect as an introduction to his entire body of work, as the title indicates.

Like many of Yevtushenko's poems, "Prologue" serves as a vehicle of self-identification. In the very first line, "I am different," the poet makes a statement that would sound self-evident and redundant had it not been written at the beginning of a new phase in Russian poetry. A new generation, led by Yevtushenko and Andrey Voznesensky, was making its voice heard, replacing the officially approved old guard which had ruled the poetic scene for decades. In that sense, the above declaration is not only prophetic but also courageous, coming immediately after the death of dictator Joseph Stalin.

The poet also declares that he does not fit in — another statement that goes beyond its nominal meaning: He does not fit into the encrusted establishment of prescribed tenets and norms. He does not fit in because "much of everything is mixed" in him — his thoughts, his allegiance, his creeds — which would be acceptable under normal circumstances but was not in his country at that time. He denies that he lacks the "integral aim" for which he is criticized; on the contrary, there is great value in being different and individualistic. He believes that this is what makes him indispensable to his society, whether or not it wants to admit it. By "greeting all movement" he welcomes constant change in life, change that alone can guarantee progress.

The restrictions the poet is forced to endure blur his horizon and sap his energy. "Frontiers are in my way," he laments in the second stanza, feeling embarrassed at not being able to visit foreign cities such as Buenos Aires and New York, stroll in London and Paris, or speak with people in their languages.

The complaint about these restrictions is followed by an even stronger complaint about not being able to express himself freely as an artist. "I want art to be/ as diverse as myself" is another of the poet's creeds, perhaps the most important one. If the freedom he is seeking brings torments and harassments, he is willing to accept them, for he is "by art besieged." In the next stanza, he enlarges upon his domain, declaring that he feels himself akin to Sergei Yesenin, a leading Russian poet of the twentieth century, to poet Walt Whitman, to composer Modest Moussorgsky, and to the artist Paul Gauguin, thus placing himself in the company of giants in all the arts.

The fourth stanza gives expression to another Yevtushenko trademark, boldness and defiance, for which is, perhaps, best known. "I like/ to defy an enemy to his face," he says openly in a way familiar to all of his "enemies." In the final stanza, he carries his defiance to the end, standing up to death itself. He sings and drinks, and he has no time to think of death; if it comes, "I shall die from sheer joy of living." It is in this joy of living that Yevtushenko finds the highest purpose of his life, for the attainment of which he is willing to defy all enemies and encourage all his brethren, in the arts and otherwise.

Forms and Devices

There is no one particular form or device that dominates "Prologue" but rather several, among which is the use of contrast. When he speaks of his frame of mind as well as his emotions, he uses contrast to underscore the complexity of human nature. He is overworked and idle at the same time, indicating that not all exertion is worth undertaking. He thinks he has a goal, yet he finds himself aimless, again pointing to the discrepancy between professed intentions and real aims. He is both shy and rude, nasty and good-natured, which is a more realistic appraisal of human nature than the insistence on either a black or white reading. He sways from West to East and back, alluding to the perennial dichotomy in the Russian mind and soul, to which he is not immune either, but whose expression has been officially suppressed. Finally, he sways from envy to delight, revealing that he is capable of a wide range of emotions. All these contrasts serve one main purpose: to show that in real life things are never black and white, as officials claim, but a combination of stands and moods often opposing one another.

Another device used in the poem, even if sparingly, is imagery. When he finds himself in a mood of exhilaration, the poet feels himself "heaped as high/ as a truck with fresh mown hay." He would "fly through voices,/ through branches,/ light and chirping,/ and butterflies flutter in my eyes,/ and hay pushes out of cracks." On another occasion, he would "love to crunch/ cool scarlet slices of watermelon" in August heat. The use of such striking images lends lyricism to Yevtushenko's poem, thus poeticizing his references to not-so-lyrical matters.

The form of the poem is consistent with the prevalent mode of Yevtushenko's poetry: free verse, its lines according to their rhythm, often in only a few words, sometimes in a cascading fashion, rhyming frequently but not according to any strict scheme. There is a built-in dramatic tension in the verses which lends itself well to Yevtushenko's powerful style of recitation.

Themes and Meanings

"Prologue" is an autobiographical poem, enabling the poet to express his beliefs and attitudes. Yet the poem is not exclusively personal. This may sound contradictory, but Yevtushenko has always been convinced of his mission as a poet speaking for his entire generation, not only for himself. Through his own declarations, he crystallizes a set of creeds for a coming generation ready to claim its own place in the sun and unwilling to accept the confines of the past. Perhaps for this reason,

"Prologue" is almost like a manifesto, a programmatic poem that can be placed at the head of any collection of Yevtushenko's poetry.

The themes that pervade the poem all circle around the poet's need to be free to express himself as he sees fit. The fact that Yevtushenko has had to work for a long time in a highly confining environment has conditioned his approach to his art. For this reason, he is often coy in his allusions, despite his inherent boldness, perhaps so as to see his poems in print. One wonders how his poetry would seem had he been able to say exactly what he wanted, and in the way he wanted to, at the time it was written.

At the same time, it would be wrong to see "Prologue" primarily as an anguished outcry of a poet shackled by an oppressive system. Many of the themes in the poem—the insistence on being different, the ebullience of youth, a thirst for life and joy of living, the confusion of contradictory forces within oneself—could be applied universally. The universality of his themes, coupled with his artistic acumen, have enabled Yevtushenko to outlive the topics of the moment and remain a leading Russian poet for decades.

Yevtushenko's pronouncement of his kinship with poets Yesenin and Whitman is of interest not only to literary historians but to the general reader as well. That he would be akin to Yesenin is not surprising, for both poets remain faithful to their rural origins while becoming urban poets later in their careers. The kinship with Whitman, plausible though it may seem (primarily because of their mutual closeness to nature), is more surprising; it brings a poet from the American prairies close to a poet from the Siberian taiga.

Vasa D. Mihailovich

PROVISIONAL CONCLUSIONS

Author: Eugenio Montale (1896-1981)
Type of poem: Lyric
First published: 1956, as "Conclusioni provvisorie," in *La bufera e altro*;
collected in *The Storm and Other Poems*, 1978

The Poem

"Provisional Conclusions" actually comprises two poems: "Piccolo testamento" ("Little Testament") consists of six sentences forming thirty undivided lines of free verse, while "Il sogno del prigioniero" ("The Prisoner's Dream") has thirty-four free-verse lines divided into four stanzas of various lengths. Each title plays upon alternate meanings of "conclusion": "Little Testament" alludes to death, the final end, and "The Prisoner's Dream" carries the political connotation of termination or liquidation. Both are written in the first person, for they present the poet's "temporary judgment or conclusions" about contemporary life.

"Little Testament" opens at night as the poet contemplates his own kindled thoughts. No ardent blaze ignited by political or religious reflection ("factory or church . . . red or black" signify Communism and Catholicism), the fragile "mother-of-pearl" iridescence springs from recollections of love. As if present, the poet tells his beloved to conserve the "powder" of these memories for the time when "every other light's gone out" and "dark Lucifer" swoops down on the "wild," "hellish" world to make the apocalyptic pronouncement, "It's time."

Hardly diminishing this frightening vision, the poet says his modest gift is "no inheritance, no goodluck charm/ to stand against the hurricanes." Yet to counteract the gloom, he goes on to reassure his beloved that "the sign was right" and will be recognized, just as each individual will recognize the truth behind his or her own thoughts and actions. Only by knowing oneself and acting according to that knowledge may the "faint glow" of good slowly catch fire and blaze again in the world.

The second poem apparently presents the same narrator imprisoned in the dark, infernal times foreseen in "Little Testament." Poignantly illustrating the persistent "faint glow" of love and humanity, "The Prisoner's Dream" opens with an introduction to an unnatural world where "you can't tell dawn from night."

Opening with the prisoner's longing for freedom ("starlings over the watch-towers/ . . . my only wings"), the second stanza then presents rapid, significant details of existence in the squalid cell. This dismal reality is escapable only through sleep and dreams of the beloved.

Abruptly disrupting even this meager comfort, stanza 3 curtly opens: "The purge never ends, no reasons given." The brutal, absurdist reality of ideologies and regimes, reigned over by "gods of plague," replaces the meanness of confined existence. Only by recanting, confessing, or "breaking down and selling out the others" may one be saved and "get the spoon/ instead of being dished up."

In the final stanza, this brutal reality merges with the liberating dream-vision.

Lying on "this piercing mattress," the prisoner imaginatively fuses with a "soaring moth" and "shimmering kimonos of light," conjuring "rainbows" and "petals" to combat prison bars and unending beatings. His thoughts rise, "only to fall back/ into the gulf where a century's a second." Physical suffering and mental delirium uncover moral crisis and self-doubt: "I don't know whether I'll be at the feast/ as stuffer or stuffing." The only certainty is that he must endure and dream, a realization which closes the poem.

Forms and Devices

The two poems are joined not only by poet Eugenio Montale's label as "provisional conclusions" but also by the similar forms and devices they share. Presented as loose, even sometimes incoherent ruminations, both open with references to the night, as the narrator ponders the perennial battle between darkness and light. Through various manifestations and images of these forces, each poem offers its own distinctive vision of the difficult, often tragic reality of modern life. In "Little Testament," this vision is structured around a nucleus of personal religious sentiment. In "The Prisoner's Dream," on the other hand, it is conditioned by the exigencies of political dogma. No doubt its focus on the public or social arena of contemporary times makes this second poem more accessible to most readers.

In large part because of their pessimistic visions, both poems are pervaded by gloom and obscurity, which the poet partially offsets through the device of symbolic imagery. Above all, Montale's images revolve around different types of illumination. In "Little Testament," for example, "flickering," "glass-grit," "faint glow," and "striking . . . match" all refer to brief, unstable fits of light, with an eventual and more constant brightness promised in references to the "tough log on a grate" and the "glow catching fire/ beneath" at the end of the poem. Images of light of equal significance can be found in "The Prisoner's Dream," such as the realistic "oily sputtering" of lamps or the fanciful "winey lantern," or even the prisoner's own metaphorical fits of mental lucidity. Through this figurative sense, especially evident in the fourth stanza, reality, dream, and hallucination become one.

Closely related to images of tenuous, shifting light are those of iridescent rainbows and spider webs. An evocative symbol of fragility and transience, "spiderweb" is present in both poems, although "Little Testament" additionally identifies it with the idea of memory. It is the rainbow, however, which is Montale's most symbolically charged image. In Italian, *iride* denotes both a rainbow and an iris; the poet uses both of these images as his own private token or emblem of fidelity, love, faith, and hope. The poet plays upon the word's multiple denotation in "Little Testament," for the second sentence associates the image with the biblical postflood rainbow representing God's covenant or promise, while in the next he treats it as a flower now crumbled to dust. This image has a much weaker presence in "The Prisoner's Dream," however, where it seems to function more as an illusion "conjured up" to transform the dingy here and now than as a complex emblem of faithful love.

The poet's vision of an ever-worsening world focuses on two equally powerful and ambiguous forces, religion and politics, which also offer their own share of imagery. Although "Little Testament" expresses an idiosyncratic form of belief, it is nonetheless full of allusions to traditional religion: Faith, hope, humility, pride, signs, Lucifer, apocalypse, salvation, and resurrection are all derived from Christian belief. Many of these same elements appear faintly and in a more abstract form within the strongly defined atmosphere of political evil in "The Prisoner's Dream."

Themes and Meanings

"Little Testament" and "The Prisoner's Dream" are complex poems about many things, all of which have multiple meanings. Montale approaches one of the major conclusions from these "judgments" — the theme of the prison-world of human existence, especially in modern times — in two different ways. In "Little Testament," the prison-world is represented as the general existential condition of humanity. The theme achieves cosmic proportions, both through its allusions to contemporary social and cultural crises of values and through its predominately religious-based imagery. In "The Prisoner's Dream," the theme is interpreted as a more concrete, specific condition, derived from the poet's own perception of the Cold War years. In both, the individual's "dark night of the soul" coincides with the world's own darkness, fanaticism, and inhumanity.

Alongside this realistic, powerfully expressed negative theme, the poet masterfully places another which is more positive but more tenuous and intangible. This theme is that of human significance, which he approaches by affirming modest, unheroic virtues such as dignity, morality, love, faith, commitment, and humanity. Montale's poems make it clear that he believes these all-important elements are no longer operative in today's society and are even in danger of being forgotten. The perceived fragility and impermanence of these significant values — indeed, even of civilization itself — is perhaps the essential message of "Little Testament."

While the poet is unable to change the threatening conditions beleaguering humanity, he can still affirm essential values in the language, images, characters, and events of his poems. Because he brings these elements to life, readers have the opportunity to experience vividly their significance and so can more readily remember and understand their importance. Also, the poet can capsulize his own personal strategy for affirmation — endure, bear witness, and create poetry out of this persistence — as he apparently does in "The Prisoner's Dream." Like the love token, his poetry perhaps "only survives in ashes," the pale vestiges of a vital, uncontainable reality, but it is valuable nonetheless. That is perhaps the central message of "The Prisoner's Dream."

Although Montale perceives all of life as "provisional" or inconclusive, he holds firm the belief that individuals must keep faith with themselves and with life. Only through decency, stoic endurance, and vigilant openness toward even the smallest signs of good can one's own humanity be realized. Montale's own self-realization occurs through communicating and transmitting, with his poetry, the human values he himself has received. Regardless of each's individual emphasis, both poems affirm the poet's own tenacious conviction that love is the refuge and shield of humanity, its only hope for enduring and transforming the prison of existence. Even though such "persistence" may only lead to "extinction," the flame still burns, the mind remembers, and the heart recognizes love, the ultimate and most enduring "sign"; humanity, like the "dream," "isn't over."

Terri Frongia

PSALM

Author: Paul Celan (Paul Ancel or Antschel, 1920-1970)
Type of poem: Dramatic monologue
First published: 1963, as "Psalm," in *Der Niemandsrose*; collected in *Paul Celan: Poems*, 1980

The Poem

"Psalm" is a short poem in free verse. Its twenty lines are divided into four stanzas, each representing a separate unit in the poem's movement. The title indicates the theme and sets the reader's expectations: This poem is a prayer, an evening song, a praise. God, whom traditional evening songs praise, is, however, repeatedly identified with "no-one" and, eventually, the poem turns out to be a song in praise of the human spirit. The context of Paul Celan's poetry and the imagery of "Psalm" also suggest that, more specifically, this poem is about Jewish people who were murdered by the Nazis during World War II. This specificity nevertheless bears universal validity and human significance.

The poem is written in the first-person plural, and, thus, the persona is actually a congregation of people. As the first line indicates, however, this congregation is dead. In obvious reference to the story of creation in the Bible, the persona declares: "No one molds us again from dust and clay, no one conjures up our dust." The word "again" betrays that a chance to live, once given, has been irretrievably lost, and the people represented by the persona have lost all hope of coming to life again.

The three lines of the first stanza, in each of which the words "no one" are repeated, end on a note of desperation. The praise of the name of "no one" in the first line of the second stanza is therefore full of shocking irony. The shift toward an upward movement nevertheless begins here as the persona associates the congregation with a flower that wants to bloom for "no one" and even wishes to glorify and court "no one." Thus, the sense of devastation introduced in the first stanza is somewhat dissipated, even though bitterness is still betrayed by the voice.

The bitter self-awareness of the congregation is continued in the third stanza as it recognizes its own nothingness that informs its own past, present, and future. The self-identification with the flower is also continued, however, and the congregation is characterized as the nothing rose and the no one's rose. Whereas the image of the rose conveys beauty, lack of value is suggested by the first metaphor and an orphaned state by the second one. The fact that this rose is "blooming" contributes to the affirmation of an inner richness and force.

In the last stanza, parts of the rose are compared to human mental and physical states and convey both much suffering and transcendence. The reproductive parts of the rose as well as the implication of many petals of its "crown" convey dynamic growth of a people, a drive toward beauty and spiritual awareness. The inner core of the rose, the pistil, is as bright as the soul. The stamen is ravaged by heaven, as if laid to waste or burned by the sun. The head of the rose, which the poet calls a crown (rendered as "corolla" in the translation) is red with "the crimson word." The suggestion of blood in the colors red and crimson is unmistakable. It emphasizes suffering, martyrdom, and untimely death. The "crimson word," sung over the thorn, suggests cries of pain and complaint as well as beauty.

Forms and Devices

"Psalm" is a complex poem because it is built upon a movement from irony to paradox and is developed through an extended metaphor that fuses with several other metaphors. The tone of irony, bitterness, and an initial sense of nihilism are relieved by overtones of mystic imagery and symbolism, which render the poem ambivalent. This ambivalence is a source of the poem's richness, as it makes two contradictory interpretations possible. The duality that pervades the whole poem allows the reader to experience overwhelming pain and despair, as well as empathy with the people who suffered devastation and untimely death. Awe and respect for them is evoked through an awareness of their inherent beauty and loveliness. Even a trace of reconciliation redeems the poem from bitterness.

The repeated personification of "no one" emphasizes divine absence. The irony that results from the suggested relationship of a silent "no one" and a congregation that is full of praise disappears as the image of the rose begins to predominate. This rose, a symbol derived from Jewish mysticism, may appear forlorn, deserted, or lost— as suggested through the metaphoric combination of this image with nothing— but it gains significance through spirituality.

For Celan, the rose, along with the image of the crown, symbolizes the people of Israel. Whereas the pistil and the stamen represent reproductive principles and therefore organic growth—and, in the context of the poem, self-generation—the petals of the rose also symbolize the members of the community or the congregation. The crown, which also may be interpreted as an image of transcendence, unites the reproductive organs of the rose, whereas in the Neoplatonic and Jewish mystical tradition, sexual union symbolizes ultimate unity and harmony, the goal of all redemptive activities. To suggest a spiritualizing principle in the rose, Celan associates the pistil with the soul or anima on the basis of its light color. The stamen, representing the male principle and thus, in this mythical tradition, the physical aspects of a human being, is envisioned by the poet as torn by intense suffering. The combination of the two suggests transcendence.

The unifying effect of the "crown" is increased by the red color, which identifies the rose with the crown and conveys both vitality and an open, bleeding wound. This effect is reinforced by the metaphor of the "crimson word" sung by the congregation, for in this context the word implies both praise and a cry of woe.

An interesting analogy may be drawn between the negative reference to God's creating abilities as manifested in bequeathing human life through addressing the dust, or, as translated, "conjuring," and the "crimson word" or loud complaint. Whereas the divine creating force of the word has disappeared, the "crimson word" of the rose remains rich with beauty and suffering, as if capable even of creating

God. Whereas this interpretation may appear ironical and shocking, in the mystical tradition creation or re-creation of God is identified with redemption.

Themes and Meanings

Celan—an East European Jewish poet whose parents and close friends were killed by the Nazis—never recovered entirely from the tragedy he experienced when barely twenty years old. He repeatedly expressed his utmost grief in his poetry and searched for a solution or answer to the extreme suffering of his people.

In "Psalm," Celan addresses the universally valid question of the relationship of the world and an infinitely absent God. Twentieth century European nihilism, frequently attributed to the German philosopher Friedrich Nietzsche (1844-1900), who declared that God was dead, also affected Celan, who, because of his traumatic wartime experiences, faced a spiritual crisis. Eventually, however, Celan came to use the resources of Jewish mysticism for probing questions raised by the suffering he witnessed and experienced. Celan nevertheless differs from mystic poets, because the mystical symbolic significance of his imagery hangs in balance with an all-but-unresolvable bitterness and despair. In "Psalm," he juxtaposes a sense of nihilism with tenets of his religion and raises a question that is hidden beneath a twentieth century convergence of cultures and tragic historical events: Can God be redeemed from the void of his infinite absence and indifference?

The poet approaches this question by fusing in the image of "no one" two different religious traditions of Judaism. In the biblical tradition, God is envisioned as being personally involved in the creation of human beings and a committed part of a covenant with Israel. For Celan, this God has disappeared. In the Judaic mystical tradition, which influenced rabbinical Judaism and was transmitted through the Cabala, the creator of the universe is an infinitely distant, nameless entity—a nonbeing who projected the chain of powers from which the world ensued. This God, envisioned as male, frequently is experienced as infinitely distant, but He repeatedly is sought out and courted by mystics, who have asserted that He is discoverable in the midst of emotional intensity. The skillful fusion of these two concepts in the image of "no one" renders "Psalm" poignant and touching: It is extremely painful to register the absence of God, and it is overwhelming to witness the immense effort of the congregation to personalize and beautify this apparently indifferent, absent nonbeing. The suggestion of the discoverability of God is nevertheless hidden in the image of the rose. As David Brierley points out in *"Der Meridian"* (1984), Gershom Scholem, Celan's primary source of Jewish mystical imagery, also traces the rose to its identity with the Shechinah, the mediator between humans and God in Jewish mythology, the anima of the world.

Ultimately, as the poem concludes with the image of the thorn, the song of the congregation remains a monologue, and the pain from which the poem derives both is transcended by vision and remains historical and real.

Marie Gerenday Tamas

PSALM

Author: Georg Trakl (1887-1914)
Type of poem: Lyric
First published: 1912, as "Psalm"; in *Die Dichtungen*, 1919; collected in *Poems*, 1973

The Poem

"Psalm" ushered in what is known as Georg Trakl's middle period, in which his poems were longer and his imagery more complex than had been the case in his previous work. The influence of the French poet Arthur Rimbaud is well documented. "Psalm" is written in long, flowing lines of free verse. In the original German, it contains the mellifluous language that ensured that Trakl would continue to be read, even if he was not entirely understood.

"Psalm" has four stanzas of nine lines each, and a single, isolated line at the end. Semantic associations between adjacent lines are not always readily apparent.

Although everything is described in the third person, the poem is highly autobiographical, as is all of Trakl's work. The title seems to indicate a devotional poem, but "Psalm" is devotional only in that for Trakl, the act of writing was a means of atoning, at least in part, for his sins.

The first stanza is a good illustration of the extreme contrasts that characterize Trakl's poetry. Four consecutive subjects are operated on by negative forces. They are extinguished, abandoned, burned, and misused. A madman dies and is replaced, exactly halfway through the stanza, by the sun god in an idyllic South Sea island paradise, an image qualified only by the closing observation that it is a paradise lost.

At first, the second stanza seems to consist of nine unrelated images. The sense of danger, though, is omnipresent, and it is clear that something horrible is happening in the last line. It is the female figures who are at risk. The nymphs have left their safe place, perhaps out of a false sense of security, for no sooner is the strange man buried than he is replaced by the son of Pan, whose strong body soaks up the heat of the midday sun. The following central line of the stanza portrays some very vulnerable little girls who, one suspects, are also of central significance.

The sister who is mentioned in the middle of the poem dominates the beginning of the third stanza. While she remains the constant focal point, there is now a fragmentation of the male personality. He appears in rapid succession as the someone of "someone's evil dreams"; the "student, perhaps a double"; his "dead brother" (in two places); and the "young novice." What happened at the end of the second stanza seems to have overwhelmed and destroyed the integrity of his personality.

Indeed, the remainder of the poem is anticlimactic, with images of ending, departure, decay, and desolation. The Church remains silent, as does the God portrayed in the last line, a *deus absconditus* (hidden god). Only the opening of his eyes indicates acknowledgment of the poet's penance.

Forms and Devices

The most conspicuous structural device in "Psalm" is Trakl's prominent use of anaphora. He employed this rhetorical device of repetition in only one other poem, "De Profundis." By setting apart consecutive subjects with the formula "It is a . . ." Trakl has heightened the evocative power of each image and has lent the poem the air of an incantation. Images that might be questioned in a more relaxed format tend to be accepted when stated so absolutely. Trakl has applied the technique to both negative and positive images. It is a compelling way of presenting the realities of his mind, and it is because his inner world is portrayed so convincingly that he is considered the foremost poet of German expressionism.

Trakl's poems are extraordinarily closely knit. He wrote them slowly, and his manuscripts show many revisions and alternative wordings. In the final version, everything is significant. Adjacent lines are associated, no matter how disparate their content may seem, and the more structurally important their position in the poem, the more interpretive weight may be placed on them. For example, the climax and turning point in "Psalm" occurs halfway through the poem, the key lines being the last line of stanza 2 and the first line of stanza 3: "A white steamer carries bloody scourges up the canal./ The strange sister appears again in someone's bad dreams." The first line suggests sadistic sex; the second line identifies the victim. Thus the peak of the poem "Psalm" captures the essence of Trakl's confession, the driving force behind all his poetry: He had an incestuous relationship with his younger sister Grete. The central significance of the sister is formally attested by her exactly central position in the poem. By adding the single extra line at the end, Trakl made her line the median, with eighteen lines before it and after it.

Numerous cross-references extend throughout the poem like long threads holding it together. The white steamer that carries "bloody scourges" at noon has its counterpart in an empty boat that moves down the black canal in the evening. There is an aural accompaniment to this event. The rooms in stanza 2 are filled with chords and sonatas, but the music stops in stanza 3 with the final chords of a quartet. Likewise, the shadows who, in the third last line of stanza 2, embrace before a blind mirror reappear in the antepenultimate line of the poem as the shadows of the damned, descending to the sighing waters.

The self-judgment implicit in the imagery indicates that this psalm was written by a poet who entertained no hope of redemption.

Themes and Meanings

The quality of Georg Trakl's poetry has never been disputed, but its meaning has eluded critics for decades. Attempts to interpret his work within the Christian context were necessarily selective. Studies of particular images found that they could mean different things in different poems. When the pieces simply did not fit together, the last critical resort was always to the biographical fact of Trakl's dependency on cocaine, which supposedly rendered the logic of his visions unreproducible. Certainly, the surface picture is often confoundingly complex.

It was not until 1985, more than seventy years after his death, that Trakl's work was decoded in a monumental psychoanalytical study by Gunther Kleefeld, *Das Gedicht als Sühne* (the poem as penance). His title, taken from one of Trakl's letters, emphasizes the highly personal nature of the poetry. Trakl did not consciously set out to construct a clever system of cryptic symbols. In fact, he himself may not have known why his poems took the shape they did. Images arose in free association out of the deep structures of a disturbed psyche, much as they do in dreams, and the psychoanalytical approach has proved to be the best method of deciphering their meaning.

The task of interpreting Trakl's poetry is simplified by the small size of the cast of characters who may appear (although in any number of forms). He deals with himself, his sister, his father, and his mother, and continually reworks his family situation.

In "Psalm," the first stanza shows (in psychoanalytical terms) Trakl's id (the unconscious, instinctual area of the psyche) yielding to the superego (the moral, social area of the psyche; seat of the conscience), the madman to the sun god, the bad boy to the good. In the second stanza, the id is buried as the stranger, but it resurfaces as the sexually charged son of Pan. The sister figure is represented by the nymphs, the little girls, and the sonatas (Grete used to play Franz Schubert pieces). They embrace, and the last two lines introduce Trakl's own verdict of sickness.

Stanza 3 shows Trakl as neither the id nor the superego, but as the very confused ego in the aftermath of the event. What has happened with the sister now seems like a bad dream, and it has had a negative affect on her as well, making her even more vulnerable than before. The music stops, and the little girl is now blind.

Trakl blamed his parents for his unhappiness, for the lack of attention and absence of control that led and allowed him to become involved with his sister. The father appears in "Psalm" as the gardener and the caretaker, and is portrayed as inept at both jobs. It is in his old asylum, in stanza 4, that dead orphans lie beside the garden wall. The orphans, of course, are Georg and Grete Trakl, who appear in the following line as fallen angels.

Finally, the mother is present in "Psalm" in the first and fourth stanzas as water, the universal female symbol. In an image with positive emotional resonance, she is the singing sea, the womb that gave rise to the sun god. This image belongs to the past; the paradise is lost. In stanza 4, she is the sighing waters to which the shadows of the damned descend. All that is left for them is the death wish, the desire to return to the inorganic state.

This poetry is not only about the troubled Trakl family. Trakl's intense imagery of psychic agony transcends his immediate circumstances and applies to all who find themselves drawn in directions that are not condoned by society.

Jean M. Snook

THE PULLEY

Author: George Herbert (1593-1633)
Type of poem: Meditation
First published: 1633, in *The Temple*

The Poem

Most of George Herbert's poems are profoundly personal. This is not to say that they are always autobiographical, although indeed one senses the force of lived experience in his most successful poems. Yet whether or not they describe Herbert's own experiences, they typically present an individual in the midst of some dramatic process of meditation, analysis, worry, or wonder. "The Pulley" is a remarkable exception, structured as an explanatory tale about the creation of man.

Herbert does not often operate on the level of myth, but "The Pulley" owes something to the classical story of Pandora's box. In Herbert's version, however, it is not all the troubles of the world that are loosed upon unsuspecting humankind by an overly curious Pandora but all the "world's riches" that are poured upon humankind by a beneficent God. In revising not only the Pandora myth but also the biblical story of Creation in Genesis, Herbert constructs a narrative that is charming and bold. The speaker imagines himself as a witness to the moment of Creation and gives an on-the-spot report of what transpired and what was on God's mind as He both gave and withheld certain gifts.

There is a touch of humor in the poem as God not only pours blessings out of a glass on his new creation but also quizzically examines and then rationalizes his own actions. When nearly all the blessings are out—secular blessings, it seems, such as strength, beauty, wisdom, honor, and pleasure—God pauses and decides to keep the one remaining treasure, "Rest." He explains himself in direct terms, and this explanation is central to the poem: God's purpose is not to mystify or torment but to instruct, and the story of Creation is intended to give insight into how one should lead one's life. If humans were given everything, including "rest," the highest jewel of all, they would become complacent and have a mistaken sense of their own self-sufficiency. They would, in short, pay devotion to "Nature, not the God of Nature."

So it is to anticipate and correct this devotional danger that God gives all the blessings but one to humankind. In a pun that is both playful and serious and is even dizzying in its meaning and effect, God concludes by saying that while the comfort of "rest" will be withheld, all the "rest"—that is, the remainder—of the blessings will be freely given. As a result, man will be "rich and weary." There is no sense of threat here, but the ending of the poem is somewhat sobering. Man's life will be one of "repining restlessness" and "weariness." Yet this will prove to be a way to God. Only in the last lines of the poem does Herbert provide enough information to understand why the poem is entitled "The Pulley": Human existence involves reciprocal forces pulling or pushing against one another, but the pull to earth will be more than balanced by the pull to heaven, and as is typical in Herbert it is not one's strength but fully acknowledged weakness, compensated for by divine strength, that sends one to God's "breast."

Forms and Devices

One of the great charms of "The Pulley" is its simplicity of language. There is an easy-going, conversational quality to the poem that turns a potentially overwhelming spectacle, Creation, into a comprehensible fable and similarly turns a potentially foreboding power, God, into a familiar friend. As in many other poems by Herbert, God speaks directly to man, and not in the form of puzzles or distant pronouncements, but in statements that are intimate, patient, and consoling. Without these latter qualities, the underlying message of the poem — that human life is invariably characterized by incessant restlessness and weariness — would not be so palatable.

The images of the poem are also simple and homely, despite the fact that the subject is potentially disturbing and complicated. God performs actions that are magical and bold: For example, in language that recalls Genesis, he commands, "Let the world's riches, which dispersed lie,/ Contract into a span." Herbert frequently plays with quick transformations of space, especially from large to small, and this sudden description of Creation as an event of tremendous concentration — the entire world, as it were, contracted into the size of a human hand, a span — is momentarily startling. Despite his astonishing power, God appears primarily as a humble artificer, working with a glass of blessings containing simple ingredients that he pours out, and there is something infinitely comforting about the fact that the divine mysteries of Creation can be understodd in terms of a common tool, the pulley.

Perhaps to reinforce the consoling familiarity and simplicity of the narrative, the poem is not very adventurous technically. The four five-line stanzas uphold a regular rhyme scheme, and the few variations in the meter are not so much complicated inversions to add tension or intensity but rather (presumably) deliberate flattenings of the lines to make them sound prosaically familiar. God noticeably does not speak in elevated language. Sincerity, not sublimity or cool austerity, characterizes his style, and this makes his assurances to man disarming and compelling.

Beneath the simplicity of the poem's language, though, is a level of complexity added by the wordplay. God apparently likes puns — or at least it makes perfect sense for Herbert to imagine God's language as embodying verbal ambiguities. A pun is a perfect figure of speech to convey the simultaneous playfulness and philosophical seriousness of the theme of "rest" in "The Pulley." This word is repeated throughout the poem not only to toy with its various meanings but also to understand fully its consequences. Peaceful "rest" is at first glance obviously a blessing, much desired by humankind, but ironically, more than any of the other blessings poured upon man, it has the capacity to distract man from his true goals, heaven and intimacy with God. For this reason, God, with great wit, allows man to keep the remainder of the blessings, knowing that they will not afford him any "rest." True rest will come only as a result of "restlessness," which will toss man upward. Herbert's choice of a concluding word is particularly shrewd and completes the wordplay of the poem: Embedded in God's "breast" is one's final "rest" (a pun more obvious in the seventeenth century spelling of "breast" as "brest").

Themes and Meanings

"The Pulley" is both a myth of origins and a moral and spiritual fable; these two genres overlap because, for Herbert, man's devotional responsibilities are perfectly consistent with and flow inevitably from who he is. Despite the brevity and simplicity of the poem, several key facts are affirmed. For example, this version of the Creation myth emphasizes the dignity of man, bestowed by a God who is thoughtful, generous, and kind. The story of Creation in the Book of Genesis is astonishing: A spiritual breath raises dusty clay to life in the form of Adam. In Herbert's poem, the Creation seems even more splendid, as man is described as the sum and epitome of all the world's riches, and God is a being who communicates easily and cordially with his creation.

Simultaneous with this emphasis on the dignity of man, however, is a carefully drawn distinction: Strength, beauty, wisdom, honor, and pleasure are necessary and vital components of man, but they are not sufficient to guarantee his spiritual health. For this he needs rest, the one quality held back by God. Man's independence, then, is qualified, but not undermined completely. "The Pulley" does not suggest that man is disastrously flawed and impotent, or that life in the world of Nature is insignificant and useless: Man's life can, after all, be "rich." It does show the limits of human powers and the liabilities of earthly existence: The inevitable human fate is restlessness and weariness.

Perpetual desire serves two extremely important purposes. First, it is an important devotional corrective, saving one from an undue concentration on Nature, the things of this world, and what is in fact only the illusion of human independence. It is all too easy to be distracted and "adore" the gifts rather than the giver, Nature rather than "the God of Nature." Since the former provide no lasting peace, however, one is thereby always redirected to the latter.

Life may thus be a series of postponed gratifications, even afflictions, but this will ultimately take one to God, the second purpose served by perpetual desire. "The Pulley" is not a poem of advice about how to change the focus of one's devotion from the things of the world to God, the author of those things. It is rather a dramatic, even magical poem that envisions a climactic union of man and God accomplished not by human intellectual power or will but simply by desire. Much like the poem "Love" (III), which concludes Herbert's sequence of lyrics in *The Temple*, "goodness" is somewhat beside the point when it comes to intimacy between man and God: Not worthiness but "weariness" tosses him to God's breast and secures his rest.

Sidney Gottlieb

THE PURPOSE OF ALTAR BOYS

Author: Alberto Rios (1952-   )
Type of poem: Dramatic monologue
First published: 1982, in *Whispering to Fool the Wind*

The Poem

"The Purpose of Altar Boys" is composed in free verse. Its forty-five lines are held together in a single stanza. The title appears to be straightforward and serious, preparing the reader for an account of the function of altar boys in the Catholic church. Alberto Rios, however, looking back from the point of view of adulthood, assumes the voice of a mischievous altar boy who has created innovations in the performance of his duties when he assists the priest during the sacrament of Communion. As the poem progresses, the word "purpose" of the title takes on the meaning of intention.

The altar boy begins by explaining the way in which the human eye is constructed for perceiving good and evil. He says he learned this from his friend Tonio at catechism, where the boys were being taught the principles of their religion. Tonio learned about the eye from his mother. The altar boy explains that "the big part" of the eye "admits good" and the "little/ black part" is for "seeing evil." He believed this because Tonio's mother was a widow and, consequently, an "authority" on such things. Because the dark part of the eye sees evil, the altar boy associates evil with darkness. He explains that this is why children cannot go out at night and why girls sometimes undress at night and walk around their rooms or stand in their windows with nothing on but their sandals.

The narrator claims that he was the altar boy who "knew about these things." Therefore, when he assisted the priest at Communion on Sundays, he believed he had his own mission. One of an altar boy's responsibilities during Communion is to hold the communion plate under the chin of each person receiving the consecrated bread of the Eucharist, called the Host, so that it cannot accidentally fall to the floor and be defiled. As the narrator expresses it in the poem, his job as altar boy was to "keep Christ from falling." While performing this duty, however, he had opportunities to accomplish his own purposes.

On some Sundays, he says, his mission was to remind people of the night before. Holding the metal plate beneath a communicant's chin, he would drag his feet on the carpet, stirring up static electricity. He would wait for the right moment, then touch the plate to the person's chin, delivering his "Holy Electric Shock" of retribution. The right moment would be when "Christ" had been taken safely into the communicant's mouth. The narrator says that the shock caused a "really large swallowing and made people think." He adds that he "thought of it as justice." On other Sundays, however, the "fire" in his eyes was different, and his mission was changed. On these days, he would hold the plate too hard against the same nervous chins, pressing upward, so he could look with "authority" down "the tops of white dresses."

Forms and Devices

In "The Purpose of Altar Boys," Rios adopts the persona of a young boy, whose essential innocence attracts the reader and contributes to the humor of the poem. This persona affects the poem's language and structure. The diction is simple and colloquial, as exemplified in "kids can't go out" and in the boy's references to the iris as the "big" part and to the pupil as the "little" part of the eye. This voice also accounts for the absence of such literary devices as simile, metaphor, and rhyme. These would give the poem a self-consciousness that the altar boy does not have. He narrates his story in a linear structure and without the interruptions of stanza breaks, as his mind moves quickly from thought to thought, image to image.

The sense of ease and speed in the narration is also facilitated by the poet's use of a relatively short poetic line, usually containing six or seven syllables. Although the lines are short, the sentences are long. Five of them take up six or more lines, and one of these extends through twelve lines. The other three sentences in the poem take up one, two, and three lines, respectively. The combination of short lines and long sentences creates a sense not only of speed but also of breathlessness—these features express the altar boy's excitement as he tells his story of good and evil, judgment and temptation.

His excitement is also conveyed by repetition. Fascinated by darkness, he repeats "at night" three times in four lines. Speaking about things that happen at night, he begins two of three consecutive lines with "That's why." The most significant occurrence of repetition, however, is the boy's use of the pronoun "I." It increasingly dominates the poem. The pronoun does not occur until line 17 and does not appear again until line 24. In the remaining twenty-one lines, however, it occurs six times. Toward the end of the poem, the word "I" ends one line and begins the next. The increasing appearance of the word reflects the altar boy's self-assertion and reveals the pride he takes in fulfilling his missions.

The poet achieves special effects with punctuation and line breaks. He uses one dash in the poem, following the word "evil," overemphasizing the word, as a boy would do. He uses a colon in "the precise moment: plate to chin" to indicate the gap across which the static electricity will jump. Line breaks also mirror the action: "To keep Christ from falling/ I held the metal plate/ under chins." The poet places "under chins" beneath "I held the metal plate," as the plate would be held under a chin. On the other hand, he places "from falling" on the same line as "To keep Christ," indicating that the boy does not allow such a fall. Another significant line break occurs in "and I/ I would look," where the first "I" represents the altar boy in his official role, and the second reflects his personal impulse. The boy's eyes move down, just as the "I" does. This is where he lets "Christ" fall.

Themes and Meanings

Alberto Rios explores the relationship between authority and experience in "The Purpose of Altar Boys." The narrator says that Tonio's mother was an "authority" because "she was a widow." As a woman, a mother, and a widow, Tonio's mother had considerable experience. She was once a virgin, a girl no older than the altar boy. Perhaps an altar boy looked down the top of her white dress. She has fallen in love, been married, experienced sex, given birth, suffered the death of her husband, and raised Tonio. Her authority derives from her experience. She told Tonio the story about the parts of the eye to protect him from temptation, to preserve his childhood innocence.

The narrator claims that he also had experience. He "knew" about girls standing naked in their windows, although he does not say how he learned this. He believed that this experience gave him the right to punish those girls with his electric shock, as well as the "authority" to look down their dresses. The altar boy's experience does not compare with the experience of Tonio's mother. He also based his authority on his position as an altar boy, presuming to derive the right to judge and punish from being the helper of a priest. He considered himself superior to the other altar boys, claiming to be "the" altar boy who "knew," and he thought of his electric shock as "Holy," although he was not vested with the authority of a priest.

The ultimate authority in the poem is the Catholic church. It is ironic, but appropriate, that the altar boy heard the story of the eye at catechism, where he was learning the church's views of good and evil. The Catholic church has some two thousand years of experience, including experience with altar boys. It knows that boys are liable to create mischief and, entering adolescence, likely to be curious about the bodies of girls. It knows that altar boys are human. Is this the purpose of altar boys: to exemplify human nature, to remind people that there is a bit of the devil, as well as the angel, in everyone?

The altar boy is a comic character, a prankster whose mischief is essentially harmless. What is harmless in a child, however, may be evil in an adult. A voyeur is not an attractive person. Far worse are people who commit murder and claim that God told them to do it; the altar boy was flirting with the sin of pride when he took upon himself the authority to judge and punish others. It is important that the poem is written in the past tense. The adult narrator has experience that he lacked as a boy. His concepts of good and evil are no longer naïve. Evil occurs during the day as well as at night, and the sin of pride is far more serious than stealing a glance down the top of a girl's dress.

James Green

THE QUAKER GRAVEYARD IN NANTUCKET

Author: Robert Lowell (1917-1977)
Type of poem: Elegy
First published: 1945; collected in *Lord Weary's Castle*, 1946

The Poem

"The Quaker Graveyard in Nantucket" is one of the noisiest poems in the English language. Robert Lowell employs a multitude of harsh sounds, broken rhythms, and recurring patterns of alliteration to reflect the poem's preoccupation with the violence and turbulence of the world it depicts.

The poem is divided into seven parts, differing in length and tone. It begins with an evocation of the violent death of Warren Winslow, one of Lowell's cousins, who was lost at sea when his ship sank during World War II; the poem is dedicated to Winslow's memory. Borrowing heavily from a description of drowning victims in Henry David Thoreau's *Cape Cod* (1864), Lowell presents a grim image of the drowned man and describes a burial at sea. He also mentions Ahab, the mad whaling-ship captain in Herman Melville's *Moby Dick* (1851), who took his ship and crew with him to a watery grave in his pursuit of the white whale.

The second section depicts the bleak site of the Quaker graveyard on the island of Nantucket, where markers record the deaths of many of the island's men who were lost at sea on nineteenth century whaling expeditions. The nearby ocean is violent, noisy, and menacing, and the gulls' cries seem to echo the cries of drowning sailors. Humans, however, are the purveyors of violence, as well as its victims, as evidenced by the "hurt beast" (the harpooned whale slaughtered by Ahab's crew).

The third, fourth, and fifth sections of the poem continue to depict the wild and violent world of the ocean in which the Nantucket sailors, including Ahab's men as well as the real Nantucketers, wreak their violence on the creatures of the sea and are violently killed themselves. Lowell introduces a religious theme, first in an ironic passage in which the drowning Quaker sailors say, " 'If God himself had not been on our side,/ When the Atlantic rose against us, why,/ Then it had swallowed us up quick.' " Clearly, they are about to be swallowed. The theme of religion is developed through references to the crucifixion of Christ, which the poem relates to the biblical Jonah, who spent three days in the belly of a whale. Jesus, Jonah, and the whale are all depicted as crucified and speared by the harpoons of the whalers.

The violence of the poem is put aside in the sixth section, entitled "Our Lady of Walsingham." At the time he wrote "The Quaker Graveyard in Nantucket," Lowell was a recent convert to the Roman Catholic faith, and this section of the poem borrows from a book describing an old English Catholic shrine in order to evoke a mysterious peace that is in sharp contrast to the violence of the rest of the poem. The sailors of the earlier segments are replaced by pilgrims who walk humbly to the shrine of Mary. The medieval image of Our Lady is neither beautiful nor expressive, but it presents an image of submission to a God whose purposes encompassed both the innocence of the crib at Bethlehem and the violent death of Christ at Calvary.

The final section is the most dirgelike. The winds are "empty," and the ocean is "fouled with the blue sailors." Humans kill and die, but the violence is ancient and somehow part of God's purpose. The last line asserts: "The Lord survives the rainbow of His will."

Forms and Devices

The violence that the poem depicts is reflected in many of the devices Lowell uses. The rhythm, for example, combines a basic iambic measure with many variations, producing a kind of ground swell that is interrupted violently on many occasions, as if suggesting a stormy sea. The lines are of varying lengths, and although all the lines of the poem contain end rhymes, there is no regular rhyme pattern.

The most noticeable aspect of the poem is the use of a variety of sound devices, ranging from alliteration to assonance and including echoes of various sounds as well as end rhyme. Most of these sounds are harsh, with hard vowels and plosive or stop consonants, but such sounds may be preceded by softer sounds. This can produce sudden sharp changes, as in the lines "ask for no Orphean lute/ To pluck life back."

The noisy quality of the poem resounds throughout, as in the hard vowel sounds and the *k* consonant sounds in lines such as "As the entangled, screeching mainsheet clears/ The blocks: off Madaket." Piled-up alliteration and echoing sounds show in the following: "This is the end of them, three-quarters fools,/ Snatching at straws to sail/ Seaward and seaward on the turntail whale,/ Spouting out blood and water as it rolls,/ Sick as a dog to these Atlantic shoals."

The poem contains a wealth of other devices, including allusions, primarily to *Moby Dick* and to Christian symbols, but also to classical mythology. There is personification of the sea; "the high tide/ Mutters to its hurt self." Lowell makes considerable use of metaphor—for example, in an image of the beach "Sucking the ocean's side" — and simile: "We are poured out like water." Such devices, however, are less important than the sounds that create the tone of the poem and provide its unique characteristics.

Themes and Meanings

Lowell's clear intention in "The Quaker Graveyard in Nantucket" is to depict the harshness and violence that he sees as conditions of all life and to provide an understanding of how religious faith can reconcile humans to the harsh conditions of life. The death of the author's cousin is related to all violent deaths at sea, and through the allusions to *Moby Dick* and the biblical appearances of whales, those deaths are connected to the deaths of other creatures—destruction that is caused by humankind.

The final two sections of the poem are intended to convey the "peace that passeth understanding" that is promised by Christianity. It is presented in the section entitled "Our Lady of Walsingham," and this peace is not easy or pretty: The image of

Mary has neither beauty nor expression, and the will of God, referred to in the final section, is not easy to understand. The reference includes the sobering reminder that "the Lord God formed man from the sea's slime" and that death has always been part of life. Worship of the Judeo-Christian God requires unquestioning faith.

The poem's final meaning, however, is anything but simple, in large part because of the variations in tone of the poem's different parts. There is a vigor and vitality implicit in the loudness and harshness of the first five sections that is muted in the final two sections. The shift to the reverence of the sixth section is almost an anticli-max, and when the poem moves from the shrine at Walsingham back to the ocean in the final section, there is a sense of fatigue almost amounting to depression. This is to some extent dissipated by the surging grandeur of the final nine lines, but the sense of exhaustion is very strong in the closing section.

The result of this is that the poem's intention to show religious faith reconciling humans to their harsh fate is subverted to some extent by the poet's fascination with what he can express in language. Lowell seems to have been in love with words and with the sounds of words, especially in his younger years, and this shows more clearly in "The Quaker Graveyard in Nantucket" than in any other poem. More vitality is instilled into the depiction of the terrors of this world than into portraying the consolations of religion, so that the fascination of the struggles of life and death outweighs any attempt to reconcile humans to their fate.

John M. Muste

THE QUALITY OF SPRAWL

Author: Les A. Murray (1938-   )
Type of poem: Lyric
First published: 1983, in *The People's Otherworld*

The Poem

Sprawl commonly denotes an unevenly extended spatial position lacking visual order, as in "urban sprawl." This fifty-line free-verse poem adapts the usage to identify a behavioral stance in which individuals exceed the limits of conventional behavior to achieve an end. The poem contains eight stanzas, each of which is an independent unit of illustration. The word "Sprawl," which begins each stanza, is the subject of a present-tense statement of what sprawl is or does contrasted with its negative image.

Many of the characters and incidents representing sprawl have the exaggerated quality of social "tall tales," but are offered in a straightforward and definite tone that invites belief. The opening incident shows sprawl to be a farmer cutting down a Rolls-Royce to make a pickup truck. The reaction of the company in trying to reclaim its image is predictably routine and bespeaks a lack of sprawl.

In the second set of illustrations, a farmer sows his fields by plane, a hitchiker is driven "that extra hundred miles home," and someone concentrates on internal being. These are acts of "sprawl" because they exceed accepted norms for a purpose that can be seen as practical. Wasteful and useless gestures such as "lighting cigars with ten-dollar notes" are not acts of sprawl.

A contrast is also drawn with "style," which has display as its goal. Sprawl extends the rules, as when racing dogs are fed "liver and beer," or when a "dozen" bananas are actually fourteen.

Acts of sprawl become expressive or powerful when words and conventions are powerless. When logger Hank Stamper, a hero figure in a film drawn from a Ken Kesey novel, faces a powerful lumber conglomerate, his eloquence consists of using his chain saw to dissect a bureaucrat's desk.

The fourth illustration turns to historical information. Sprawl is always on the side of the individual but "is never brutal," as was Simon de Montfort in his revolt against Henry the Third.

All human activities leave room for sprawl. Among those parts of poetry that qualify as sprawl, the poet humorously includes the nonexistent fifteenth to twenty-first lines of a sonnet. He continues to tease the reader, stating that, though he is familiar with paintings possessing sprawl, "I have sprawl enough to have forgotten which paintings."

Sprawl is a semiheroic stand against authority that may be seen as "criminal presumption" by those with a group identity. The sixth stanza mentions the Borgia Pope Alexander proclaiming the division between the Spanish and the Portuguese "New World" as such a questionable example.

The actors in the next-to-last stanza are Australian eccentrics, such as Beatrice Miles. A street person, she reputedly traveled by taxi from Sydney to Melbourne on coin donations from impromptu recitations. Sprawl is thus elevated to a state worthy of public pride. The poet applauds the independence of spirit that leads such people to follow their impulses.

The final stanza discusses sprawl and its possible effect on society. Sprawl is subversive in a mischievous way. It endures only if it is not taken seriously by those it mocks. The poem ends in a somber warning: "people have been shot for sprawl."

Forms and Devices

Stanzaic organization is a conspicuous element in the framework of "The Quality of Sprawl." Free verse is often organized according to word and line placement that avoids recurring patterns in favor of rhythmic effects and visual configurations. In many unrhymed poems, stanzaic division is irregular or nonexistent.

By comparison, the discursive content of this poem is presented in eight orderly stanzas of roughly equal informational importance. The basic component of all stanzas is the complete grammatical sentence. Phrases do not dangle or drift loosely. Most are integrated within sentences as clauses. Word groupings in longer sentences are regulated by means of the correct use of commas and parentheses, though some internal quotation marks are left out.

A large variety of sentence length and structure is used. The five lines of the first stanza are a single, elongated compound-complex sentence with three clauses. A short, simple sentence, "Sprawl occurs in art," opens the fifth stanza. While the stanzas range between five and nine lines, the number of grammatical sentences in each varies from one to five.

Every stanza can be read independently. No sentence or idea is continued from one stanza to the next, nor are there intricate transitions between the stanzas. In place of such links, a basic internal organization is repeated. Each stanza contains one central statement about sprawl followed by a discussion focusing on an example of this aspect of sprawl. An internal balance is formed with a corresponding glimpse of what is never sprawl. The word "sprawl" is used to begin each new stanza, producing a visual uniformity that further connects the individual stanzas. The final stanza alone breaks this pattern by adding "No" to its first line.

Despite this reliance on the conventions of written composition, Murray maintains the liveliness of natural speech. He sustains a tone of congeniality, choosing vocabulary that is never didactic or argumentative, creating an impression of immediate understanding between reader and author. This is necessary to ensure that sprawl is accepted as an existing human characteristic, not a function of Murray's reactive imagination. The audience is, therefore, addressed in language that is specific rather than general, with examples that are concrete rather than abstract. The car that is blowtorched into a utility vehicle is identified by brand name. The "lighting" of a cigar "with ten-dollar notes" is called an act of "idiot ostentation and murder."

The few places where language is distilled beyond the commonplace stand out.

The first instance (stanza 6) is the use of a Latin term, "*In petto*," in place of more everyday words such as "secretly" or "to himself." An ordinary reader would need to look up this term, especially since it is the hinge on which the example of Pope Alexander's act of sprawl turns. Another atypical line, "And would that it were more so" (stanza 7), is notable for its fervor as well as its poetic syntax.

The overall good humor with which Murray entertains as he informs offsets the more serious tone that surfaces at the poem's conclusion. The poem remains a light handling of a theme that Murray believes is worth serious consideration. He accomplishes this by using a lively and diverse array of subjects—from folk wisdom to British painting, from Catholic history to the author's own kinfolk—that provide pictures of sprawl in action.

The anecdotal approach, rather than one of full narrative richness, presumes acceptance and precludes close analysis. Vignettes are offered in a quick succession of cartoonlike drawings of sprawl. These are focused by means of a contrasting negation of sprawl within each frame. The overall effect is that of a good-natured piece of entertainment with a serious theme.

Themes and Meanings

The theme of this poem is the resilient spirit of the individual who refuses to be rendered helpless by the norms of society. Despite Murray's disclaimer that "Sprawl is really classless" (stanza 7), this poem is very much about class. The hero is the "little person," the average citizen who does not normally control fate but who, on occasion, seizes a chance to make a forceful personal statement. The unspoken villain is the establishment, which evokes conformity to rules even when they are meaningless or makes decisions on a scale that negates individual preference.

Murray presents sprawl as inherent in certain types of actions regardless of motive or consequence. The first story, for example, is clear, but many details are left out. One can imagine that there is some reason, such as a dispute or the age of the vehicle, behind the transformation of the luxury motor car into a mundane truck, but such background detail remains unnecessary. The degree of success achieved by Hank Stamper's response is similarly irrelevant. The emphasis is on the largesse of spirit that connects such diverse acts as "farming by aeroplane" and going far out of the way to take home a hitchhiker.

From the outset, there is no attempt to offer a concise, dictionary-style definition of "sprawl" as used by the author. No exact synonyms are given. Such a verbal approached is avoided. In its place, a lively, often satirical, extended definition is formed, example by example.

"Sprawl" here is a noun of adjectival fullness, describing and defining a certain group of actions and reactions that will seem immediately familiar to most readers, even those who do not engage in such behavior. Its application is to any nonroutine human response that blends the grandly inelegant with the forcefully expressive once-in-a-lifetime gesture. "Sprawl" colors human actions in glaring neon hues that break through the routine sameness and the dull everyday necessity to "fit in."

Murray begins and ends by applauding sprawl. Sprawl is noticeable but not showy. It may be inelegant, but it is not disgusting. Inventiveness and practicality merge with stubbornness and independence in sprawl. It endures because it encourages action and makes people feel good about themselves.

Karla Sigel

QUESTION AND ANSWER IN THE MOUNTAIN

Author: Li Po (701-762)
Type of poem: Lyric
First published: wr. c. 753, as "Shan chung wen ta"; in *Li T'ai-po ch'uan-chi*,
   1717; collected in *The Penguin Book of Chinese Verse*, 1962

The Poem

There are two other alternative titles for this poem in some existing editions, but neither is as apt. The first, "Answer to a Question," is too general, whereas the second, "Answer from the Mountain, to a Worldly Person," is too explicit.

The poem begins with an innocent question, which can be translated differently depending on which of the two variant texts is used. According to one text, the line can be rendered as: "You ask me what I am doing dwelling in the Emerald Mountain." In the second text, the line would be: "You ask me why I intend to dwell in the Emerald Mountain." The first reading specifies dwelling in the mountain as a fact, whereas the second suggests that the poet is contemplating doing so. The distinction between the two readings will have a significant bearing on the rest of the poem.

To answer the question, the poet writes that "I smile but make no reply, for my heart itself is at leisure." In the variant text, the poet simply says nothing instead of making no reply. Although the wording "make no reply" echoes the title of the poem appropriately, saying nothing could be an interesting reading because it suggests that the poet does not wish to be bothered by the question at all. This reading is more consistent with the sense of serenity expressed in the phrase, "for my heart itself is at leisure."

Having handled the question in one way or another, the poet begins to muse upon the pleasures of the idyllic world. In the last two lines, Li Po describes a locale with peach blossoms floating along the stream "into the distance." The variant text for line 3, which has the peach blossoms flow "in a meandering manner" instead of into the distance, is visually more pleasing but less meaningful, since the whole point of the stream is that it is a conduit into a horizon lost to the mundane world. In this realm, the poet concludes, there is a different heaven and earth not belonging to the world of human beings.

The relatively large number of varying texts and titles for this brief lyric suggests that the poem may have been popular enough to be widely circulated and thus corrupted in the process. The variant texts for the poem appear to be a minor issue, as in each of the three instances the difference involves one word (in Chinese) only. As pointed out above, however, the one-word difference in line 1 would require one to read the whole poem differently. If dwelling in the Emerald Mountain is already a fact, the poem would be a descriptive record; if it is only a matter of the poet's contemplation, then the whole poem would be a psychological projection.

Forms and Devices

"Question and Answer in the Mountain" is written in the seven-character, truncated-verse format. It does not employ the matched couplet usually found in "recent-style" Chinese poems. Although this is not an irregular practice, it gives one the impression of "craftlessness" and freedom from formal constraints—which are some of Li Po's virtues as a poet.

The poem employs several rhetorical devices. The first is the question-answer situation commonly found in Chinese writings, including poetry and religious (Taoist and Buddhist) dialogues. The device is effective for writers who intend to demonstrate some sort of truth, and Li Po's poem obviously has a similar purpose. The second rhetorical device is found in line 2, where a negation (not having words to say) is juxtaposed with an affirmation (having leisure at heart), with the latter being reinforced as the sharper focus. Because line 2 does not really answer the innocent question in line 1, a tension is suddenly created for the next two lines to resolve. Finally, there is also a paradox in the poem: Although the poet has no answer to offer his interrogator, he has in fact answered the question in the end.

More important than the rhetorical maneuvers mentioned above, an allusion is used in the last two lines. In general, allusions are an indispensable resource for Chinese poets because explicit or implied references to historical figures, places, or events could give the poem an ornamental texture or thematic accent. In Li Po's case, he alludes to a tale by T'ao Ch'ien (also called T'ao Yüan-ming) entitled "The Peach Blossom Spring." The story describes how a fisherman, following the trail along a peach-blossomed stream, reaches a secluded farming community. The people of this land, thanks to their ancestors who escaped the turmoils of the Warring States era, have been left alone to enjoy their idyllic life for hundreds of years, undisturbed by the vicissitudes of the dynasties outside. Having been entertained, the fisherman leaves, but somehow his strange encounter becomes public knowledge, thus jeopardizing the lost horizon. In the end, however, no one is able to relocate the secluded community. In his poem, Li Po not only compares the Emerald Mountain to the Peach Blossom Spring figuratively, but he also objectifies the desire to get away from the mundane world and lead the life of a recluse.

Themes and Meanings

In approximately 743, Li Po served as a court poet (in effect a courtier) in the capital Ch'ang-an. Because of the scheming, the favoritism, and above all, the demoralizing intrigues that are part and parcel of courtly life, he resigned from his post. Between 744 and 755, he traveled around the country, visiting many places before reaching Hsüan-chou in 753, where he stayed for some time and wrote the famous poem, "A Farewell to Li Yun in the Xie Tiao Pavilion." During his tours, Li Po could have seen foreboding signs of the An-Lu rebellion, which was to break out in 755 and decimate the country on a massive scale. "Question and Answer in the Mountain" was probably written shortly before 753 while the poet was visiting the Emerald Mountain, in modern day Anlu County, Hubei Province.

The poem is a classic example of how intellectuals in traditional China might have dealt with the frustrations of public life if they did not wish to be enmeshed in it, and this is the real question beneath the surface of "Question and Answer in the Mountain." In general, when times are favorable, intellectuals would go into public service and carry out their duties according to the precepts of Confucianism. Once the commitment proves impossible to sustain (because of the corruption of the court), however, they would abandon the official life in order to return to the fields and farms, or travel among the mountains and rivers—in effect becoming hermits. It should be noted that cultivating one's own gardens and traveling casually are important metaphors in Taoism, which is a central component of Li Po's philosophy of life.

In the contexts outlined above, the first main theme is therefore the withdrawal from public life and its accompanying pleasures, particularly a sense of freedom and leisure. This is also the real answer conveyed by the smile and the silence in line 2. Considering Li Po's experience with the court, it is no accident that his poem invokes the poet-recluse T'ao Yüan-ming of the Chin Dynasty, who set an example for intellectuals of integrity. The first two lines of the poem, indeed, seem to echo T'ao's fifth poem of the "Drinking Wine" sequence.

Because of the landscape setting associated with reclusive life, the congeniality of nature is another important theme in Li Po's poem. Defining human experience positively, the landscape provides the poet with an alternative existence that is both cathartic and fulfilling. Furthermore, the allusion to T'ao Yüan-ming's fable makes it clear that the actual landscape of the Emerald Mountain and the fictional space of the Peach Blossom Spring eventually coalesce into a "utopia." Desirable as it is, this "utopia" is nevertheless characterized by an inherent irony of which Li Po may have been aware: The ultimate truth about the Peach Blossom Spring is that the premise of its sole existence is the real world being torn apart by war. Although the An-Lu rebellion had not yet broken out when Li Po wrote about the different heaven and earth in his newfound world apart from men, it would seem that he was diagnosing and divining the problem of his time accurately.

Balance Chow

RABBI BEN EZRA

Author: Robert Browning (1812-1889)
Type of poem: Dramatic Monologue
First published: 1864, in *Dramatis Personae*

The Poem

"Rabbi Ben Ezra" is a long poem of 192 lines expressing Robert Browning's optimistic philosophy of life regarding both youth and old age. Youth is a time of struggle for glimpses of God's omnipotence in an imperfect world. Old age can usher in the wisdom of spiritual maturity that comes from recognizing divine perfection behind earthly imperfection and from perceiving God's unbounded love as well as God's omnipotence.

Abraham Ibn Ezra (1092?-1167) was a Spanish rabbi who, in his middle years, was driven by persecution from Spain into a life of travel and scholarship. He was a theologian, a philosopher, a linguist, and a scientist. A strong believer in immortality, he found the second half of his life much more productive and satisfactory than the first half. The ideas of the poem are Browning's, and they are not always in accord with the rabbi's actual sentiments.

The first stanza of the poem enunciates the philosophy of the whole work and begins a series of exhortations encouraging readers to look forward to the aging process that brings a mature faith in God's providence to take what is defective and partial in this world of seeming limitations and to make all right and whole.

Stanzas 2 through 9 refuse to chastise youth for the frustrated ambitions, doubts and confusions, and unsatisfying pleasures that serve the useful purpose of redirecting human striving for higher spiritual goals. Humankind was born to struggle and aspire and not to rest, as animals do, in a satiety of low material pleasures. A divine spark energizes the human heart into undertaking a quest for infinite satisfactions centered in God.

Stanzas 10 through 19 note that the experience of youth, with its glimpses of God's power and perfection, prepare for the greater wisdom of old age and the discovery of God's perfect love during the evolution of humans from brutes to spiritual beings whose struggle for oneness with God continues even in the hereafter. Therefore, let all that makes up humans — youth and age, body and soul — be cherished in their evolving spirituality and quest for the divine.

Stanzas 20 through 25 affirm that the perception of ultimate truth in old age transcends the disputations of youth, the disparate convictions of confused thinkers, or the voguish values of the masses. On the contrary, knowledge of the "Right/ And Good and Infinite" rests on our intimations of immortality and those faint "Fancies" or intuitions of something immeasurably greater, too often ignored by the vulgar populace.

Stanzas 26 through 36 elaborate on the biblical metaphor of God as the divine potter who molds the clay of a human's spiritual nature on the spinning wheel of the world of time and transient matter ("He fixed thee 'mid this dance/ Of plastic circumstance"). Under the divine fashioning of the struggling and striving human clay, humans are ultimately wrought into a heavenly chalice of spiritual perfection for the slaking of the thirst of their Creator. Thus, human life in youth, age, and death has a providential purpose of attaining spiritual perfection.

Forms and Devices

"Rabbi Ben Ezra" is a dramatic monologue of thirty-two stanzas, each consisting of six lines with an experimental rhyme scheme (*aabccb*). The prevailing meter is iambic trimeter ("Grŏw óld ălóng wĭth mé!"), but the rhyming third and sixth lines in each stanza employ iambic pentameter ("Thĕ lást ŏf lífe, fŏr whích thĕ fírst wăs máde"). The musical effect of short and long lines of iambic beats is an alternating staccato and legato (smooth) sound system that parallels the sense of the poem's alternating concern with dynamic yearnings and divine satisfactions, where human yearnings have their ultimate rest. Consonance and assonance permeate the poem ("Grow old along with me!/ The best is yet to be").

The primary paradox of the poem is the reconciliation of the oppositions of earthly imperfection and divine perfection by affirming that doubt and limitation teach humanity faith in ultimate spiritual fulfillment ("For thence,—a paradox/ Which comforts while it mocks"). Metaphors abound. Human aspirations are implicitly compared to plucking flowers (lines 7-9), admiring stars (lines 10-12), and waging chivalric war (lines 79-84). Throughout the poem, the dichotomy of the material and spiritual sides of human nature is metaphorically expressed through the contraries of "clod" and "spark"; brutish "beast" and "god in the germ"; and "flesh" and "soul, in its rose-mesh." These metaphors, in turn, feed into the poem's climactic metaphor of the potter (God) molding clay (a human's spiritual nature) on a spinning wheel (the world of time and transient matter) to transform humanity into a heavenly chalice of spiritual perfection, slaking the thirst of the Creator.

Two biblical passages inspired Browning's metaphor of the potter. First, Isaiah 64:8, "But now, O Lord, thou art our father; we are the clay, and thou our potter; and we are all the work of thy hand." Also Romans 9:21, where Paul asks, "Hath not the potter power over the clay, of the same lump to make one vessel unto honour, and another unto dishonour?"

Browning was a modern master of the dramatic monologue, a poetic form in which a single person speaks, often at a moment of crisis, for the purpose of revealing both the self and the society conditioning the speaker. "Rabbi Ben Ezra" is not typical of Browning's best dramatic monologues, because the poem is less a revealing portrayal of the speaker and his age and is more a declamatory presentation of the author's optimistic, faintly Neoplatonic Christian philosophy of life.

The language and syntax are characteristic of Browning's elliptical, rough, and even grotesque style that so appealed to modernist poets of the twentieth century and that captured the dynamic incongruities of Browning's aspiring, struggling humanity in an imperfect world. For example, line 24 is typically difficult, rushed, compressed, and experimental: "Irks care the crop-full bird? Frets doubt the maw-crammed beast?" Its labored phrasing communicates the question: Do care and doubt bother the bird and brute whose bellies are full? The answer is no. Only a heaven-starved humanity needs more than finite satisfactions.

Themes and Meanings

"Rabbi Ben Ezra" is a poem about a Jewish thinker who sums up Browning's optimistic vision of an imperfect, heaven-starved humanity searching through youthful doubts and trials for mature intimations of immortality that come in old age as a prelude to optimum spiritual fulfillment after death.

According to Browning's philosophy of life, God created an imperfect world as a testing-ground for the full and final realization of human nature (with its immortal soul) in a heaven of spiritual perfection. Browning's optimism was not blind; it was continually being tested by his awareness and acceptance of the evils of the world and human nature ("Then, welcome each rebuff/ That turns earth's smoothness rough"). The optimism that once made "Rabbi Ben Ezra" a favorite of Victorian fans of Browning, however, eroded the poem's popularity among twentieth-century readers accustomed to harsher cultural realities and put off by the bouncing exhortations and affirmations in the verses. Underlying the poem's theme of ultimate spiritual perfection behind apparent mortal limitations are three contrasting motifs of age and youth, godlike human and brute, and potter and clay.

The works of Abraham Ibn Ezra that Browning was most likely to have known were commentaries on the Old Testament. Although elements of Ezra's philosophy are expressed in the monologue, Browning did not attempt to capture the spirit of medieval thought, but rather to express his own vigorous optimism tinged with Neoplatonic Christian idealism.

"Rabbi Ben Ezra" explores problems of faith and doubt, spirituality and evolution (for example, Darwinism) that troubled Browning's Victorian contemporaries. In particular, the speaker's rejection of low pleasures in the human quest for true happiness may be Browning's dismissal of the hedonism in Edward FitzGerald's *The Rubáiyát of Omar Khayyám* (1859), which had similarly employed the metaphor of the potter and the spinning wheel.

Thomas M. Curley

THE RAVEN

Author: Edgar Allan Poe (1809-1849)
Type of poem: Ballad
First published: 1845, in *The Raven and Other Poems*

The Poem

"The Raven" is a ballad of eighteen six-line stanzas with decidedly emphatic meter and rhymes. The ballad is a nightmarish narrative of a young man who, bereaved by the death of the woman he loved, compulsively constructs self-destructive meaning around a raven's repetition of the word "Nevermore," until he finally despairs of being reunited with his beloved Lenore in another world.

Narrated from the first-person point of view, the poem conveys, with dramatic immediacy, the speaker's shift from weary, sorrowful composure to a state of nervous collapse as he recounts his strange experience with the mysterious ebony bird. The first seven stanzas establish the setting and the narrator's melancholic, impressionable state of mind. Weak and worn out with grief, the speaker had sought distraction from his sorrow by reading curiously esoteric books. Awakened at midnight by a sound outside his chamber, he opens the door, expecting a visitor; he finds only darkness. Apprehensive, he whispers the name Lenore and closes the door. When the tapping persists, he opens a window, admitting a raven that perches upon a bust of Pallas (Athena).

In stanzas 8 to 11, the narrator, beguiled by the ludicrous image of the black bird in his room, playfully asks the raven its name, as if to reassure himself that it portends nothing ominous. He is startled, however, to hear the raven respond, saying, "Nevermore." Although the word apparently has little relevance to any discoverable meaning, the narrator is sobered by the bird's forlorn utterance. He assumes that the raven's owner, having suffered unendurable disasters, taught the bird to imitate human speech in order to utter the one word most expressive of the owner's sense of hopelessness.

In stanzas 12 and 13, the narrator settles himself on a velvet cushion in front of the bird and whimsically ponders what the raven meant by repeating a word he inevitably associated with thoughts of the departed Lenore. At this point, the grieving lover, in anticipation of the raven's maddening repetition of "Nevermore," begins masochistically to frame increasingly painful questions.

Imagining a perfumed presence in the room, the narrator, in a state of growing agitation, asks the raven whether God had mercifully sent him to induce in the poet forgetfulness of the lost Lenore; the inevitable response causes the narrator to plead with the raven—now addressed as a prophet of evil sent by the "Temptor"—to tell him whether there is any healing in heaven for his grief. The raven's predictable answer provokes the grieving lover, now almost in a state of maddened frenzy, to ask bluntly whether his soul would ever be reunited with Lenore in heaven. Receiving the horrific "Nevermore" in reply to his ultimate question, the distraught narrator demands that the raven, whether actual bird or fiend, leave his chambers and quit torturing his heart; the raven's unendurable answer drives the bereaved lover into a state of maddened despair. The raven becomes a permanent fixture in the room, a symbolic presence presiding over the narrator's self-inflicted mental and spiritual collapse.

Forms and Devices

"The Raven" is Edgar Allan Poe's most famous poem, not only because of its immediate and continued popularity but also because Poe wrote "The Philosophy of Composition," an essay reconstructing the step-by-step process of how he composed the poem as if it were a precise mathematical problem. Discounting the role of serendipity, romantic inspiration, or intuition, Poe accounted for every detail as the result of calculated effect. Although the essay may be a tour de force, informed readers of the poem—from the nineteenth century French poets Charles Baudelaire, Stéphane Mallarmé, and Paul Valéry to such modern poets as Allen Tate and T. S. Eliot—have recognized the value of Poe's essay in understanding the poem's forms and poetic devices.

Poe's analysis of the structure and texture of "The Raven" is too detailed to consider at length (and some of it must be taken with several grains of salt, allowing for considerable exaggeration on Poe's part); however, his essay sheds light on three important aspects implicit in the poem's form: its conception as a theatrical performance; the narrator's anguished involvement in making meaning by obsessively asking increasingly self-lacerating questions; and the function of the maddening, incantatory rhythm and rhymes that help cast a mind-paralyzing spell over both the declaiming narrator and the reader.

Although the principles of brevity and unity of impression or effect that inform the poem rest on Poe's aesthetic theories, derived from the facultative psychology of his time (the world of mind separated into faculties of intellect, taste, and the moral sense with crucial implications for the form and substance of poetry and romance), it is more helpful to see the contribution of this severe economy of means to the histrionic qualities of the poem. The persona narrates the poem as a kind of dramatic monologue, carefully arranging the scene of his chamber and the stage properties for maximum theatrical effect: the play of light and shadow from the hearth, the esoteric volumes, the silken, purple curtains, the door and window opening onto a tempestuous night offstage. There is also the dramatic juxtaposition of the black talking bird perched on the white bust of Pallas over the chamber door, the velvet cushion on which the narrator sits facing the raven, and the lamplight throwing shadows over the narrator's soul "floating on the floor," at the frenzied climax of the poem. Even the pivotal refrain that keynotes the poem's structure contributes to the artistic effect "in the theatrical sense."

The most original device of the poem is the way the narrator unconsciously arranges his questions. He begins nonchalantly with a commonplace question; under the hypnotic influence of the raven's cacophanous, melancholic repetition of "Nevermore," and driven by both the human thirst for self-torture and a superstitious mind, the bereaved lover luxuriates in sorrow by asking more distressful questions until the inexorable answer becomes intolerable, and he melodramatically sinks into maddened despair.

The nightmarish effect of the poem is reinforced by the relentless trochaic rhythm and the arrangement of the ballad stanzas into five lines of octameter followed by a refrain in tetrameter. This combination, along with emphatic alliteration, allows for strong internal and end-rhymes, resulting in a mesmerizing syncopation of redundancies as inescapable as the sonorous refrain. This incantatory repetition creates an aural quality that helps force a collaboration between the poem and the reader, a maddening regularity aptly conveying the speaker's disintegrating reason, while contributing to the theatrical effect of the poem as histrionic performance.

Themes and Meaings

"The Raven" objectifies Poe's belief that the artistic experiencing of a poem is an end in itself. As both poet and critic, Poe attacked two trends that he found equally disastrous: what he called "epic mania" (using the length of a poem as an index to its power and significance) and the "didactic heresy" (taking the explicit moral or philosophical meaning of a poem as its chief value).

Although Poe's aesthetic theories, set forth in such essays as "The Poetic Principle" and "The Philosophy of Composition," rely on a romantic theory of the imagination (as filtered through the writings of Samuel Taylor Coleridge and the temperament of Poe), the gist of his art is targeted toward the poem as experience. According to Poe, the intellect craves truth (the sphere of philosophical, rational discourse), and the moral sense craves duty (the domain of didactic writing), whereas taste thirsts for beauty (quenched only by poetry with its musicality and, therefore, its indefinite pleasure, and by romance with its more definite pleasure). Hence, a poem, in providing an indefinite, pleasurable aesthetic experience, requires a sense of complexity (all means including rhythm and sound adapted to a predetermined end) and a suggestive undercurrent of meaning.

In speaking of "The Raven," Poe declared that an intended undercurrent of meaning first becomes apparent in the metaphorical "Take thy beak from out *my heart*, and take thy form from off my door!/ Quoth the Raven 'Nevermore!'" The raven thus becomes "emblematical of Mournful and Never-Ending Remembrance." Fortunately, the poem's thematic significance transcends this limited intention.

The undeniable power of "The Raven" comes from the inexplicable, overwhelming sorrow at the heart of the poem, conveyed through the narrator's theatrical passion, grief, and, finally, insane desperation. The reader, involved in the complicity of the poem's design, sees the narrator as existing operatically, on a stage, outside the normal relations of space and time, and moving from the barely plausible to the realm of fantasy. The sensitive narrator's apparent passivity and the pounding rhythm create the emotional logic of a dream, in which things happened to him that he cannot change, only experience. Yet he is paradoxically involved in promoting his own psychological disintegration by posing a crescendo of self-destroying questions whose answers were the illogical repetition of a single word, croaked by a non-reasoning creature. Through his compulsions, he participates in constructing the unendurable meaning of eternal loss and separation from the one object of his desire. The drama of this loss of sanity is unforgettable as the reader surrenders to the histrionic performance which is the poem.

Clifford Edwards

REASONS FOR ATTENDANCE

Author: Philip Larkin (1922-1985)
Type of poem: Lyric
First published: 1955, in *The Less Deceived*

The Poem

"Reasons for Attendance" is a short poem of twenty lines that is divided into four cinquains with regular rhyme scheme based primarily on slant rhymes. The title hints at Philip Larkin's multiple concerns in the poem. He ponders why the young couples with "flushed face" move "to and fro" inside the dance hall while he remains outside. Similarly, he considers why he, despite his protests that he does not need the happiness inside the hall, is drawn "To watch the dancers" — that is, to "attend" to them, in the archaic sense of "give heed to."

"Reasons for Attendance" begins with the speaker standing outside "the lighted glass" feeling compelled to watch the dancers inside. For the remainder of the poem, Larkin alternates between the perspectives of the observer outside and the dancers inside the hall. In the third line of the first stanza, he shifts from himself to the particulars of the dancers, who shift "intently" and "Solemnly on the beat of happiness."

The second stanza brings another shift in perspective, as the poet focuses on what he senses ("smoke and sweat" and "The wonderful feel of girls") as he attempts to penetrate the atmosphere inside. The first line of the stanza ("Or so I fancy") raises the possibility that the earlier sensations described inside the dance hall were only what the poet's "fancy" projected onto the scene.

Beginning with line 2 of the second stanza, the poet presents the two competing motivations that inform the poem — sex, seen by many as "the lion's share/ Of happiness," and the "lifted, rough-tongued bell" of art, which demands a separateness of its followers. In the third and fourth stanzas, Larkin seems to resolve the conflict by asking that the dancers and the detached observer be allowed to follow their own "voices" — the dancers to follow the "trumpet's voice" of communion and sexuality, and the speaker, the "individual sound" of his muse's bell. He concludes that "both are satisfied."

With the last line of the poem, however, the poet undercuts this apparent resolution by raising the possibility that neither party has found happiness: "If no one has misjudged himself. Or lied." This ambivalence saves the poem from the kind of easy truce between competing ethics that Victorian readers admired and contemporary readers may find too pat in Alfred, Lord Tennyson's "Ulysses": "He works his work, I mine."

Forms and Devices

In "Reasons for Attendance," the poet uses ambiguity and paradox to suggest his uncertainty over the choices he has made and his ambivalence toward the dancers. In the final line of the third stanza, the poet moves toward a clear declaration of his position concerning human choices: "It speaks; I hear." "It" seems to refer to the vague concept in the stanza's second line — "that lifted, rough-tongued bell." Sensing that the reader will not be able to understand the significance of the bell, Larkin parenthetically identifies it as "Art," only to withdraw certainty with his qualifier "if you like." If the bell is art, the statement bridging the third and fourth stanzas seems deliberately ambiguous: "others may hear as well,/ But not for me, nor I for them." May hear what? the reader might ask, since the "others" in the poem — the young dancers — have heeded the trumpet's call to communion, not the voice of art. When the poet concludes "and so/ With happiness," the reader can only wonder, and what with happiness? since "so" apparently refers to the preceding ambiguous statements about hearing.

The poet ends with a final instance of ambiguity, this time a pair of demonstrative pronouns presented in parallel positions, neither with a clear referent: "Therefore I stay outside,/ Believing this; and they maul to and fro,/ Believing that." The poet has worked himself into a state of confusion concerning his own motives and implies that the young dancers experience a similar confusion.

Larkin creates a sense of the uncertainty he feels about the world inside the "lighted glass" of the dance hall through a series of paradoxes. The young dancers move "on the beat of happiness," yet they shift "Solemnly." The poet juxtaposes the "smoke and sweat" inside the dance hall with the "wonderful feel of girls." He also creates a paradox in his use of a lion metaphor: The sexuality enjoyed by couples may be "the lion's share/ Of happiness," but the young couples "maul to and fro."

Instead of letting his confusion rage, Larkin remains detached, controlling his emotions through a number of poetic devices. In the second stanza, when the poet senses his own anxiety over the possibility that sex holds "the lion's share/ Of happiness," he distances himself by shifting to the purposely pretentious tone of the third stanza: "What calls me is that lifted, rough-tongued bell/ (Art, if you like)." Larkin also reins in his fears by using a consistent meter (iambic pentameter) and relentlessly adhering to his chosen rhyme scheme (albeit most often through less obtrusive slant rhyme). Finally, the poet guards against his own emotions by using understatement throughout the poem: "It speaks; I hear," "and so/ With happiness," "both are satisfied," "Or lied."

Themes and Meanings

The central concern of "Reasons for Attendance" is the choice between competing ways of life — a life of human connection and sexuality, and the detached, isolated life of the artist/misanthrope. In this poem (as in Robert Frost's "The Road Not Taken"), the decision-making process itself is dramatized for the reader. In Larkin's poem, the reader sees what Mikhail Bakhtin calls the "dialogic imagination" at work as separate "voices" — the "trumpet's voice" and the "rough-tongued bell" — struggle to present their competing claims.

After noting how he answers the trumpet call of the dance hall, the detached poet becomes more and more engaged by the movements of the "flushed face" dancers until he can actually "sense" the "smoke and sweat" beyond the glass. Finally seduced by thoughts of the "wonderful feel of girls," he is forced to ask himself, "Why be out here?" At this moment, the voice of individuality is compelled to counter with "But then, why be in there? Sex, yes, but what/ Is sex?"

Triggered by the mention of sex, Larkin the individualist plunges ahead to proclaim his judgment of the notion that supreme happiness is possible only through sexuality: "Surely, to think the lion's share/ Of happiness is found by couples— sheer/ Inaccuracy, as far as I'm concerned." Forced by the break in stanzas after the word "sheer" to wait to hear the poet's final assessment, the reader can almost feel Larkin struggling to choose the right word to express his disdain. Through the device of enjambment from one stanza to another, Larkin creates the turn of the poem. Poised at this moment of indecision, the reader has been led by the emphatic words "Surely" and "sheer" to expect an outburst of contempt for the notion that social contact is superior to individual happiness. Instead, either under the influence of his competing voice or in fear of the passionate crescendo of emotions in the preceding lines, the poet retreats to understatement—calling the notion "inaccurate" — and assumes the detached, pretentious tone that dominates almost until the poem's end.

In fact, from this turn in the poem until the final line, Larkin is able to create what Bakhtin calls a "centripetal force": The two voices seem to reach a resolution in which each accepts the beliefs of the other and both are "satisfied" with their own choices. Larkin even seems to underscore this controlled harmony by resorting in the final stanza to exact rhyme rather than slant rhyme for the first time in the poem.

The final line of the poem ("If no one has misjudged himself. Or lied."), however, destroys the poem's logical and formal harmony, setting off again what Bakhtin would call the poem's "centrifugal force." Larkin's honesty (the same unflinching clear-sightedness that pervades many of the poems in *The Less Deceived*, the monograph in which "Reasons for Attendance" appears) raises the possibility that either the dancers or the poet have been self-deluded in their happiness. Which of the two parties is "the less deceived"? Larkin's honesty at the poem's end might lead the reader to conclude that the poet is less deluded than the solemn, mauling dancers. Yet the use of the masculine "himself" (though ostensibly a generic pronoun) and the dramatization of the poet's self-deception in the course of the poem lead the reader to speculate that the poet, though less deceived than at the poem's beginning, is still deceived himself.

Janice Moore Fuller

RECESSIONAL

Author: Rudyard Kipling (1865-1936)
Type of poem: Meditation
First published: 1897; collected in *Recessional and Other Poems*, 1899

The Poem

"Recessional" contains five stanzas of six lines each, with the first and third lines and the second and fourth rhyming. Following each quatrain there appears a rhymed couplet, which remains the same in the first four stanzas, then changes in the fifth. The closing couplet issues an even firmer admonition to underscore the warning that is extended in the previous refrain.

A recessional is a hymn or piece of music that is sung or played at the end of a religious service. From one perspective, the title dictates the form of the poem, which follows the tradition of the English hymn. More significantly, though, the title may be taken ironically. The poem was written in 1897, the year of Queen Victoria's Diamond Jubilee, which turned into a celebration of the British Empire. "Recessional," seems to herald the end of the Empire rather than to assure its long life.

In the opening quatrain, the poet speaks to the "God of our fathers" and acknowledges Him as the Lord of all that the British control. The couplet that follows asks that God's spirit be with the poet and his proud, vain countrymen unless they fail to understand that permanence and salvation can be found only in "Thine ancient sacrifice," not in temporal things: "Lord God of Hosts, be with us yet,/ Lest we forget—lest we forget." The poet then continues what is essentially a prayer, and in each stanza he speaks more directly to the empire builders themselves. In the second stanza, for example, he reminds them that rulers depart and only God remains. This idea he reinforces in the third and fourth verses, which take up the fleeting nature of pomp, power, and pride.

The final stanza emphasizes even more strongly that such worldly accomplishments as the Empire, no matter how valiantly sought and guarded, transform into mere dust when placed alongside the eternal nature of God. The closing couplet, different from those that have ended the preceding four stanzas, warns the British of boasting and foolishness, and supplicates God for mercy: "For frantic boast and foolish word—/ Thy mercy on Thy People, Lord!"

Forms and Devices

Today Rudyard Kipling is not considered a fashionable poet, in part because of the even rhythms and rhyme that characterize his work, but those very forms and devices for which he is now often criticized make many of the poems pleasantly readable, especially when presented aloud. Certainly, he was neither an innovator nor a major influence on English poetry, but many of his varied poems provide an accessible and often amusing history of the British Empire. He was a master of the dramatic monologue, as illustrated in a poem such as "Gunga Din," and he could handle the ballad form with good effect.

From a technical standpoint, however, "Recessional" stands apart from the poems that record the brighter side of the Empire. In this poem Kipling departs from his usual methodology and adapts the form of the hymn to suit his own purposes. The English hymn owes its origins to the eighteenth century poet Isaac Watts (1674-1748), and those who came after Watts followed the patterns set down by him. Kipling also remains faithful to the established forms and devices.

First, the hymns were usually addressed to God, who is called by various set names. Kipling follows this format and employs many of the prescribed titles: "God of our fathers," "Lord God of Hosts," "Judge of the Nations." He uses the formal "Thy" and "Thine" throughout. An expression such as "awful Hand," which appears in the first stanza, is also typical, even though it jars modern readers who may not know that "awful" once meant "full of awe" and served aptly to describe God.

This stilted language, so characteristic of the hymn, is not only exercised to name the varied attributes of the divine being but is also used to describe material objects. For example, Kipling in the final stanza pictures a gun as a "reeking tube and iron shard." In the first stanza, rather than calling the Empire by name, Kipling chooses the metonymic device of "palm and pine" to represent the vast regions the British dominate; later he conjures up great stretches of the Empire by the simple words, "dune and headland."

Echoes from the King James Version of the Bible also find their way into the language and imagery of the hymn. Kipling follows this dictate as well by speaking of the "dust that builds on dust" and referring to an Old Testament city, Nineveh. The fourth stanza draws on a direct reference from Romans in the New Testament to point out how the British erroneously considered themselves superior to those they ruled.

Finally, the hymn requires what might be called stock words to depict human-kind's folly in contrast to divine wisdom. Kipling fulfills this demand as well, when he damns the Diamond Jubilee of Queen Victoria for being full of "tumult," "shouting," and "pomp" and admonishes the celebrants, whom he sees as "drunk with sight of power," speaking in "Wild tongues that have not Thee in awe."

Kipling, then, has relied on the versification and diction of the traditional English hymn, which for the most part does not constitute great poetry. This undistinguished form and its devices — noble in their own manner — may give Kipling's poem an old-fashioned air and may even at first obscure its timeless truths. Once "Recessional" is seen as a subversion of the very pattern it employs, the irony becomes apparent and the poem gains resonance. Although the hymn tradition that serves as the basis for the poem is intended to praise, Kipling has done quite the opposite, condemning the excesses of Empire and those caught up in an orgy of nationalism.

Themes and Meanings

At the time that "Recessional" was written, the British boasted that the sun never set on their Empire, one of the most extensive, powerful, and prosperous exercises in imperialism that the world had ever known. That Kipling observed the celebration of an empire—surely thought to last a thousand years—by titling his poem "Recessional" suggests that he foresaw an end to British dominion over such far-flung places as great parts of Africa and the West Indies, Australia, Canada, New Zealand, and India. Even though this gloomy assessment disappointed those who thought of Kipling as a defender of the Empire and led to criticism, he was right after all. In fact, even at the time of the Diamond Jubilee in 1897, cracks had started to appear in the imperial shield. There had been the 1857 mutiny against the British in India, and the Boer War in South Africa would start in 1899; as well, nationalism was on the rise in settler countries such as Australia. World War I weakened the Empire further, and World War II brought about its dismantling—by the 1950's, the Empire was indeed only the "pomp of yesterday." Kipling predicts this collapse in his disparaging reference to the glorious exercise in dominion that occurred when bonfires were lighted simultaneously around the world to observe the anniversary of Queen Victoria's accession to the throne; the line that calls up this event is less than triumphant: "On dune and headland sinks the fire."

Two lines in the fourth stanza allude to the British attitude toward the subjects who populated their Empire: "Such boastings as the Gentiles use,/ Or lesser breeds without the Law." This allusion is not altogether clear without reference to its biblical source, Romans 2:14: In Paul's epistle to the Romans, he warns the Gentiles that they are not exempt from the holy law, but like the Jews are subject to the "judgment of God." Particularly appropriate is the earlier verse (2:11), where Paul states: "For there is no respect of persons with God." At the basis of Empire lay the idea that the British were superior to those they ruled and were not subject to the same restrictions as the "lesser breeds"—Kipling's ironic description of the British subjects, black and white, who dwelled in the stolen land on which the sun never set. The Anglo-Saxon superiority so cherished by the British had apparently been granted them by their Christian God. The spread of Christianity figured prominently in the business of Empire, but even the embrace of the official religion did not confer British superiority on the Indian or African.

While the poem may be read satisfactorily in its historical context as a death knell for the British Empire, it can also be approached as a religious poem that summons humankind to shun earthly delights and with "An humble and a contrite heart" direct attention toward eternal values. The Empire then becomes a metaphor representing worldly things that turn to dust, even if their glitter attracts a boasting and foolish people.

Robert Ross

THE RED WHEELBARROW

Author: William Carlos Williams (1883-1963)
Type of poem: Lyric
First published: 1923, as "XXII," in *Spring and All*; as "The Red Wheelbarrow,"
 in *Selected Poems*, 1949

The Poem

"The Red Wheelbarrow" is a brief lyric written in free verse. It is composed of
four stanzas, each consisting of two short lines. The entire poem contains only sixteen words, four words in each stanza. The lyric "I" does not appear, placing the
reader in direct contact with the images of the poem. These are presented one by
one in short lines, which slow the reading and focus the reader's attention on each
bit of information in a sequence that suspends completion of the scene until the very
last word. The surprise implicit in this arrangement is particularly present in the
poem as it was first published, without a title, as poem number "XXII" in *Spring
and All*. In that book William Carlos Williams alternates passages of prose expressing his theories of poetry with groups of poems illustrating those theories.

The poet begins with an impersonal statement, composed of abstract words: "so
much depends/ upon." This stanza creates suspense by raising the question, What
depends on what? This is partly answered in the second stanza: "a red wheel/ barrow." In contrast to the words of the first stanza, each word here, except for the
article "a," evokes a sense of impression. By dividing the word "wheelbarrow" into
its parts, "wheel" and "barrow," and by breaking the line after "barrow," the poet
slows the reading, which helps to imprint the image on the reader's mind. It also
makes a wheelbarrow less familiar than usual, its wheel separated from its barrow, a
tray with two handles at each end for carrying loads. Implicit here is the original
idea for the invention of a wheelbarrow.

In the third stanza the poet begins to provide a context for the wheelbarrow in the
natural world with the information that it is "glazed with rain/ water." It might be
thought that the word "water" is superfluous. By separating the word "rain" from
"water" with a line break, however, the poet continues the slow motion and suggests
that the rain has just stopped. The word "glazed" implies light shining off the film
of water still present on the red paint of the wheelbarrow. The sun has come out.

The fourth and final stanza completes the scene. The wheelbarrow is "beside the
white/ chickens." The color white contrasts with the color red, which intensifies
both colors and suggests bright light. The sentient chickens contrast with the inert
wheelbarrow. The chickens are moving, and the scene comes alive. Human beings
do not appear in the poem, but they are implied, as it took people to domesticate
animals and invent machines.

Forms and Devices

Williams has excluded most of the forms and devices traditionally associated with poetry in the composition of this poem. He rejects the convention of beginning each line with a capital letter; he does not employ a traditional form; he avoids writing in an established meter; and he does not use rhyme. He does not use words for their connotations or associations or write in elevated language. He excludes similes, metaphors, and symbols. Even the subject of the poem is mundane, a wheelbarrow not being the sort of thing likely to inspire aesthetic contemplation or reveal great truth. The term "anti-poetry," sometimes applied to Williams' work, is valid only in reference to characteristics such as these.

Williams relies almost entirely on images to communicate the meanings of "The Red Wheelbarrow," and the poem exemplifies the principles of Imagism, a literary movement originated in London by friends of Williams, the American expatriate poets Hilda Doolittle (H. D.) and Ezra Pound. Imagist poetry presents things directly, using only words essential to the presentation, and is composed in free verse. Although Williams sometimes used the term "Imagism" and "free verse" in reference to his work, he was intent on creating an American poetry distinct from English poetry, and he distanced himself from the expatriates, substituting the term "Objectivism" for "Imagism" and developing his conception of the variable foot to distinguish his versification from free verse.

Although the images in "The Red Wheelbarrow" refer to objects in the external world, Objectivism also applies to the poem as an object itself, made out of words and comparable to a painting made out of paint. Williams knew and was influenced by such visual artists as Alfred Stieglitz and Charles Demuth. He believed that a poem can be a painting and a painting can be a poem. "The Red Wheelbarrow" creates a visual scene in the reader's mind, and the first stanza, "so much depends/ upon," functions like a frame for the picture. It says, "Look at this." A painting is seen, however, all at once, while the poem occurs image by image, line after line, having a duration in time.

The poem is intricately structured in repeating patterns. For example, there are four words and three stressed syllables in each stanza. Stanzas are arranged in two lines each, the first containing three words and two stressed syllables, the second containing one word and one stressed syllable. The poem also exemplifies the variable foot. Each line is a poetic foot, and each foot is to be given the same duration in reading. This results in a pause following the second line of each stanza to make up for the extra stressed syllable in each of the first lines. Variations in rhythm also result from the number and placement of unstressed syllables. For example, the unstressed syllable in the third line of the poem, "a red wheel," comes before the two stressed syllables, while in the fifth line, "glazed with rain," it comes between the two stressed syllables.

Themes and Meanings

What "depends upon" a red wheelbarrow, white chickens, and rain? The reader is aware of the usefulness — in the case of rain, the necessity — of these things in the external world. The things referred to in the poem are also particular instances of types and classes of things—the wheelbarrow being a machine, for example, on which life also depends. Furthermore, sensations, feelings, emotions, thoughts, and ideas depend on such things. As the poet expresses it in his poem "A Sort of a Song," "No ideas/ but in things." The faculty of the mind that has ideas is the imagination. "The Red Wheelbarrow" is about the relationship between the imagination and reality.

In *Spring and All*, Williams explains that the imagination is the opposite of fantasy; it penetrates fantasies to reveal realities. It clears away personal and conventional associations and meanings that human beings have attached to things, and to the words that represent them, enabling human consciousness to perceive the things of reality as directly as possible. In *Spring and All*, Williams writes: "To refine, to clarify, to intensify that eternal moment in which we alone live there is but a single force—the imagination."

The poet creates such an experience for the reader in "The Red Wheelbarrow." The imagination is itself a force of nature that creates things like poems and wheelbarrows, just as nature creates rain and white chickens. The reader experiences the poet's imagination in the process of making the poem, making a thing out of words to stand in relation to the reader as would an actual experience of the scene represented in the poem. Williams does not employ the lyric "I" of the poet's personality or use the conventions and devices traditionally associated with poetry. This allows the reader to focus on the words and images of the poem. Williams' strategies also seek to dissolve the personal ego of the reader. Forgetting self, the reader achieves a moment of pure awareness.

It is the poet's mind that the reader experiences, as it selects and arranges the words of the poem, revealing the ideas implicit in them. The words depend on the things and the processes they name for their existence and meaning. In this light, the nonimagistic words in the poem are particularly interesting. The images name things and their visual qualities, but what is the difference between "a" red wheelbarrow and "the" red wheelbarrow? What ideas are referred to in the prepositions "on," "with," and "beside"? What is the meaning of "depends"? The ideas expressed by these words have been discovered by the human imagination in its contemplation of things and the relationships among them. Language depends on things, and civilization depends on language.

James Green

A REFUSAL TO MOURN THE DEATH, BY FIRE, OF A CHILD IN LONDON

Author: Dylan Thomas (1914-1953)
Type of poem: Lyric
First published: 1945; collected in *Deaths and Entrances*, 1946

The Poem

"A Refusal to Mourn the Death, by Fire, of a Child in London," a poem of twenty-four lines divided into four stanzas of six lines each, follows the rhyme scheme *abcabc*. The title indicates the poet's rejection of conventional means of responding to death. The refusal takes on greater force as it confronts the senseless casualty of a child to war; the fire refers to the firebombing of London during World War II.

The poem is written in the first person, and more is revealed about the poet who speaks than about the child who has died. The poet declares that not until he himself dies will he declaim the child's death. He rejects somber elegies, with their toxic spirituality; in dying, the child has united with the elements from which life springs and therefore is no longer prey to death.

The poem opens boldly with an extended adjective— "mankind/ making/ Bird, beast and flower/ Fathering and all humbling"—that modifies "darkness." The image locates the origin of life in death. The poet thus evokes at the start the natural cycle of birth and death. The darkness signals the "last light breaking"—light indicating consciousness—as well as the stilling of the "sea tumbling in harness," or the blood surging through the body. Death, then, extinguishes both the psychic and physical signs of an individual life.

This loss is more accurately a transformation: Single life diffuses into universal life. After death, one must "enter again" the "Zion of the water bead" and the "synagogue of the ear of corn." Rather than personal immortality, humans are destined for incorporation into dynamic, elemental bonds or assemblages of freshly sprouting life. Once metamorphosed, the poet can convey the child's experience in death, embodying the substance and vitality of nature itself.

Gripped by this awareness, the poet views customary rituals of mourning as sterile and hollow. To presume to honor the child with such pieties is to "murder" her humanity; to dare to sanctify her "innocence and youth" is to "blaspheme" the Incarnate Christ. With the phrase "the stations of the breath," the poet alludes to "the stations of the Cross," a ritualization of Jesus' suffering—again fusing life ("breath") and death.

In death, the girl joins life—that is, the "long friends," those long dead and forever alive—the "grains beyond age," or the seeds and sands of time, and the "dark veins of her mother," or the earth, veined with rivers. The water of the "riding Thames," London's river as the child is "London's daughter," is "unmourning"; it is the water of renewal, vital and teeming with life. Water quenches fire and nourishes seed, and just as rivers pour into the sea—all water being one—individual life flows into universal life, all life being one.

The ambiguity of the poem's last line, "After the first death, there is no other," suspends contraries in a vision of wholeness. Nature is compelled toward regeneration; therefore, while a death is final, life itself is eternal.

Forms and Devices

Fellow poet Conrad Aiken has called Dylan Thomas a "born language-lover" with a "genius for word magic." Thomas' passion for words is revealed in his conjuring of their sensual appeal as well as their connotative power.

The texture of the poem is enriched by the sound pattern woven by the poet. Besides the tight rhyme scheme, alliteration, as in "mankind making," "last light," and "sow my salt seed," helps draw the reader's senses into the world of the poem.

The poet also chooses words for the richness of their associations: "Zion," "synagogue," "pray," "sackcloth," "blaspheme," and "first death" are all radiant with religious significance. Juxtaposition of such terms with natural imagery—"water bead," "ear of corn," "sound," "valley," "grains"—indicates Thomas' understanding of the sacramental force of nature: The symbols of religious myth and ritual owe their potency to a link with primordial, natural realities.

The poet communicates such visionary insight with his complex imagery. "Zion of the water bead," for example, merges a symbol from religious legend, "Zion," with an original metaphor inspired by nature, "water bead." The complexity of Thomas' imagery renders it dynamic; the image provokes a reader to resolve the tensions between its disparate parts. Readers' preconceptions of science and religion, nature and myth, and past, present, and future are dramatically challenged.

As envisioned by the poet, human and natural life are of the same stuff. He envisions the human body as a microcosm of nature; the circular system is "the sea tumbling in harness." At the same time, he personifies nature: "grains" are "friends," and London's earth has "dark veins."

Themes and Meanings

Thomas' poetry has an almost revelatory power, in which meaning is experienced in the act of either creating or re-creating (that is, reading) the poem. The sound, rhythm, and visual impact, as well as psychological force, of the words have a transforming effect on the imagination. The violent shifts of perspective that the poem achieves help make one receptive to its visionary, ultimately healing power.

Thomas' concern with the creative process is evidenced in his own description of his "dialectical" method:

> An image must be born and die in another; and any sequence of my images must be a sequence of creations, recreations, destructions, contradictions. . . . Out of the inevitable conflict of images . . . I try to make that momentary peace which is a poem.

The poet's struggle is that of the creative imagination attempting to name the unnamable — that is, the mysteries of existence. The poem confounds contradictory images of life and death, sacred and profane, human and nonhuman, and the one and the many in an attempt to capture the inexhaustable fecundity and resilience of life. It climaxes in a statement which is itself a paradox: Death is final and yet is not, ultimately, definitive.

The poem's vision of the protean unity of all things transforms grief into wonder. This insight is affirmed both by ancient belief that life has eternal regenerative power and by scientific theory that matter can never be destroyed but only transmuted — into energy.

Amy Adelstein

RELIGIO LAICI

Author: John Dryden (1631-1700)
Type of poem: Verse essay
First published: 1682

The Poem

Religio Laici (a layman's religion) represents John Dryden's tentative and candid examination of major religious issues of his day. From the title, one might expect a personal confession of faith. Instead, Dryden examines the principal contemporary religious currents in England and, although he reveals only general points about his own beliefs, he clearly expresses his adherence to the Church of England. The poem, consisting of 456 lines of heroic couplets, divides into several logical sections.

In the beginning, Dryden eloquently points to limitations on the power of reason in religion, stressing that even the ancient philosophers, despite all their wisdom, could discover no adequate foundation for religion through their intellectual efforts. Because he shared with his contemporaries a profound respect for the intellectual attainments of the classical Greeks and Romans, this line of reasoning effectively prepares the groundwork for Dryden's rejection of Deism, the rational religion of his own day. A summary of basic Deistic tenets (lines 42-61) precedes a formal rejection of natural religion.

Dryden suggests that any light the Deist sees originates in revelation, not from man's intuitive knowledge as the Deists assumed, and that, in any case, a lesser being such as man cannot atone for his own sins through his own efforts (lines 62-125). Only an unfallen being, Dryden urges, would be adequate to the task. Defending the Bible as the true source of religious revelation (lines 126-167), Dryden cites specific factors that support its authority: its antiquity, its narrative consistency, the conviction and courage of its authors, external confirmation from other sources, its style, its success despite its demanding ethics, and its acceptance despite persecution.

The Deist renews the debate that it is unjust that so many who never had an opportunity to receive revelation have been lost. Dryden agrees that this is a grave charge, yet he thinks that through divine mercy many who never know the true religion might yet have been saved (lines 168-223).

As this point, the poem takes a different approach to the question of scriptural authority by discussing Father Richard Simon's *Histoire critique du Vieux Testament* (*Critical History of the Old Testament*), first published in 1678 and translated into English in 1682 by Henry Dickinson. In a note in his text, Dryden explains that this portion is a digression, though it returns him to the authority of Scripture versus tradition, a central difference between Protestants and Catholics. Since he has already argued for the authority of the Bible, Dryden has laid the groundwork for parrying a newer and more recent challenge. Through meticulous scholarship, Si-

mon demonstrated that translators had so loosely and inaccurately translated biblical books that their claim to serve as a basis for faith was seriously compromised.
His purpose was to induce readers to turn to the authority of the Roman Catholic
Church as an infallible guide. Dryden acknowledges that Simon's points are cogent
in many instances but believes that the translations are sufficiently accurate on matters of genuine importance. He asserts that Scripture is clear on essential points and
rejects the view that an infallible church exists. While Dryden does not entirely
exclude reliance upon tradition, he points out that generally the most reliable is the
most ancient. Thus, tradition should be considered, but more trust should be placed
in the authority of the most ancient church fathers.

Excessive reliance on tradition, Dryden charges, has caused the Catholic Church
to deny the laity access to the Bible (lines 356-397). Yet making the text available
had the unfortunate effect of causing individuals to become overzealous and to run
to extremes of contention and sectarianism (lines 398-426). Rejection of tradition
thus led to extremes of private interpretation and ensuing religious strife.

In the conclusion of the poem (lines 427-456), Dryden recommends moderation
based upon the realization that necessary points of faith are few and plain. He further suggests that disputed points might be settled through the authority of the earliest and least corrupt of church fathers and that an individual who differs from
others on doctrine can promote the interests of society as a whole by keeping personal beliefs private.

Forms and Devices

In his lengthy prose introduction to *Religio Laici*, Dryden comments on the style
appropriate to a poem of its kind:

> If anyone be so lamentable a critic as to require the smoothness, the numbers, and the
> turn of heroic poetry in this poem, I must tell him that, if he has not read Horace, I
> have studied him, and hope the style of his *Epistles* is not ill imitated here. The
> expressions of a poem design'd purely for instruction ought to be plain and natural, and
> yet majestic; for here the poet is presum'd to be a kind of lawgiver, and those three
> qualities which I have nam'd are proper to the legislative style.

Casting himself in the role of an instructor and teacher, Dryden is content to eschew
poetic ornaments and figures in favor of a direct, plain style.

The poem employs the heroic couplet, Dryden's preferred verse form, with few
variations. Major structural divisions are usually indicated through verse paragraphs. Although most of the couplets are end-stopped, the norm for this stanza
pattern, a large number end with less than a full stop so that the grammatical unit
carries over to additional lines. This extension of the grammatical unit enables Dryden to pursue a line of reasoning smoothly to its end, taking into account some of its
complexities. Dryden's expansion of the normal limits of the couplet is one key to his
skill at reasoning verse.

In Dryden's heroic couplets, metrical departures are limited to two major ones, and both can be observed in *Religio Laici*. By occasionally adding a line to form a triplet, Dryden breaks the steady rhythm of the couplet. The break is even more effective when he makes the third verse a hexameter and creates a climactic effect, although among the seven triplets in *Religio Laici* few create an impressive rhetorical climax. The satiric tone of the following, expressing disapproval of excessive and individual reliance upon Scripture, may represent the triplet at its most effective in the poem:

> The spirit gave the doctoral degree;
> And every member of a company
> Was of his trade and of the Bible free.

The triplet's final verse, a hexameter for emphasis, achieves subtle poetic effects through balance and the use of zeugma, an unusual scheme for Dryden.

The second variation, use of a hemistitch or "half line," occurs only once in the poem. As a precedent for this metrical variation, Dryden cites Vergil, probably erroneously, for modern critics believe that the short lines in the *Aeneid* (c. 29-19 B.C.) are actually incomplete verses. Dryden uses the hemistitch to achieve an effective climax in the following passage:

> Those giant wits, in happier ages born,
> . . . .
> Knew no such system; no such piles could raise
> Of natural worship, built on pray'r and praise
> To One Sole GOD.

The final verse of only four syllables draws the reader up short; emphasis is further heightened by accents on three of its four syllables.

Throughout the poem Dryden uses schemes of repetition, such as balance and antithesis, yet his style remains for the most part simple and unadorned, at least by comparison to his other long poems in heroic couplets. In large measure, he assumes the stance of the debater, answering objections from the Deist on the one hand and the Catholic on the other. On occasion, Dryden personifies his adversary and gives him a direct quotation. The effect is clearly to stack the argument in Dryden's favor, since his opponents have no opportunity to attack his own moderate positions outlined near the poem's conclusion. When he presents his own views, he speaks in the first person, in a tone that is both reassuring and restrained. In both prose and verse, Dryden was a master of the art of taking the reader into his confidence.

Not all the diction is informal and colloquial, however; the most striking departure from the plain style can be found in the poem's opening twenty-two lines. In stately, slow rhythms, verses adorned with similes and metaphors and with schemes of repetition achieve a studied, majestic effect as Dryden explores the limitations of reason. The careful arrangement of sounds creates a tone of solemnity appropriate to Dryden's subject—the inadequacy of reason in religion. The verses remind the reader that Dryden is indeed capable of the heroic style that he has agreed to abandon. Paradoxically, while Dryden rejects reason as inadequate, he employs it as fully as possible in support of his major arguments throughout the rest of the poem.

Themes and Meanings

Although Dryden acknowledges the limits of reason in religious inquiry, his objective is to persuade the reader by presenting a rational, moderate argument. As he says in his preface, men are to be reasoned into truth. His portrayal of the Church of England and its theological stance reflects the longstanding view of the church as a *via media*, a middle way between extremes. Dryden is content to uphold general beliefs, such as the authority of Scripture and atonement, and leave other points vague.

The occasion for the poem is not known, though it is possible that, as poet laureate, Dryden thought it prudent to distance himself from the rising current of Deism, or rational religion, which appealed to his age. Like many Englishmen of the Restoration, he shared the view that extremes in religion brought calamity to society, though unlike the Deists, he was unwilling to distance himself from Christianity.

He disagrees with Deism on two basic assumptions. First, he rejects the view that basic religious truths are innate and articulable through reason. If that were so, Dryden argues cogently, the ancients would have discovered them. Second, he argues that following the fall, man's reconciliation with God cannot be achieved by man himself. The Deists, rejecting the idea of original sin, logically denied the need for atonement. On the other hand, Dryden agrees with the Deistic view that to condemn those who lived before or outside the Christian tradition seems unjust. Dryden's answer is to view the matter with tolerance and to suggest that divine mercy, in some manner, may well extend to everyone.

His eloquent defense of Scripture paves the way for rejection of the arguments raised by Simon's work on the Old Testament. Instead of attacking specifics, Dryden addresses the writer's motive, believing that the author sought to discredit the Bible in order to persuade men to accept Catholic oral tradition. While acknowledging some errors in biblical accounts, Dryden maintains that the text is adequate on essential beliefs and points out dangers in man's reliance upon tradition.

The rejection of extreme Protestant belief is brief by comparison. Dryden thinks that extremes of individualism have been the result of too much reliance upon individual interpretation of the Scripture, a condition that leads to sects, dissent, and strife. He suggests that men consult their own church's views on particulars of belief and ancient tradition.

Dryden is more concerned with defending a middle-of-the-road position in religion than with making any original contributions of his own. From this position, he discredits movements he believes to be socially dangerous, subversive, and disruptive. While attacking what he regards as dangerous extremes, he carefully avoids consideration of any specific doctrines of religion, as if to suggest that the Christian tradition permits many shades of belief and that tolerance of differences represents the best attitude.

Stanley Archer

RELOCATION

Author: David Mura (1952-   )
Type of poem: Meditation
First published: 1982; collected in *Breaking Silence: An Anthology of Contemporary Asian American Poets*, 1983; revised in *After We Lost Our Way*, 1989

The Poem

"Relocation," a poem of forty-seven lines, has four major sections separated by asterisks. Within each major section are three four-line stanzas, with the exception that the first section has only two stanzas and that an italicized haiku concludes the final section. The poem's dedication reads, "for Grandfather Uyemura," the central character in the poem. It is his several "relocations" that the poem describes. The physical removals from Japan to America, within America, and back to Japan are sometimes voluntary and sometimes coerced, and they result in either exhilaration and freedom or depression and oppression.

David Mura uses the format of the poem to deliver a sketchy biography of his grandfather, recounting the most significant events in his grandfather's adult life. The poem also indirectly traces the emotions with which Mura's grandfather responds to those life experiences and, even more indirectly, Mura's own emotional reactions to those events that predate his own birth.

The first section begins with an expository stanza that makes reference to an Asian custom prevalent around the 1920's. Asian men who had immigrated to America to seek their fortunes would send to their home countries a picture of themselves as a way of advertising for a bride of the same ethnic background. They would pay the one-way passage to America of any eligible woman who would be lured across the ocean by the picture and promise of marriage. Because the couple would not have previously met, the woman thus based her entire future happiness on the merit of a snapshot, and there were often unpleasant surprises at the dock if the man had misrepresented himself. Grandfather Uyemura, however, was so handsome that he did not hide behind a picture but returned to Japan in person to claim a bride. He was able to sail back to America with his arms around his chosen mate.

In section 2, Mura recounts his grandparents' success in establishing a happy life in their new country. Through industry and hard work, Grandfather Uyemura has bought a greenhouse where he grows orchids and roses. He also has enjoyed a certain amount of luck in the gambling houses.

The mood shifts away from happiness and good fortune in section 3, however. World War II breaks out, and the Japanese people living in America, including Grandfather and Grandmother Uyemura, are herded by the government into various "relocation camps" for the duration of the war. Instead of their pleasant home and greenhouse, the couple now lives with other Japanese-Americans in barracks surrounded by guards and barbed wire. Grandfather Uyemura is forced to plow fields and eat meals in a common mess hall with his wife.

The war has ended for some time by the final section, and the couple has a son whom they have named Kitsugi. He, however, adopts American ways with a new name — Tom — and a new religion — Christianity — which confuses and disappoints Grandfather Uyemura, a Buddhist. When his wife dies, Grandfather Uyemura returns to Tokyo and composes haiku in his old age.

Forms and Devices

Although all stanzas but the final haiku have a consistent number of lines that are roughly the same length, the poem breaks from conventional form because the lines do not rhyme. Grandfather Uyemura himself breaks from tradition in that he returns to Japan in person rather than trusting a snapshot to deliver a life partner to him.

His early adult life is lucky. His exuberance and good fortune are shown in the shining chrome of his Packard, at which he proudly beams. There is also an invincibility evident in the second stanza: After a lucky night at gambling, he greets even the thorns on the roses. He will not let hurtful things bother him. His imprisonment in the relocation camps with other Japanese does not defeat the spirits of either him or his wife. Their strength is that they have each other — for companionship and love — and their heritage.

At dinner, Grandfather Uyemura folds an origami crane out of a napkin, to the amusement and rapture of his wife. Besides signifying flight or freedom of spirit as any bird imagery would do, the crane has long symbolized for cultures ranging from China to the Mediterranean three other qualities: justice, longevity, and the good and diligent soul. The poem shows that Grandfather Uyemura possesses all three of those traits. Though treated with gross injustice, he unquestioningly does what he is ordered to do; he outlives his wife; and he is a good person who works hard. In Japanese, the name he has chosen for his son means "prince of birds."

An important poetic device that Mura uses is ambiguously purposeful enjambment (when the grammatical, logical, and syntactical sense of a poetic line both continues into the next line and also gains an additional meaning by pausing at the end of the first line). The first occurrence of this device is in lines 9 and 10. If one reads without pause to the first comma, the main idea is that Grandfather Uyemura was able to purchase his greenhouse through hard word and diligent saving. If the reader pauses instead at the end of line 9, the word "field" is sensed as a noun of location rather than an adjective. Imagining Grandfather Uyemura's greenhouse "on a field" emphasizes the concept of land that is important to the poem — specifically, the new land of America that challenges such immigrants as Grandfather Uyemura.

Another instance of enjambment occurs in the final four-line stanza in lines 42 to 44. At this point, Grandfather Uyemura's defiance has become resignation; his wife has died, his son seems more American than Japanese, and he himself is returning to Japan. If these lines are read with attention to the commas — not pausing at the ends of the lines — the picture that evolves is of Grandfather Uyemura, thin and cranelike, sitting in a chair and writing poetry. If, instead, the reader pauses at the end of line 43 and considers "spent" as an adjective rather than as a transitive verb, the implication is that old Grandfather Uyemura is himself spent, defeated by an unjust life in his new country. From such a stance, though, poetry finally emerges, and such a voice signifies a spiritual strength despite an emaciated physical body.

Themes and Meanings

Two important themes are central to an understanding and appreciation of the poem: movement or relocation and the larger issue of the clash of Japanese ethnicity with American culture.

The bird imagery in the poem, beginning with the screech of seagulls at the dock when Grandfather Uyemura meets his future wife, symbolizes the flight that characterizes the grandfather's life: immigration, return to Japan for a bride, return to America to seek his fortune, forced relocation in the internment camp, and return to his homeland. Putting down roots in a new country has not been possible for Grandfather Uyemura (although there are indications that it will be for his son), whose adult life has been marked by a continual pattern of flight. He is like the origami crane that he himself designs.

As the poem's title, "relocation" names what once must have been Grandfather Uyemura's sought-after personal goal. By the end of the poem some twenty years later, though, his return to his place of birth and to composing a verse form that is particularly Japanese indicate that American culture has not assimilated him and that he has settled on his culture of origin as his ethnic identity. As early as stanza 2, "pale ghosts" are gathering, which may be read as *hakujin*, or white people, that surround the Japanese couple in America. (The practice of labeling non-Asian people as "ghosts" is given extensive treatment in the works of another Asian-American writer, Maxine Hong Kingston.) On a less literal level, the pale ghosts could symbolize the ghosts of the grandfather's Japanese ancestors who will not let him rest until he returns to his home and his heritage.

Confined by Caucasian guards in the camp, Grandfather Uyemura outwardly submits to hard physical labor on one hand, but on the other hand silently defies his imprisonment, which he will not allow to break his spirit. He keeps his gaze on the "west," toward Japan, and mutters under his breath "Baka" to the guard. Mura does not gloss this Japanese expression, which is slang for "idiot" or "dumbbell." The grandfather is not giving in, and Mura also seems resistant toward catering too much to a non-Japanese reader.

Grandfather Uyemura has long cultivated the earth — as a field hand working to buy his greenhouse, then in the camp working a mule-driven plow. He has perhaps pruned the bonsai tree, which he writes about in his haiku, as he has nurtured his American orchids and roses. It is ironic, Mura implies, that the grandfather, at the hands of white America, has not been tended and nurtured with equal care and respect. His belief that "the Buddha always ate well" is at once a retort to his son's Christian crucifix that bears a gaunt and dying Jesus and a justification for himself, emaciated and aged, to return to Japan.

Subsequent to appearing in *Breaking Silence: An Anthology of Contemporary Asian American Poets* (1983) as one of hundreds of poems written by fifty Asian-American poets, "Relocation" appeared in Mura's first book of poetry, *After We Lost Our Way* (1989), under the title "Suite for Grandfather & Grandmother Uyemura: Relocation." The more recent version uses richer and more enigmatic imagery and shows Grandfather Uyemura contemplating remarriage after returning to Tokyo. The rest of the narrative lines, including the final haiku, are retained, however.

Mura discusses his own writing and concerns in his prose autobiography, *Turning Japanese: Memoirs of a Sansei* (1991). Awarded a writing grant that allowed him to spend 1984 in Japan, Mura describes his own search for cultural identity. The book is a meditation on difference and assimilation as well as a telling portrait of modern Japan.

Jill B. Gidmark

REMEDIES, MALADIES, REASONS

Author: Mona Van Duyn (1921-   )
Type of poem: Lyric
First published: 1970, in *To See, To Take*

The Poem

"Remedies, Maladies, Reasons" is written in a loose iambic pentameter form and is composed of fifty-eight couplets that rhyme obliquely. The last line in the poem which rhymes with the previous couplet, stands alone. There are three sections in the poem: The first thirty-six couplets form the first part; couplets 37 through 58 compose the second; and the single concluding line is a separate section of its own. The title serves as a synopsis of the poem: The speaker searches for reasons why her mother was so obsessed with her daughter's and her own physical maladies, and she wonders, in part, whether her mother's remedies were effective.

Mona Van Duyn and her mother are placed at the center of this lyric poem written in the conventional first person. This is not a persona poem; the speaker is the poet, and she is reflecting on her own past. The first section records chronologically Van Duyn's personal history, but the history is limited to the speaker's health and how the mother and daughter respond to it. The first sentence explains the dilemma: Van Duyn "nearly died/ at six weeks from nursing a serum" her mother had taken, so her mother becomes extremely overprotective of her, even when she grows up. "Girl Scouts, green apples, tree climbs, fairs," everything the "other kids" enjoyed, were off limits to her. Van Duyn describes herself as her mother's "one goose" that refused "to fatten" despite her mother's attempts to poke food into her daughter's mouth until she gagged. Enemas, mucus, mineral pills, bowels, and sore throats are the subjects of the mother-daughter discussions; the seemingly unhealthy relationship focuses solely on the daughter's health.

Van Duyn behaved in a submissive manner, partially because she "was scared to die," until she finally fought back as a junior in high school when her mother, in disciplining her, was "Breaking/ another free yardstick from the drygoods store/ on a butt and legs still bad." She continued rebelling in college, learning "how to tear up the letters" in which her mother gave her the customary advice: "for my sake please don't do it . . . don't try it . . . don't go . . . !" Years later, after Van Duyn had married and begun her career, when she returned to her mother's house to tend her ailing parents, she still heard the same litany: "Don't you dare go outside that door without your sweater!" The poet imagines that her mother can see on her daughter's shoulders, only "the weak, rolling head of a death-threatened baby."

In the beginning, section 2 turns the focus away from the mother's obsessive fascination with her daughter's health and concentrates on the mother's self-scrutiny; the self-scrutiny is limited to the world of the senses. Van Duyn's mother apparently has little interest in struggling for spiritual or psychological truths. She charts the levels of "blood in the snot," marvels at the smell of her sweat or urine, chronicles "the gas that makes her 'blow up tight as a drum,' " and counts the times she vomits: "I puked four times, and the last one/ was *pure bile!*"

Despite listing all the obvious shortcomings of her parent, Van Duyn remains fond of her mother, and, in her mind's eye, she can "still see the mother [she] wanted, that [she] called to come,/ coming." The poem closes with tremendous tenderness after all the "suppurating, rotting, stinking, swelling,/ . . . shrieking, . . . oozing." The emotional warmth, in the end, outshines the body's powers and failures.

Forms and Devices

Poets often write in couplets to draw the reader's attention toward the pairing going on in the poem; in this case, Van Duyn is drawing together mother and daughter, life and death, grief and tenderness, sickness and health, youth and age, accurate vision and hallucinations. The couplets also serve a more grounded purpose: In a particular rhyming couplet, the poet often tries to join words or ideas that are meant for each other. Van Duyn is a master of this. She rhymes "ate" and "toilet" and thereby heightens the intake/outflow obsession of the mother. "Oil" and "bowel" are linked by sound and function. The mother "marvels" at the "smells" her stinking body makes. It is marvelous to rhyme and find beauty in the beastly flesh. Rhyming also points out oppositions: The young Van Duyn wanted to "hike," but she was denied permission and forced to wear the shoes of the "chronic" invalid.

Van Duyn also yokes disparate ideas or images through her metaphors and comparisons. The poet describes her mother as a "Homer of her own heroic course" whose catalog of maladies and remedies echoes, humorously, Homer's own examples of bloody encounters and noble endurance. Van Duyn stays with the epic journey motif and describes her mother as an Odyssean character: "Keeping her painstaking charts, first mariner/ of such frightful seas, she logs each degree and number." The metaphor is funny but not cruel; the mother is on an epic journey toward death, but she only charts the number of times she "pukes" or the number of units of penicillin her doctor prescribes. The classical allusions end with another mock-heroic picture: The mother consults an oracle (a mysterious and sometimes dangerous action in ancient Greece), but here she consults only "the eight shelves of the six-foot, steel,/ crammed-with-medication oracle."

The final coupling takes place between the two different pictures the poet has of her mother. Van Duyn says, initially, "I know what she is, I know what she was:/ a hideous machine that pumps and wheezes." Her mother is a disgusting, stinking machine for "students to learn/ the horror, the nausea, of being human." The poet, however, draws the poem to a close with a typical gesture: She counters the mood by saying, "And yet. . . ." The qualification comes in the form of a reversal: The mother, looked at now, is "an attractive woman" and is the kind of mother the poet actually wanted. The formal device of the couplets makes the reader anticipate some sort of yoking or linking, and Van Duyn delivers on the promise that her formal choice suggests: Her mother is terrible and tender, both a horror and a blessing.

Themes and Meanings

"Remedies, Maladies, Reasons" is a love poem. It examines a mother's overbearing love for her daughter and the daughter's attempt to come to terms with her memories of that, at times, misdirected love. It is also a poem of praise, however, a character study of a woman — warts, snot, bile, belches, mucus, gas, and all.

Van Duyn, in college, away from the cloying love of her mother, is able, for the first time, to bear "like a strange bubble the health of [her] body/ as [she] walked the fantastic land of the ordinary." In this poem she is able, perhaps for the first time as well, to appreciate her mother as a larger-than-life character, one motivated by love. She is able to see, by the poem's close, what it is like to walk in the land of love's hallucinations.

The third section of this poem is a single line that has a double meaning. The line simply says, "Do you think I don't know how love hallucinates?" This line explains how the mother can be both a "suppurating, rotting, stinking, swelling . . . machine" and an "attractive woman." The love the mother felt for her daughter forced her to hallucinate about all the horrors that could befall her once-sickly child; but, on the other hand, love also allows the daughter to see the mother as something other than a sick flesh machine. Love purifies vision; the warts and all, accented so terribly in the first fifty couplets, are removed by the power of love. The loving mother is loved. She is attractive because of that love.

These hallucinations of love could, however, have another meaning. The poet imagines her mother "armed with pills, oils, drops,/ gargles, liniments, flannels, salves, syrups,/ waterbag, icebag," doing heroic battle, over her daughter's bed, with the Enemy — death. Van Duyn imagines that the mother will always drive her Enemy "from every sickening place where he hides and waits," but this is the ultimate hallucination. The Enemy always must win eventually, and that is the final terror of the poem. The daughter must be separated from her mother by death, and Van Duyn must also be separated from "the fantastic land of the ordinary" by death. The love one feels from a mother and for a mother may allow one to imagine an escape from death's sting, but the fantasy cannot last long. Van Duyn knows that it is only a hallucination when she imagines death always defeated. She knows that life, regrettably, is coupled with death.

Kevin Boyle

REMEMBERING TITIAN'S MARTYRDOM
OF SAINT LAWRENCE

Author: Jorie Graham (1951-   )
Type of poem: Lyric
First published: 1982; collected in *The Pushcart Prize, VIII*, 1983

The Poem

Although American, Jorie Graham grew up in Italy and received much of her education in Europe. "Remembering Titian's Martyrdom of Saint Lawrence," like many of Graham's poems, comes from her Italian experience. The poem describes a religious painting by the Renaissance painter Titian, a painting that exists in two versions. In both versions, the painting's foreground features Saint Lawrence, who reclines on a grill with a fire burning beneath him. In the earlier version of the painting (completed about 1557), the martyrdom is set in front of a temple façade, while in the later version (painted 1564-1567 by Titian and his workshop), the martyrdom occurs in an open archway. Smaller differences between the two versions abound. (In the painting's second version, for example, the human figures that surround Saint Lawrence are more grotesque, and two cherubs holding a crown descend from the sky.)

As Graham remembers the painting, she seems to be blending details from the two versions. This conflation may be unintentional, or she may be repainting Titian's martyrdom to suit thematic purposes of her own.

"Remembering Titian's Martyrdom of Saint Lawrence" is very much like the many other poems about paintings in Graham's second volume of poetry, *Erosion* (1983). In these poems, Graham describes a painting in detail but often freely alters these details, perhaps fulfilling what she calls in an interview her "rage to change" what is fixed and finished. The poems about painting—fitting into a subgenre of lyric poetry called ecphrastic poetry—follow a typical pattern of description modulating into meditation. The clearly meditative sections of Graham's ecphrastic poems often involve sudden plunges into metaphysical questioning about time and eternity, for instance, or permanence and impermanence, or the relation between spirit and flesh. Many critics of Graham's poetry have called her a philosophical poet, a very apt description as long as it does not imply that her poems are abstract or unsenuous. Graham is, though, one of the few contemporary poets who acclaims abstractions because she feels that they are messengers of silence and implicitly mark the failures of language.

Forms and Devices

In "Remembering Titian's Martyrdom of Saint Lawrence," Graham remembers most vividly the roiling smoke of the painting and its dominating lights—red from the fire, which flickers eerily and searchingly over the helmets and breastplates of the soldiers and the body of Saint Lawrence; and a blue light, which streams from the heavens and penetrates smoke and flame to brand, as the poem says, "even the meanest/ twig or/ fingertip." The lights of the painting irradiate not only Saint Lawrence and every detail of the painting but also the painting's circumambient air and, most intensely, the viewer of the painting:

> See
> how the two lights
>
> twine, over my face,
> my hands.
> Every pocket will be
> found out,
> every hollowness
> forgiven.

It is the way in which the painting's lights search out the viewer that most amazes and troubles the speaker of the poem. The blue and red lights are so lurid and searching that it is the viewer rather than the saint himself that must suffer the painting. The saint is, paradoxically, untouched by his own martyrdom: "Even the excitements/ of the smoke/ glide over him/ unshadowing." It is the viewer who is touched, ultimately examined, and judged by the painting.

Graham uses this and other paradoxes to begin what finally becomes an argument with the painting, a deep objection to its intervention in the life of humanity, which is by nature impermanent and vulnerable, unlike the marble-bodied saint that Titian depicts. The saint in the painting ultimately becomes, for the speaker, an affront to humanness.

Besides the poem's use of paradox and its intensification of the imagery and lighting within the Titian painting, Graham reconfigures or figuratively displaces what she calls the "rivers" of light in the painting, turning these into a kind of Heraclitean, ever-changing river of the world. At the poem's structural crux in stanza 13, the speaker defies the saint, saying she would not want to be like him—untouched by the elements, impervious to the flames. Graham turns her devotions from the saint to the transitoriness and genuinely immolating qualities of the world. "I would not be that man/ in the fire," she says, then asks whether there is a stream "whose banks don't/ come away/ into its muscular spirit,/ whose love/ doesn't scour its own bed,/ roil its mud/ with sky."

This crux in the poem is structurally its most important feature. The aspects of poetry—stanzas, line breaks—that are usually used as formal controls or indicators of content are by Graham, here and in much of her work, employed in an almost nominal fashion. The free verse stanzas have great visual symmetry, but the logic of the poem typically straddles stanzas; similarly, line breaks often occur where sense would seem to militate against them. Formally, Graham's poems are often like a temple in ruins.

In the short line poems of *Erosion*, Graham's use of stanza and line seems to rupture deliberately both cadence and sense, a device that seems to call for a broken reading, one that cuts against the firmly articulated argument of the poem. The very short lines (ranging in this poem from one to, at most, six or seven words) also create a great blank space around the poem. Graham has said that poems need white space because white space, like abstractions, suggests silence.

Not surprisingly, she admires the versification of William Carlos Williams, whose sense of line may be a model for her own. In an essay called "Some Notes on Silence," Graham says that she likes to think of the poetic line as "otherwise skeletal notes rising in a very large empty cathedral." This description seems applicable to "Remembering Titian's Martyrdom of Saint Lawrence."

Themes and Meanings

Toward the end of the poem, Graham seems to be imagining the ascension of the saint into the heavens. As he rises on the blue river of light that flows from the sky, the speaker's feelings are of both awe and indignation, as she demands of the saint how he can know and judge humankind: "how can you know/ when you see us," she asks, "the terrible deficit/ we work into? . . ." These lines express the speaker's anger that this saint and his world could presume to exercise judgment over the living.

The postulate of the painting—that there exists an immutable world, an immutable body—is ferociously rejected. The speaker almost plunges her hands into flame to feel the human condition and to deny the argument made by the painting. Human life is not like the lives of the martyred saints, which can, so the painting suggests, be reconfigured and redeemed in the light of a flawless heaven. No, humans, for the speaker of the poem, work into a "terrible deficit." For humans, there can be no reparations or reimbursements, only, as the poem says earlier, the muscular spirit whose progess through the world scours its own passage, roils mud into the sky, and finally incinerates itself.

The thematic concerns of this poem echo, but interestingly vary, a perennial modern theme, the idea that perfectness is grossly discordant with the life of humanity. Like William Butler Yeats, Wallace Stevens, and Sylvia Plath, to name only a few of her predecessors, Graham finally says that humans live in a world of changes, and most painful ones. The rebellious, muscular rejection of perfection is perhaps the distinctive tonalty that Graham adds to the music that surrounds this theme.

Anne Shifrer

REMEMBRANCE

Author: Emily Brontë (1818-1848)
Type of poem: Lyric
First published: 1846, in *Poems by Currer, Ellis, and Acton Bell*

The Poem

Except for its brevity, Emily Brontë's lyrical poem "Remembrance" contains all of the characteristics of an elegy. Its subject is the mourning of the death of a beloved; the poem is meditative; the poet attempts to come to terms with the death of her lover from the past; finally, there is some evidence that the poet accepts her loss and finds solace, at long last.

The persona of the poem may or may not be Emily Brontë herself. Biographers have tried unsuccessfully to identify a young man from her youth whose death could have later given occasion to the writing of the poem. Whatever the case, the first person narrator addresses her dead lover, mentally though not literally, at his graveside some fifteen years after his burial. She remembers and thus observes a "remembrance" as she comes to terms with his death, trying—still trying—to give him up.

The first two stanzas are each questions addressed to her only lover, many years dead. "Have I forgot to love thee?" she asks, after letting the reader know that he is "cold in the dreary grave." Her first problem is to determine if enough time has passed to "sever" her loss. Whether she has forgotten to love him is an ironic question, since the act of remembering him is of itself an act of love. She then, in the second stanza, asks herself if her thoughts still "hover" to his grave far away.

In the third stanza, she asks her dead lover to forgive her if she now forgets him. She indicates that her loyalty to him is in question because of her intentions to bury him at last. "Other desires and other hopes" beset her, causing her to recognize functional displacement of his love although there is no operative displacement. She next records that "No later light has lightened up my heaven." The poet, or at least the persona of the poem, has not in fifteen years genuinely reexperienced any aspect of her relationship with another person. The speaker of the poem does, however, indicate an acceptance of his death, and she tells how she has survived in a universe without his love. His death has caused her "golden dreams" to perish; she records that she proceeded in life "without the aid of joy."

In the last two stanzas, she recognizes that her passion for him is identifiably "useless." Accordingly, she has "weaned" her soul, not from him, but from "yearning" for him. The grave, then, belongs more to her than to him, because her own life has been buried in and with his body. Finally, she dares not think of him, an indulgence in "Memory's rapturous pain." The poem ends with a question: How could she "seek the empty world again," having once experienced him but now absolutely unable to recapture his love? She cannot do so, and thus will languish eternally in a state of lingering.

Forms and Devices

Brontë wrote "Remembrance" in accord with conventions of poetry at the time in that the work itself is mechanically, though masterfully, balanced. The eight stanzas have a neatly observed rhyme scheme of *abab, cdcd, efef*, and so on. Odd-numbered lines usually contain twelve syllables, although some are clipped to eleven. Even-numbered lines consistently have a ten-count rhythm. The poet makes occasional use of alliteration ("forgive if I forget," "No later light has lightened," "while the world's tide,") and assonance ("existence could be cherished," "wish to hasten").

The effectiveness of the poem, however, does not depend upon use of convention. Rather, her evocation of a series of images not only makes impressions but also conveys meanings. The poem starts with "Cold in the earth and the deep snow piled above thee," manifesting at once the most powerful feeling of the work. Not only is the poet mentally and spiritually visiting the grave of her dead lover, but also both she and the reader realize the finality of death and the hopelessness of recovery.

The first two stanzas of the poem record questions, as does the final line. Has she forgotten him, and, having known him, can she now or at any time "seek the empty world again?" The first two questions are true questions; the final one is itself an answer: No, she cannot forget him nor can she "seek the empty world again." Such an effort is pointless, for death is final and her love irreplaceable.

The middle stanzas contain an "if-but-then" structure, which forms the heart of these sentiments. In the fourth stanza, she considers what would happen "if" she succeeded in forgetting him. The seventh stanza expresses the "but," or objection, to her assertion: The "Despair" which could set in was "powerless to destroy" her feelings. The "then" part of the equation shows that she has maintained control over herself and her passion, which she now recognizes to be useless.

The poet maintains balance both in terms of the meter of the lines and in the overall structure of the poem. Images of death pervade both elements and abound throughout: Time is an "all-severing wave"; thoughts can and do "hover"; "brown hills have melted"; the "World's tide" bears her along. Brontë's effort has been to embed her thoughts in a series of images in order to force herself to try once again to be at peace with her love's death.

Themes and Meanings

"Remembrance" is not so much a poem about death as it is about the eternal hopelessness of its acceptance. Death cannot be undone; its repercussions cannot be altered, and its totality cannot be mitigated. Its reality continues to affect her own life to the extent that the poet claims that the tomb of her love is more hers than his. "Remembrance" disputes and denies the common idea that time heals all wounds. Herein, the poet is fixated in a time that shows little if any movement onward, even as she recognizes the irrevocability of its — and her own — passing. Life does not go on: Life has stopped.

The persona of the poem records her fifteen years of effort to accept and live with the death of her love. She cannot forget him; she cannot turn to another. She cannot, consequently, live again meaningfully in the world around her. The only apparent reality is her memory, which still controls and dominates not only her thoughts and feelings but also her actions. Intellectually, the poet knows the error of her ways. She recognizes the futility of worshiping cold snow, and she knows that the distance in time of fifteen years should afford her some relief. One aspect of her nature truly wants to overcome his loss and to redefine her existence as one in which "change and suffering" are not the only constants. Such dreams, though, can only perish. She remains entrapped in a life of union with one dead, and inescapably so.

Arguably, the poet's entrapment is of her own making. There is an intense pleasure on her part derived from knowing that her love for the dead youth is in fact absolute. She prides herself in knowing that she is "Faithful indeed" as a "spirit" — not a person — who "remembers" after all these years. Her "Remembrance" is the vitality of her life blood, a manifest, lamentable treasure.

The poet, then, does not accept death so much as she accepts her own condition: She will remain fixated in her quiet despair, continuing to pay obeisance to a love that can be actualized only in her memory. It is perhaps futile and vainglorious for her to exist in such a state. She protests that she has made every attempt to rid herself of the consequences of his death, yet she would not go on. She is clearly unable to resurrect him bodily; only in memory can she keep him the main part of her being. In this realm, then, "Remembrance" exists not as a futile entrapment but as an honorable tribute in an elegiac fashion. The world is indeed "empty" and she should not seek it again; rather, she should continue to bask in the glory of the grave, inevitably not capable of emotional involvement with another.

It is worthy and honorable for her to keep alive the memory of someone whom she had loved; it is admirable for her to believe that his love has meaning and still defines her after all these years. The poem's meaning, however, can be determined by focusing closely on the last two lines. "Anguish" (at his death) is described as "divinest." The poet loves, finally, not her dead love, but her love of him. She cannot resurrect him, but she can keep alive her love for him, which is exactly what she does. It is because of her love for such "anguish" that she will not move into the "empty world again."

Carl Singleton

REMOVE THE PREDICATE

Author: Clark Coolidge (1939-   )
Type of poem: Lyric
First published: 1987, in *American Poetry Since 1970: Up Late*

The Poem

To the casual glance, this poem reads like an anecdote that someone on quaaludes is trying to tell. While there are enough components to encourage one to make the usual kind of sense, a quick glance shows that these components are at times displaced, distorted, or diffused. Re-readings reveal these first impressions to be accurate but inadequate. The author was anything but language-impaired or addled by drugs. Yet even as one traces symmetries that can scarcely be thought unintended, something of one's early impression remains: One is reminded that any use of language is bound, by the nature of words, to be "language-impaired"—words push back and interfere with those meanings one had intended before trying to formulate them on the page. As trace upon trace of deliberation manifests itself and an intellectual picture begins to form—the way a photograph develops in a dark room—something is still withheld. Words and reality seldom coincide exactly; the effect is like shadowy areas in the snapshot, which throw other parts into bright relief.

First to stand out will probably be the coincidence of the poem's beginning and end each having to do with knowing. While one is not told who "they" (line 1) are, one is invited to equate them with "the old" (as in the phrase "the known is old," in the last line), which leaves for "us" the appellation "new." From the first two, and the final, lines alone, it is easy to construct some such meaning as "the old possess a knowledge that is useless to us; what is known already must belong to the old; what is unknown is what is new, and that is our province." "We," presumably, are the young. When this conclusion is applied to the poem as a whole, considerable evidence appears in its support. For one thing, this soliloquy or meditation takes place in Rome, a very old city, and one that strikes the speaker as being "all built of under"—surely, in one sense, of layers of history. Again, readers are told that "All the vaunted/ spears of time . . . , buried in a . . . heap/ under the cats' mistakes [are] nothing," which also supports the initial conclusion concerning this poem's primary meaning. It is a short step to the formulation "Yank comes to Rome, rubbernecks, says 'So what?,' goes home."

This interpretation, however, while certainly derivable from the poem, is not the poem. In order to derive the message, one must overlook or discard other pieces of the work. When so much has to be omitted, one must consider the likelihood of complications, including the complication of authorial irony. One way to read this poem is as a dramatic monologue; one need only recall the work of Robert Browning to remember the likely gap between speaker and author in this type of poem. Clark Coolidge could well be impersonating an attitude—even possibly one he had himself held. Looking closer, one finds oppositions between old ways and new in which the underlying sympathy seems to lie with the old, as where "that one pure spring" appears to be preferred to "my/ millionth trattoria." Again, the penultimate line might suggest that a coin (as it were) is being "palmed," that the side one had thought was correct might prove to be wrong. The poem is so fraught with baffles, however, that there can be no general agreement as to such speculations.

Forms and Devices

Part of the noted deliberateness of this poem occurs in the regularity of the stanzas, two of five lines and two of six; the lines, too, approximate one another in length, even though the poem has no conventional rhythm or rhyme. The first three lines, for example, each contain ten syllables—the "classic" number, that of the iambic pentameter line. Instructively, however, these lines never become iambic pentameter. It is as if the tension between old and new noted in the content were also embedded in the form: old syllable-count, new meter. Perhaps one should not too quickly dismiss the matter of end rhyme: The first four lines of stanza 2, for example, have identities of assonance.

While the syntax may strike an unprepared reader as extraordinary and difficult, to those familiar with Coolidge's earlier poetry it will, by comparison, seem almost normal. Early in his career, the poet wrote works—*The Maintains* (1974), *Polaroid* (1975)—that were hailed as "non-referential"; something of his view of his own writing may be obtained by considering the following extract from his piece on a fellow poet, Larry Eigner: "an invisible & steadying "is" behind everything . . . all particles in the pile soon to reach/ *nounal state* . . . the word "air" & its immediate prepositioning . . ./ these 'scenes' don't exist, never have . . . the poem is built// each line/ equals/ its own completion// and every next line/ its consequence." The approach, one notices, is by way of the mechanics of language and not the psychology of the individual nor the arrangement of society. While to the tyro "Remove the Predicate" may seem difficult in a quite unaccustomed way, to the reader familiar with Coolidge's work from the outset, this recent poem seems at once fairly predictable (the emphasis is on language; the title focuses on a part of speech) yet surprising, because of the large amount of normative coherence constituting it. Here is no parade of words stripped (apparently, anyway) of syntax, as in "one on below out until within/ through once those even since/ you the what says kinds/ bolt what hence when such both"—to quote from *Polaroid*—but instead something that very nearly fails to draw attention to itself via the difficulty presented by the arrangement of its words.

Yet even though "Remove the Predicate" appears to be a poem interpretable by older methods than would ever serve with his earlier work, if one keeps in mind the history of Coolidge's poetry, one will beware of imposing orders upon the arrangements of a man who has indicated, by precept and example, that words (no matter how juxtaposed) already provide an order to which the shuffles and grunts of syntax are in no way a superior wheeze.

It is true that if one removes "dope," "fault," and "fear weed" from the first stanza, one can feel well on one's way to completing a graspable sense of the sentence; however, the poem inserts and insists on those words. The apparently reachable clarity must prove an *ignis fatuus* if one is required to remove pieces of the poem in order to achieve it. Despite his movement towards the normative between the early and this later work, Coolidge proves reluctant to go the entire distance; for him, the relation of reality to language must always be questionable, and this will always be seen in his writing, whether obviously or subtly. The reader will always, if remaining honest to each word as well as to the composition they suggest overall, be forced to acknowledge that ideas of the real, on the one hand, and of the poem, on the other, should stay open to question.

In this poem, certainly, symmetries are recognizable: There are two stanzas of five lines each and two of six lines each; the first three lines each have ten syllables, enforcing a measure that subsequent lines will be heard as obliging or departing from; and "consistency of place and time" affirm the sentences and much that they contain. Yet there is a point beyond which these assembled symmetries cannot take one, an ideal order to which, despite their promises, they cannot deliver the reader. This surely is the point of the poem's devices.

Themes and Meanings

There are considerable chunks of apparently meaningful syntax in "Remove the Predicate." The poem may lack one single overarching meaning—most of Coolidge's poems do, since he has set his face against such—but to do its dance, the poem needs a number of partners. It needs the initial question, in order for the rest of the poem to have something to catch against, like a flywheel; it also needs those other pieces for the flywheel to drive. There appear to be themes: the theme of the past being of no possible use to the present, and the idea that the opposite of that opinion may also be true.

The clearest statement one can make about this poem is that when in Rome, one finds much "built of under"—of meanings and materials beneath other such items—and will "look under things" while there. Elements of the surreal complicate the plot. "Documents" that are "cut and parcelled/ out of well water" cannot occur in nature. "Hoops of tell" and "fear weed" also exist only in language, although one can surmise metaphorical meanings for them. That will remain a personal and private act. Common agreement can hardly be the hope of the poet when writing those phrases.

Quite the opposite is true. The matter of personal knowledge being largely tacit informs Coolidge's operations, creating poems that defy a unified interpretation. One must replace the predicate with oneself.

David Bromige

REPORT FROM THE BESIEGED CITY

Author: Zbigniew Herbert (1924-   )
Type of poem: Lyric/meditation
First published: 1983, as "Raport z oblężonego miasta," in *Raport z oblężonego
   miasta;* collected in *Report from the Besieged City and Other Poems*, 1985

The Poem

"Report from the Besieged City" is a dramatized meditation on aggression,
ethics, and civil autonomy. Zbigniew Herbert employs long lines of free verse, in
contrast to the rather clipped rhythms of many of his other poems. The poem consists of forty-nine lines, divided irregularly into verse paragraphs that vary from
single lines to groups of ten and eleven. The piece is voiced for an imagined persona
who is much like Herbert himself, but also a compiled transhistorical witness to the
invasions that have taken place in Poland and elsewhere over the last thousand years.

The title makes one think either of a news report from a war zone or of a logbook
or military journal. The "Besieged City" does not refer to any particular place—
although Herbert makes reference to past events in Warsaw and Gdansk—but
stands instead generally for all cities and hometowns that have ever suffered through
tyranny or invasion; the city here is a locus, a recurrent figure or image, through
which Herbert explores the issues of civil responsibility, community, and social
action.

The poem begins with the speaker or persona, a citizen of the Besieged City,
recounting how he, unable to participate actively in the defense of his homeland, is
given the "inferior role" of recording the events of the struggle. Herbert contrasts
the writer or poet to what he sees as a fundamentally better social role, that of the
soldier or activist.

Despite his doubts about the significance of his words, the speaker of the poem
makes a brief attempt at a journal, marking "the rhythm of interminable weeks" in
a list of seven dateless days. He records tortures, humiliations, and diseases
alongside the minor victories and defeats that characterize a drawn-out battle. In the
face of endless repetitions of terrible events, record-keeping becomes absurd, and its
readership, dulled by accounts of atrocity after atrocity, can only be bored, as the
speaker realizes: "all of this is monotonous. . . ."

Although the speaker wants to "avoid any commentary" and write only about
"the facts," his tactics change in the seventh verse paragraph. He becomes, rather
than a characterless transmitter of information, a critical thinker, commenting freely
on what he has seen and heard under siege, creating for himself and his readers a
widened sense of historical context for the struggle at hand, comparing his own
battle to those waged against the invaders and exterminators of other times: "Goths
the Tartars Swedes troops of the Emperor regiments of the Transfiguration." All
these nations at one time sought to invade, conquer, or partition sovereign Poland.
(The "regiments of the Transfiguration" were members of the Russian regular stand-

ing army, under Czar Peter I in the late seventeenth century.) The speaker situates himself and his people among those who have been overrun by outsiders, nations which, though resolute in their autonomy, lost their struggles. The names in this list are more contemporary than in that of the invaders: "the defenders of the Dalai Lama the Kurds the Afghan mountaineers." Herbert recalls oppressions and invasions by China, Iraq, and the Soviet Union.

The speaker also allows his own emotions to creep into his account, recalling with bitter irony how, under siege, his countrymen have raised a "new species of children" who know, instead of fairy tales, only stories of war and killing. He resents the hands-off efforts of other countries to send aid and realizes the inherent solitude of the struggle for autonomy anywhere. Responsibility, for Herbert, has an existential basis, rooted always in the insurmountable solitude of human existence.

Herbert concludes his poem by focusing on this solitude. Should the City itself fall and only one citizen escape its swelling cemeteries, that citizen would still carry the City—that is, its sovereignty and its sense of community and civil liberty— within himself. He will, Herbert tells us, "be the City." No matter if the siege ends in physical defeat, all hopes for future justice abide in "our dreams," the one realm to which tyrants and oppressors have no access.

Forms and Devices

Herbert's style is distinctive. Characteristically, he uses little or no punctuation in his poetry. Sentences and rhetorical or grammatical units are demarcated only by line breaks. Often, Herbert compresses two or more sentences into a single unit, yielding a sense of urgency and rhythmic fluidity: "yet the defense continues it will continue to the end." The content of a line is never obscured by such effects, and its meaning may even be enhanced; oppositions and elaborations flow together, creating a shifting web of poetical checks and balances, as the mind of the poem's speaker plays back and forth over the events of "the siege" and his "commentary."

The formal basis of Herbert's poetry is opposition. "Report from the Besieged City," along with other poems from the same volume, is composed of several layers of balanced or embedded contraries. Herbert sometimes uses the rhetorical scheme of antithesis to achieve this balance, placing antonyms in a grammatically parallel relationship, as in "cemeteries grow larger the number of defenders is smaller" or "if the City falls but a single man escapes." The poem's speaker sometimes contradicts himself; he would "avoid any commentary," he asserts, and yet he "would like to inform the world" of his despair and outrage. Countertensions and oppositions permeate the texture of this poetry.

This rhetorical balancing act is matched by a wider, conceptual field of oppositions. The active, fighting life is contrasted sharply by the speaker to the secondhand experience of the chronicler or poet. Activism and criticism, physical struggle and contemplation, and factuality and commentary are all held in tension within the poem. The external conflict between the attackers and the defenders—the tyrannical "barbarians" and the autonomous city dwellers—becomes a correlative of another, internalized conflict, as the speaker struggles to reconcile suffering and righteousness in his "report." His writing, on the one hand, as a record of the tortures of "interminable weeks," provides a means of informing the world and of justifying the struggle, but, on the other hand, his work does little or nothing to alleviate the pain of that struggle or to stop the onslaught of extermination and defeat. The poem may well be only a gesture of futility.

This inherent duplicity leads the speaker to doubt himself: "I record—I don't know for whom—the history of the siege . . . I know it can't move anyone." The only hope the speaker retains comes in the form of a paradox, bodied forth in the figure of the "exile"—one cut off from all community and society—who somehow carries the values of the City, which for Herbert constitute the actual City, within himself. The antithetical structures and contraries of the entire poem have been compressed into this single, contradictory figure at its close, who is at once solitary and all-encompassing.

Themes and Meanings

"Report from the Besieged City" is in many ways a pessimistic poem, predicting only the inevitable defeat and collapse of the City—a bastion of personal freedom, community, and positive social values—and affirming only the insurmountable solitude of human existence. If Herbert holds out any hope in the face of oppression and injustice, it lies in the "dreams" of the last line of the poem, which alone remain unhumiliated and unbetrayed. In the original Polish of that line, the verb *zostały*, which is translated here as "have been," can also have the sense of "remained" or "stayed behind." Herbert writes not so much about success or heroism or a new-found personal liberation as he does about remainders and leftovers. For him, an essential core of values exists within all human beings—the "City" that even exiles still carry inside themselves—that cannot be exterminated. Paradoxically, in terms of this poem, we come to experience the undefeatable quality of that essence only in humiliation and defeat; those who know nothing of siege and struggle at first hand, those full of "comfort and good advice," are, for Herbert, out of touch with the values and the dreams of freedom that motivate the poem's speaker and his fellow citizens.

Herbert's poetry is, then, ruthlessly ironic. Longing for a world of human liberty and productive community, he recognizes the inevitability of degradation, humiliation, and defeat. His humility has some roots in Christianity; the paradoxes of Pauline thought—which glorifies weakness as strength, submission as victory, and finds in death a new life—are remarkably similar to those in Herbert's poetry. For Herbert, however, humankind remains largely unredeemed, and liberation, whether theological, philosophical or political, is merely the property of "dreams." He finds no new life, but instead buries deep within himself only the faintest glimmer of hope.

Kevin McNeilly

REQUIEM

Author: Anna Akhmatova (Anna Andreyevna Gorenko, 1889-1966)
Type of poem: Lyric
First published: 1963, as *Rekviem;* collected in *The Complete Poems of Anna Akhmatova,* 1990

The Poem

Requiem is a poem sequence composed over a twenty-year period; it includes four sections of introduction, ten numbered central parts, and two epilogues. The title comes from the Catholic funeral service. *Requiem in pacem* is a Latin phrase that means "may the soul rest in peace." Many great pieces of music have this title; for example, the Requiems of Wolfgang Amadeus Mozart, Johannes Brahms, and Gabriel Fauré. The phrase may refer to a specific person or to the general concept of peaceful rest for the dead. The poet speaks in the first person, intimately, of an experience shared by many in her century: waiting outside a prison wall to be let in to speak with a beloved person inside and to bring him a food package. The poet's son was held in a Leningrad prison for seventeen months in an official attempt to force Akhmatova to write pro-Stalinist poetry.

The poem moves from a general statement that the poet stayed with her people through the difficult times, not running away in exile to a safe place, to memories of her son's sudden arrest, detention, and sentencing, to visions of death and spiritual comfort, closing on a meditation about the poet's relationship to her nation.

The opening four lines set the tone of sorrow and loyalty. The poet has chosen to suffer with her Russian people during the dark years of terror. A prose explanation then describes the scene outside the prison when a woman recognizes the famous poet and asks, "Can you tell of this?" The poet replies, "Yes, I can." This part is dated "April 1, 1957, Leningrad." The introductory "Dedication" salutes the women who stood with her outside the closed prison gate for so many hours. She wonders where they are now, her companions in suffering.

"Prologue" sets the scene—Russia in the period of Stalin's Terror (the 1930's), when "only the dead could smile" and innocent millions of ordinary people lived in dread of police arrest. Typically, Anna Akhmatova does not name the dictator. She does not need to. In part 1, she recalls her son's arrest from her home at dawn: The younger children are crying, and the candle before the religious icon is burning. Akhmatova retained her Russian Orthodox faith throughout her life although the Soviet government was vigorously opposed to religion. She recalls other periods in Russian history when women suffered from the political persecution of their loved ones. In part 2, she begins to slip into a confused mental state brought on by the intense pain of her concern for her son. She is alone and ill; her husband has been killed, and now her son has been arrested. In part 3, she describes the increasing disintegration of her spirit. She asks for oblivion. This part is dated 1940, the height of the Terror.

In part 4, in a mood of nostalgia, the poet recalls her happy childhood. She grew up in a home in the czar's parkland—it is an intense contrast to the prison where so many lives are ending. In part 5, an enormous star foretelling death hangs overhead. The mother has been waiting outside the prison each day for seventeen long months. Delirium is described in part 6. The weeks fly by like single nights, and the poet thinks about her son and death. "The Sentence," part 7, describes the poet's feelings when her son's sentence is pronounced. She must survive by killing her feelings, her memory. She will keep busy. This section is dated June 22, 1939.

The last three sections—8, 9, and 10—resolve the experience of intense pain with religious consolation. She welcomes death, since it will come anyway. A partial madness relieves her spirit. She submits to it, lets it carry away the suffering. Part 10, "Crucifixion," recalls Christ's agony on the cross and his concern for his mother. This poem is dated "1943, Tashkent," where Akhmatova lived for a time during World War II. Epilogue 1 returns to thoughts of the women outside the red prison wall. She remembers their faces, the look of terror in their eyes. Epilogue 2 honors the women with the completed poem; their scream will be heard through the poet's words. If the nation ever erects a statue to the poet, it should be placed in the prison square so that no one may forget the anguish caused by political oppression.

Forms and Devices

References to religion and nature pervade this lament. In an anti-religious Communist state, Akhmatova speaks as a believer in Christian rituals and faith. She mentions the icon (a holy picture of a saint) on the wall in the arrest scene. Remembering Christ's crucifixion helps her bear her agony at the loss of her beloved son. Her loyalty to Russia throughout this terrible period implies an eventual reconciliation. The Christian message of forgiveness is felt as she refrains from accusation or protest, and accepts her suffering.

Natural elements echo the moods of the poem. The flow of the quiet and majestic river Don expresses the flow of time. Rustling leaves set to music the excitement of suspense. Siberian storms greet the exiles in prison camps. Stars shine on her and light fills empty rooms. The last image, of a stone statue to the poet placed in the prison square, recaptures the act of suffering: Ice melting in winter becomes her tears from "the motionless lids of bronze." Suffering has turned her to stone, but around the statue doves of peace are cooing, and the river that symbolizes Leningrad's life, the Neva, flows by. The great world of stars, rivers, and mountains dwarfs human ills. A variety of meters and rhymes reflects the changing moments of the poet's experience. The early prose passage is a device that Akhmatova used in other poems. The formal meters and rhymes act as a constraint on the overwhelming emotion. For example, the final Epilogue is in rhymed couplets, indicating harmony and order within a world of chaos and brutality.

Themes and Meanings

Requiem has a history as chaotic and yet enduring as its theme. No Russian in

Joseph Stalin's time could think of publishing or even committing to paper such a protest to official injustice. Akhmatova trusted one person to memorize her poem. It was smuggled out of Russia and published in Germany in a bilingual German-Russian edition. It was also brought clandestinely to the United States. ·

Before the Communist revolution in 1918, Akhmatova was already famous. Then came decades of silence. Her first and second husbands both died as political prisoners, as did many of her close friends and fellow poets. *Requiem* records the experience of her son's imprisonment against the background of previous terrible losses to the political abuse of power.

It is typical of Akhmatova's greatness that what she relates in a modest and personal tone resonates in the experience of millions of people in this century. In the tradition of Russian aristocrats who fought for democracy in the nineteenth century, she suffered censorship but spoke for other silenced people. On the first level, *Requiem* voices a single mother's grief: Akhmatova's son, Lev Gumilyov, is in prison. On the second level, the poem addresses the women who stood with her, bundles in hand, outside the closed gates of the Leningrad prison.

A third level of meaning comes when one considers similar situations in other countries, such as the plight of the "madres de la plaza" in Argentina, who gather to protest silently the "disappearance" of their children in the years of military government. The American organization Mothers Against Drunk Drivers (MADD) reflects the message of *Requiem:* Women can stand together to protect their children.

The poem draws on the model of Christian redemptive suffering. It does not try to rationalize or analyze the causes of suffering, but lives the experience fully in solidarity with others, showing human love enduring in the face of evil. Akhmatova's loyalty to the nation is never questioned; temporary evils are overcome by acknowledged suffering and by poetry that outlasts the dictator.

Doris Earnshaw

REQUIEM FOR THE PLANTAGENET KINGS

Author: Geoffrey Hill (1932-   )
Type of poem: Sonnet
First published: 1959, in *For the Unfallen*

The Poem

Geoffrey Hill's poem "Requiem for the Plantagenet Kings" is one of a series of lyrics in an elegiac mood which appears in an early group of poems ironically entitled *For the Unfallen* (1959). The requiem focuses on events and figures of the turbulent medieval period dominated by the formidable Plantagenet rulers of England, (1154-1399), and postulates a curious, paradoxical vision of them that questions the one-dimensional view given by history (which is concerned with cause and effect).

The ironic tone of the poem is immediately evident in the title, since the premise that these restless and energetic kings could ever rest in peace seems a contradiction in terms. A requiem (rest), the introit to the service for the burial of the dead, seems almost precipitant, since the Plantagenets' influence extended far beyond their mortal lives.

Nevertheless, the poet does constrain them tightly and succinctly in a sonnet form, although varying the rhythm of the usual iambic pentameter and freely employing half-rhymes. The bonds are burst as well in the opening four-line stanza of general observation, usually reserved for the conclusion of a sonnet. Indeed, the lines might stand as a terse epitaph, but they lack the abstract elegance and formal diction usually associated with such a commemoration. There is no flattering summary of the Plantagenets' lives and deeds as soldiers, lawgivers, or champions of justice; there is, instead, a suggestion of the wild, wasteful prodigality not only of their lives but also of the age in which all victories seemed Pyrrhic. Despite the "Ruinous arms" (line 2), the death, and the blood, there did emerge the concept of the just war (for good or ill) and the idea of an order, called the state, achieving constitutionality. If history is a book read backward and is the final judge, the first stanza suggests a temporal evaluation of the reigns. "Men, in their eloquent fashion, understood," despite the traumas of life and the kinetic frenzy of the period.

The Plantagenets, often given to violent outbursts of temper and rash action, were determined to possess and keep their inherited lands on the continent, but the kings of France were equally determined that they should not. In a contest of wills, the legality of the Plantagenet claims became a spurious excuse for what was essentially a matter of pride, rapacious greed, and the joy of proved arms.

In the second and longer stanza, their temporal roles fulfilled and temporal judgment pronounced, they lie, entombed in the dust and decay of their mortal frames. "Relieved" now of their souls, they await yet another judgment. All the pride of arms and vitality has been translated into a panoply of past glory and the frozen beauty of Gothic chantries where men praise their lives and where monks— whose services have already been recompensed—pray in perpetuity for the repose of their souls. Only doomsday will render the higher judgment of their actions, when "the scouring fires of trial-day/ Alight on men."

Forms and Devices

In a variation of the Shakespearean sonnet, Geoffrey Hill creates a web of diction whose complexity is very like that of William Shakespeare's own. The irony, however, which gives an enigmatic quality to Hill's work, is singularly his own.

Irony, "the act of dissembling," is not intended in this poem to mislead or obscure but to subject the Plantagenets to a prismatic light that catches a fuller portrait than is afforded by a simple reading of historical events or a formal biography. Startling and oblique, the facets of the prism reveal, not only a multitude of accepted views of their reigns, but the emotional, psychological, and intellectual response of the poet, thus becoming fused in the experience which is the poem.

The prism is largely, and most frequently, a product of the exactness of the poet's diction. This is not to say that only a single meaning can be read in it, but rather that its precision and compression—so that the ambiguity of the word refracts—allow many meanings to coalesce. In the first line of the poem, for example, the curious image, "the possessed sea," presents not only the primary image of the sea but also the unexpected adjective, "possessed." How so possessed, becomes the question that can be answered only in the hint of at least two diametrically opposed ideas. Certainly the poet means, on the one hand, that the Plantagenet kings thought of themselves as owning the English Channel, which stood between them and their French possessions; on the other hand, the kings were also peculiarly "possessed" by it, in the sense of being obsessed with their rights to the land often denied them. Furthermore, the term "sea" for the English Channel may allude to the Caesars, who thought of the Mediterranean as *mare nostrum* ("our sea"), thus suggesting their grandiose ambitions, even, perhaps, mastery; it may also, possibly, be a reference to the exalted opinions the Plantagenets had of themselves. The irony is most pointed when considered in context of the last lines of the poem, implying that the "sea," after much carnage, really possesses them all—all who were venturous enough to seek to possess the other shore.

This intricate ambiguity of diction is matched only by the poet's agility in the use of the metaphor (implied comparisons). It would seem the height of irony, for example, to refer to the "chantries" as "caved." The very ornateness of the church architecture, however, so surprisingly compared to a cave, elicits the recognition that caves were the first burial chambers of primitive man. To compare them here, therefore, is to impose a dimension of humanity upon the otherwise formal distancing in the deaths of kings. Since the conclusion of the poem is decidedly Christian in tone, it should be remembered that the bloodied body of Christ was placed in something very like a cave; thus, the image links all humanity with the divine. The poem concludes, as it began, with the image of the sea, a traditional symbol of eternality into which the print of the "daubed rock" (blood?) tells of the Plantagenets' passage in the flux of time.

Themes and Meanings

Two themes are interwoven in the text of "Requiem for the Plantagenet Kings." The first of these, a traditional motif, *sic transit gloria mundi* ("thus passes the glory of the world"), is a poignant recognition that all in the material world is subject to the depredations of time, which shows little mercy to man or his works. The Plantagenets lie "secure in the decay/ Of blood," as the poet observes.

The plaint appears in the early doom-laden poetry of the Anglo-Saxons (*The Seafarer, The Wanderer, The Ruin,* c. mid-eighth century) and continues as a familiar theme in English poetry. It is particularly suited to medieval sensitivities, since the bitter contrast of splendor and squalor, of dream and reality, the ideal and the base, was acutely painful. The juxtaposed images in the poem, for example, of the gross reality of war, as in "the sleeked groin, gored head," and the grace of the "well-dressed alabaster" by which the Plantagenets were remembered, harmonize by a strange, subtle metamorphosis which time and art can also mercifully unfold. Geoffrey Hill suggests that the transmutation by art of raw experience preserves something of man and his work.

Inextricably linked with the first theme is an exploration into the paradoxical nature and meaning of history with which Hill struggles and returns to in his later works, *King Log* (1968) and *Mercian Hymns* (1971). Like other poets of the twentieth century, he has been compelled to accommodate to the findings of twentieth century physics, particularly the relationship of space and time and its unsettling implications for reading, writing, and understanding history. It is the tension created when the older views, traditional and religious, form a Gordian knot in "Requiem for the Plantagenet Kings"; the ambiguity of Hill's diction, unresolved and complex, mirrors not only his own, but twentieth century man's bewilderment and uncertainty.

On the one hand, to paraphrase Heraclitus, if you cannot step into the same river twice—that is, you, like the river, are changing from moment to moment—then history can only be history of that moment; hence, the poem, with its simultaneity of presentation. The ultimate reality of the world is change. On the other hand, if humankind is the instrument of a greater transcendental will, it may be part of a larger design whose meaning is obscured in the divine. The question is, then, were the Plantagenets ministers or scourges of the divine will, or were they simply the flotsam and jetsam of the flux of time? Geoffrey Hill's closing of the poem would suggest that only the end of time can possibly reveal the solution to the puzzle.

Maureen W. Mills

RESOLUTION AND INDEPENDENCE

Author: William Wordsworth (1770-1850)
Type of poem: Lyric
First published: 1807, in *Poems in Two Volumes*

The Poem

"Resolution and Independence," known in manuscript as "The Leech Gatherer," is a poem of 140 lines divided into twenty stanzas. The published title suggests the thematic moral learned by the speaker from an encounter with the leech gatherer, who supplies the manuscript title.

The poem is written in the first person, the speaker probably being the poet himself (when he was about to be married), who describes a strange experience he had one spring morning when he met an old man while walking across an English moor. The first two stanzas set the scene of an animated landscape filled with sounds of birds and rushing water, sights of bright sunshine reflected from wet grass, and a rabbit kicking up a mist as it runs away. The poet says, in the third stanza, that he was as happy as the scene he surveyed.

Yet unexpectedly, and suddenly, he fell into a deep melancholy, which he describes in the fourth and fifth stanzas. He is perplexed about his strange sorrow, which contrasts so strongly with the scene about him and his former happiness. In stanzas 6 and 7, he considers the plight of persons (perhaps like himself) who have spent their lives without much consideration for anything except their own happiness; two great poets, Thomas Chatterton and Robert Burns, illustrate the fate of those who begin in joy and end in great sadness.

In this meditative mood, the poet sees with surprise, in stanza 8, a very old man. The old man seems as solid as a great stone placed atop a hill; at the same time, he seems mysteriously out of place, the way a sea animal might if it has been found somewhere on land. The poet passes from these comparisons in stanza 9 to observe in stanzas 10 and 11 that the old man is a pathetic example of human suffering, one who searches for leeches in pools of water. These he might collect and sell for medical uses by physicians of the time.

Finally, in stanza 12, the poet speaks to the old man, asking how he makes his living, and hears a reply in stanzas 13 through 15. What strikes the poet, however, is not the substance of the old leech gatherer's remarks, but rather the style of his speaking. In stanza 16, therefore, the poet realizes that he has not understood what the old man has been saying, so he has to repeat his question in stanza 17.

The leech gatherer is patient with the young poet, so he repeats his answer in stanza 18—that he gathers leeches from the pools on this barren moor. The effect of this encounter, produced by both the style and substance of the old man's remarks, is described by the poet's words in the last two stanzas: He is troubled, as if in a vision, with the image of the old man as a rebuke to himself for not being stronger, for not being more resolute and independent. In the future, when he feels again the temptation to fall into melancholy, he will remember the example of this old leech gatherer, whose fortitude will guard the poet against further temptations of despair.

Forms and Devices

The poem acquires its tone of solemnity and ritual encounter from its use of a stanzaic form associated with ceremony and seriousness: the rhyme royal (sometimes called the Chaucerian stanza, because Geoffrey Chaucer used it in several of his poems in the fourteenth century). This is a stanza of seven lines which are arranged to rhyme *ababbcc*. "Resolution and Independence" makes one change from the traditional form, because it adds an extra metrical foot to the seventh line to make a stanza of six iambic pentameter lines, concluding with a line of iambic hexameter (to echo the way the Spenserian stanza concludes). This additional, longer line brings each stanza to a thoughtful, self-reflective conclusion that provides a basis for renewed consideration and progressive self-examination to open each successive stanza.

Self-reflective meditation is dramatized by the encounter between poet and leech gatherer, as each seems puzzled by the strange behavior of the other. Since the form of the poem is controlled by the poet, his own strangeness is objectified by the reflection of his consciousness in the appearance of the other person. The dramatic encounter becomes an occasion for self-awareness for the poet. There is a hint of narrative to the poem, because the poet tells a story with a beginning, middle, and end to outline the plot of a young man's growing up: It is thus a form of initiation and springtime renewal.

The poet's interest in the old man's formal style of speech is a sign of the poet's professional interest in language. The poem is highly metaphorical, creating an inner landscape from the imagery of the external setting, as when the opening stanza describes the brooding stock dove to convey a double sense of "brooding": darkly thinking and warming to create new life. The sounds and signs of spring and morning, with rain and running water, yield to images of shallow pools in which the old man hunts for leeches. Most impressive, at the center of the poem's form is the device of the double simile in stanza 9: Here the psychological impact of the old man's appearance is conveyed by a comparison with a "huge stone" atop "an eminence," and the stone itself is compared with "a sea beast crawled forth." Several qualities of the old man's significance are suggested: his peculiar appearance amid so much solitude, his condition of alienation, his fortitude, and his independence.

By the end of the poem, the old man has been internalized by the speaker, so that the poet's mind becomes haunted by the memory of the leech gatherer as a monument to endurance, integrity, and resolution. The devices whereby this is accomplished are figurative uses of language which are metaphors of substitution, as the old man's voice sounds like water and his very body is turned first into a rock, then a sea beast, a cloud, and finally a dream, as the poet transforms him into a figure of his own mind.

Themes and Meanings

At the heart of the poem is the question of whether the poet will become a responsible human being, independent of others for his own happiness. He realizes that his essential quality of mental or spiritual identity cannot rely upon an external environment for its continuing strength. At first, the speaker feels at one with the happy springtime setting, but when he falls suddenly into despair, he is puzzled into a crisis of confidence in himself. Then, when he has most need, the old man appears as if "by peculiar grace" to serve as an admonishment.

All that occurs in the poem is a consequence of the poet's sense of need, apparently without cause. The powers of mind, as imagination, usurp the poet's consciousness of everything that surrounds him, including the leech gatherer, making it difficult for the poet to keep hold of the external reality through which both he and the leech gatherer move. In this is the theme of mental experience transcending physical limitations. Yet the poet's imagination seizes upon the details of the encounter to nourish itself, to create a self-reflecting image for the poet to study as a lesson in resolution and independence.

The poet needed to feel self-reliant just as he was nearly falling into helpless and mysterious despair. The leech gatherer supplied what the poet needed, because the poet had the imagination to make use of the encounter. The meaning of the poem is that the human mind transcends the natural environment upon which it has been accustomed to depend and from which it can draw spiritual and mental nourishment, even though the lesson of transcendence is not without its mysteries and pains of dislocation. Every human being is, like the old man and, as the poem demonstrates, like the young poet, lonely and alienated from the rest of nature, because a human being is essentially different from natural being. Nevertheless, in a triumphant exercise of imaginative self-reflection, "Resolution and Independence" celebrates the human capacity to make use of the natural and to learn from sympathetic responses to fellow human creatures.

Themes of vocation, maturation, and creativity are embodied in the poem's texture of natural imagery, dramatic awareness of human pathos, and narrative recall of a momentous morning's adventure. Although the poem is not one of those which William Wordsworth called "lyrical ballads," it nevertheless achieves the lyrical shape of those famous poems, because it makes its meaning a song of subjective achievement through a shaping of the objects of circumstance. Mind makes meaning from environment; environment does not make meaning for mind.

Richard D. McGhee

RETURN

Author: Octavio Paz (1914-   )
Type of poem: Lyric
First published: 1976, as "Vuelta," in *Vuelta (1969-1975);* collected in *The Collected Poems of Octavio Paz, 1957-1987,* 1987

The Poem

The 168 lines of "Return" are divided into 7 stanzas of unequal length. "Return" marks Octavio Paz's return to Mexico City after serving as Mexico's ambassador to India between 1962 and 1968. He resigned this post after the massacre of Mexican students at Tlatelolco in 1968. The Lopez Velarde epigraph, which refers to the destruction of the Catholic provinces during the Mexican Revolution, calling the country "the subverted paradise," mirrors Paz's revulsion at seeing modern Mexico debased by a megalomaniac government and compliant citizens.

The first stanza is an objective rendering of the speaker's walk through the streets of Mexico city and Mixcoac. The speaker's tone is pleasant as he views "bougainvillea/ against the wall's white lime." The setting assumes the qualities of a painting except for the lines "Letters rot/ in the mailboxes," which is the only negative image in the stanza and a reference to a lack of communication. The mention of Mixcoac, the Mexican home of Paz's infancy, and the lines "I am walking back/ back to what I left" connect the reader to the speaker's remembered past, a past that has all but vanished.

In the next stanza, the speaker loses contact with the external world. His objective state turns within as his body and spirit dissolve. He speculates about death in Mexico City under the "pounding fist of light." The speaker wonders what it would be like to die in a city office or hospital or on a city pavement and concludes that such a death "isn't worth the pain." Pedestrians become unimportant, just as the speaker feels himself to be. Existence is nothing more than "mist."

The third and fourth stanzas vividly depict the suffering of an entire population. The educational system, religious institutions, and business enterprises all appear to share the movie theaters' "ghost populations of desire." The people of the city help promote the decay of the culture with their sordid, middle-class desires, which lead only to suffering. The speaker implies that the nature of this suffering leaves the city's citizens with no haven. He denounces several professions, claiming that their members are too selfish to save their culture. People are called "buffoons," "coyotes," and "satraps." Those who should serve, including members of the military and the civil government, do not.

The next stanza examines the result of human corruption. No longer does the speaker focus upon the people but upon the modern wasteland created by them. Decay, poverty, and death are the by-products of the modern dilemma in which gardens "rot," people are "urban nomads," and poverty-ridden districts and shanty towns are laced by "thoroughfares of scars." At the conclusion of the stanza, the speaker states, "City/ heap of broken words," indicating that all promises and hope for a renewed life have disintegrated.

In the sixth stanza, the fractured society is shown as having lost a common language. "Yesterday's news" becomes "more remote/ than a cuneiform tablet smashed to bits." A shared language (closer to a shared system of belief) becomes an anomaly. Without this language, there can be "no center." The society's recovery depends on a way of communicating that will include all Mexicans. Yet the only reality that the bankrupt culture honors is the dollar sign, which is stamped "on every forehead," a reference to the greed of individuals who have become noncommunicative islands of personal suffering.

The final stanza begins with a feeling of frustration as the speaker comments, "We are surrounded/ I have gone back to where I began." The epigraph had suggested that paradise has been lost, but the speaker is not willing to judge things in terms of "success or failure"; the Chinese sage mentioned by the speaker would answer that it is an error to judge things in this manner. The speaker proclaims that the city "is not a subverted paradise/ it is a pulse-beat of time," implying that his personal reflections and declarations have no actual meaning outside the poem itself.

Forms and Devices

"Return," with its "Time/ stretched to dry on the rooftops," owes much to surrealism. The tone of the poem leaves the reader with several horrific images of modern Mexico City. As the speaker moves from one fantastic observation to the next, using a stream-of-consciousness technique, the reader is rarely allowed a static vision of the speaker's surroundings. At times, memory is mixed with observation, and the result is a blurring of the line between reality and the speaker's imagination and past.

Imagery occupies an important position in "Return." The vividness of this imagery adds to the surreal quality of the poem as well as to the atmosphere of decay. Personification, metaphor, and simile aid Paz in creating this surreal mood. Ash trees and the wind "whistle." The "sun's spread hand" creates "almost liquid/ shadow and light." The sun of midday is a "pounding fist of light." Colleges and temples possess "genitals." Ideas become "swarms of reasons shaped like knives." The buildings of Mexico City are described as "paralytic architecture," and the nation's streets become "thoroughfares of scars/ alleys of living flesh."

Enjambment is used with great success in the poem. Paz employs little punctuation. The ideas of the poem are controlled by the placement of lines on the page. The images, however, are constantly overlapping. The free-flowing pattern created by enjambment adds to the overall dreamlike quality of the work. Nightmarish images are placed in close proximity. Since Paz examines the sometimes enigmatic nature of memory as well as reality, enjambment allows him to blend and distort many of these images. In turn, this blending of images emphasizes the ambiguous nature of memory. Without convenient stopping points, the reader is forced to follow the speaker's observations in rapid succession.

The use of poetic devices to achieve a level of experience that combines the past, present, and even the future adheres to the speaker's desire to reach a point where such divisions are indistinguishable. Paz's methods are directly tied to his thematic intent. Without these poetic devices, the poem would be less effective.

Themes and Meanings

"Return" functions on a variety of thematic levels. The nature of memory, the function of time and self-imposed boundaries, loss of purpose, decay in the modern world, and the power of the imagination all play important roles in the poem.

Ostensibly, the poem appears to focus on the speaker's return to Mexico. His displeasure with what he sees is apparent as he assembles a host of urban wasteland images that are fused with his memory. At one point he comments, "I am in Mixcoac," the place of his infancy. He states, "I am walking back/ back to what I left/ or to what left me." The speaker's memory of his homeland is not distinct from his visions of modern Mexico. He indicates that his past has become part of his present, a present that does not offer the remembered sanctity of childhood.

The speaker's exposure to Mexico City and its corruption greatly disturbs him. He sees that his people, along with their institutions, have failed. Traversing the city, he moves deeper into the very fabric of Mexican culture. His once-objective observations are tinged with infuriation and bitterness. Yet the speaker does not view his people without pity. He sees the common man and woman partially as victims, citizens whose institutions and culture have betrayed them. Nevertheless, the modern Mexican wasteland is a creation of the speaker's compatriots, whether villains or victims. The speaker senses the enormity of their failure as he glides from one image of despair to the next. His surroundings become dehumanized, and the speaker eventually loses his body and spirit to these surroundings. At one point, he exclaims, "We are surrounded." His apprehension for the future of Mexico and his accompanying sense of futility only accentuate modern Mexico's predicament.

The circular nature of the poem is evident when the speaker states, "I have gone back to where I began." In a sense, the title of the poem speaks of a return to the beginning of the poem. The reader as well as the speaker must restart their individual attempts to discover meaning. The speaker bemoans the fact that the Mexican people no longer have a philosophical center upon which to focus. So the reader is locked into a circular pattern that lacks finality. There is no center for the reader. Each person, within a separate sphere of existence, circling without any fix on a center, can do nothing but search for a focal point, something that the speaker has claimed is lost. The cyclical nature of the poem and existence itself prove to be obstacles in reaching any specific end.

The conclusion of the poem presents the reader with a new dilemma. The speaker denies the previous thematic content of the poem by commenting, "It is not a subverted paradise/ It is a pulse-beat of time." The speaker cancels assumptions about theme or meaning by informing the reader that the poem does not signify anything except what the reader brings to the poem. There are questions that the speaker asks about the modern wasteland and the meaning of life in that wasteland; there are, however, no absolute answers. He comments, "I walk without moving forward/ We never arrive/ Never reach where we are/ Not the past/ the present is untouchable," illustrating that he does not know the answers to the questions he himself has posed.

The poem transports the reader beyond the construct of linear time. The past is lost; the present is never the present, because linear time forces it immediately into the past. Divisions become ephemeral. The power of the imagination and the workings of the poet's memory convey to the reader the many possibilities of an existence without boundaries. In a sense, the poem restores the reader by engaging him or her in the creative process. The return of the poem's title becomes representative of a renewal of spirit that the poem brings about as well. The wasteland does exist, but the power of the imagination transcends that wasteland.

Robert Bateman

THE RETURN

Author: Ezra Pound (1885-1972)
Type of poem: Lyric
First published: 1912, in *Ripostes*

The Poem

The apparent simplicity of this twenty-line poem belies its mysterious subject and persona. Its short lines, straightforward diction, and compelling rhythms pull the reader forward through a series of striking images, but at the poem's end, he or she is nowhere nearer to discovering the dramatic situation.

Most scholars agree that "The Return" is about the return of the ancient, pre-Judeo-Christian gods to earth, but others argue that the poem describes the retreat, the "anabasis," of a once-mighty army. Either interpretation fits, although the "Gods of the winged shoe" in the third stanza suggest the former reading. In either case, "The Return" portrays the passage of a group of formerly heroic beings, now weary and worn out by their anxieties. The persona watches them pass and describes their slow, uncertain movement. He seems to be calling others to witness the defeated return of this godlike host.

Line 1 suggests that the persona was present when these hero-gods were at the zenith of their power or that he is at least knowledgeable about their former glory; the fact that they have "returned" implies an earlier journey. If these are indeed the ancient gods who held sway before the advent of modern religions, then the assumption is that monotheism has conquered but not yet destroyed them. The less mysterious interpretation—that these are warriors returning after years of hard campaigning—would also account for the persona's description of the defeated, but still awe-inspiring, host.

The speaker describes the exhausted pace of the returned heroes. Their slow, "wavering" step in stanza 1 is the result not only of their simple physical enervation but also of their moral collapse. Although these beings have not met with formal defeat, their long struggle has drained them of self-confidence and psychological strength. Their uncertainty, moreover, suggests that they have no real destination; in their absence, they have lost their former home.

Stanza 2 continues the description of their march. At one time, they moved forward in confident phalanxes, but now they have been reduced to a mass of stragglers, returning "one by one." The implication is that each being has been reduced to an isolated individual who no longer draws power from their combined might. Once again, the persona stresses the emotional climate that hangs over the returnees: Some nameless fear makes them hesitant. He contrasts their timidity with their original appearance of inviolability.

In stanza 3, the speaker continues his description of the heroes' former strength. They seemed to take flight in their eager movement forward. Supernaturally powerful hunting dogs, their "silver hounds," accompanied them, and in their keenness, the dogs sniffed the air and strained at their leashes. The characterization of this former greatness continues in stanza 4. The persona summons up the full-throated hunting cries of the beings, the swiftness and ruthlessness of their hounds, and the ominous excitement of the hunt. In the final stanza, however, the speaker returns to the present: The dogs lag on their leashes and the beings who hold them are pale and drained.

Forms and Devices

"The Return" is written in free verse, having no set number of beats per line, no recurring rhyme scheme, and no regular stanza pattern. Although it is certainly not the first instance of free verse in Western literature, it has been said that the poem marks the start of the free verse "movement" that has dominated English-language poetry in the twentieth century. Moreover, "The Return" is widely praised as a model of the form, an example of the supple power of free verse when its "freedom" is fully under control.

Yet, despite the poem's label as free verse, individual lines use a variety of complex rhythms, including variations on ancient prosodic patterns. The rhythmic pattern of the final stanza, for example, mimics the classical "adonius" meter, often used in Greek heroic poetry; this same rhythm is similar to that used in older English-language liturgical writing.

The key thing to note, however, is the way that Ezra Pound has wed his theme to his prosody: As the poem describes the straggling return of defeated heroes, its rhythms mirror the hesitant pace of their march. Stanza 1, for example, accomplishes this conjunction of theme and rhythm in two ways: through internal rhythms and through the curtailments at the ends of lines. Line 1 is broken midway by a semicolon (the line's caesura), causing a pause in the reader's forward movement. Yet the line is also punctuated by strong stresses, beginning with its first word, "See," which is in turn followed by two unstressed beats, "they return." The initial stress acts as an exclamation calling the persona's hearers to witness the heroic column as it passes, but the two succeeding unstressed beats and the following midline break are a kind of letdown, mirroring the disordered step of the returning gods. Immediately, however, the speaker regains his awe and repeats the opening "see," thereby pulling his hearer's attention more strongly to an event that is important to him.

At lines 1 and 3 of this stanza, the syntax is unnaturally broken between an adjective and its modified noun, causing the reader to stop and "stumble," matching the slow, unrhythmic pace of the gods. This break and pause is reinforced by the meaning of the separated words: "Tentative" ends line 1 before it can be joined to "Movements," beginning line 2; "uncertain" cuts short line 3 before it can modify "Wavering" in line 4. The resulting rhythm exactly reproduces the footfalls of defeated men as they step uncertainly forward, pause, look around, and stumble on.

This device is repeated in stanza 2, where the speaker describes the movement of snow blown by shifting winds. In this metaphor comparing the gods to the light, powerless snow, line 3, ending with "hesitate," itself "hesitates" before it continues on to line 4, completing the thought—"And murmur in the wind."

In contrast to the broken, uncertain rhythms of stanzas 1 and 2, stanzas 3 and 4 describe the godlike heroes as they were in the past, full-blooded, keen, and "inviolable." Stanza 4, for example, begins with the repeated hunting cry, "Haie! Haie!," a double stress that underscores the power and unity of the gods as they hunted during their golden age. This line is followed by a series of repetitions in lines 2, 3, and 4 (a parallelism): The speaker is eager to recall the gods' splendor to his hearers, and he does this by underlining their heroic attributes through the repeated "These were . . ./ These . . ./ These were. . . ."

The other crucial formal device in "The Return" is its vivid sensory imagery. In fact, the poem is an example of Imagist method; Imagism was a poetic theory, largely created by Pound himself, that sought to emphasize highly charged visual, tactile, and olfactory impressions instead of distinct subject matter, so that the images themselves would join directly to tell the poem's story. Here, the persona carefully describes the "trouble" of the returnees' "pace," their "pallid" appearance, and their straggling, isolated march. The snow metaphor in stanza 2 reinforces this collection of images. In contrast, the "silver hounds" of stanza 3 and the hounds' keen scent in stanzas 3 and 4 bolster the once-glorious appearance of the gods, while the dogs' slack leashes of the final stanza mirror the enervation of defeat.

Themes and Meanings

Pound was one of many thinkers and writers at the end of the nineteenth and the beginning of the twentieth century who believed that the Judeo-Christian religious tradition had crippled the spiritual and psychological life of many people. He believed that the otherworldly, self-renouncing tendency of monotheistic religions had caused people to ignore the world around them, making them dull and ridden with guilt.

Yet, Pound also believed that, under the surface, modern human beings still retained an older belief in a polytheistic universe where godlike spirits dwelled in springs, trees, mountains, and fields. Throughout his poetic life, Pound reasserted this conviction in an attempt to refresh the minds and senses of twentieth century urbanites cooped up in their cities and penned in by their guilt.

"The Return" is an expression of this belief in the continuing reality of humankind's ancient gods. Although these beings, as the poem portrays them, have been defeated, they are by no means dead. In "The Return," Pound, through his persona, calls out to his readers in an attempt to gain their attention: The gods still exist for those who have eyes to see them.

Generally, this poem has an elegiac tone: Even as Pound reasserts the continued existence of the gods, he acknowledges their lost vitality. Thus, the poem struggles with two contrasting themes: the isolated, forgotten status of the gods in the modern era and the memory of their ancient splendor. Pound acknowledges that the gods at the zenith of their power were neither kindly nor merciful. These were superhuman beings with ferocious, superhuman passions. The gods were hunters, perhaps of human souls, and their strengths were those associated with predators—keen senses, an aptitude for violence, power, and speed. Yet these same attributes, Pound seems to say, are ones that humans have lost in the modern world. For all their faults, the ancient gods lived in close association with humans, imparting to mortals these full-blooded immortal traits. In contrast, contemporary human beings live in a universe remote from their all-seeing, omnipotent, monotheistic God, whose ultimate characteristics humans cannot share.

The poem ends hesitantly, akin to the stumbling pace of the returning gods. Perhaps, the final stanza implies, the gods have fallen so low that a recovery of a polytheistic world view is impossible. In the modern world, both humanity and its ancient heroes have grown weak, pale, and slow.

John Steven Childs

RETURN TO MY NATIVE LAND

Author: Aimé Césaire (1913-   )
Type of poem: Lyric
First published: 1939, as *Cahier d'un retour au pays natal;* translated as *Return to My Native Land*, 1968; collected as *Notebook of a Return to My Native Land*, in *Aimé Cesaire: The Collected Poetry*

The Poem

   Return to My Native Land is an extended lyric meditation (1,055 lines in the original French). Aimé Césaire wrote the first version in the late 1930's, having completed his studies in France, upon his return to his native Martinique (revised versions appeared in 1947 and 1956). Although the general mode of the poem is lyric, it mixes modes frequently. It has some epic qualities, especially evidenced by the narrator who, as an epic hero should, is trying to embody in himself the best qualities of his race. Further, about half the poem is written in prose.

   The poem can be generally broken down into three parts. The first part is an examination of the poet's native Martinique, and particularly its capital, Fort-de-France. In the second part, he reacts, often negatively, to the people and history of this land. In the third, he learns not only to accept but also to embrace the people and spirit of his native land.

   Césaire is often associated with the French Surrealist poets, and even a brief glance at the poem reveals why. In the first full paragraph, he tells a cop to "Beat it"; then, in a quick rush of images, he turns toward paradises that are lost to such people as the cop, nourishes the wind while rocked by a thought, and unlaces monsters—among other things. Such images have the impossible, dreamlike quality characteristic of Surrealism, and this quality keeps up throughout the poem. Overall, the poem does have a narrative shape, which is not characteristic of Surrealism, and as these images in the beginning suggest, the overall thrust of the poem involves the speaker's attempt to unleash the spirit of his native land which has been hidden, and imprisoned, and made to look monstrous by the subjugation of imperialism.

   The key phrase in the first section of the poem (most of which is written in prose) is the phrase that begins many paragraphs, and indeed, the poem itself: "At the end of the wee hours." Literally, this phrase refers to the time immediately before sunrise and suggests someone who has been up most of the night, throughout the wee hours. Figuratively, the phrase suggests someone on the edge of an insight that is slowly dawning. Indeed, what the reader finds in this first section is an exploration of the city which focuses on observations of how the land's history of rule by France has twisted and distorted it.

   The reference to "Josephine, Empress of the French, dreaming way up there above the nigger scum," is a good example of the type of image to be found in this section. It refers to a statue of Josephine, robed in the manner of the Napoleonic empire, which does in fact stand in the center of the public square of Fort-de-

France. The statue seems to pay no attention to the "desolate throng under the sun," meaning the people of African descent who populate Martinique, and the populace feels no connection to her. She is a symbol of the French empire, and a reminder to the people that their culture and ethnicity is considered second class in this city.

Other recurring phrases also provide a clue to what holds the various images of this section together: "this town sprawled flat," "this inert town," the narrator repeats several times, to emphasize the idea that this is a town paralyzed in certain ways by colonialism. Other images of the town crawling, of life lying prostrate, and of dreams aborted also give the sense of a people struggling against a paralyzing burden.

The second section of the poem begins when the narrator thinks about going away and examines the other people he could be. In this section, the poem switches back and forth between free verse and prose. Though not all the possibilities of who he could be are examples of who he would want to be, some are. At one point, for example, he fantasizes himself returning to the "hideousness" of this land's "sores" and presenting himself as a redeemer, someone who can speak of the freedom that the native population has never known.

This leads him to consider the grim despair of the lives of these people he would save. "Who and what are we?" he asks, and tries to give this question as large (rather than as specific) an answer as possible. He identifies with all the Africans in his past, the ones who lived lives his own European sensibilities consider pagan, as well as with a man who was dragged "on a bloodspattered road/ a rope around his neck"—a clear reference to enslavement.

This section is full of lines in which the narrator seems to be shrinking from his heritage. When he exclaims, "So much blood in my memory!" he is genuinely overwhelmed by the violence of this past. Similarly, when he says, "I may as well confess that we were at all times pretty mediocre dishwashers, shoeblacks without ambition," he is truly troubled by how effective the colonial occupation of his land has been in aborting the dreams of his people. This disappointment with his people and his land comes to a focus when he finds himself smiling mockingly at a black whom he sees as "comical and ugly"—because he realizes he is looking at this man through the eyes of the imperialists who have controlled his country.

Recognizing this, he is forced to recognize the extent to which he has been participating in the victimization of his native land simply through accepting the values and customs that the French have imposed on them, and he vows to change. "I will deck my natural obsequiousness with gratitude," he says, meaning that he will no longer bow to the values he has been taught (those values that tell him that the Martinicans of African descent can be viewed as second-class citizens) but will actively embrace his people, happy for who they are.

This last third, with its revolutionary spirit of optimism, contains the lines that were to become central to the artistic and political negritude movement of the 1940's, 1950's, and 1960's: "My negritude is not a stone, its deafness hurled against the clamor of the day . . ./ my negritude is neither tower nor cathedral/ it takes root in the red flesh of the soil/ it takes root in the ardent flesh of the sky." That is to say, his negritude, his blackness, is not a weapon nor a construct to hide behind; rather, it is something organic and alive and a part of the land in which he lives.

From this point on, the tone of the poem is one of almost unbounded acceptance of his land, his people, and his heritage. The pain of "the shackles/ the rack . . ./ the head screw," which is the type of pain that earlier in the poem seemed almost over-whelming, is not denied here, but it is seen as pain that can be accepted. The work of man, he sees, "has only begun," and though this presages more hard work ahead, it is a fundamentally positive thing because it means that the present order, in which blacks in his land feel the need to bow down not only to whites, but to white culture, is a temporary and passing order. "The old negritude," he says several times, "pro-gressively cadavers itself" — meaning the old sense of what it means to be black is dying. The work that the last third of this poem announces as begun, is the work of celebrating all the forms and contradictions of the new negritude (meaning the new way of being a black person) that is being created.

Forms and Devices

One use of form in this poem that a reader cannot help but notice is the way the poem mixes prose and free-verse passages. In the first section, when the narrator is providing a general overview, the dominant mode is prose; in the second, when he is wrestling with his own sensibility, prose and verse are mixed; and in the last section, when he is trying to achieve a new sensibility, the dominant mode is verse.

A closer look at this movement in the poem provides some insight into what the poet is doing. Many of the verse passages, especially early in the poem, are actually lists of images or people. The prose passages also contain such lists, but putting these lists into verse seems to be a way of focusing on each individual item in the list, as if the narrator is trying to clarify his thoughts by examining them closely. As the poem continues, free verse becomes the dominant mode of discourse, as if to call attention not only to what is being talked about, but the language itself. The implica-tion seems to be that this new creative spirit of negritude the narrator is trying to achieve is an inherently poetic spirit, one that will take strength from the rhythms and sounds of language.

A dominant metaphor holding the poem together is the image of an awakening. As already mentioned, the phrase "At the end of the wee hours" implies not only a town that is about to awake but also an artistic sensibility that is on the verge of awakening to the realities of living in an imperialist society. As the poem pro-gresses, he awakens not only to the reality of the history of enslavement, brutality, and cultural subjugation that the people of his native land have endured, but also to the vitality of their spirit. While at the beginning of the poem the town is viewed as inert, toward the end, the town is viewed as lively and the people as dancing. Not only has the town come awake, but the speaker's sensitivity to the life of the town has also awakened.

Although there are passages (especially some of the prose passages) in which the narrator seems to be Césaire himself, it would be a mistake to assume that the narrator of this poem can, in all cases, be identified as Césaire. Rather, it might be more correct to say that this is a narrator who speaks for Césaire. That is to say, Césaire the poet has created a persona that embodies his own sensibility. To complicate this further, one of the ways that he expresses his sensibility is by speaking of the whole history of his people as contained in himself (as Walt Whitman often did in his poetry). This comes through especially in passages such as the one that begins by discussing "tadpoles hatched" by his "prodigious ancestry" and goes on to list the dead places of his soul that have been created by the uprootings and violence suffered by his ancestors.

Themes and Meanings

Although the central thematic concern of the poem is the importance for the person who lives as the subject of a colonized land to decolonize his or her own mind and sensibility, one of the central paradoxes of the poem is that it is written in French, the language of the colonialists, not in the native Creole of the Martinican population. Indeed, in their brief introduction to *Aimé Césaire: The Collected Poetry* (1983), Clayton Eshleman and Annette Smith point out the paradox that Césaire, the spokesperson for decolonizing the mind, who was later to become mayor of Fort-de-France, the city on which he focuses in *Return to My Native Land*, apparently never thought of Creole as a suitable language for his poetry.

Further, the traditions from which the poem seems to borrow are largely the traditions of French literature. Not only does the poem's rush of bizarre and often grotesque images seem to place it in the context of French Surrealist literature, but also, as Eshleman and Smith also note, the images of hardship and misery seem to owe much to such images in the works of Victor Hugo, the great French novelist of the nineteenth century, whose works Césaire read as he was growing up.

A partial resolution of this apparent paradox can be seen through an analogy to the writers of the Harlem Renaissance of the 1920's, who were also greatly influential in Césaire's poetry. The images of people from the whole history of the black race that the narrator includes and identifies with, may remind readers of Langston Hughes's early poem, "The Negro Speaks of Rivers"; similarly, the ending of the poem, in which he speaks of transcending the binds and confines that have been placed on his people, bears a similarity in tone and spirit to another Langston Hughes poem, "I, Too, Sing America," which talks of the inevitability of African Americans being included in the mainstream of American life.

Similarly, the type of revolution that Césaire seems to be advocating in this poem is not a revolution that results in the violent overthrow of the past; rather, it is a revolution through inclusion. Toward the end of the poem, the narrator speaks of rallying dances to his side, including the "it-is-beautiful-good-and-legitimate-to-be-a-nigger-dance," as if to say that he wants to celebrate who he and his people are and can be, not dictate who they cannot be or what they should not do.

Shortly thereafter, he says, "bind me with your vast arms to the luminous clay/

bind my black vibration to the very navel of the world/ bind, bind me, bitter brotherhood." The image of being bound, which earlier implied slavery, has been transformed here into an image of connection to the natural world and to other people. He does not want to forget or forsake his connection to the white-dominated French world. Rather, he wants to have the chance to accept his connection to this world on his own terms, and in a life-affirming way, rather than have the terms of this connection dictated by imposed power structures.

To put this more directly, the task this narrator takes on himself is the task of defining for himself a concept of his own negritude, starting from the realities that have been imposed on the black population of his native land by white, European colonizers. The fiery optimism of the last section of the poem, with its unqualified lines of acceptance such as "I accept . . . I accept . . . totally, without reservation," is the optimism of someone who has learned he can see beauty and create life even from within the ruins of a system that has defiled the life and beauty of his land and people.

Thomas J. Cassidy

RHAPSODY ON A WINDY NIGHT

Author: T. S. Eliot (1888-1965)
Type of poem: Lyric
First published: 1915; collected in *Prufrock and Other Observations*, 1917

The Poem

"Rhapsody on a Windy Night" is a lyric poem in free verse. It is divided into six stanzas that vary in length from nine to twenty-three lines each, with a separate closing line at the end of the poem. In one way, the title seems to reflect the poem's form, since in music a rhapsody is an irregular, unstructured piece. The poem at first appears to be an uncontrolled jumble of oddly juxtaposed images in lines and stanzas of irregular length, with no consistent rhyme scheme but with scattered rhymes, repetitions, and variations throughout. "Preludes" and *Four Quartets* (1943) are other poems showing T. S. Eliot's interest in using musical forms.

From another perspective, the title is ironic, since the label "rhapsody" suggests a mood of enthusiasm or frenzy that the poem does not convey. A situation that could be romantic—a midnight stroll in the lamplight and moonlight—is actually dominated by images of sterility, decay, isolation, and despair. Moreover, the only sign of the wind is found in the two lines stating that the street lamps "sputtered," although the wind is emphasized in the title and is an important image associated with decay and spiritual emptiness in other poems, such as "Preludes" and "Gerontion."

"Rhapsody on a Windy Night" is written in the first person, but the reader learns less about the speaker as a distinct personality than he or she does in Eliot's other early monologues, such as "The Love Song of J. Alfred Prufrock." On his nocturnal walk, this speaker does not express his thoughts or emotions directly or effusively, as one would expect in a "rhapsody." As he passes a succession of street lamps, moving in and out of their pools of light, he seems controlled by their commands to consider the sordid images in the streets and the distorted images thrown up by his memory. In the last stanza, he obeys mechanically as the lamp, illuminating the entrance to his apartment, orders him to return to his daily routine and prepare for bed.

The speaker's strange nocturnal visions are unified by some fairly consistent patterns, as the first or second line of each stanza (except the third) marks the time from midnight to four in the morning, and each stanza (except the first and third) quotes the lamps that direct his observations. He notices and remembers a woman with a torn and stained dress lingering in a doorway; the moon appearing as a similar aging, diseased woman; a cat licking up butter; eyes peering through shutters; dry geraniums; and stale smells of chestnuts, females in closed rooms, cigarettes, and cocktail bars. Although the memory interjects other images that seem out of place—such as driftwood, a useless rusted spring, a child grabbing a toy on a quay, and an old crab gripping a stick—the images all are united through the dominant characteristic of twisting or distortion. This "crowd of twisted things" culminates in the speaker's final sensation as he is compelled, at the poem's end, to return to everyday life— "The last twist of the knife."

Forms and Devices

Eliot believed that poetry must be difficult in order to reflect the complexity of modern civilization. He also believed that the poet's first concern should be his language. He wrote that "the only way of expressing emotion in the form of art is by finding an 'objective correlative'; in other words, a set of objects, a situation, a chain of events which shall be the formula of that *particular* emotion" (*The Sacred Wood*, 1920). A poem such as "Rhapsody on a Windy Night," therefore, does not explain feelings or thoughts in any general, conventional way. Readers must work to discover the complex patterns of meaning, sound, and structure underlying the stream of bizarre and banal images that make up the poem.

Metaphors and other figures of speech provide one method for connecting disparate images. The first two stanzas contain the most complex figures of speech, as abstract ideas about the nature of memory give way to the concrete objects that dominate the poem. The memory has floors that can be "dissolved" under the influence of midnight and moonlight, preventing it from dividing perceptions logically or precisely. Time and memory become concrete when the midnight spell on the memory is compared to a madman shaking a dead geranium. As rational memory is destroyed and nonrational forces take control, strange combinations of images are shaken from the depths of the memory.

Other similes connect different sensory experiences. Light and sound are combined when each street lamp "Beats like a fatalistic drum," reinforcing the incantatory rhythm of the poem and anticipating the speaker's realization of his own entrapment in a futile existence. Then the personification of the street lamps, with their ability to order the speaker to observe what they describe throughout the poem, gives him a detached, impersonal perspective that reflects Eliot's determination to break away from the lyrical subjectivity of nineteenth century Romanticism. The speaker receives impressions from the objects lighted in the street and his memory responds with free associations, comparing (in stanza 2) an open door to a grin and the corner of an eye to a crooked pin.

The rest of the poem consists of more fragmentary juxtapositions of images, with fewer explicit connections provided by similes, but with other poetic and linguistic devices helping to make connections. Eliot rejected the label *vers libre* (free verse) when it implied absence of pattern, rhyme, or meter. Although there seems to be something undisciplined or unexpected in the way lines and sentences are developed in this poem (suggesting subconscious or involuntary utterances), there is a complex interplay of syntactic patterns, semantically related words, internal rhymes, intermittent end rhymes, alliteration, and other sound patterns linking the woman in stanza 2, the woman in the moon in stanza 5, the particularly fragmented details of the branch and broken spring in stanza 3, and the glimpses of human and animal actions in stanza 4.

By stanzas 5 and 6, the romantic idea of incantations is replaced by a monotonous effect in these patterns and repetitions. The parallel lists of dry and stale images, the short imperatives, and the rhymes and alliteration that create ironic links in "Cologne" and "alone"; "Mount," "Memory," and "key"; and, finally, "life" and "knife" emphasize the limitations of memory and the mundane, isolated lives of individuals.

Themes and Meanings

Although "Rhapsody on a Windy Night" appears to be organized according to the hours of night, the sequence of impressions in the poem is dictated by psychological connections more than by chronology. The influence of the French philosopher Henri Bergson is evident when the speaker lets his memory synthesize unconsciously and spontaneously (rather than analyze rationally or logically) and when he seems repelled by the idea of blind reflex actions — the kind of automatic and empty motions that unite the cat licking rancid butter, the child with vacant eyes grabbing a toy, the crab gripping a stick, eyes peering through shutters, a woman twisting a paper rose, and his own mechanical preparations for bed.

This creative process of the memory, however, leads to nothing hopeful for the speaker, as the futile action of shaking a dead geranium implies. All the images that are so imaginatively synthesized are twisted or distorted in some way. Some are literally twisted concrete objects — a branch, a broken spring, a torn hem, and a crooked pin — while other objects take on unusual properties or configurations — street lamps beat like drums and speak, sand stains a dress, an eye "twists like a crooked pin," and a cat "flattens itself in the gutter." Some involve twisting motions or sensations, including the smells that "cross and cross across her brain." Still others are distorted by deterioration — the rusted spring has lost its strength, the butter is rancid, and the moon is a woman with infirmities ranging from feeble eyesight and a face cracked with smallpox to a loss of memory. His experience of new kinds of associations with these "twisted things," along with the vacant eyes, the stale smells, and the confinement of "shuttered rooms," only makes the speaker more horrified at the sterility and decay of everyday life by the end of the poem.

Many of these images show the influence of the French Symbolist poets of the late nineteenth century, especially Jules Laforgue, from whom Eliot borrowed the geranium and lunar images, the idea expressed in the line of French, and the poem's cynical attitude. As Gertrude Patterson observed in *T. S. Eliot: Poems in the Making* (1971), this is one of the early poems that deal with a single emotion rather than multiple, conflicting feelings; Eliot's attraction to the slums resulted in the expression of "consistent disgust at the life of the city." "The last twist of the knife" is the speaker's realization that sleep can only prepare him for an existence more empty and monotonous than the observations and memories he has experienced in the streets.

Tina Hanlon

THE RIVER-MERCHANT'S WIFE: A LETTER

Author: Ezra Pound (1885-1972)
Type of poem: Dramatic monologue
First published: 1915, in *Cathay*

The Poem

Ezra Pound's adaptation of a poem by Li Po, an eighth century Chinese poet, is a dramatic monologue spoken by a sixteen-year-old girl. It is written in open verse in the form of a letter from the wife of a river-merchant to her husband, who has been away from their home for five months.

The opening of the poem conveys both immediacy and continuance. The first line begins with the word "while" and presents an image of the wife as a young girl. The second line starts with the word "I" and contains an image of the girl playing at the moment when she met her future husband. The effect that is created is a feeling of recollection which draws time's passage across the consciousness of the present. The focus is shifted from the "I" to a memory of "you." The first stanza concludes with the couple merging into "we" — "small people" who lived in a village in a state of unreflective innocence.

The second stanza begins a triad of quatrains that recapitulate the three years of their marriage. In the first of these, the girl remembers herself at fourteen as severe, contained, and shy at the moment of the ceremony. She seemed to be acting out of obligation. Then, at fifteen, she began to relax and remembers that she "desired" to join her husband in both temporal and etherial realms, recognizing the immediate call of the physical as well as the transcendant appeal of the eternal. Her question that concludes the third stanza is a compression by Pound of a tale of a woman who waited on a tower for her husband's return. In his cryptic reference, he implies that the woman is content to be in her husband's company or to be by herself. The fourth stanza moves to the present, and the wife is now sixteen. Five months ago, the river-merchant had departed on some unexplained journey. He has covered considerable distance in both geographic and temporal terms, and the wife expresses her unhappiness.

The last section of the poem, an extended stanza of ten lines, is located entirely in the immediate present. It is a powerful expression of the wife's feelings and an attempt to demonstrate to the river-merchant how she has grown into a mature and more complete stage of love. Her references to the seasonal changes in the natural world indicate that she no longer entertains a concept of a theoretical love which is "forever and forever and forever" but has realized that nothing can exist outside of time. The image of mosses in an accumulation "too deep to clear them away!" suggests the effect of time's passage, and the image of "paired butterflies" shows that she is aware of love's delicacy and fragility. Her maturity is registered by the extremely powerful use of the only active verb in the poem: Her statement "They hurt me" refers to seasonal changes and their consequences. Her reflective utterance

"I grow older" summarizes the range and scope of time that the poem encompasses.

The last part of this stanza contains a reversal of mood. Demonstrating her resiliency and depth of character, the wife now addresses her husband as an equal partner. Adopting an almost businesslike tone but maintaining her care and concern, she expresses her confidence in herself by declaring that she too will leave the protection of their home in order to meet him along the river Kiang. The willingness to travel along the river herself solidifies the relationship, and the reference to Cho-fu-Sa (Pound's version of the Chinese *Ch'ang-feng-sha* or "long wind beach") is a specific commitment to a particular place, rather than the previous nebulous "forever" of the second year of her marriage.

Forms and Devices

Pound wrote that "An 'Image' is that which presents an intellectual and emotional complex in an instant of time." Pound believed that the essence of this method, called Imagism, had been captured by the Chinese ideogram, which fused picture and meaning in one symbol.

The striking opening image of "The River-Merchant's Wife" captures an entire cultural epoch. Pound originally used the American slang "bangs," but the taut language of "hair was still cut straight" is an accurate rendering of the ideogram and of the appearance of young Chinese girls of that era. This image is followed by one of the river-merchant as a boy, his masculine aspects immediately established by his appearance "on bamboo stilts, playing horse" while she follows the traditional feminine activity of "pulling flowers." Their early sensual attraction is implied by the boy parading around her and "playing with blue plums."

The playful imagery of the first stanza is abruptly replaced by images of unease and uncertainty when the couple are actually married in her fourteenth year. She is presented as "scowling," "bashful," and never laughing. The wall is an image of enclosure and her desire to "mingle" their dust forever suggests claustrophobia and internment. The psychological condition of their first year of marriage has been precisely evoked.

When the river-merchant departs during the third year of their marriage, the images show how the girl's sense of herself, her marriage, and the world are evolving. The river imagery ("swirling eddies" and "narrows") indicates the dangers of the outside world. The husband, previously on stilts, now drags his feet under the pressure of responsibility. The wife's sorrow is accentuated by seasonal references, the moss grown "too deep to clear" both a sign of time's passage and a symbol for the weight of loneliness. The "paired butterflies" remind her of her single state, and her vision of them "already yellow with August" is a projection of her sense of accelerated time.

The final image of the poem is a parallel one in which the wife and her husband are both depicted on the river Kiang, its "narrows" demarking it as a place of menace. They are moving toward each other, their resolve to overcome obstacles a testament to the possibilities of a future in which the separate "I" and "you" of the poem will be joined as an unstated "we" — a union quite different from the separate lives of the "we" in the first stanza. This transference completes the cycle of shifting personal pronouns that functions as a frame for the imagery. From the introduction of the individual "I" and "you," to Pound's brilliant inversion "I married My Lord you" (which combines direct address with continuing personal consciousness), to the series of almost accusatory you's, to the use of the third-person "they" to indicate fate in the last stanza, the variants anchor the images and reinforce their meanings.

Themes and Meanings

Pound's introduction of poetry by Li Po into the Western literary canon was a part of his program to increase cultural awareness. Pound viewed "criticism" in the largest sense to include versions of literary creation, such as "criticism by translation" and "criticism in new composition." His adaptation of "The River-Merchant's Wife: A Letter" was designed to open the field of early Chinese civilization to Western eyes, and he succeeded so well that T. S. Eliot remarked on the appearance of *Cathay* (1915) that it "invented Chinese poetry for our time." Some professional sinologists attacked Pound for his lack of accuracy, but he dismissed their inability to appreciate the power of his poetry and his approach to translation.

Pound was interested in innovative uses of familiar forms, and he admired Robert Browning's employment of dramatic monologue to capture the spirit of a moment in historic time. Pound believed that Browning's work permitted a combination of the "human" or distinctly personal and the cultural, or socially resonant. Such crucial elements of "The River-Merchant's Wife" as the correspondence of human emotion to natural setting, the representation of the eternal cycle of the seasons as time's passage and human growth, and the linking of romantic intensity with restraint and composure are products of Pound's fusion of Browning's methods and Li Po's artistry.

Ford Madox Ford commented that "the poems in *Cathay* are things of supreme beauty. What poetry should be, that they are." Pound took the ultimate vessel for expressing feeling — the lyric — and used its full capacity for transmitting essential human emotions within the mode of the dramatic monologue. Pound's fervent proclamation that "nothing matters but the quality of affection" is the primary principle of his philosophy of composition and is at the heart of the appeal of "The River-Merchant's Wife." Without striking false notes or falling into sentimentality, Pound has shown that what he loved well — language, culture, and art — remains as his poetic legacy in his finest work.

Leon Lewis

THE ROAD NOT TAKEN

Author: Robert Frost (1874-1963)
Type of poem: Lyric
First published: 1916, in *Mountain Interval*

The Poem

"The Road Not Taken" is one of Robert Frost's most familiar and most popular poems. It is made up of four stanzas of five lines each, and each line has between eight and ten syllables in a roughly iambic rhythm; the lines in each stanza rhyme in an *abaab* pattern. The popularity of the poem is largely a result of the simplicity of its symbolism: The speaker must choose between diverging paths in a wood, and he sees that choice as a metaphor for choosing between different directions in life. Nevertheless, for such a seemingly simple poem, it has been subject to very different interpretations of how the speaker feels about his situation and how the reader is to view the speaker. In 1961, Frost himself commented that "The Road Not Taken" is "a tricky poem, very tricky."

Frost wrote the poem in the first person, which raises the question of whether the speaker is the poet himself or a persona, a character created for the purposes of the poem. According to the Lawrance Thompson biography, *Robert Frost: The Years of Triumph* (1971), Frost would often introduce the poem in public readings by saying that the speaker was based on his Welsh friend Edward Thomas. In Frost's words, Thomas was "a person who, whichever road he went, would be sorry he didn't go the other."

In the first stanza of the poem, the speaker, while walking on an autumn day in a forest where the leaves have changed to yellow, must choose between two paths that head in different directions. He regrets that he cannot follow both roads, but since that is not possible, he pauses for a long while to consider his choice. In the first stanza and the beginning of the second, one road seems preferable; however, by the beginning of the third stanza he has decided that the paths are roughly equivalent. Later in the third stanza, he tries to cheer himself up by reassuring himself that he will return someday and walk the other road.

At the end of the third stanza and in the fourth, however, the speaker resumes his initial tone of sorrow and regret. He realizes that he probably will never return to walk the alternate path, and in the fourth stanza he considers how the choice he must make now will look to him in the future. The speaker believes that when he looks back years later, he will see that he had actually chosen the "less traveled" road. He also thinks that he will later realize what a large difference this choice has made in his life. Two important details suggest that the speaker believes that he will later regret having followed his chosen road: One is the idea that he will "sigh" as he tells this story, and the other is that the poem is entitled "The Road Not Taken" — implying that he will never stop thinking about the other path he might have followed.

Forms and Devices

In his essay "The Constant Symbol," Frost defined poetry with an interesting series of phrases. Poetry, he wrote, is chiefly "metaphor, saying one thing and meaning another, saying one thing in terms of another, the pleasure of ulteriority." His achievement in the poem "The Road Not Taken" is to bring these different uses of metaphor into play in a delightfully ironic balancing act. That is to say, the speaker solemnly uses the metaphor of the two roads to say one thing, while Frost humorously uses the speaker as a metaphor to say something very different.

The speaker is a solemn person who earnestly believes in metaphor as a way of "saying one thing in terms of another." The speaker uses the details, the "terms," of a situation in nature to "say" something about himself and his life: that he has difficulty making a choice and that he is regretfully certain that he will eventually be unhappy with the choice that he does make. When he first considers the two roads, he sees one as more difficult, perhaps even a bit menacing ("it bent in the undergrowth"), and the other as being more pleasant ("it was grassy and wanted wear"). Even in taking the second path, though, he reconsiders and sees them both as equally worn and equally covered with leaves. Changing his mind again, he believes that in the future he will look back, realize that he did take the "less traveled" road after all, but regret "with a sigh" that that road turned out to have made "all the difference" in making his life unhappy. The speaker believes that in the future he will be haunted by this earlier moment when he made the wrong choice and by the unfulfilled potential of "the road not taken."

In contrast to the speaker, Frost uses metaphor to "say one thing and mean another." That is, Frost presents this speaker's account of his situation with deadpan solemnity, but he uses the speaker as a specific image of a general way of thinking that Frost means to mock. The speaker first grasps at small details in the landscape to help him choose the better path, then seems to have the common sense to see that the two roads are essentially equivalent, but finally allows his overanxious imagination to run away with him. The reader is meant to smile or laugh when the speaker scares himself into believing that this one decision, with its options that seem so indistinguishable, will turn out someday to be so dire as to make him "sigh" at "all the difference" this choice has made. Frost's subtle humor is most likely what Frost was referring to when he described the poem in 1961 as "tricky," for the Thompson biography documents two letters Frost wrote near the time of the poem's publication (one to Edward Thomas and one to the editor Louis Untermeyer) to convince these readers that the poem is meant to be taken as a joke on the speaker and as a parody of his attitudes.

Themes and Meanings

"The Road Not Taken" is an excellent example of what Frost meant by "the pleasure of ulteriority" in his poetry. That is, the poem offers an entertaining double perspective on the theme of making choices, with one perspective fairly obvious and the other more subtle.

Considered through the perspective of the speaker himself, "The Road Not Taken" is an entirely serious, even a sad poem. It expresses both the turmoil of making a choice and the depressing expectation that the choice he makes between seemingly equal options will turn out for the worse—is in fact going to make an even greater difference for the worse than seems possible when he makes the choice.

Considered from Frost's perspective, on the other hand, "The Road Not Taken" is a humorous parody of the speaker's portentous habits of mind. Frost's 1931 essay "Education by Poetry" offers further clarification on this point. In it, he wrote that people need to understand that all metaphors are human constructs that "break down at some point"; people need to "know [a] metaphor in its strength and its weakness . . . [h]ow far [one] may expect to ride it and when it may break down." From this perspective, the main problem of the speaker in "The Road Not Taken" is that he tries to ride his metaphor too far and too hard. Although he sees it break down early in the poem (in that he actually cannot see any real difference between the two roads), the speaker persists in thinking that the road is "less traveled" in some way that he cannot see and that this difference will lead to dire consequences later on.

One other common interpretation of the poem deserves brief consideration: the view that the poem is a celebration of nonconformity, an exhortation to the reader to take the road "less traveled." In this interpretation, the title is seen as referring to the road that the speaker does take (which is "the road not taken" by most other people), and the speaker is seen as ultimately exultant that he took the road "less traveled," because it "has made all the difference" in enhancing his life. To consider the validity of this interpretation, one must put aside Frost's stated intentions for the poem—an act that many critics consider is sometimes justified because an author's intentions cannot be seen as fully controlling the impression made by a literary work. Aside from the issue of Frost's intentions, however, this interpretation still conflicts with many salient details in the poem. One problem with this view is that the speaker can hardly be praised as a strong nonconformist if in the middle of the poem he can see little difference between the paths, let alone vigorously choose the road "less traveled." Another problem is that he imagines telling his story in the future with a "sigh," an unlikely gesture for a vigorous champion of nonconformity.

In 1935, Frost wrote on the subject of style that "style is the way [a] man takes himself. . . . If it is with outer seriousness, it must be with inner humor. If it is with outer humor, it must be with inner seriousness. Neither one alone without the other under it will do." "The Road Not Taken" is a notable example of Frost's own sophisticated style, of his ability to create ironic interplay between outer seriousness and inner humor.

Yet the humor of the poem also has its own serious side. This humor conveys more than merely the ridicule found in parody: It also expresses an implied corrective to the condition that it mocks. This condition is that the speaker sees the course and tone of his life as determined by forces beyond his range of vision and control. Frost implies that if the speaker were able to see himself with some humor, and if he were able to take more responsibility for his choices and attitude, he might find that he himself could make "all the difference" in his own life.

Terry L. Andrews

ROCK AND HAWK

Author: Robinson Jeffers (1887-1962)
Type of poem: Meditation
First published: 1935, in *Solstice and Other Poems*

The Poem

"Rock and Hawk," one of Robinson Jeffers' most often reprinted short poems, has been regularly identified as one of his signature pieces—that is, it presents, in simple, direct form, one of his main themes. That theme has been called "Inhumanism." It is based in the concept that humans, far from being the central point of reference in the cosmos, are a minor component of the process, significant only because they are capable of damage out of proportion to their importance. The idea is Darwinian, growing out of Jeffers' post-college researches in medicine and biology. It can be considered an early statement of the radical environmental attitude.

The poem accomplishes this by presenting what it calls a "symbol": a falcon perched on an ancient, massive rock high on a headland. In this symbol, the poem states, "Many high tragic thoughts/ Watch their own eyes." This complex allusion draws several ideas together. On one level, thoughts of high tragedy have conventionally been those that best represented the values of human civilization, those qualities that humans prized. Here they "watch their own eyes," as if distrustful of their own motives. Second, in one high tragedy, that of Oedipus, the hero literally pierces his eyes because of the horror he has been forced to discover about himself. Finally, if thoughts of high tragedy are thus suspect, their eyes betray fundamental human hypocrisy. The rock juts out, the single prominent figure in this landscape; nothing else can live there. The implication is that the rock has life of its own, or at least participates in a life. Its survival proves this; earthquake and storm have worn all else down. On this rock rests a falcon.

Jeffers passes then from establishing the scene to meditating upon it. He states that this is the proper emblem of the future, superseding those of Christianity and Mormonism. The image of rock and hawk together demonstrate the polar potentialities of existence: life in hawk, death in rock—both secure and balanced states in the cosmic cycle. Further, both remain remote from human interference and human misinterpretation. Because they incarnate and reflect the values that accept life and death as parts of the span of existence, they teach humans to imitate them to grow into the totality of the cosmos.

The balanced attitudes that rock and hawk illustrate are those of "consciousness" and "disinterestedness." Both are necessary, as both life and death are necessary, and each is dependent on the other. These transcend human values, as this emblem outfaces tragedy. Tragedy may help humans draw success out of partial failure; theoretically, it teaches survival. Jeffers argues that complete survival will come only after incorporation of the union of rock and hawk, the combination of "the falcon's/ Realist eyes and act" with "the massive mysticism of stone."

Forms and Devices

Robinson Jeffers is remarkable among modern poets for his simplicity of presentation. He uses a minimum of effects, preferring, like his biblical models, to rely on basic devices to project his themes. "Rock and Hawk" is no exception. It is one of Jeffers' "short line" poems, in which he forsakes his customary preference for long lines—those with more than five stresses. This poem presents seven three-line stanzas, each with three stresses spaced irregularly.

This stark simplicity serves his subject well. It is doubled by his diction. The poem first announces that it centers on a symbol, thereby spelling out what it is doing. It follows this with an arresting phrase and a classical figure: In this symbol, "high tragic thoughts/ Watch their own eyes." The figure is a double paradox— thoughts cannot literally watch, and things cannot in any case look at their own eyes. The figure reminds one of the celebrated passage in William Shakespeare's *Julius Caesar* (c. 1599-1600) in which Cassius asks Brutus, "Can you see yourself, Brutus?" Jeffers uses the figure to suggest a number of things, chief among which is probably that Western culture's conventional ways—the high tragic ways—of looking at things may not be enough.

The second stanza presents the first part of the symbol, the rock, standing "where the seawind/ Lets no tree grow." This personification is important. It suggests that control resides in the entire natural process rather than in some god or force. The rock is characterized by a double epithet: "Earthquake-proved, and signatured/ By ages of storms." The first suggests not only that it has stood the test of time but also that it incorporates design features that surpass all the works of humans. The second uses back-formation to create the image of impersonal names—again, not human—carved into the surface, a testimony of the controlling natural process.

The persona employed in the poem now asserts itself. It chooses this image for itself, not for humankind. This reminds the reader that humans are the emblem-making animal. This symbol, fashioned by nature, transcends humans, unless they reject their earlier limited symbols to join the entire natural order in this.

The remainder of the poem presents a series of paired abstractions, epithets, and images to reinforce and translate the central symbol. This simple structure underscores Jeffers' simple but daring point. Reiteration drives the point home. Humans must learn from the natural order, but not by simply imposing their will and short-sighted values upon it. To show this, Jeffers inverts personification. He confers "realist" eyes on the falcon, not to suggest that it possesses human rationality, but to say that man needs to relearn the "fierce consciousness of the predator." Similarly, the rock displays "massive mysticism;" it is not the bemused contemplativeness of humans, who assume indifference and superiority, but the total submission of stone.

Themes and Meanings

Jeffers' themes are overt, but this does not mean they are always easy to discern or assess. In part, the reason for this is that the poet's philosophy—the so-called Inhumanism—is so stark, bleak, and uncompromising. It is not entirely novel;

Shakespeare certainly anticipated some of his negativism in *Hamlet* (c. 1600-1601), and Jonathan Swift devastated the notion of the inherent goodness of humankind. Jeffers, however, exceeds both in refusing to find any independent redeeming value in the species. For him, humans are simply another part of an evolved complex. Far from inheriting a right to dominate, humans will be lucky to survive. They will only survive if they recover the vision of the complex itself, to consider with clear-eyed, personal indifference the health of the whole.

This requires accepting the roles of either hawk or rock without dissent. Undoubtedly this is difficult. Anyone would rather eat than be eaten. Jeffers feels that it is exactly this egocentric human-first attitude that must be overcome if the entire biomass is to survive. Left unchecked, humans will continually inflict damage on the system in order to pursue their private, limited objectives. Over the long term, these repeated injuries will unbalance the system to the point that everything, including humankind, is destroyed. This progressive deterioration is inevitable unless humans learn to change.

Jeffers accepted this theme as his personal poetic mission, developing aspects of it in a series of poems both short and long. Here he is most concerned with demonstrating the shortcomings of the tragic ideal, a prime motivator of human behavior in our civilization, with reference to the universal attitude he espouses. Thus, he begins by promising to reveal "a symbol in which/ Many high tragic thoughts/ Watch their own eyes." Near the end of the poem, he describes "the falcon's/ Realist eyes" as one pole of the new emblem with which humans should replace that of tragedy. Presumably, the contrast will reveal the shortcomings of the old human view.

The final lines of the poem suggest these deficiencies. The two poles, rock and hawk, will be immune to failure and success. Jeffers implies that the view which considers any human participant is ultimately destructive of the whole. Any art or literature that makes the hero of tragedy its ideal figure fosters this view. Aristotle suggests in his *De poetica* (c. 334-323 B.C.; *Poetics*) that the lesson of tragedy is double. The first point is that even though the hero fails, one learns from the hero's mistakes. The second is that even the hero can be sacrificed for the good of society. As long as human society is viewed as in twofold competition, with other species and with other societies, such a lesson is probably useful.

Jeffers contends, however, that at this point in evolution, this lesson and view are not only wrong but are dangerously wrong. Take away the central assumption of tragedy, that humans are the central and moral determinant of the universe, and one sees that humans are only one more part. Final survival depends on this recognition.

James Livingston

ROMAN SARCOPHAGI

Author: Rainer Maria Rilke (1875-1926)
Type of poem: Sonnet
First published: 1907, as "Römische Sarkophage," in *Neue Gedichte*; collected in *New Poems [1907]*, 1984

The Poem

"Roman Sarcophagi" is a sonnet consisting of four stanzas broken down into two quatrains followed by two tercets. In the original German, the rhyme scheme follows a pattern that runs *abab*, *cddc*, *efe*, *efe*, and the lines average ten syllables in length. The title refers unambiguously to the poem's subject, ancient stone coffins, often ornamented with carvings, in which the Romans buried the dead.

Two pieces of information are crucial to a proper understanding of this poem. First, the word "sarcophagus" comes from two words in the ancient Greek that together mean "flesh eater." As the *Oxford Universal Dictionary (3d ed.)* notes, "sarcophagus" originally referred to a kind of stone that was supposed to devour decaying flesh. Eventually, it came to refer to coffins made from this stone. Second, in the years preceding the publication of *New Poems*, Rainer Maria Rilke made several visits to Italy. Always attentive to the historical and cultural details of the places he visited, Rilke at one point discovered, as Robert Bly explains in *Selected Poems of Rainer Maria Rilke* (1981), that "In the middle ages, Italian farmers . . . would knock the ends out [of the sarcophagi] and line them up so that they became irrigation canals, carrying water from field to field." Between these two pieces of knowledge, Rilke will weave his poem.

The opening stanza begins abruptly, as though the poet were speaking with some urgency in the midst of an ongoing meditation. Addressing the reader in the first-person-plural "we" form, the poet refers to a general condition that both presumably share. Referring to the ruins of the antique sarcophagi, the poet affirms that, like them, reader and poet alike "are scattered out and set in place." Yet, unlike the sarcophagi, human beings also share common negative emotions that the poet identifies as "thirst," "hatred," and "confusion." All these qualities "dwell in us," and taken together they indicate that being human is somehow to be lacking, is somehow synonymous with being unfinished.

The notion of "dwelling" leads gracefully into the second stanza, in which the poet shifts from describing the shared human qualities of the living to depicting the actual sarcophagi and the contents they once held. The poet names the accoutrements that once accompanied the dead into their coffins, the "rings, glasses, ribbons, and images of gods," which, in their reality as things, strike a vivid counterpoint to the negative, amorphous human qualities described in the first stanza. Among these distinct and definite things a human being once lay, a "slowly loosening something" that in death perhaps acquired a completeness that it lacked in life.

In the third stanza, the poet plays specifically on the etymological origins of "sarcophagus," describing the bodies as "swallowed by those unknown mouths." Rilke further plays on this image by making an imaginative leap from the "mouths" of the coffins to the "brain that one day will make use of them," a reference that perhaps on the most literal level refers to the farmer who eventually will invent a new use for them.

In the concluding stanza, the poem becomes starkly literal as the sarcophagi complete their transformation from ritualistic vessels for the dead to practical vessels for irrigation of the farmers' fields. The poem closes with an image of moving water rendered with a simple and sensuous clarity.

Forms and Devices

Rilke's subject matter is conducive to a rich exposition. In his intertwining of the etymological history of the word "sarcophagus" with the actual history of the sarcophagi, he is able to generate a series of surprising images and transformations. In a certain very real sense, "Roman Sarcophagi" was a poem waiting to be found, and Rilke seems happy to let the inherent poetic richness of his subject reveal itself. As is clear from the first-person-plural "we" of the opening stanza, the poet here, as so often in *New Poems*, gives the reader the impression that he is merely pointing to some meaning already present in the world. For Rilke, it would seem, the task of the poet is not so much to make meaning for the reader as it is to recover and share a communal meaning that is already "out there," waiting to be found.

Yet the reader should not be seduced too easily, for one can argue that Rilke's ability to see the potential buried within his subject, along with his apparently effortless ability to render this shared meaning, is precisely the measure of his mastery as a poet. A close reading of "Roman Sarcophagi" reveals that the poet carries a few selective details and figures through a series of imaginative transformations from stanza to stanza.

Most notably, the etymology of "sarcophagi" suggests to the poet an image of the coffins as mouths. In the first stanza, the one ostensibly least focused on the story of the coffins themselves, the poet describes the "unfinished" nature of human life in terms of "thirst." In the second stanza, he draws a comparison between the confusion or thirst of living humans and the "slowly loosening something" of the Romans in the coffins — it is as though the confusion of life only slowly vanishes after death as the indefiniteness of the human body gradually dissolves among the definite objects placed alongside it. Finally, in the third stanza, the body is completely swallowed by the coffin-mouths, and in the fourth fresh, shining water runs through the coffins.

Through this developing cluster of images, the poet has shown how "thirst" might "dwell" in people, just as the decaying body dwells in the coffin. With the movement of water through the transformed coffin, the human "thirst" of the first stanza finally has been quenched.

On the surface, it would seem that Rilke is attempting a direct, almost objective presentation of his subject, but further reflection demonstrates that the poem works by means of a chain of details selected from the subject at hand in order to present the reader with a startling, almost miraculously ironic transformation as the human "thirst" of the opening stanza is eventually quenched by the water the farmers use for irrigation. Rilke presents the objective history of the sarcophagi but does so through selective images that emphasize processes of death, decay, and eventual rebirth.

Themes and Meanings

Often in Rilke's *New Poems* it seems as though the poet in observing his subject is attempting to look into a mirror. Yet the thing that is regarded throws back an image not of the poet's self but of all that the self is not. In other words, the striking otherness of the observed subject provides the poet with a way of understanding what it means to be human, precisely because the subject itself is something beyond the human. In "Roman Sarcophagi," the poet describes human life as confused and unfinished. As is clear from Rilke's other work, to be incomplete is a source of both great pain and great joy, for if one is incomplete this means merely that more life is to come; in short, one's very lack of completion is simply the negative side of one's potential for growth. Continually throughout his career, Rilke's poetry explores the ways in which people grow and change over the course of a life. For Rilke, growth is always synonymous with life itself, and failure to grow is a kind of death.

Hence, in Rilkean terms, the Romans buried in the sarcophagi become fully completed human beings only as they gradually dissolve among the artifacts buried with them. Hundreds of years later, when the farmers break the ends out of the coffins and place them end to end as irrigation canals, any trace of the bodies the coffins once may have contained has disappeared as they are transformed from ritualistic vessels for the dead into wholly practical vessels for bringing water and life to the crops. Whereas once the coffins contained the dead, they now bring water—bright, shining, animate—the most elemental of life-giving substances.

In telling the story of the transformation of the sarcophagi, it seems that Rilke has hit upon the perfect image for describing a metamorphosis from life to death to new life again, a new life figured in the image of the flowing water with which the poem closes. Such a passage seems all the more vivid and believable because of the strikingly literal terms in which Rilke renders it.

Vance Crummett

SADNESS AND HAPPINESS

Author: Robert Pinsky (1940-   )
Type of poem: Poetic sequence
First published: 1975, in *Sadness and Happiness*

The Poem

"Sadness and Happiness," the title poem of Robert Pinsky's first collection, is divided into thirteen sections, each of which contains five unrhymed quatrains. The title of the poem is, simply, the subject of the poet's meditation: He considers the sadness and happiness in his own life and in the lives of others.

The poem is written in the first person. Pinsky discusses his own life, the career choices he has made, and his family. The poet is not speaking through a persona; part of the poem's success derives from Pinsky's attempt to remove all masks and speak, with wit and candor, from his heart.

The first section is typical of the entire poem. In it, Pinsky addresses large philosophical themes, and he balances these with specific events or memories. He begins the poem by suggesting that, in memory, it often "becomes impossible/ to tell" sadness and happiness from each other. This is a theme to which he will return often in the poem. Sadness and happiness are "Crude, empty" terms, but he uses them because "they do/ organize life." Others, including the "sad American/ house-hunting couples with kids," may use closet space to organize their lives, but Pinsky prefers the abstractions of sadness and happiness for his purposes. Pinsky moves easily somehow from the notion of closet space to "*post coitum triste*," or the sadness following intercourse. This discursiveness is typical of the poem; if the poem follows a pattern at all, it is the mazelike pattern of associative thought.

The second section follows the sexual meditation. Pinsky notes that the " 'pain' and 'bliss' " of early courtly love sonnets were based in part on the speaker's desire "to get more or better" sex, but Pinsky sees that " 'Bale' and 'bliss' merge" even in sexual relations. Sadness and happiness cannot be separated, partially because the memories of sexual pleasures are joined by "absurd memories of failure."

Passing through historical allusions to the "muttered babble" of "Korsh, Old Russia's bedlam-sage," and the musical references to the "sex-drowsy saxophones" of the blues, Pinsky arrives, in sections 5 and 6, at his relationship with his wife. The noises in the historical and musical asides give way to the sounds of a particular memory Pinsky has of his wife. While driving with her, everything he sees, apart from his wife, seems ambiguously "full of emotion, and yet empty—/ . . . all empty/ of sadness and happiness." In Central Square in Cambridge, Massachusetts, Pinsky meets the Salvation Army brass band, the "farting, evil-tempered traffic," "young girls begging," and "filth spinning in the wind." Everything seems empty, except for his wife.

Memories of his wife slip into recollections of previous women with whom he was involved. He asks " 'some lovely, glorious Nothing,' Susan,/ Patricia, Celia" to forgive him for his "past failures"; he also wishes he were without a past. He would like only his wife, without the other "foolish ghosts" of the past, to urge him "to become some redeeming/ Jewish-American Shakespeare."

In section 8, he recalls his romantic, adolescent dreams, his fantasy of becoming "a vomit-stained/ ex-Jazz-Immortal, collapsed/ in a phlegmy Bowery doorway." Instead, he has become a poet with a normal life, a wife and daughters. He then imagines himself as a type of prophet who would like to address the Central Square crowd, "the band,/ the kids, the old ladies awaiting/ buses, the glazed winos." His imagined speech to them is a comic mixture of the hortatory tones of T. S. Eliot and Ezra Pound; his harangue, however, just as it begins to gather steam, trails off. Instead of continuing his attack on the "city of/ undone deathcrotches," he attacks himself, reflecting on his perverse ability to enjoy "air pollution . . ./ even the troubles of friends."

Pinsky stays with the Central Square environment in section 10 and wonders whether the "two bright-faced girls" should win his admiration as they cross the square with their "long legs flashing bravely above/ the grime." He continues the meditation in section 11, concluding that "the senses/ are not visionary, they can tug/ downward."

Recalling with pride a "sandlot home run" leads Pinsky to a recollection also of his errors, the "poor throws awry/ or the ball streaming through,/ between my poor foolish legs." This recollection of the ballfield leads to the final thoughts in the poem, a meditation on the Spanish word *polvo*, or dust, which in the poem comes out of the "reddish gray/ powder of the ballfield" and leads to the dust that bodies turn into in death. Pinsky concludes with a complaint against the impermanence of life. For Pinsky, "It is intolerable/ to think of my daughters, too, dust" or of his wife changed into "*el polvo*." He decides that humans are "desperate to devise anything" to "escape the clasped coffinworm/ truth" of art or nature.

Forms and Devices

Pinsky attempts to name, or at least discuss, some organizing principle for the vagaries of life, and his formal choices reflect the difficulties of this task. It would seem at first glance that this poem, with its division into sections and quatrains, is very regular, or at least predictable in some way, but Pinsky works against the structure he imposes on the poem. The sections are not ironclad divisions; rather, they are permeable boundaries. Pinsky, in fact, ends only one section (the last, section 13) with a complete sentence, while all the others spill over into the section that follows. Stories or digressions do not end because a section ends, but continue and trail off, finally, in a subsequent section.

Images or memories also are not confined to one particular section of the poem. In sections 2 and 3, Pinsky speaks of Petrarchan love poems and chivalric trophies, and admits, in a distanced way, that he

                                      stood
                    posing amiss while the best prizes

                    of life bounced off his vague
                    pate or streamed between his legs.

In section 12, the inflated Petrarchan image becomes appealingly pedestrian when the poet recalls his sandlot baseball days: the "agony of recalled errors . . ./ . . . poor throws awry/ or the ball streaming through,/ between my poor foolish legs." Nothing remains fixed in the poem.

Even words will not hold steady. In the closing sections, Pinsky speaks of "*el polvo*," which is the "reddish gray/ powder of the ballfield," but also the dust on which a girl dances in the Cervantes poem and the dust that his daughters and his wife will become in death. It is difficult to organize or structure a philosophy when everything seems to be in flux, and nothing—not even the formal structuring device of quatrains and sections—can halt it.

The game that Pinsky's wife uses to organize life, the "invented game,/ Sadness and Happiness," also offers little consolation. Pinsky brings this point home by noting at the start of the poem that it is often "impossible/ to tell one from the other in memory," and then reemphasizing the idea by a formal and unusual device: Pinsky will never allow the words happiness or sadness, or their synonyms, to stand alone in the poem. The two emotions are always joined somehow, usually within a line or two. When discussing "*post coitum triste*," he says he is happy not to have experienced it often. He says that with no past, he would be happy "or else/ decently sad." When he sees the "gray sad leaves" falling in autumn, he thinks they "can bring/ joy, or fail to." And when crossing the bases after hitting a home run, he conflates the two again by recalling the "happiness/ impure and oddly memorable as the sad/ agony of recalled errors."

The poem emphasizes the inability of humans to fix things in place by showing the slippage possible between concepts, simple words, images, structuring devices like sections and quatrains, or the present and the past.

Themes and Meanings

This typically modern, elliptical poem that in its discursiveness resists precise meaning addresses the oldest theme in literature, present as far back as the *Epic of Gilgamesh* (c. 2000 B.C.): humans attempting to deal with their mortality. The poem, in parts, is a verse autobiography, but all the memories of the past lead to the final vision of the future, in which all Pinsky's family—and the poet himself—will be dead. The poet speaks of "that romantic/ fantasy of my future bumhood" that he held in adolescence; in maturity, however, the only fantasy he has of his future is the prospect of an inevitable death.

How does one counter one's impermanence? Pinsky's wife plays the "Sadness and Happiness" game with the children to help them organize and stabilize life, but Pinsky points out the dangers in that generous approach. People are, in Pinsky's words, "desperate to devise anything . . .// to escape" life's transitory nature. Yet Pinsky does not offer the reader much ease from the burden. William Shakespeare in his poems offered his loved ones permanence through art, suggesting, in Sonnet 18, that "So long as men can breathe, or eyes can see,/ So long lives this [poem], and this gives life to thee." Pinsky is not so glib or cocky. His art simply records the anguish and the muted pleasures of living in a world of impermanence. He offers his wife and children his sadness, but he cannot offer them immortality through art.

The poem attempts to ward off the powers of death—the change that "all/ changes breedeth"—by listing with wit all the minute particulars of a man's life, from his baseball days and early failed romances to his dreams of grandeur in addressing and working a Central Square crowd. All the attention to the stuff of life, however, even the two girls' "long legs flashing bravely above/ the grime," brings Pinsky to a philosophical moment that seems akin to Platonism. He believes that

> it takes more than eyes
>
> to see well anything that is worth
> loving; that is the sad part, the senses
> are not visionary, they can tug
> downward, even in pure joy.

Yet Pinsky is wedded to the senses, even while he is perfectly aware of their limitations. The poem does not offer the reader a vision of a Platonic realm; it only critiques the world of the impure senses. Pinsky, in the end, is a poet who sees the world and its transience clearly, mourns appropriately, and continues to make song, attempting, with wit, to fashion sense out of a world that constantly eludes him.

Kevin Boyle

SAILING TO BYZANTIUM

Author: William Butler Yeats (1865-1939)
Type of poem: Lyric
First published: 1928, in *The Tower*

The Poem

"Sailing to Byzantium" is a short poem of thirty-two lines divided into four numbered stanzas. The title suggests an escape to a distant, imaginary land where the speaker achieves mystical union with beautiful, eternal works of art.

"Byzantium" is a loaded word for William Butler Yeats, a word rich with meaning. "Byzantium" refers to an earlier Yeats poem by that title and to the ancient name for Istanbul, capital of the Byzantine empire of the fifth and sixth centuries. In his prose work *A Vision* (1925), Yeats wrote that Byzantium represents for him a world of artistic energy and timelessness, a place of highly developed intellectual and artistic cultures. It represents a perfect union of aesthetic and spiritual energies; Yeats wrote, "I think that in early Byzantium, maybe never before or since in recorded history, religious, aesthetic, and practical life were one." To historians of art, Byzantium is famous for its multicolored mosaics inlaid with marble and gold. Often the mosaics depict Christ or other religious figures in symmetrical arrangement with two-dimensional, impersonal facial expressions.

The first stanza describes a country of "sensual music," presumably Ireland, but representing any place dominated by living for today. As an old man, the poet at once celebrates the fertility and joyful images of teeming fish, birds, and people but despairs of their temporal ignorance. Caught in the endless cycle of birth and death, these living beings overlook certain "monuments of unageing intellect" that the poet seeks to explore.

The old man reflects on himself in the second stanza, calling himself a scarecrow on a stick without much physical vigor. What he lacks in body he compensates for in desire to express himself through singing. Singing (his poetry) will allow him to transcend old age. The spirit of his poetry will carry him to Byzantium, a magnificent and holy city.

The third stanza presents the speaker standing before a golden mosaic, pleading that the Byzantine sages and "God's holy fire" will illuminate his soul. He realizes that his heart is trapped inside a fleshly creature that will soon die; the poet wants to leave this world and enter the world of timeless art through his song — poetry.

The fourth stanza develops the contradiction that a human being cannot leave this world while occupying a body. The poet desires to merge with the elaborate, gold-inlaid Byzantine mosaics and become like a bird perched on a bough, serenading sleepy emperors and nobles for all eternity. Preserved in this mythic form, the poet can observe past, present, and future, rejoicing in his artistic immortality.

Forms and Devices

"Sailing to Byzantium" follows an ottava rima stanza pattern, which usually consists of eight eleven-syllable lines rhyming *abababcc*. Italian poet Giovanni Boccaccio is credited with inventing the form. Sir Thomas Wyatt and George Gordon, Lord Byron, popularized it in England. Yeats, however, modifies the form to suit his own purposes, using ten syllables instead of the original eleven and using slant rhymes instead of exact ones. In lines 1 and 3, for example, different vowel sounds prevent "young" from rhyming exactly with "song."

Yeats constructs his poem around one major opposition: the mortal world of the flesh versus the golden world of eternal art. One of Yeats's major themes in poetry is that no one can make a choice of absolute certainty between precise opposites. The two realms depend on each other for what they mean, as in the case of Ireland with its teeming animal life and the medieval imperial city of Byzantium. Yeats juxtaposes a natural, mortal world driven by the cycle of life and death with an impersonal, immortal world of art. The speaker yearns to detach himself from the temporal world of his body to find himself inside "the artifice of eternity."

Two metaphors running throughout the poem—birds and singing—point to the differences between Ireland and Byzantium. The bird has long been a spiritual symbol, as in the dove from scripture. The birds in the trees in stanza 1, references to a bird's flight in stanza 2, and the bird "set upon a golden bough to sing" in stanza 4 emphasize the difference between a sensual, physical world of spiritual ignorance and a timeless world of spiritual revelation. The image of the bird in flight in stanza 3 is a pervasive gyre symbol appearing in many of Yeats's later poems. The whirling, coiling motion and the use of the verb "perne" are Yeats's adaptations of the noun "pirn," a small cylinder originally made of a hollow reed or quill on which thread or yarn was wound. Yeats means to imply the merger of his soul with the spiraling bird's flight, just as the poet wishes to lose his soul in the eternal world of art.

The metaphor of music-making and song as poetry establishes Yeats's desire to make his own Byzantine mosaic in verse, where his spirit might be preserved for all eternity. The poet looks at one gold mosaic in stanza 3 and pleas for the sages to "be the singing-masters of my soul," to teach the poet how he might be similarly able to step out of his aging body.

Elements of song pervade Yeats's poem. The old man dreams of the songs he shall make if, by merging with voices of sages and Byzantine art, he can transcend the restrictions of mind and body. The reader should note the alliteration of *g*, *s*, *l*, and *p* consonants and the assonance or recurring vowel sounds in stanza 4 that reflect the music of language.

References to folk legend, myth, and symbol abound in "Sailing to Byzantium." Throughout his career, Yeats worked symbols into his poetry, giving a universality to ostensibly topical poems. The bird images stand for transcendence, immortality, and the spirit. As another example, the "golden bough" of stanza 4 may refer to both Sir James George Frazer's work in comparative mythology, *The Golden Bough* (1890), and to classical Roman poet Vergil's *Aeneid* (c. 29-19 B.C.), in which Aeneas plucks a golden bough in order to descend into Hades.

Themes and Meanings

Yeats's poem offers fertile ground for inquiry into the realms of language, structure, imagination, myth, and symbol. Many critics have written about "Sailing to Byzantium," and the poem seems almost inexhaustible in its supply of ideas. Yeats published "Sailing to Byzantium" when he was sixty-three, so the theme of the life cycle and the differences between youthful exuberance and sterile old age certainly inform the poem. Yet to suggest that Yeats's only concern is his approaching death seriously undervalues the richness of the poem's symbols.

The poem's major theme is the transformative power of art: the ability of art to express the ineffable and to step outside the boundaries of self. Some concrete details of the poem might be read autobiographically, such as the speaker's desire to leave his country, references to himself as an old man, "a tattered coat upon a stick," and having a heart "sick with desire/ And fastened to a dying animal." Although an old man, the speaker still feels the desire to sail to Byzantium and metaphorically to transcend the sensual music of Ireland. He wants to transform his own consciousness and find mystical union with the golden mosaics of a medieval empire.

The poet pleads with the sages in the mosaic to open the door and allow him entry into their world, where he might reflect on past, present, and future. With his body discarded, the poet's concept of time changes. He is no longer the victim of a biological cycle but has liberated himself into a new world, capable of reaching over all eras. The poet leaves behind a temporal world of ignorant lust and physical celebration to gain the perspective of eternity.

Another of the poem's broader meanings is the paradox of consciousness and the body. Yeats entertains the idea that consciousness might continue outside the restrictions of mind and body. The poet's body falls apart, yet his facilities of imagination, soul, and spirit are still passionate and alive. Individuality fades away as the body dissolves in old age, and the poet finds himself reincarnated as a golden bird. This new form exceeds the realms of individuality because it merges with eternal art, the Byzantine mosaic.

While one may be tempted to read "Sailing to Byzantium" as only about the division between mind and body, Yeats's theme of transformation goes far beyond this simple dichotomy. The poem also represents the idea that art supersedes nature. The poet avoids the necessary return to dust by joining "the artifice of eternity." Great works of art, poetry, and song whose spirit expresses great desire have the power to overcome nature. In another poem, "Byzantium," Yeats discusses the relationship between transcendent art and the human hands that made it. "Sailing to Byzantium" explores many levels of aesthetic, spiritual, and intellectual transformation through which the poet journeys far beyond his native land.

Jonathan L. Thorndike

SAINT JUDAS

Author: James Wright (1927-1980)
Type of poem: Sonnet
First published: 1959, in *Saint Judas*

The Poem

"Saint Judas" is a nearly Petrarchan sonnet, in nearly regular iambic pentameter, with an unusual rhyme scheme. Its title suggests that its contents, as well as its form, will represent a modification of tradition, since anyone familiar with the story of Judas Iscariot, apostle and betrayer of Christ, will be surprised to see him canonized in the title of the poem as "Saint Judas." The title simultaneously stimulates curiosity and encourages an open mind for the unorthodox interpretation of character that follows.

The sonnet is written in the first person. Readers of James Wright's later, more confessional poetry will expect the speaker of the poem to be Wright himself, but "Saint Judas" instead takes the point of view of the infamous traitor of the title. It is important to note that the persona of this poem is not to be confused with Saint Jude, another of Christ's apostles, who is known by the Catholic church as the patron saint of desperate cases. The Judas referred to here is the apostle Judas Iscariot, whose story, as it is traditionally told, appears in the Bible in Matthew 27:3-5. Like Robert Browning's murderer in "Porphyria's Lover," or Vladimir Nabokov's child molester in *Lolita* (1955), James Wright's "Saint Judas" is a character who could only arouse sympathy by being seen from the inside.

The narrative of the poem begins in the octave, where the reader finds Judas on his way to commit suicide. He has been momentarily sidetracked by the suffering of a man who has been beaten by a "pack of hoodlums." In his rush to help and give comfort, he forgets himself and his problems. He even forgets the sordid bargain in which he had earlier betrayed Christ to the Roman soldiers in the Garden of Gethsemane for thirty pieces of silver. Most important, he forgets his overwhelming despair.

In the sestet of the sonnet, Judas rushes to the recent victim of brutality, drops his rope and his suicidal intent, ignores the soldiers for whom he had so recently committed the highest treason, and succors the unfortunate man in his arms. It is then that he remembers the last supper that he had with Christ and the traitorous kiss with which he turned Christ over to the Romans. Even though he is haunted by these damning memories, even though he sees himself as "Banished from heaven" and "without hope," he still "held the man for nothing" in his arms. The poem ends with a poignant image of selfless humanity and absolute generosity of spirit.

Forms and Devices

"Saint Judas" is a pivotal poem in James Wright's canon. It is a stylistic bridge between the 1950's formalism of his first two books, *The Green Wall* (1957) and

Saint Judas (1959), and the freer, more colloquial verse of his later volumes, *The Branch Will Not Break* (1963) and *Shall We Gather at the River* (1968). This sonnet, which is both the title and the last poem of *Saint Judas*, is a powerful farewell to the traditional rhyme and meter of his early mentors, Edwin Arlington Robinson and Robert Frost, and a tentative welcome to the stark, unadorned diction and powerful imagery of his contemporaries, Robert Bly and William Carlos Williams.

"Saint Judas" relies heavily on the traditional poetic strategy of literary, historical, and religious allusion. Many of Wright's later poems deal with society's outcasts—the drunks, the murderers, the lonely, the alienated, and the discarded—but in "Saint Judas," Wright has taken on the Herculean task of vindicating the archetypical villain and outcast of Western culture: Judas Iscariot. Poets who use allusions know that they risk losing the attention of readers who do not have the requisite cultural background. "Saint Judas" will mean very little to the person who is unfamiliar with the life of Christ and his mercenary betrayal by one of his own disciples with a hypocritical gesture of affection. Traditional poets have always been willing to take the risk that using allusions entails in order to bring even stronger pleasure to those readers who are prepared for the intellectual challenge. It is a risk of which modern poets have become increasingly wary. "Saint Judas" is the last of Wright's poems in which he is willing to rely so completely on the power of archetypical material to inform his verse. It is the last of his poems that would inspire a critic to compare his work with Wordsworth's.

In "Saint Judas," Wright mixes a traditional use of allusion to older literature with the colloquial language of contemporary America. Despite its two-thousand-year-old subject, there is nothing archaic about this poem. Wright refers to the men who brutalize the "victim" of the poem as "hoodlums." He says that Judas forgot his "name," his "number." These simple, direct words force the reader to see the plight of Judas in modern terms. It is not enough, the diction suggests, to have compassion for the historical "Saint Judas"; it might also be necessary to reassess one's opinion of the downtrodden and the condemned of this time.

Themes and Meanings

"Saint Judas" is fundamentally a moral poem that deals with two of Wright's favorite themes: alienation and despair. Judas is alienated from the rest of humanity because of his despicable crime; the reader knows that he despairs, because at the opening of the poem, he is on his way to kill himself. Is there any hope? That is the unusual question that Wright thinks to ask, and it is the kind of question that distinguishes him from so many of the fashionably nihilistic poets of the 1960's. The poem seems to answer: Where there is life, there is hope.

Wright chooses to imagine a Judas who is outside the traditional theological context, who faces his life and death like any other man, and who makes moral choices right up to the moment when he must inevitably swing upon the ash tree. This Judas, confronted with another's suffering, does not play the role of the predictable villain of melodrama, but instead is envisioned as caught up in an act of humanity so complete that he loses himself entirely. If Judas Iscariot is capable of this, what acts might the man on death row be capable of performing? What might anyone be capable of doing?

"Saint Judas" is not only a reassessment of common notions of "the good man" but also a cautionary tale. It warns one not to judge others too harshly. Many people do not doubt that Judas Iscariot must be burning in hell; religion and common sense both seem to confirm this easy verdict. Wright, however, wants his readers to question what anyone can really know about the state of another's soul. One must wonder whether one fatal act condemns a man forever and whether there can be redemption through human kindness. Can even the worst criminal have a moment of goodness? The answer to all of these questions, from Wright's point of view, is made clear in the title, in which he sees Judas as an essentially good man, frail and prone to error like so many others. He made a terrible mistake, but he need not despair, because God, unlike man, is merciful in his judgments.

Cynthia Lee Katona

THE SALUTATION

Author: Thomas Traherne (1637-1674)
Type of poem: Lyric
First published: 1903, in *The Poetical Works of Thomas Traherne*

The Poem

In the contemplative lyric "The Salutation," Thomas Traherne celebrates the wonder of life through the eyes of a first-person speaker who has only recently become aware of life's gifts. The lyric consists of seven regular six-line stanzas, forty-two lines total. What begins as a celebration of existence becomes by the end a religious poem in praise of the creator.

In the first stanza, the speaker addresses parts of his physical body—limbs, eyes, hands, and cheeks—to inquire why they were originally hidden from him. Where, he asks rhetorically, was his speaking tongue? The questions imply a commonplace theme in Traherne's poetry: the pre-existence of the soul. He implies that the parts of his body have also been hidden from consciousness, that they too have been in existence. Thus what is celebrated is in one sense not pre-existence but a newly acquired mental awareness of existence.

In the second stanza, the speaker acknowledges that his pre-existence was unconscious, that he remained thousands of years beneath the dust in "Chaos" and now welcomes his lips, hands, eyes, and ears as newly discovered treasures. Acknowledging in the third stanza that he has been nothing, the speaker also welcomes sensory pleasures as joys he has discovered and experienced. Stanza 4 lauds the richness of these joys, comparing them metaphorically to gold and pearls. To the speaker it appears that human joints and veins contain more wealth than all the rest of the world.

Stanza 5 represents a major change of emphasis, a pivotal point in the lyric, for the speaker who has celebrated his sensory pleasures now reflects upon them as gifts from God. From nothingness, the speaker has arisen into a world of greater objects and substances—earth, seas, sky, day, sun, and stars. All of these, he declares, become his—presumably because he celebrates them, reflects upon them, and admires them.

In stanza 6, the speaker expresses his conviction that God has prepared all the wonders of the world for his existence and that all creation serves him. Mythically like an Eden, wide and bright, the world created for the speaker brings with it an assurance that God has adopted the speaker as his son and heir, that he has received title to a great legacy.

In the final stanza, the speaker rejoices in the novelty of his existence, the strangeness of all things outside himself that were created for him. The world is "fair," its contents "Treasures" and "Glories." The greatest wonder is that all was created for one who once was nothing. The speaker thus celebrates the creator through praise of the creation and through his understanding of its purpose.

Forms and Devices

Among the poem's most creative conventions is the introduction of the first-person speaker. In the first stanza, reference to his "Speaking Tongue" suggests that he has just begun speaking, like an infant who has become aware of his own body and senses and is struck with wonder at their power. The speaker does not remain at that stage, however; he quickly develops a sense of his being and of mental categories (abstractions) such as time. He is able to admire the universe outside himself and to discern the purpose of its creation. Optimistically finding everything created pleasant and good, he celebrates the creator through celebrating creation. Throughout his development, the speaker maintains a tone of naïve and innocent wonder as he celebrates himself, the world, its purposes, and the creator. Thus, Traherne presents a developing intellect from childhood to maturity, but the speaker retains the child's sense of wonder and optimism throughout. In his Eden there is neither a serpent nor a Fall; the fictive speaker's mind develops and expands without any awareness of guilt and sin.

Each of the poem's six-line stanzas, rhyming *ababcc*, exhibits an unusual metrical pattern: two iambic feet in line 1, four in line 2, five in line 3, three in line 4, and five in lines 5 and 6. Traherne also uses repetition to create emphasis and conviction. In the final stanza, the word "strange," or one of its variants, occurs six times, employing the schemes of repetition called "ploce" and "polyptoton." The device creates a tone of incantation that urges acceptance of the poem's message.

The poem's diction is simple, even plain, reminiscent of the Puritan plain style of the seventeenth century. Adjectives such as little, fair, bright, glorious, and wide are typical of the poem's simple and basic vocabulary. Nouns, on the other hand, suggest biblical origins of the plain style and add to the religious and elemental emphasis created by the poem: God, Eden, dust, gold, glories, joys, eternity, chaos, abyss. The rich imagery is dominated by sight images, some quite general, others specific and vivid. Earth, seas, light, and day contrast with the more specific gold, pearl, cheeks, and limbs.

Figures of speech seem conventionally chosen in order to make abstract ideas more concrete or to heighten the reader's sense of value. The limbs of boys, for example, become sacred treasures, and the world as prepared by God becomes a glorious store.

Themes and Meanings

Although Traherne belongs among the Metaphysical poets, he is among those Metaphysicals more accurately termed meditative or contemplative poets. "The Salutation" best fits the contemplative poem designation, for its speaker does not engage in a disciplined, structured meditation for the purpose of self-improvement. Instead, he turns his attention to objects outside himself in order to cultivate a sense of wonder and praise their existence. For its effect, the poem depends upon the reader's ability to share his profound sense of naïve wonder when viewing his own existence and that of the external world.

Although the speaker assumes a kind of quiescent pre-existence of the soul, this theme is more subdued than in other Traherne poems, such as "Wonder" and "Shadows in the Water." The speaker views himself as having existed beneath dust and chaos for thousands of years, as having been nothing. Such a minimal conception of pre-existence heightens the wonder by contrasting the speaker's state with the richness and diversity of life on earth. Through identifying himself with dust and nothingness, the speaker magnifies his existence.

Like many lyrics, this one belongs among those that praise external nature and contemplate Dame Kind, with a view toward belonging or uniting with nature, as the more conventional mystic seeks unity with God. The poem attempts to portray all being as miraculous — a source of contemplation — and it conveys Traherne's own sense of wonder at the mystery of life. It follows his assumption that to praise and celebrate creation, to unite with it, is somehow to possess it. Contemplation, an individual act, enables him to view the world as created for man the individual, and the speaker seems to realize that only through contemplation can he experience a truth of this kind: "The Sun and Stars are mine; if those I prize."

The wonder and mystery that the speaker celebrates are made partially understandable through his grasp of divine purpose, a canon of faith with the speaker. The speaker can believe that everything was created by God not merely for man as a species but also for himself as an individual. Thus one finds in the poem a mystical version of Protestant individualism. Instead of the more common Puritan version in which the anxiety-ridden individual considers himself the center of a powerful drama of God and Satan struggling for his soul, with the outcome in doubt, Traherne presents the drama of the individual celebrating and seeking union with a totally benign creation, serenely assured that all is directed by God.

In an anthropocentric perspective, he views all of creation as a preparation for his own existence. Resorting to the myth of creation, the speaker depicts the world as an Eden prepared by God for a single soul and as evidence that he has been chosen as God's heir. In this Eden one finds no trace of the Fall, no evidence of fallen nature, only a fair creation prepared by God for man's benefit. The speaker naïvely expresses his own response to the strangeness in the form of a concluding paradox:

> But that they mine should be, who nothing was,
> That Strangest is of all, yet brought to pass.

In addition to celebrating the wonders of creation, the poem focuses on the drama of the individual soul. Just as he perceives no evidence of the pain and suffering of life, the speaker feels little unease regarding his own salvation. Yet as God's heir he must play his part in the mythic Eden of creation. Salvation is an individual matter, and the speaker appears to find a key element as one involving optimistic praise and identification of the self with creation.

Stanley Archer

SAME TIME

Author: Octavio Paz (1914-   )
Type of poem: Meditation
First published: 1962, as "El Mismo Tiempo," in *Salamandra (1958-1961)*;
   collected in *The Collected Poems of Octavio Paz, 1957-1987*

The Poem

"Same Time" is a long poem of 184 lines in free verse. Its format represents a break with Octavio Paz's early practice; under the influence of Stéphane Mallarmé, he had begun to think of a poem as a visual object. Accordingly, he emphasized white space through the use of short lines, occasionally allowing a single word to suffice for the line. Except for question marks, the poem has no punctuation. The title introduces one of the poem's chief themes: time's movement in relation to the individual and to poetry.

The first-person narrator inhabits a city of ceaseless flux, an impersonal flow of traffic in which glimpses may be had of people, for example, the couple by the iron railing and the nameless old man talking to himself. The city has alternately fascinated and repelled poets since Charles Baudelaire (1821-1867). Paz was captivated by T. S. Eliot's use of the theme in *The Waste Land* (1922). Poets are intrigued by the phenomenon of an individual consciousness boxed in by millions of other individuals with whom there is no communication: "To walk among people/ with the open secret of being alive." The poem was written in Paris, but memory takes the narrator to Mexico City, where the cars become trolleys carrying passengers from the Zócalo, Mexico City's main square, to the suburbs.

The narrator invokes the memory of walking Mexico City's pitted streets during the rainy season, June to September. His eyes lift to the clouds racing through the Mexican night sky, and their shape enraptures him; they become "Mistresses of eyes." Unbidden, a word comes to mind: "alabaster." The moment represents a transition from passive onlooker to user of words: The poet will make "castles of syllables." Writing—the creation of poetry—supplies an identity to this single person surrounded by millions.

Today, in the flow of the city, the poet still writes, shuttling words back and forth across the page, but with a newfound perspective: The world exists independently of him. The lyrical "I" is only one pulse beat in the throbbing river of humanity. Advice given by two philosophers, Mexico's José Vasconcelos and Spain's José Ortega y Gasset, reinforces the need for thinking and meditation in order to give meaning to life. Writing is a solution. To record the beauty of the world, the sun sinking into the river, the feminine cluster of grapes, revives the poet.

In these moments of beauty, time may be preempted. Images return, even though time does not, and their recurrence supplies a sense of continuity. When the words for poetry appear, there takes place a fullness of presence, of time within time that is a moment of transparency.

Forms and Devices

To show that there may be another kind of time within the chronological time that defines all living creatures, Paz resorted to a spiral-like poetic form. The poem's lack of punctuation means that the conventional grammatical signposts (commas, periods, semicolons) will not be present to convey a linear approach. Less circular than *Piedra de sol* (1957; *Sun Stone,* 1963), which opens and closes with the same lines, "Same Time" nevertheless begins and ends in a way that suggests a movement from a point—the stillness outside the city—to a similar point at a higher level of consciousness: "time within time/ still/ with no hours no weight no shadow/ without past or future." The effect is reminiscent of a spiral whose movement is accentuated by the abundance of empty spaces facing the readers' eyes. One also can note how the negation of the first line, "It is not the wind," is echoed in the closure, "It is not memory."

A single-word line provides special emphasis. "Lit," "bird," and "clouds" suggest the lightness that is pointing toward "alabaster" and, ultimately, "transparency." "Alabaster" occurs at the midpoint of the poem. On one level, it is an allusion occasioned by Paz's reading of Rubén Darío's *Prosas profanas* (1896; *Profane Hymns and Other Poems*, 1922): "Heavenly alabaster inhabited by stars:/ God is reflected in such sweet alabaster." This is the reason for the word's favored position, for it is such sweet whiteness that prepares the way for the evocation of transparency. "Alabaster" appears alone twice, and it represents an axis in the poem after which the narrator discovers an identity through poetry and heightened perception.

Effective images are scattered throughout: Some are clearly based on a real or remembered moment, such as the "blackbird on a gray stone," and some are ambiguous, such as "three leaves fall from a tree." The memory of the streetcars stimulates a cluster of metaphors. The "trolley-poles" call to mind "Black rays," their sparks are "small tongues of fire," and the noise they make on the way to the suburbs is compared to crashing towers. Other isolated metaphors sparkle throughout this long poem: The sweep and grandeur of poetry (or music) is captured in "castles of syllables"; the roundness of grapes suggests "feminine clusters."

As the narrator walks mentally through the cities of his life, he remembers many objects: trees, cars, houses, a dog, a bird, the fig tree. For the most part, these objects exist as images in the poet's memory, but occasionally they acquire the status of symbols. The sky is omnipresent, clear (without "a wrinkle"), filling up with clouds that hint of gestation and prepare for the near-miraculous appearance of the word "alabaster." Paz has prepared the reader for the various symbolic meanings of this word: purity, lightness, beauty, softness, celestial presence. This symbol, in turn, converts into the "word," which for Paz means poetry, music, art, and creativity.

Anaphora, the repetition of words or phrases at the beginning of a line, is used at the beginning and end of the poem. "It is not the wind," it is not the sea, but "It is the city," and at the conclusion, one reads that "It is not memory," but "It is transparency."

Themes and Meanings

"Same Time" is a showpiece for several of Paz's favorite motifs: seeing, writing, and time. The tradition of the poet-seer, an individual with special ways of seeing, goes back to the European Romantics. Paz's version of it is shaped by his experiences in Mexico and India and his vast knowledge of Western literature. ·

The recurring moment of transparency in Paz's poetry refers to those seconds in which his vision allows him to see beauty in great detail and glimpse extraordinary relationships between words and objects. It is unsummoned, as he says, but perhaps triggered by another word ("alabaster") or object ("cloud"). With this opened eye, the poet explores beauty, his gaze "sustains loveliness" and seems to affect a change upon his notion of time. Moments of transparency for Paz are not unlike those moments of epiphany mentioned by James Joyce and explored in loving detail by Spanish poet Juan Ramón Jiménez.

Transparency provides the optimum moment in which poetry can crystallize. The "thin unsummoned transparency" that appears in the middle of the poem facilitates creativity, a fact that the poet has long recognized ("You said") but not always adhered to ("You made nothing"). In these states of lucidity in which light (and here one must think of the strong sunlight of his native Mexico) passes through all barriers, the poet can build castles out of syllables.

The heightened sense of awareness that Paz calls transparency bestows on the moment a sense of presence. This intuition of otherness is not memory, the poet carefully notes, but rather it is as if time had acquired a new dimension. Within the relentless chronological nature of the time that defines people may be another time in which the phenomena of the world are weightless (like the bee that does not cast a shadow in the Jorge Luis Borges story "The Secret Miracle"), and the time neatly divided into past, present, and future melds into something indivisible. In such an instant, one is spared the need to talk about time passing: "Perhaps time doesn't pass/ images of time pass." T. S. Eliot, whose poetry deeply impressed Paz, begins "Burnt Norton," the first of the *Four Quartets* (1943), with a similar meditation on the nature of time that includes the lines: "If all time is eternally present/ All time is unredeemable."

There is no need to reclaim time if such visions can be granted to poets and their readers. "Same Time" points to this moment: "It is not the wind . . . it is not memory . . . it is transparency."

Howard Young

SAN ILDEFONSO NOCTURNE

Author: Octavio Paz (1914-   )
Type of poem: Lyric
First published: 1976, as "Nocturno de San Ildefonso," in *Vuelta (1969-1975)*;
collected in *The Collected Poems of Octavio Paz, 1957-1987*, 1987

The Poem

"San Ildefonso Nocturne," written in free verse, is divided into four stanzas of unequal length. Octavio Paz once again uses punctuation, a practice that he had abandoned in previous books. He also returns to the circular form he introduced so successfully in 1957 in *Piedra de sol* (*Sun Stone*, 1963). "San Ildefonso Nocturne" begins with the poet viewing through the window of his room a garish display of neon advertising in an unnamed city. Parts 2 and 3 move into the narrator's past as a boy in Mexico City, and part 4 closes with the poet once again in his room watching the neon advertisements flashing in the night. In *Sun Stone*, the same six lines open and close the poem; in "San Ildefonso Nocturne," a similar effect is achieved through the repetition of a scene—the poet at the window.

In his hotel room, the narrator sees the neon lights of advertisements spray the blackness of his window. Preoccupied as always by communication, he connects the advertising signs with the syllable clusters he is putting down on his page. The words turn into ants; there is a tunnel that will lead him somewhere. "What does it [the night] want?" he asks at the conclusion of part 1.

The night wishes to summon him to Mexico City in the year 1931, when he would have been seventeen. Squinting lights contrast with the neon glare of part 1. Pockets of characteristic poverty greet his eyes; children cover themselves with unsold newspapers. A lascivious clatter of heels, metonymy for a woman of the night, provokes two allusions explained by the poet. The lines "*a sky of soot/ the flash of a skirt*" are taken from the Mexican poet Ramón López Velarde, and the French phrase "*C'est la mort—ou la morte*" ("It is death—or the dead woman") comes from Gérard de Nerval's sonnet about Artemis, the huntress. Both allusions suggest prostitution.

The poet now refers specifically to San Ildefonso, a college built by the Jesuits in the seventeenth century, and his memory evokes the buried idols and canals of the Aztec city of Tenochtitlán covered by present-day Mexico City and its vast central plaza, the Zócalo. He recalls two novels he read as a boy, Fyodor Dostoevski's *Bratya Karamazovy* (1879-1880; *The Brothers Karamazov*, 1912)—thus the reference to Alyosha K (Karamazov), the saintly one of the brothers—and Stendhal's *Le Rouge et le noir* (1830; *The Red and the Black*, 1898), whose hero was Julien Sorel.

Part 3 recognizes that the man who writes is the small boy, and the narrator bemoans the failure of his generation to have any positive effect upon the world. Part 4 stresses the power of language, as Paz is seen again writing at the window, and introduces a new personage, his sleeping wife; she represents nature, and with her he can lose his fear of death as he flows with her body.

Forms and Devices

Paz achieves his circular structure by means of many devices. Not only does the scene remain the same, but also the vocabulary duplicates itself. The poem commences with an unusual use of the verb "to invent": "In my window night/ invents another night." A few lines later, the city "invents" the lights, and in part 4, the sleeping wife "invents herself." This motif contributes to the circular motion of the poem. Paz also reprises metaphors and sometimes translates them. What were "Sign-seeds" in the city's night window are flatly stated at the closure of the poem to be part of the "commercial sky." The "high-voltage calligraphy" of the first scene goes through the stage of "squinting lights" in the evocation of the poet's adolescence to the straightforward description of reality's "commercial sky."

From his reading of T. S. Eliot's *The Waste Land* (1922), Paz learned about allusions and the practice of footnoting them, which he does in the case of the quotations from López Velarde and Nerval. He takes it for granted, however, that his readers will understand the references to Alyosha Karamazov and Julien Sorel. Part 2 contains buried allusions to Eliot's "Burnt Norton" ("galleries of echoes") and *The Waste Land* ("broken images").

The metaphors that describe the neon lights are especially arresting. Their profusion suggests a convulsed carnival; the endless flickering contained within forms "nomadic geometries." They represent a tension in the poet's mind ("false heaven/ hell of industry") and beckon with the promise of the benefits of progress and the predicament it brings.

Movement between various points of time is one of the poem's most intriguing aspects. The poem is about a series of returns, and it is significant that it appeared in a collection that Paz called *Vuelta* (*Return*, 1987), an account of his coming back to Mexico after years of living in the Far East and Europe. The first point in time is the present of the narrator, and the city whose lights he contemplates, although unnamed, is probably Mexico City. The tunnel at the end of part 1 will lead him to a point in adolescence, and the space is the Zócalo, Mexico's huge main square ("vast as the earth"). The Zócalo is rich in reminders of his country's colonial past (the cathedral's façade is a petrified garden), but it also sits upon the site of the ancient Aztec capital Tenochtitlán in an area once covered by canals. The transfer made by the reader and narrator is expressed in the line "sun turned to time,/ time turned to stone," in which the elements of life (sun), time, and history (stone) blend together.

The nocturne is haunted by history — that of the narrator and his friends — full of friendly ghosts that in his memory become flesh.

Themes and Meanings

One of the resonant words of this poem is the verb "invent." The night invents another night, the city invents signs, streetlights invent yellow pools of light, and the sleeping woman invents herself. More than an example of personification, Paz's use of *inventar* underlines the sense of magic and heightened awareness that has always concerned him as a poet. He intends the verb to carry its basic meaning, "to come across suddenly" (like the moments of transparency in his other poems), which implies the use of the imagination, another faculty that fascinates him.

The poem affords its author a chance to take stock of himself and to compare the present-day author, halfway through his life, with the seventeen-year-old crossing the Zócalo. The literary heroes he remembers bear special significance. Alyosha Karamazov and Julien Sorel assisted him in the invention of bolts of lightning to hurl against the century, and they stand for two sides of the poet himself: Alyosha, the pure in heart, stands as a buffer between his family and the world; and Julien, the ambitious hero from the provinces, has an enormous drive to succeed.

The "we" in this section refers to Paz and his cohorts, who, like all young idealists, made up in virtue what they were lacking in humility. As is usually the case, however, their desires for reform were betrayed by their own weaknesses as well as, in the case of Mexico, the entrenched strength of the system. Paz carries denouncement to the level of hyperbole, a zigzag of reconciliations, apostasies, recantations, and bewitchments.

He refuses to accept the possibility of blame. History itself, he writes, is the error. This assertion presumes that outside the accumulation of failures generally recorded by history there is an intimate sort of history — "everyone's anonymous heartbeat" — which is unrepeatable and identical. This core of personal human experience allows the poet to assert that "Truth/ is the base of a time without history."

It is such moments that the poet Octavio Paz has tirelessly sought and described. That is why he writes. Faced with the Hamlet-like dilemma of thought versus action, he chooses "the act of words." In the making of poetry, he enters once again into history, but neither as a direct participant nor as a mere bystander. He sees poetry as a "suspension bridge between history and truth" (events and intimacy), a way of coming and going — slightly frightening, as are all suspension bridges over the canyon between thought and action.

At the conclusion of part 4, Paz introduces one of his most important themes: the glory of the female body and the love that it represents. The union of individuals in love (the "truth of two," as he calls it in *Sun Stone*) redeems the individual from oblivion. Gazing at the form of his sleeping wife, he believes her to be copying nature, its islands and lagoons (such was Tenochtitlán when the Spaniards came). He knows that truth does perhaps lie outside of history: It is "the palpable mystery of the person."

Howard Young

A SATIRE AGAINST MANKIND

Author: John Wilmot, Earl of Rochester (1647-1680)
Type of poem: Satire
First published: 1679; collected in *Poems on Several Occasions by the Right Honourable the E. of R——* , 1680

The Poem

"A Satire Against Mankind," sometimes called "A Satire Against Reason and Mankind" or simply "Satire," is one of John Wilmot, Earl of Rochester's best-known poems. Written in iambic pentameter with a slighly irregular rhyme scheme (rhyming couplets occasionally give way to triplets), it is a humorous but bitter denunciation of human nature and all its vain pretensions to wisdom and virtue. The first forty-five lines of the poem form a general reflection on the failings of reason, which misleads and deceives man. Man believes himself to be eminently wise, but he is in fact the greatest of fools. Reason is compared to an *ignis fatuus* (literally a "false fire," or will-o'-the-wisp) that leads man through the treacherous landscape of his own mind. Clever people who profess to be "wits" are singled out for particular criticism, wit being decried as "vain frivolous pretence."

Rochester then introduces an interlocutor, a "formal Band, and Beard," or conventional, venerable clergyman, who agrees with the speaker in the poem that wit is abhorrent, but who takes issue with him for railing against mankind and reason in general. This interlocutor praises man as being made in God's image and possessing a soul, which, he says, raise man above the beasts by allowing him to comprehend the universe, Heaven, and Hell.

The speaker retorts that man is a mite who presumes to compare his brief life to the infinite. Man makes up his own cosmic mysteries and then solves them. The speaker is contemptuous of philosophers who prefer their cloisters to the wide world, and who spend their time thinking because they are incapable of doing.

The speaker distinguishes between false reason and right reason, which exists only insofar as it governs action and helps man enjoy life. This "right" reason comes from the senses; for example, the speaker's right reason tells him to eat when he is hungry, whereas mankind's more common false reason says to wait until the clock indicates that it is the hour to dine. The speaker will allow that there is some value in reason if it is this right reason, but that mankind, in general, is still contemptible. Man, he says, is worse than beasts who act on instinct. Beasts prey on other beasts for food, but man preys on other men by betraying them wantonly, out of hypocrisy and fear. Man lusts for power to protect himself from other men. The concept of honesty is laughable, because if a man is honest he will be cheated and despised. Politicians, he says, are venal and corrupt, and raise their friends and family rather than promote the good of the country. Churchmen are sinful hypocrites who preach heartily against sin but are really grasping and adulterous.

In the final stanza, the speaker claims that there may exist a humble, pious, honest man, and if he were to meet such a man he would be glad to recant this whole diatribe and pay homage to honesty; yet if there is such a man it would only prove that "Man differs more from man, than man from beast."

Forms and Devices

Rochester supports his satire with vivid and sometimes fanciful images and metaphors, many of which extend for line after line. His images are often deliberately ridiculous, so as to point out the ridiculousness of man's pretensions. When he describes reason as "an *ignis fatuus* of the mind," for example, he describes how it leads the stumbling follower through "fenny bogs, and thorny brakes," over "Mountains of whimseys" to a "boundless sea" where he tries desperately to stay afloat on books and to "swim with bladders of philosophy." Some of the humorous comparisons are more barbed; wits, he says "are treated just like common whores,/ First they're enjoyed, and then kicked out of doors." Combining his criticism with humor makes it more palatable to the reader, and ensures that the poem is more a clever satire than a vicious diatribe.

Rochester's intent is not entirely to amuse, though. Many of his images are wickedly persuasive as they expose the darker side of human nature. He compares men to beasts who are armed by nature with teeth and claws, and says, "Man, with smiles, embraces, friendships, praise,/ Unhumanely, his fellow's life betrays." He chooses as his examples of mankind the types who are supposed to be the most just and least self-interested of men. The statesman, he says, should "his needful flattery direct,/ Not to oppress, and ruin, but to protect." Instead, the statesman is proud and corrupt, receives bribes, and advances his family's interests over the country's. Clergymen receive the same satirical treatment. Rochester asks, "Is there a churchman who on God relys?/ Whose life, his faith, and doctrine justifies?" Rochester's answer is an emphatic no. The clergyman, he says, "from his pulpit, vents more peevish lies,/ More bitter railing scandals, calumnies,/ Than at a gossiping are thrown about." Clergymen are moreover proud, licentious, and greedy. By choosing as his particular subjects figures who should be examples of virtue in the community, Rochester broadens his satire from the individual to society.

Themes and Meanings

Rochester lived at the dawn of the Enlightenment, a time when new scientific discoveries and new ways of thinking were sweeping aside long-held traditional beliefs. Rochester was probably very familiar with Thomas Hobbes's *Leviathan* (1651), and much of his poetry seems to reflect a Hobbesian influence. It was in Rochester's era that the traditional notion of man being at the center of a divinely ordained universe, in which God took an active and pervasive interest, was replaced by a new vision of the cosmos as a vast, impersonal world, in which the role of man was minor. God was still a presence in this new vision, but He was seen as being like a clockmaker; He created the world, set it in motion, and sat back to watch impartially as it operates.

In such an intellectual environment, doubt of man's importance and distrust of, or contempt for, older ideas of man's divine nature were common in literature. "A Satire Against Mankind" is a compelling and particularly dark enunciation of these doubts. Rochester mocks mankind for thinking that the gift of reason raises him to a status close to the divine: "This supernatural gift, that makes a mite,/ Think he is the image of the Infinite:/ Comparing his short life, void of all rest,/ To the Eternal, and the ever blest." He sneers at man's intellectual pretensions: "This busy, puzzling, stirrer up of doubt,/ That frames deep mysteries, then finds 'em out."

Rochester does not reject mankind and his pretensions to reason as completely worthless, however; he expresses a firm belief in man's ability to know his immediate environment, via his senses. In this sense, he is a true product of the Enlightenment, in that he trusts empirical evidence and observable experience above all metaphysical speculations. He says: "Our sphere of action, is life's happiness,/ And he who thinks beyond, thinks like an ass." Rochester objects to man's presumption in believing that he can understand cosmic mysteries and the nature of the universe simply because, as a human, he is capable of thought.

Rochester's satire seems to spring as much from pain at man's weakness as from contempt for his follies. The final stanza is a kind of apology (in some early texts it is shown as a separate addendum to the main part of the satire) in which Rochester says that meeting a truly virtuous, modest, and pious man would readily convince him to revise his views on mankind. One senses that he truly wishes to discover such a good man and would be glad to "adore those shrines of virtue" if he could. Yet even such a paragon would not entirely convince him of mankind's redeemability; if such a man did exist, it would only prove that there is more difference among individual men than there is between man and beast. The whole poem, despite its stinging criticism of man's vice and weakness, is tinged with sadness at man's imperfections and his inability to make sense of anything beyond his immediate sensory perceptions. At the end of man's life, Rochester says, "Old age, and experience, hand in hand,/ Lead him to death, and make him understand,/ After a search so painful, and so long,/ That all his life he has been in the wrong." It is this heartfelt undertone of pain and sorrow at man's condition that tempers the vitriolic condemnation of man and makes "A Satire Against Mankind" both a classic statement of the ethos of Rochester's era and a timeless meditation on the nature of man.

Catherine Swanson

SCENTED HERBAGE OF MY BREAST

Author: Walt Whitman (1819-1892)
Type of poem: Lyric
First published: 1860, in *Leaves of Grass*, third edition

The Poem

In "Scented Herbage of My Breast," as in the other poems in the collection entitled *Leaves of Grass*, the poet Walt Whitman adopts a mask or persona through whom he speaks. The voice of this persona assumes various tones, usually ones that suggest a robust, celebratory, all-embracing stance toward life. In this particular lyric poem, the persona addresses himself to herbage, or grass, a symbol that is at the heart of the volume of poetry in which this poem appears.

The speaker begins by noting the timelessness of the grass, whose perennial roots are not frozen in the winter and whose blooms reappear every year. Looking at this grass, the persona says that he is reminded of both death and love, two realities that are, for him, beautiful and reminders of still another reality, life. As he muses on the relationship among beauty, death, and life, he observes that he is unable to prefer death or life, for he sees them as intricately connected by the cycle of life-death-life that pervades Whitman's poetic vision.

His reflections on this cycle compel him to announce his role as a spokesperson for himself and his comrades. As if he is blowing a bugle, initiating a drum roll, and raising a flag, the persona announces his intention: "I will say what I have to say by itself,/ I will sound myself and comrades only, I will never again utter a call only their call,/ . . . I will give an example to lovers to take permanent shape."

Following this announcement, the persona makes a subtle shift in the "you" whom he addresses. Up to this point, he is addressing the grass, but now he speaks to death, stating that he sees death as "the real reality." Additionally, he sees that the cycle of life-death-life has a special time frame, one in which life "does not last so very long" and death lasts "very long" — these two words being the final words of the poem.

This lyric thus moves from a specific symbol — "Scented herbage" — toward the abstraction that is death. The speaker begins his song by singing to this specific symbol, and he concludes by addressing the general, abstract notion of death. Whitman's poetic mask expands his vision from material to spiritual reality, from the particular to the universal, from the individual to the universal.

Forms and Devices

In the center section of "Scented Herbage of My Breast," the speaker refers to the grass as being "Emblematic and capricious blades." Those two adjectives suggest the ways in which the poet views both symbolism and voice, two aspects of this poem and other poems that are critical to Whitman's techniques.

Like many of his nineteenth-century contemporaries, including Ralph Waldo

Emerson, Whitman was interested in objects as emblems or symbols. Grass, and what Whitman described as the "leaves" of grass, became his emblem, or visible sign, of an invisible reality. By describing this emblem as a part of the natural world and a part of his own physical being — the "Scented herbage of his breast" — he was able to emphasize the way in which grass symbolizes the cyclic quality of nature and the persona's similarly cyclic quality. Life yields to death, which contributes to new life.

The voice that sings of this cyclic quality is as capricious as the grass that is described in that way. If capriciousness suggests qualities of unpredictability and fickleness, then the voice in Whitman's poem does indeed possess those qualities. It begins with the gentle observation about grass and the reflective comment that the speaker will think later about the meanings of this "Scented herbage." Repeating the phrase "I do not know," the speaker suggests an exploratory approach, a thoughtful posture.

This reflective voice yields to a much bolder stance when the speaker issues an order to the grass: "Grow up taller sweet leaves that I may see! grow up out of my breast!/ Spring away from the conceal'd heart there!" As a result of getting a clearer view, the poet sees his role of singing, on behalf of the human community, a song of death and life, and so he announces his role of singer/spokesperson for all.

The poetic voice then assumes still another tone, this one different from the original exploratory stance and the subsequent commanding and announcing tones. In the final lines of the poem, the persona seems to have become one who has made meaning out of the symbol he was examining. Despite words that suggest tentativeness in the last lines — "perhaps" and "may-be" — the speaker sounds certain: He knows that death lasts as long as immortality, for death is a part of the cycle in which life and death, one and the same, last forever.

Themes and Meanings

One of the best ways to approach the many meanings of this lyric poem is to see where it fits in the collection in which it appears, *Leaves of Grass*. It is one of approximately fifty poems that appear in a section entitled *Calamus*. Whitman explained the reason he entitled his section as he did: "Calamus is the very large and aromatic grass, or rush, growing about water ponds in the valleys — spears about three feet high; often called Sweet Flag; grows all over the Northern and Middle States. The recherché or ethereal sense of the term, as used in my book, arises probably from the actual Calamus presenting the biggest and hardiest kind of spears of grass, and their fresh, aquatic, pungent bouquet."

This notion of aromatic grass explains why Whitman would describe his major symbol as "Scented herbage," and it suggests why he would add the reference to his breast. For Whitman was, in many ways, a poet of the physical, physiological body, and his poetry is replete with references to the human anatomy and to songs celebrating the beauty and strength of the body. In this poem, the persona is indeed rhapsodizing over the aroma, the hardiness, the life that is symbolized by the grass and that is inherent in the human body.

The persona is also singing of comradeship, a theme that connects the cluster of poems in the *Calamus* section of *Leaves of Grass*. Many critics have analyzed this section as suggesting ideas about relationships among male lovers, and this may, perhaps, be the focus of the persona's attention. Yet the more universal focus is also clear: a call to connections between the visible and invisible worlds, between the individual and community, between the self and the other, between death and life.

Marjorie Smelstor

THE SCHOLAR-GYPSY

Author: Matthew Arnold (1822-1888)
Type of poem: Pastoral
First published: 1853, in *Poems*

The Poem

"The Scholar-Gypsy" is a pastoral poem, in twenty-five ten-line stanzas, based on a legend recounted by Joseph Glanvill in *The Vanity of Dogmatizing* (1661). Matthew Arnold supplies the essential elements of the legend in lines 31 through 56 of the poem.

The poem opens on a pleasant August afternoon, with the poet-shepherd dismissing his companion shepherd to take care of his usual pastoral chores, bidding him to return at evening when the two will renew their quest. Meanwhile, the poet waits in a pleasant corner of a field filled with colorful flowers, lulled by the distant sounds of sheep and workmen; trees shield him from the sun as he looks down on the university town of Oxford.

The poet picks up Glanvill's book and rereads the tale of the talented but poor scholar who left his studies at seventeenth century Oxford to learn the mystic secrets of the gypsies. Rumors persisted that the scholar was seen occasionally; in stanzas 7 through 13, the poet imagines that the scholar is still glimpsed by shepherds, by country boys, by Oxford riders returning on the ferry, by young girls, by reapers, by a housewife darning clothes at the open doorway of a lonely cottage, by the blackbird, even by the poet himself. These seven stanzas primarily evoke the pastoral countryside around Oxford.

Making a quick turn at stanza 14, the poet ceases to daydream and realizes that it has been two hundred years since Glanvill's story and that the scholar is certainly dead and buried. The poem then turns again, at the beginning of stanza 15, where, by his imaginative leap, the poet realizes that the scholar still lives in spirit and imagination. From here until the last two stanzas, the poet presents contrasting images of the life of the still-living scholar, free to pursue his quest, against the lives of ordinary mortals. These contrasts are present in almost every stanza of this section, usually with the scholar presented first, and modern man second. The scholar possesses an "immortal lot" because he has not wasted his spiritual and psychic energy on the changes and schemes of mortal men. He left the world young and fresh, firm in his resolve, secure in his vision, self-sufficient; he still seeks his one goal, the spark from heaven. Man also seeks the spark, but it fails to appear; even the wisest sage can tell only of wretched days and misery. Modern life is a disease, and the poet repeatedly urges the scholar to fly from all contact with ordinary mortals and to continue to nurse his unconquerable hope that someday the spark will fall.

In the final two stanzas, which act as a sort of parable, the poet compares the urgent necessity for the scholar to flee to the action taken by a Tyrian trader who finds his usual territory increasingly overrun by lighthearted Greek traders. Recognizing the Greeks as invaders of his native city, Tyre, the trader turns his ship about, sails west from the Peloponnesus, through the Mediterranean, to beaches outside the Straits of Gibraltar, where he finds new customers among the dark Iberians who come to examine his wares.

Forms and Devices

With its formal language and stanza form, "The Scholar-Gypsy" displays many of the characteristics of an ode. This stanza form may well have been suggested to Arnold by that employed by John Keats in "Ode to a Nightingale" and "Ode on a Grecian Urn." In addition, the lush imagery of the more pastoral parts of the poem may also owe something to the example of Keats.

There are important dichotomies in the poem which influence the overall structure. The poem tends to fall into two separate but related parts, reflecting the two quests documented in the poem. The first part, the first thirteen stanzas, deals primarily with the quest of the poet for the scholar; the second part, the remaining stanzas with the exception of the final two, deals with the quest of the scholar (and of Arnold) for the spark from heaven, the mystical moment of insight. The first part, along with the two final stanzas, contains most of the pastoral language in the poem, while the second part is marked more by poetry of statement as well as by a different tone.

As in much of Arnold's best poetry, it is the imagery that carries the burden of meaning and emotion. There is the contrast in the language of the two parts mentioned above; but in the second part itself, there is an even more important division, one that leads to the expression of one of the poem's major themes. One finds, in almost every stanza, language that characterizes the life of the scholar: "immortal," "fresh," "undiverted," "firm," "unclouded joy," "gaily," "unconquerable," "enchanted," set off against language used to describe the modern intellectual plight: "exhaust," "numb," "sick," "doubt," "half-believers," "casual creeds," "vague," "wretched," "misery," "sick," "palsied," and others. This contrast adds up to convey to the reader a powerful emotional understanding of the intellectual life of Arnold's day, with its uncertainty and strife.

The effect of the imagery is probably most concentrated in the final two stanzas. Here Arnold intends the extended image of the Tyrian trader to sum up the poet's advice to the scholar to fly all contact with ordinary mortals. This final summarizing extended image is a hallmark of many of Arnold's poems and clearly a common poetic practice for him. Similar images may be seen in "Dover Beach," "Sohrab and Rustum," "Tristram and Iseult," "Rugby Chapel," and others. In "The Scholar-Gypsy" the closing image is probably also intended, with its return to lush pastoral imagery, to calm the reader after the vigorous and biting denunciation of the modern world.

The pastoralism of the poem is perhaps its most noticeable aspect. Unlike so many poets who return to the traditional Arcadia or to a generalized sort of rural serenity, Arnold has naturalized, or domesticated, his pastoral. Arnold uses a very specific countryside, that around Oxford, as the locus for his poem. All the places mentioned in the poem are real places, well-known to Arnold and to many Oxford students. Arnold often walked the countryside described and often returned to it for refreshment. In his days at Oxford, Arnold was frequently accompanied on his walks by his close friend, the poet Arthur Hugh Clough; for the two of them, many of the local places, as well as the legend of the scholar-gypsy itself, acquired special, personal meanings.

Themes and Meanings

The pastoralism of the poem leads immediately to several themes. Most generally it represents, as it does for many poets, an escape from the intolerable world of court or affairs. Arnold certainly romanticizes the Oxford countryside, attributing to it his happiest days. Against this romantic background, then, Arnold places the quest for and of the scholar-gypsy, which gives added significance to the background. As a broad generalization, the scholar (and Arnold) seek the meaning of life. Since for Arnold Christianity was dead, and there seemed nothing to take its place as giving meaning to life, the result is a constant search and intense loneliness and emptiness in life. Another general way of phrasing all this is that it presents the wisdom of the heart against the wisdom of the head. The head sees the true condition of the modern world, but the heart is drawn to the simpler, more unified life represented by the scholar and Oxford.

The poem itself is much more specific. The countryside is a specific one, well-known and loved by Arnold; the legend of the scholar-gypsy had special meaning for him. The scholar represents a side of Arnold that was at odds with the way in which he had to live his life. Arnold felt himself tugged to and fro by the demands of the world. He believed sincerely that his need to function in the modern world had killed him as a poet. His status as a family man, as an inspector of schools, and as the self-dedicated instructor of the middle-class obliged him to live and work in the world of hurry, change, and debate, while he desired calm and singleness of purpose. It is worthy of note that the only italicized words in the whole poem are in line 152, "Thou hadst *one* aim, *one* business, *one* desire"—emphasizing the poet's desire for singleness of purpose.

While Arnold certainly seeks something that will supply meaning for life, what the poem specifically emphasizes is that the poet seeks a *way* of life analogous to that of the scholar. The scholar is free, dedicated, not pulled about by the daily concerns of modern life—and thus he has a kind of immortality. In this connection, it is to be noted that Arnold is hardly concerned at all, in the images of the poem, with the physical side of modern life, with commerce and trade, with large cities and bustling crowds, with mass culture and the cheap and tawdry. The poet's concern is with the intellectual life, with having something secure onto which to hold, with being in command of one's own soul and intellect. The poem clearly suggests that dedication to the quest is even more important than its resolution.

Finally, for a full appreciation of how seriously Arnold took these issues and this quest, "The Scholar-Gypsy" must be read in conjunction with his later poem "Thyrsis," a pastoral elegy for the death of his friend and fellow poet, Arthur Hugh Clough. The poem is deliberately connected to "The Scholar-Gypsy" by being only one stanza shorter, by the use of exactly the same rhyme scheme and stanza form, and, most important, by being set in exactly the same landscape and using again the figure of the scholar, which clearly meant so much to both Arnold and Clough.

Gordon N. Bergquist

SCHUBERTIANA

Author: Tomas Tranströmer (1931-   )
Type of poem: Lyric
First published: 1979, as "Schubertiana," in *Sanningsbarriären*; collected in
   Tomas Tranströmer: Selected Poems, 1954-1986, 1987

The Poem

"Schubertiana," a poem whose title refers to nineteenth century Austrian composer Franz Schubert, consists of five numbered stanzas of varying length. Stanzas 1, 2, 4, and 5 contain from six to ten lines each; the central stanza, stanza 3, is conspicuously shorter, having only two lines. The poem is written in free verse, but, with the exception of the last two, the lines are extraordinarily long.

The poem begins with an evocation of New York City: its skyscrapers, teeming crowds, fast-paced life, squalor, and occasional violence. The poet, speaking in the first person, moves without transition to an intuitive observation: "I know too— without statistics—that right now Schubert is being played." Not only is Schubert's music being played somewhere, but it is more real to someone, the poet asserts, than anything else—more real than the giant city, its masses, or its misery. The musical performance is certain, even without empirical evidence.

The second stanza abruptly shifts the scene and focus. The biological foundation of all life is evoked in a reference to the physiological structure of the human brain and the swallows' return from South Africa (Transvaal) to Europe, or, perhaps more specifically, to Sweden, to precisely the spot where they had nested the year before. Against the background of the wonderfully intricate structure of the human brain and the seeming miracle of swallow navigation, Schubert, "a fat young man from Vienna, called 'the little mushroom,' " is described as such a consummate musician that he could encompass the signals of an entire life in a few ordinary chords of a string quintet and get a river to flow through the eye of a needle.

This string quintet is the bridge to the third and fourth stanzas. While the quintet plays, the poet walks home through a humid forest, falls asleep, passes weightlessly into the future, and knows that plants have thoughts, that the mind permeates all life. The fourth stanza describes the various kinds of trust that are necessary in the contemporary world: trust in the natural world, in social institutions, and in the equipment of daily life. Yet none of these merits the trust universally placed in it. The quintet, though, testifies that something, though never clearly and directly identified, is worthy of human trust.

Only the fifth and final stanza deals entirely and specifically with music. While a Schubert piano duet plays, its true heroic character is noted. This, however, is not the music for people who are not true to themselves or try to set a price on everything. The long, sinuous melodies in all their developments and varying modulations do not reflect or accompany those who forsake, betray, or compromise themselves or human nature.

Forms and Devices

Although the poem is about Schubert's music, it does not make use of devices that traditionally have been associated with lyric musicality. Even in the original Swedish, there are no strong rhythmic patterns, concentrated repetitions of sounds, or especially euphonious combinations of sounds. The language is, in fact, rather colloquial. One way of looking at the poem's musicality is, however, in terms of the description of Schubert's music in the last stanza. There his melodies are described as long — as opposed, for example, to the short and concentrated rhythmic motifs often found in the music of Ludwig van Beethoven — and as remaining themselves through all changes, modulations, and developments.

The same could be said of the structure of the poem. The lines of "Schubertiana" are extraordinarily long, resembling the long melodic lines in Schubert's work. They have, moreover, no parallel in Tomas Tranströmer's other poems, except his well-known collection *Östersjöar* (1974; *Baltics*, 1975), which was published shortly before "Schubertiana." The underlying structure of each stanza is also similar to Tranströmer's description of music that remains fundamentally itself even though undergoing many changes. In each stanza, the poet speaking personally describes an experience or perception — New York City, the physiological structure of the brain and the swallows' miraculous return, the walk through the forest, the question of trust, and the playing of the piano duet — followed by his understanding of the remarkable way in which Schubert's music relates to these extremely diverse situations. Although the situations change, the basic pattern remains the same: Personal experience or insight is juxtaposed to an important aspect of Schubert's music. Since the musicality of this poem is not strongly linked to the sounds of the original Swedish — although there are, to be sure, connections — the musicality can well be seen and understood in translation.

Another reason the poem works so well in English is that its basic strategy is one of comparison, particularly unexpected, even surprising, comparisons. After emphasizing the massive size, the frenetic lifestyle, the chaos, and the brutality of New York City, the poet without preparation or transition makes the startling observation that he knows intuitively that someone is performing Schubert. It should be noted that Schubert is best remembered for his extraordinary gift of melody and his rich, evocative harmonies embodied in his songs (*Lieder*, in German) and works for small ensembles or solo instruments. These small-scale chamber works, which are so melodically and harmonically rich, are abruptly juxtaposed to and astoundingly encompass in their own way the sprawling, chaotic city. Similarly, the incomprehensible complexity of the brain and the swallows' astounding migration over thousands of miles is contrasted to a few simple chords of the string quintet into which the signals of an entire life are distilled. It is the string quintet that, in the shortest and most contracted stanza of the poem, accompanies and stands in stark relief against the disquieting yet seminal insight that mind is not unique to humankind but pervades all the natural world. In the fourth stanza, Tranströmer points out that in order to live daily life without sinking through the earth, great trust must be placed in many aspects of the ambient world. Yet, this trust that is so necessary is unmerited in comparison to the trust that the music of a Schubert quintet invites—trust that is compared to the banister that leads through the dark. In the last stanza, the playing of a simple Schubert duet is juxtaposed to the awareness and understanding of the integrity of the music and the personal integrity that it demands.

Themes and Meanings

"Schubertiana" is only one of Tranströmer's many poems that, either directly or indirectly, refer to music and reveal his intense interest in music. Although Tranströmer is a psychologist by profession, he is an accomplished pianist, and Schubert is one of his favorite composers. His other poems dealing with musical themes include "C Major," "Allegro," "Nocturne," "Slow Music," "Brief Pause in the Organ Recital," and "Carillon." The purpose of "Schubertiana" is not to imitate music or to attempt to re-create a musical experience in words, as many other poets have done; rather, Tranströmer explores the role of Schubert's music, particularly in human existence, but at the same explores the role of music more generally.

Tranströmer argues that music is not merely an embellishment or adornment of life. Schubert's music is, on the contrary, something that lies at the foundation of human existence. It has to do with the ground of all being and the way in which human beings extend their understanding beyond empirical experience toward this ground that ultimately must remain unknown. It has often been pointed out that Tranströmer maintains a remarkable openness to the unknown. He does not allow his mind to be enclosed by systems, ideologies, or dogma. In the last lines of his poem "Vermeer," for example, a prayer is addressed to cosmic emptiness, but the response that is whispered is "I am not empty, I am open."

"Schubertiana" juxtaposes Schubert's music to a sampling of the most extreme aspects of modern life, and, in so doing, the true nature of the music reveals itself. Schubert's music in its own mysterious way is more real than the physical and social reality of New York City, the hard realities of life in that city notwithstanding; it is more marvelous and awe-inspiring than the complexities of the human brain or than the swallows' ability to return home. This music, though, is more than heightened reality or the object of marvel and wonder: It is revelatory. It breaks down the boundary of time, allowing the arresting insight that plants are rational beings, that they have thoughts, and mind, thus, is infused throughout the natural universe. Schubert's music, moreover, is such that it more fully deserves human trust than any of the institutions or conventions of modern life. The music, though, makes ethical demands. In order for any individual to experience these remarkable qualities, music requires absolute personal integrity; it cannot tolerate duplicity or dissemblance. When its demands are met, however, Schubert's music partakes of the fundamental essence of human existence to the extent that it can accompany the individual from the depths of existence upward toward destiny.

Steven P. Sondrup

THE SEAFARER

Author: Ezra Pound (1885-1972)
Type of poem: Lyric
First published: 1912, in *Ripostes*

The Poem

"The Seafarer" is a poem in free verse consisting of some one hundred lines or half-lines, as dictated by the fragmentary nature of the original Anglo-Saxon poem (c. 800). Since the poem is a nearly literal translation, it cannot be analyzed in terms of modern prosody, such as stanzas, rhymes, and meter. Indeed, in the original, spellings vary and punctuation is nonexistent. The poem has, however, a well-modulated movement that derives from a central feeling of isolation, fearfulness, and somber reflection on the human condition and man's fate.

Writing in the first person, Ezra Pound assumes the persona of the anonymous original poet, and therefore, as translator, achieves an immediacy of mood that transcends time and place and speaks with immediacy to his present-day reader.

Pound begins as does the original poet, with an address to the reader: "May I for my own self song's truth reckon." This directness bears witness to the oral tradition of the poem and the poet's intimate approach to his reader, and earlier, his audience. I shall tell you the truth, he says, as I have known it. He continues with a descriptive scene of chilling bitterness, both figurative and literal, in which he pictures the harsh realities of the seafaring life. He dramatically elicits the terror evoked on "Narrow nightwatch nigh the ship's head/ While she tossed close to cliffs." The passage—of some considerable length, and indicating the importance that the sea-farer places upon such a harrowing recollection—concludes with a vivid image of the miserable cold in which the air "hung with hard ice-flakes," and indicates his own isolation. The staccato cries of the birds of the sea and air offer but a meager companionship, and prove a poor substitute, with their "sea-fowls' loudness," for the laughter he has once known; the "gannet's clamour" serves for his games, the "mews' singing," for the comradeship of the hall. Above this desolate scene, the seafarer relates, "the eagle screamed/ With spray on his pinion."

In the stream of consciousness that follows, other memories provide a wrenching contrast to the seafarer's present situation. He envies the life of the land-dweller who will never know his hardship but will also never appreciate the beauties of the earth as does he: the joys of spring when "Bosque taketh blossom," and even the homelier joys of a "winsome wife." The call of the sea, however, is strong. The "lone-flyer," the very bird whose scream he found distressing, becomes the bird who calls him back, and "Whets for the whale-path the heart irresistibly."

The final movements of the poem are, in both style and content, traditional elegiac passages such as those found in many Anglo-Saxon poems. Within these lines are expressed the universal fears and griefs of all people—the passage of time, the loss of old friends, and the futility of life, which must end with death. The world shall be as if the seafarer had never been; even the deeds of warrior and poet cannot forestall death.

Forms and Devices

Although Pound does not adhere strictly to the accentual pattern (four strong beats to the line) that was obligatory for an Anglo-Saxon poet, he does maintain, since it is "from the Anglo-Saxon," many features and characteristics of the earlier prosody. The sea dominates the Anglo-Saxon worldview, and nowhere is it more vivid than in the imagery of "The Seafarer," where it is shown in all its turbulence and power to inspire terror in those who dare to venture into its unknown regions. Despite the sea's omnipresence in the Anglo-Saxon consciousness, the poet is constricted by the limitations of the language. His vocabulary is spare (there are only two denotative words for sea: *see* and *meres*), and he must therefore contrive, for the sake of variety, metaphors and similes; that is, comparisons that will adequately express his mood. The earlier poet uses kennings, which are combinations of familiar words. The skill of the poet is judged by his imaginative use of this device. In "The Seafarer," for example, the technique is richly evident in such substitutions for sea as "the whale's acre," "the whale-path," and "the salt-wavy tumult." Similarly, ice is transformed into "ice-flakes," hail into "corn of the coldest."

If Pound fully utilizes the vitality of the diction of the earlier poet, he also fully employs another of the conventions of the original, the use of alliteration (the repetition of initial consonant sounds within a given line). For example, "Bosque taketh blossom, cometh beauty of berries" fairly bursts with the ripeness of the season, whereas the contrary mood of old age is echoed in "Grey-haired he groaneth, knows gone companions." The line nearly creaks and wobbles under the burden of its message.

Although these prosodic features are common in the verse of the anonymous Anglo-Saxon poet and in Pound's translation, they are not the only features. The commonality is also struck in the recurrent motifs—that is, the recurrent patterns of events or moods and feelings. The traditional *ubi sunt* and *sic transit* motifs are used with great effectiveness to close the poem. In the first of these (*ubi sunt*, or "Where are?") passages, lyric in character, the poet looks about him, remembers the joys of the past with his companions, and, in a desolate tone, realizes that not only has all changed, but he has also been deprived by death of many he has loved. This theme is frequently followed, as it is in "The Seafarer," by a related theme— the *sic transit gloria mundi* ("thus passes the glory of the world") theme—in which the poet notes the brief span allotted to humankind from eternity's store of time. Whether by misadventure or old age, everyone, rich or poor, king or peasant, must meet death at the end of the final voyage.

Themes and Meanings

In the concluding lines of this very personal elegy, the seafarer of the poem becomes an Everyman figure. As he journeys far from his home into the unknown, he is alternately filled with the exhilaration of Ulysses and the despair of Job, as he ponders the dangers of life and the finality of its conclusion. The seafarer is all men who do not understand their beginnings, whose purpose remains obscure, and whose immortality exists only in the memories of those who come after. The warrior seeks fame in great deeds, the poet perhaps in his own song, but—as the poet suggests—all may be vanity.

In the Anglo-Saxon world, there was no comforting thought of Christian salvation or heaven, and the reader is offered none here. The cruel hand of fate, amoral and rigid in its law, oppresses and finally sweeps everyone away into the void of nothingness. The anguish inspired by inescapable death is still felt strongly in the modern world, where many have abandoned faith. Modern man, the product of a technological and scientific society, searches just as anxiously for meaning in life as did his ancient counterpart. Within months of the first publication of this poem (in 1912), Pound was to question man's fate still further as World War I began. A dark foreboding colors the work of many poets and writers of the early twentieth century, as diverse in character as Pound and Thomas Hardy, as T. S. Eliot and Wallace Stevens.

Ezra Pound, as one of the founders of the Imagist movement, rejected the staid metrical patterns that had dominated Victorian and early twentieth century poetry. It is clear from "The Seafarer" that he had broken the bonds of this dominance by turning to other criteria by which poetry might be judged. In rejecting rhyme and stanza and creating a line whose length was determined by the breath unit or by natural colloquial speech patterns, Pound facilitated the entry of free verse into the lexicon of poetry. The powerful sound devices and the striking imagery inherent in the original "The Seafarer" became a hallmark and technique found not only in Pound's later work, but in twentieth century free verse generally.

Maureen W. Mills

THE SEARCHERS

Author: Tomas Rivera (1935-1984)
Type of poem: Meditation
First published: 1976, in *Ethnic Literatures Since 1776: The Many Voices of America*

The Poem

"The Searchers" is a long free-verse poem in seven sections. The title refers to the central theme of the poem: the constant movement of migrant workers as they seek not only work but also truth and dignity. Tomas Rivera presents them as embodying the questing spirit of the Americas, though they are often denied their legal and monetary due. Because the poem deals with the abuse of and discrimination against the migrant workers (Chicanos), the injurious effects of prejudice are a central concern. Though the poem does present the Chicanos as expressing the elemental identity of the Americas, the poem indicates that rejection of the people and their culture has turned them inward, searchers for a truth that can sustain one during adversity and misfortune.

Section I introduces the images of the earth in which the workers search for their history and their humanity, as well as for their livelihood. Throughout the rest of the poem, Rivera draws on the experience of the migrant worker to illustrate his belief that the earth and those who work it will endure. They will find within themselves "the passion to create/ of every clod and stone/ a new life/ a new dream." Their search is based on the perfection of the seed of the newborn child, which is the beginning of all life. Only bigotry and repression can, temporarily, negate the promise of the beginning.

Sections II and III extend the meaning of the word "searcher" to those who look for the past from which they have been separated by oppression and, equally important, to those who look into the face of the inevitable, death, a mystery that is suggested in loneliness and desire. The will to endure is questioned and tested.

Section IV begins the delineation of social repression and injustice that continues through Sections V and VI, in which the poet introduces the names and experiences of some of those who died. These passages poignantly celebrate the survival, the conquest, of these people. They are never alone—in life, in death, or in memory. That they belong to the greater experience of the Chicano is the final assertion of the poem.

Sections V and VI proclaim the solidarity of the people and their culture. The individuals who died (such as Chona, who died giving birth in a sugar-beet field, or Kiko, who died in Italy in World War II) are the martyrs. In their struggles for freedom and dignity, they were destroyed and became points of reference for those who lived after them. Section VII ends the poem with the assertions that people—and race—are greater than death and that the Chicano will continue to search. It is the search for truth and personal dignity that is central to humanity itself.

The movement of the poem from lyric to narrative and back to lyric occurs as Rivera develops his idea of passion: the celebration and acceptance of life. The passion includes pain, but the pain nurtures and deepens the passion as the individual is recalled as someone whose life was never solitary. The experience of the migrant worker necessitated that many people live and travel together. Rivera presents this as closeness, not as crowding. From the closeness came sharing and understanding.

Forms and Devices

The poem is written in both English and Spanish, indicating the bilingual nature of the Chicano. Rivera leaves in Spanish songs and sayings that belong to the community. In them, as well as in the English segments, images of food and relatives, frightening and abusive experiences become metaphors for the human experience. The simplicity of image and language is consciously intended by the poet to relate his subject to the most fundamental conditions of human life. Yet by giving the central word of the poem ("searchers") a value that grows from those who search for work and bodily sustenance to those who search for history, dignity, and religious meaning, he gives great value to even the most common of words, such as bread or a kiss. They become a way of searching. He avoids similes and symbols that would take the reader's attention away from the experience of the people. In addition, he uses the work, food, and love necessary for life to give sacred value to such objects as bread and milk. When he mentions items indigenous to the workers — novenas, rosaries, *pan dulce* ("sweet bread"), trucks — he does so to indicate that even the most commonplace of objects and events can tell the story of a people. These objects are significant to the Catholic Chicano workers. He also mentions people with whom he himself worked. They, too, are expressive of their people, though they are never symbolic — they never stand for something other than themselves.

The poem is generally a lyric; yet it exceeds the intent and tradition of the lyric; "The Searchers" has the sweep of an epic, even though it is much shorter. It tells the history of a people — their trials and conquests; it describes their travels and their way of life. In doing all this, the poem resembles the fiction written by Rivera. His fiction told of the lives of the migrant workers, but it included songs and strong visual images that allowed the reader to experience the spirit of the people. The poem accomplishes the opposite by telling of spirit in image and song, yet forcing the reader to confront the actual experience of the migrant worker through the examples that are presented narratively.

Themes and Meanings

The poem has its origins, perhaps, in the ballad, from which come the lyrical line and the repetition of sounds that combine music and words to make poetry. The ballad also provides the subject: the tale of death and struggle. It resembles contemporary versions of the Mexican *corrido*, a traditional song telling of love and passion, struggle and death. In "The Searchers," Tomas Rivera relates his poem and the lives of migrant workers in the United States to the cultural traditions of Mexico, yet his poem and its characters belong to the United States. His poem, in form, language, allusion, and theme relates a bicultural society that is distinct from the two societies that served as its progenitors.

Though echoing the themes of hope and compassion that occur in so many of Rivera's poems, "The Searchers" places them in the broader context of the Chicano and of Rivera's own philosophical inquiry. By combining meditation with narrative, Rivera extended the poetic resonance of images of workers and the Chicano that are found in many other poems. In "The Searchers," however, he achieves a form that combines the facts of a particular group with the eternal poetic quest for the meaning of life. The elements of danger and death, the struggles to remain alive and to retain dignity, provide an unusual force and poignancy.

This poem is a meditation on the necessities of life by a poet who had struggled to live, who had fought prejudice and ignorance, yet a poet who was not embittered. As author of the poem, he is the essential searcher, and his poem charts his search from fields and migrant worker camps to the spirit.

Frank L. Kersnowski

THE SECOND COMING

Author: William Butler Yeats (1865-1939)
Type of poem: Lyric
First published: 1920, in *Michael Robartes and the Dancer*

The Poem

"The Second Coming," an intense, lyrical poem of twenty-two lines, addresses a listener prepared to expect useful insight into the meaning of history. Instead, the poet offers a disturbing prophecy of cultural dissolution. The homey, commonplace images of everyday life are merged with an apocalyptic revelation about a new order that portends instability and chaos among humankind. By the poem's last line, the reader senses the impending arrival of something hideous and devastating to human freedom and harmony, an effect wrought by the poet's skillful inversion of familiar symbols and the promise of catastrophe delayed.

The poem can be conveniently divided into three movements: lines 1 through 8, 9 through 17, and 18 through 22. The reader is led progressively through a series of ever more ominous prophecies of upheaval and social discord. Each image is derivative of common religious sentiment of the poet's time, expressed in familiar biblical cadences yet riven with sinister import.

William Butler Yeats begins the first movement with the mysterious image of a falcon turning and turning in a "widening gyre," a radiating spiral, increasingly beyond the reach of its falconer/guide. Outside his command and direction, the falcon can neither be controlled nor diverted in its motion.

As a result of the falcon's centripetal break from both instinct and training, "things fall apart" in the observer's sensory world, and "the center cannot hold"; hence, the poet declares, "mere anarchy" will be "loosed upon the world." The ones who might have stood against social deconstruction "lack conviction," while the ones who will share the spoils of this moral collapse "are full of passionate intensity." "The blood-dimmed tide" slaughters "the ceremony of innocence," and the reader faces the prospect of nightmarish violence. To relieve temporarily the tension of this dire forecast, at line 9 the poet issues a plea for deliverance from the nameless evil about to occur: "Surely some revelation is at hand." His repetitive cry, however, serves only to register the inevitability that no deliverer will arise to defeat the foe: "Surely the Second Coming is at hand!" There Yeats parodies the New Testament doctrine of Christ's return from heaven to Earth to judge the wicked and save the redeemed. Offered up is a much different "second coming" that proffers no element of worthy anticipation for faithful earthly inhabitants.

The "*Spiritus Mundi*," or spirit of the world, cannot quite envision the grotesque shape forming with "lion body and the head of a man" in the desert, its presence noted only by "indignant desert birds" who cannot fathom its significance. Its sphinxlike inscrutability will either surprise or destroy those who seek to resolve its mystery.

In the final movement, lines 18 through 22, "The Second Coming" turns expectation into fearful dread as the poet adorns his prophecy with the portent of disaster and universal human suffering. "The darkness drops again," and "Twenty centuries of stony sleep" are interrupted by the newly awakened monster. A "rocking cradle" has nurtured the "rough beast," whose identity is shrouded in ambiguity in the poem's last line. The beast "Slouches toward Bethlehem to be born," inexorably creeping toward its destiny as the genesis of civilization's ultimate nemesis.

Forms and Devices

The key image in the first movement of the poem is the "gyre," a device used by Yeats to exemplify his theory of history. The falcon's orbit away from the falconer suggests a conelike, ever-widening spiral, as the poet establishes his cyclical view of civilizations passing through growth, maturation, and eventual overthrow by the forces of history. The image is left intact, however, only until line 3, when, in one of the poem's more powerful, memorable lines, Yeats announces history's demise: "things fall apart; the center cannot hold." Poetic image melts into prosaic exposition as history and the conventional ways in which it may be understood are rendered impotent by the violence wrought by the "mere anarchy" that is unleashed.

"The Second Coming" works as a series of nightmarish images presented sequentially and then summarily upended by the poet's mournful, deliberate commentary on their significance. Rhythm and pacing merge to create a breathlessness in the reader that approximates that of one seeking to escape a nightmare only to discover that one is already awake. Carefully chosen verbs such as "drowned," "vexed," and "reel" carry the tone of impending doom while pushing the reader forward to the poem's climax.

Crucial to the success of this effect is Yeats's skillful juxtaposition of biblical metaphor, inverted in its meaning, and pagan history. The first and second advents of Christ were familiar and benevolent landmarks in the historical mindset of Yeats's original readers—perhaps in a way that they no longer are to many Westerners. The poet's decision to link this Christian commonplace with the ancient riddle of the sphinx creates an unbearable tension in the poem's second movement. Notably, it is the *Spiritus Mundi* and not the *Spiritus Sanctus* (Holy Spirit) who is unable to discern the significance of the lion-man forming in the desert. The spirit of Judeo-Christian faith is absent or banished from the landscape, unable to assist in recovering the vision necessary to countermand this invasion by an alien consciousness.

The poet thus subtly paints the portrait of a secularized humankind no longer in tune with the purposes of God, its respect for the wisdom of the ancient world waning. Emptied thus of interpretive as well as recuperative powers, the reader faces the blank canvas of history, left only to wonder aloud "what rough beast . . . slouches toward Bethlehem," the birthplace of Christ, "to be born?" This ironic counterpose of knowledge and ignorance, discernment and blindness, gives the poem its lasting power to challenge and amaze later generations of readers who still seek illumination of history's meaning in the work of poets.

Themes and Meanings

Yeats believed that human history could be marked in twenty-century intervals. As the birth of Christ ended the reign of Greco-Roman culture, Yeats prophesies in the poem the end of Christianity's dominance over human philosophy and the Western social order in the twentieth century. Clearly, then, he uses the second-coming motif as a reference to a new incarnation other than Christ's that will displace Christian civilization with something less beneficent and conducive to human progress.

Like many turn-of-the-century artists, Yeats felt some ambivalence toward this apparent change in the human order. Ostensibly restricting the artistic imagination with its legalism and fixed moral code, Christianity also provided the metaphors of creator, creativity, freedom, and order that allowed the poet the sense of power to shape the world through words. In the aftermath of Christianity's reduction to mere theology or, worse, mere politics, the poet is forced to become simply one more observer, disarmed by social forces of his authority to address the issues of his times.

Though eccentric in his views of history, especially as set forth in the obscure and perplexing prose work *A Vision* (1925), Yeats was troubled by the overthrow of Czar Nicholas in Russia by the Marxist-Leninists and the apparent rise of Fascism in Europe. These events all portended to him a new "dark ages." Thus, many commentators view the poem as Yeats's prediction of the rise and triumph of totalitarianism in the early stages of the twentieth century.

Understood in this way, the "rough beast" of the poem embodies the lurking authoritarianism of governments and movements that place ideology above individual freedom and dignity as the basis for polity and social order. Often seen as messianic by their followers and supporters—hence the apocalyptic associations with Christ and his Second Coming—such political parties exploit the yearnings of oppressed or disenfranchised peoples for "self-government" ("the ceremony of innocence is drowned"). Their rhetorical hold on the public imagination is aided by the faithless and the feckless ("the best lack all conviction, while the worst/ are full of passionate intensity"); by calculated redefinition of what the "self" means, the people's aspirations are thwarted once the new regime is in power.

In "The Second Coming," the self is exemplified in the falcon that can no longer "hear the falconer"; no "revelation" is forthcoming except that of anarchy unbound. In the poet's view, the absence of either the inward sense of destiny and purpose (the falcon's instincts) or the outward witness of history and civilization (the falconer's call) unleashes a "blood-dimmed tide" of human misery that awaits despotic exploitation. At this symbolic Bethlehem, Westerners thus await a new incarnation whose interest will not be humankind's salvation but rather its subjugation.

Bruce L. Edwards

THE SEEKERS OF LICE

Author: Arthur Rimbaud (1854-1891)
Type of poem: Lyric
First published: 1891, as "Les Chercheuses de poux," in *Reliquaire*; collected in
  Collected Works, Selected Letters, 1966

The Poem

"The Seekers of Lice" is a twenty-line poem divided into five quatrains of Alexandrines with a rhyme scheme of *abab*. The title suggests an unpleasant topic, playing against the beauty of the poet's words. Sensory images are everywhere in the poem. In the first line, "the child" is introduced; his forehead is covered with "the red torment" caused by the lice. Two "tall gracious sisters" appear "with delicate hands and silvery fingernails." In the second quatrain, these sisters remove the child from his bed and seat him by an "open window." The child is bombarded by the visual sensations of the outside natural world and the sensual fingers of the sisters running through his infested hair.

The child is experiencing more than the removal of the lice, however; he is being tenderly loved by these "tall gracious sisters." In the third quatrain, the child hears the sisters singing through their breathing and whistling as they suck in their saliva. The images and the very words used express the child's heightened auditory experience. The images from the third quatrain are surreal; the child is almost in a trance. He is under the spell of the sisters as they caress his predicament away. The last line of the third quatrain includes "the desire for kisses." The child's experience has taken on an erotic quality. The fourth quatrain describes how he hears the sound of the sisters' black eyelashes "blinking." He smells a "perfumed stillness" while "royal nails" squash "the gray and lazy lice." In this quatrain, the child continues to be overpowered by sensual experiences. He not only inhales the perfume, but he also hears the "crackling" of the lice being squashed. The child is baffled and confused about how to respond to what is happening to him.

Whereas the first quatrain began with "When," the fifth and last quatrain begins with "Then." The situation presented at the beginning of "The Seekers of Lice" finds its resolution in this last quatrain. The first line speaks of the "wine of Idleness." The child is moving ever closer to the realm of rapturous delight. In addition to the wine, there is "the delirium of a mouth-organ's sigh" in the second line, which, combined with the first line, tips the scales beyond self-control. Pain and pleasure are intertwined, and the child cannot help but feel, in the last line of the poem, "an endless need to cry."

Forms and Devices

The power of "The Seekers of Lice" is generated by its musical quality, which plays against the unpleasant reality of the poem's subject. The poet walks a fine line without ever making the poem seem morbid. The rhyme scheme enhances the elegant quality of the poem; the *abab* rhyming makes the poem seem songlike. The reader is swept up in the rhythm as the sensual images weave their spell. The poem begins with "When," almost as a fairy tale would begin with "Once upon a time." As in some fairy tales, the inviting language disguises gruesome happenings.

The child in "The Seekers of Lice" is confronted with a sensual experience that almost overwhelms him. The "tall gracious sisters" have "delicate hands and silvery fingernails" which will move through his hair in search of the "lazy lice." The poem is much more than the mere squashing of lice. Arthur Rimbaud begins the poem by adding surreal touches, as when the child hears the sisters breathe and makes it out to be singing; when they draw in their saliva, it becomes whistling. The poet takes great care in the progression of his images. In the opening lines of the first and second quatrains the child is identified by the genderless term "child," whereas in the opening lines of the third and fourth quatrains, the child is identified as "he." The sisters of the first quatrain become "They" in the second.

Sound, smell, and sight are everywhere in the poem, creating sharp contrasts that show the poet's skill at dramatizing, at setting up finely woven scenes. The experience for the child is one of total sensual release, and Rimbaud employs alliteration to add to the trancelike quality of the poem. "The Seekers of Lice" moves to its emotional conclusion in which "Then" is the first word of the last quatrain, signifying that there will be a resolution. "Wine of Idleness," "delirium," and "slow caresses" bring the child to a heightened sense of happiness that leads to "an endless need to cry." The subject of the poem is all but lost in the delicacy of the ending. "The Seekers of Lice" is a song that sings both sweetly and sadly.

Themes and Meanings

In 1870, Arthur Rimbaud had become tired of living in Charleville, France, with his domineering mother. He wished to set off for Paris and taste a new life that he could only imagine. He was merely sixteen at the time, yet his poetic genius was on the verge of full flower. A teacher by the name of Georges Izambard had become a friend and adviser of young Rimbaud when Izambard was teaching in Charleville. Izambard encouraged Rimbaud by being sympathetic to his situation and his poetic need to expand his horizons beyond the provincial life of his hometown. Rimbaud did escape to Paris, but there he was arrested, since he did not have enough money to pay the full fare. Izambard was contacted, and he sent money to bail Rimbaud out of prison. It was arranged that the young rebel would travel to Douai, which was northwest of Charleville, and stay with Izambard's aunts. He spent two enjoyable weeks with the Gindre sisters before he was forced to return home to Madame Rimbaud.

This episode is important in relation to "The Seekers of Lice," which Rimbaud wrote when he was no older than eighteen. The "tall gracious sisters" introduced in the poem are the Gindre sisters, and—almost certainly—the child is Rimbaud himself. The sisters most likely gave the runaway child tender care that probably both excited and confused him. His experience with his own mother was not of the same kind. The child came to these two women in need of being rid of the lice that had infested him at his previous location. At sixteen, Rimbaud was in the throes of being awakened erotically. The world of the senses is both intriguing and frightening, and the adolescent wishes to recapture the innocence of childhood even as he yearns to explore the sensual world. Because of the Franco-Prussian War, the schools in Charleville had to be closed down, so Rimbaud's formal education came to a halt. The Gindre sisters served to educate the young poet, in a different way, in the fresh-air world of Douai.

It speaks to the genius of Rimbaud that he was able to encapsulate his experience with these two older women in such an intriguing fashion. The reality of why the child is being caressed never quite disappears totally, but the surreal and sensual images almost win the day. The poem is particularly effective because of the emotional power of its contrasting images. The subtlety of the tenderness expressed speaks to the young Rimbaud's realization of how wonderful it can be to be under the care of concerned females. Inspired by his two weeks in Douai, he wrote a delicately beautiful poem on a distasteful subject. In so doing, Rimbaud harkened back to the beautiful and disturbing poems of Charles Baudelaire.

Michael Jeffrys

SELF-PORTRAIT IN A CONVEX MIRROR

Author: John Ashbery (1927-   )
Type of poem: Meditation
First published: 1975, in *Self-Portrait in a Convex Mirror*

The Poem

"Self-Portrait in a Convex Mirror" is a long poem in free verse, its 552 lines divided into six verse paragraphs of unequal length. The title refers to a 1524 painting by the Italian artist Francesco Mazzola, also known as Il Parmigianino. "Self-Portrait in a Convex Mirror" makes the poet's thoughts about Parmigianino's painting the focus for a different kind of self-portrait, a self-portrait in words.

Although a poet may use the first person as the voice of a persona, a character whose outlook and experience are quite different from the poet's, in "Self-Portrait in a Convex Mirror," the voice is John Ashbery's own. The poem represents the poet thinking out loud, revealing the processes of his own mind as he considers Parmigianino's self-portrait.

In the first verse paragraph, Ashbery quotes from Giorgio Vasari's *Lives of the Most Eminent Painters, Sculptors, and Architects* (1550). Vasari describes how Parmigianino painted his self-portrait on half of a ball of wood as if his face were reflected in the surface of a convex mirror. In the resulting painting, Parmigianino's right hand appears to be thrust forward "as though to protect/ What it advertises." Describing the painting, the poet is also interpreting it, finding in it several paradoxes: a surface which appears to have depth, a "soul [that] is not a soul," and "Affirmation that doesn't affirm anything."

The second verse paragraph suggests an interruption in Ashbery's meditation. In fact, each verse paragraph represents a break in the poet's attention as his thoughts move toward and away from the painting. As Ashbery's attention draws away from the painting, he makes more comparisons between Parmigianino's self-portrait and the poet's own mind. The painting becomes a "mirror" for the poet's thoughts. By painting a picture of himself, Parmigianino has captured for the future the illusion of the present moment, an illusion which the poet tries to duplicate in words.

In the third verse paragraph, the poet meditates on the present depicted in the painting, until his experience of the painting becomes like a dream. The poet awakens from this "dream" into his own present, less fixed and idealized than the present in Parmigianino's painting. It is easier, the poet says, to imagine the future or to remember the past than to gain perspective on the chaotic and elusive present.

As the poet's thoughts drift away from the painting, in the fourth verse paragraph—the poem's shortest—he calls the painting to mind again, thinking of it as a surprising concept, "the first mirror portrait." At first the painting appears to be an optical illusion, a mirror reflecting the poet's own face rather than Parmigianino's. Recognizing that illusion, the poet imagines that he has surprised the painter at his work. As the poet looks into the painting, he is looking into Parmigianino's world and therefore into the past.

In the fifth verse paragraph, the poet wonders if the painting will survive into the future and still be in style, as it has already survived the time since Parmigianino painted it. Ashbery sees Parmigianino's self-portrait as a metaphorical mirror in which each viewer, including those in the future, may find things that are as much in the viewer as in the painting.

The sixth and last verse paragraph, by far the poem's longest, turns back to the painting. Questioning the role that love plays in Parmigianino's painting, Ashbery comes back to the present. The "explosion" of details here and now is "so precise, so fine," that "We don't need paintings or/ Doggerel written by mature poets." Yet the present, with "no margins," seems not to exist when contrasted with "the portrait's will to endure."

The self-portrait was "a life-obstructing task" because it forced Parmigianino away from the pleasures of the present to paint a picture that looked into the future. As a result, however, "This past/ Is now here," in "the painter's/ Reflected face." The poet's present in "April sunlight" in a room in New York City is mingled with the painter's present in the past and in memory.

Forms and Devices

Ashbery's poetry is often regarded as difficult. Written in free verse, "Self-Portrait in a Convex Mirror" represents what is sometimes called the stream of consciousness. Ashbery's free verse challenges accepted notions of poetry. One of his earlier books, *Three Poems* (1972), is actually written in prose, partly to question the boundaries between poetry and prose. The spontaneous and open style of "Self-Portrait in a Convex Mirror" permits Ashbery to imitate both the precision and the vagueness of what flows through his mind. Because it represents the processes of his mind reflecting on the painting, Ashbery's poem is often allusive and ambiguous.

For many years, Ashbery worked as a writer and art critic for *Art News*. "Self-Portrait in a Convex Mirror" includes allusions to art and art criticism as well as to music (composer Alban Berg's comment on "a phrase in Mahler's Ninth" symphony) and to literature (William Shakespeare's *Cymbeline*, c. 1609-1610). When Ashbery incorporates direct quotations from prose works in his poem, he is scrupulous about mentioning the sources of quotes. As the poet transcribes the processes of his own mind, however, he draws upon what he knows, without stopping to explain every reference.

By permitting paradoxes and ambiguities, the poem's inclusiveness adds to its difficulty. When Ashbery says that Parmigianino's picture is "life-obstructing," that statement challenges its context in the poem. Works of art in general, including the poem, are more often thought of as life-enhancing. In order to capture the present, Parmigianino's "obstruction" must stop it. Paradoxically, when it is stopped in a work of art, the present becomes the past, but it also looks into the future. The poet's self-consciousness about the processes of his mind allows him to question his own preoccupations as he holds up the mirror to his consciousness.

When Ashbery ambiguously mentions "The shadow of the city" in the fifth verse paragraph, the city is Rome, where Ashbery says Parmigianino was painting (but not the self-portrait) while the city was being sacked by the imperial forces of Charles V of Spain in 1527. The city is also Vienna, where the poet says he saw the painting with a friend in 1959. Finally, the city is New York, where the poet is now writing the poem. That the sack of Rome was still in the future when Parmigianino was painting the self-portrait is an example of the subtlety of the poet's concern with time.

A key pun in the poem is Ashbery's reference to speculation, which comes "From the Latin *speculum*, mirror." In a sense the poem is all speculation, as Ashbery holds Parmigianino's painting to the mirror of the poet's own mind. Speculation leads to ambiguity. Because the painting explains nothing, it permits contradictory interpretations. The poet wonders, for example, if Parmigianino's hand in the painting is held forth as a shield or as a greeting.

Ashbery heightens the ambiguity of certain sentences by using unclear pronoun references. The poet begins, "As Parmigianino did it," leaving the reader to figure out that "it" refers to the self-portrait in the poem's title. Here, as elsewhere in the poem, the pronoun "it" implicitly includes both self-portraits, Parmigianino's painting and Ashbery's poem. The poet avoids saying "I" until the second verse paragraph (preferring, for example, "the attention turns" to "my attention turns"), when he says "I think of the friends." "Self-Portrait in a Convex Mirror" uses these oblique references to imitate the evasions of the painted self-portrait.

Like the painting, the poem at once identifies and does not identify. How does the poet know that the face in the painting is Parmigianino's? How does the reader know that the identity behind the poem's is Ashbery's? Parmigianino's painting is not identical with Parmigianino any more than writing is identical with thinking. In "Self-Portrait in a Convex Mirror," the phrase "As though to protect/ What it advertises" seems to describe Ashbery's style as much as Parmigianino's painted hand.

Themes and Meanings

"Self-Portrait in a Convex Mirror" is a poem about identity and time, especially about the elusiveness of the present. The differences between Parmigianino's self-portrait in paint and Ashbery's self-portrait in words cause the poet to question art's distortions. Because works of art attempt to make time stand still, they inevitably distort the reality they seek to portray. Perhaps the simplest statement one can make about the poem is that it works out the differences between a painted self-portrait and a poetic one. If Parmigianino's self-portrait is a "snapshot" of his face at a given moment, Ashbery's self-portrait is a moving picture of his mind working in time. Parmigianino's portrait circumscribes the painter's identity more straightforwardly than the poem does. By describing, imitating, and challenging the painting, Ashbery's poem questions the limitations and ambitions of art.

Both the painter and the poet try to capture the elusive present. To do so, both must ignore the details around them which multiply into infinity. Instead of trying to describe everything he sees, the painter focuses on something in particular—in this case, his own reflection. A painting such as Parmigianino's has a central figure, the subject of the painting, but also at least a minimal background of incidental details. Instead of describing his own face, however, the poet describes the painting. Because it takes more time to read Ashbery's self-portrait than it does to look at Parmigianino's, the present in the poem seems more fluid than it does in the painting.

Even when the poet's mind seems to wander, the subject of the poem is still Parmigianino's painting; the poet, however, has more difficulty knowing what to exclude than the painter did. In the sense that the poet could go on responding to the painting, Parmigianino's painted self-portrait is closed and Ashbery's verbal one is open. In Ashbery's self-portrait, the central subject is the poet's mind, or what fills his mind as he thinks about Parmigianino's painting. The incidental details—the poet's speculations about the painting—are the central figure. Nevertheless, Ashbery's returning again and again to the painting gives "Self-Portrait in a Convex Mirror" an anchor that some of his other poems seem to lack.

The poem is an interior rather than an exterior self-portrait. The poet can see with perfect clarity in Parmigianino's picture what the painter looked like on a certain day. Yet the poet has no explanation of the painter's inner being, his thoughts, except what the poet can "read" in the painting. Where the painting is circumscribed and fixed, the poem is loose and fluid.

Ashbery's self-portrait has several vagaries. The poem assumes familiarity with Parmigianino's painting, so it includes no concrete description of the face in the convex mirror. It also never describes Ashbery's own face. Nor does it make clear whether Ashbery has a copy of Parmigianino's painting before him as he writes. He quotes two art critics without explaining whether he is quoting from memory or open books. Words referring to time appear throughout the poem, but the poet never states explicitly the time of the poem's composition. These vagaries suggest the flow of memory and the uncertainty of identity.

The limitations of Parmigianino's invented convention both create and frustrate the inclusive identity Ashbery tries to portray in the poem, which is itself an attempt to see both Parmigianino's and Ashbery's identities in Parmigianino's faked mirror. Art is illusion, giving apparent permanence to something that does not exist except in the work of art. In another sense, the picture exists only when one looks at it, "its room, our moments of attention." "Self-Portrait in a Convex Mirror" moves into "the distance between us," between Ashbery and Parmigianino, between perception and interpretation, between art and audience, and therefore between Ashbery and the reader.

Thomas Lisk

SEPTEMBER 1, 1939

Author: W. H. Auden (1907-1973)
Type of poem: Lyric/meditation
First published: 1939; collected in *Another Time*, 1940

The Poem

"September 1, 1939" consists of nine stanzas of eleven lines each. The title refers to the beginning of World War II, the day that Adolf Hitler invaded Poland. W. H. Auden uses the occasion to write a farewell to the 1930's and to meditate on the social and psychological causes of war.

The poem is written in the first person, with the poet addressing the reader directly. Auden claims to be writing the poem in a bar in midtown Manhattan. While the setting may seem, at first, inappropriate for a serious subject, it is typical of Auden, as well as of many other modern poets, to take a detached point of view — even when their subjects are profoundly important to them. The mood or tone of the entire poem is established in the first stanza. The poet reports directly his feelings of uncertainty and fear for the future, as well as his distrust of the socialist schemes of the 1930's that failed to prevent the recurrence of war.

In the following three stanzas (2 through 4), Auden characteristically gives an intellectual analysis of the causes of the war. Two years earlier, in "Spain 1937," he had used the occasion of the Spanish civil struggle to treat war as a psychological rather than a political phenomenon. Similarly, in "September 1, 1939," he observes that European cultural history is a madness that erupts repeatedly in war. The second stanza affirms the historical and psychological explanations: the emphasis, beginning with Protestantism, on man as an economic being, and the belief that psychopaths like Hitler are created by abuses they suffer in childhood.

Auden next shows how impervious each historical age is to others and how each fails to learn from its predecessors. In the third stanza, the poet refers to the ancient Greek historian Thucydides, who wrote the first history of a war, the Peloponnesian. Thucydides believed that because human nature did not change, such conflicts would be repeated in every age. Auden not only affirms Thucydides' belief, but he also gives the recurrence of war a psychological motive: Humans actually want to experience pain, not avoid it. In the fourth stanza, Auden refers to statesmen who, in all ages, foolishly rationalize war until they are ultimately forced to admit what Thucydides knew: All war reduces to motives of imperialism.

The next three stanzas (5 through 7) become more personal in tone as the poet describes the inhabitants of the bar. Like him, they are typical urbanites who huddle, build defenses against reality, and share a "normal" desire that is impossible to gratify: to be loved exclusively by another human being. Average citizens commit themselves to this impossible goal as determinedly as governments pursue the game of war.

In the eighth stanza, the poet portrays himself not as a common bar patron but as a higher voice of authority. In a poem ("In Memory of W. B. Yeats") commemorating the Irish poet William Butler Yeats, published just six months previously, Auden had asked whether poets could ever, through their verse, alter a course of events. In that poem and in this one, he reaches the same conclusion: All the poet can do is state truths. The truth Auden offers in the eighth stanza was to cause him great difficulty and lead him to remove first this stanza and then the entire poem from his collected works. The last line of the stanza— "We must love one another or die" — Auden changed once to "and die" (for Oscar Williams' reprinting in *The New Pocket Anthology of American Verse from Colonial Days to the Present*, 1955). Yet then Auden decided that both versions were dishonest, since all die anyway.

The last stanza offers a humane and hopeful tone that is absent from the rest of the poem. The poet becomes not a seer but merely one of many citizens who desire a just society. He offers not a sweeping truth but a modest prayer: to reject the prevalent mood of despair and thereby affirm that life is purposeful.

Forms and Devices

Auden is regarded, because of his style, as a poet of logic rather than emotion. He was one of the first modern poets to reject the nineteenth century Romantic concept that reading poetry should be a sensuous experience and a way to reach emotions that could not be explained by reason. Auden argued that images in poetry could show a "one to one correspondence . . . grasped by the reader's reason"; poets did not have to use symbols that suggested multiple meanings or relationships (*The Enchafèd Flood*, 1950).

One feature of Auden's poems, especially in the 1930's and early 1940's, is his frequent use of adjectives to modify neutral or abstract nouns. Another device is to attach an active or colorful verb to a flat or prosaic subject noun. For example, the 1930's are "a low dishonest decade," pain is "habit-forming," and skyscrapers, like tall people, "use Their full height" to impress.

Another way that Auden makes his lines poetic is to transfer adjectives from the words they logically modify to other words in the sentence. It is the readers' job to unscramble the sentence and make it prosaic. For example, New York's rush-hour morning commuters, who give the city its dense workaday population, are described as "dense." Tall buildings that blindly, or unwittingly, "proclaim" are "blind."

In "September 1, 1939," Auden was influenced by Yeats's poem about the Irish rebellion, "Easter 1916." The diction and rhythm of Yeats's poem are echoed, for example, in lines 6 through 11 of Auden's first stanza. The short lines of Auden's poem, usually of six or seven syllables, echo Yeats's of seven or eight.

Though Auden came to regret Yeats's influence on his poems, he never slavishly followed him. Auden's use of rhyme, for example, is subtler and much less regular. Auden is fond of slant (or half) rhymes: life/leaf, grave/grief, fear/expire. Seldom does a pattern of end rhyme last throughout a stanza. Auden frequently uses half-rhymes within lines, as in stanza 5, where the *f-r-t-m* sound pattern of the phrase "fort assume" is answered in the next line by "furniture of home." The incremental repetition of words or phrases, used infrequently, helps Auden to make transitions. At the end of the fourth stanza, a metaphor—the "face" of Imperialism—is transferred to human "Faces along the bar." "Face" is the only word repeated in the entire poem.

Themes and Meanings

"September 1, 1939" records Auden's rejection of some of the ideologies of the 1930's, most notably Marxist socialism. His direct statement in stanza 8, "There is no such thing as the State," sums up what the poem has been building to from its beginning. The "clever hopes" of stanza 1 refer mainly to socialist economic schemes that most of the British intelligentsia espoused after World War I. Such schemes had not diminished the growth of a capitalist economy nor improved the lot of the working class but, worse yet, merely aggravated the social conditions under which totalitarianism flourished.

Auden, however, blames more than one decade. From the time of the Reformation ("Luther until now"), the humanity of man has been diminished. The fascist despair of the 1930's was also the accumulation of such Western philosophical views as Thomas Hobbes', for example, that human life was nasty and brutish.

In "September 1, 1939," Auden's early interest in Sigmund Freud begins to combine with an emergent affirmation of Christianity. Explaining how to account for modern monsters such as Hitler, Auden offers not simply a reductive Freudian approach but a Christian precept. Exploring Hitler's childhood ("what occurred at Linz") is a Freudian tactic to prove scientifically the simple Christian truism of the Golden Rule given at the end of stanza 2.

"September 1, 1939" also expresses themes developed in other works of the period by Auden. In *Letter to Lord Byron* (1937), Auden argues the Freudian/Marxist determinism that behavior is determined unconsciously by instinctive needs, such as hunger and love. In "September 1, 1939," the poet affirms that belief in the problematic eighth stanza: "Hunger allows no choice." The biological need for love is the "error bred in the bone," a desire that can never be fulfilled.

In a later work, "The Prolific and the Devourer," Auden wrote that while a "change of heart," a turning away from Fascism, would not save the world, historical development would nevertheless produce a change of heart. Both failure and success increase human understanding. It is this moderate optimism—which has become known as liberal humanism—that emerges at the end of "September 1, 1939." From the humanist E. M. Forster's essay, "What I Believe," Auden borrows the image of "points of light," noting that their appearance is "Ironic." These points are the "Just," a category very close to the Christian righteous, who emerge out of nowhere (some vast darkness) to "exchange . . . messages" of hope and affirmation. The ending becomes a description, then, of exactly what Auden has done in "September 1, 1939": One of the Just, he has shared his "message" with the reader.

Alvin Sullivan

SESTINA: ALTAFORTE

Author: Ezra Pound (1885-1972)
Type of poem: Dramatic monologue
First published: 1909, in *Exultations*

The Poem

In some respects, this poem is not only old-fashioned but archaic — quite differ‐
ent from the modern free-verse poetry for which Ezra Pound is famous. For one
thing, as the poem's title indicates, the verse structure is that of the sestina, a form
invented by the Provençal poets of the early Middle Ages. For another, the speaker is
Bertran De Born, a medieval warlord.

The sestina is a complex seven-stanza verse form: The first six stanzas are six
lines long, and the seventh stanza, the "envoy," is three lines long. The first six
stanzas all use the same set of concluding words in their six lines, but these recur‐
rent words shift position as the stanzas progress so that the word that ended line 1 in
stanza 1, for example, ends line 2 in stanza 2, line 4 in stanza 3, and thus the pattern
continues. In a sense, these recurrent ending words take the place of rhyme in giving
structure to the stanzas. In this sestina, the ending words are "peace," "music,"
"clash," "opposing," "crimson," and "rejoicing."

In the lines appearing before the first stanza, Pound provides some background
information to help the reader make his or her way through this difficult verse form.
"Loquitur" means "speaker," in this case "En" (Sir) Bertrans De Born. In *La di‐
vina commedia* (c. 1320; *The Divine Comedy*) Dante portrays De Born as a "stirrer
up of strife," a characterization that fits his remarks in the poem that follows. "Ec‐
covi!" is Italian for "here you are," which is addressed to the reader, as is the follow‐
ing line, "Judge ye!"; Pound is inviting the reader to make his or her own judgment
about whether Dante's condemnation of De Born was fair. Finally, Pound provides
three key background facts: The setting for the poem is De Born's castle Altaforte;
the person to whom De Born is speaking, "Papiols," is De Born's "jongleur," or
court singer/poet; and "The Leopard" is an emblem of Richard the Lionhearted.

In stanza 1, De Born rages at Papiols, who evidently is his confidant, that the
"South" (of France) is too peaceful: He is a warrior, only happy in battle. In fact,
during De Born's lifetime the many small fiefdoms of France were often at war with
one another and with the forces of Richard of England, who was also lord of much
of France. For noblemen such as De Born, warfare was the only honorable occupa‐
tion (winning a war with a neighboring fiefdom was also the principal source of
income). So although the peace that has fallen on Provençe at the opening of the
poem is probably only temporary, De Born chafes at being kept from the exercise of
his profession.

De Born is so warlike that, as he says in stanza 2, even summer thunderstorms
make him happy. Tempests and lightning remind him of war in that such storms
disturb the tranquillity of sunny summer days. He imagines that the thunderclouds

are engaged in combat and that heavenly beings clash their swords.

The reference to heavenly war in stanza 2 leads naturally to the reference to hell in stanza 3. De Born petitions the hellish powers to grant him strife; he longs to hear the neighing of war-horses and the clang of armor. As far as he is concerned, the concentrated experience of an hour of battle is worth a whole year of peaceful pleasures.

In stanza 4, he returns to the theme of warring nature. The crimson dawn sky reminds him of blood, and the rays of the rising sun appear to be spears in combat against the night. In stanza 5, De Born turns to cursing peace-lovers. Such men, according to him, are weak-blooded and "womanish," and he relegates them to rotting in inactivity. Only in battle, he claims, does a man prove his worth: Peaceful men are not men at all, and he "rejoices" in their deaths.

Once again, in stanza 6, De Born summons Papiols to accompany him to war, specifically against the forces of "the Leopard," King Richard of England—and once again, he damns those who would try to make peace between De Born and his enemies. Stanza 7 acts as a reprise of the preceding themes: De Born yearns for the "music" of battle, prays for combat, and condemns peaceful living.

Forms and Devices

The sestina's highly structured pattern of end words dominates other aspects of this poem's form. Imagery is especially affected by the connotations surrounding the words "peace," "music," "clash," "opposing," "crimson," and "rejoicing."

In fact, clusters of imagery may be grouped about a division of the six words into two sets or about oppositions between individual couplings of the words. "Peace, music, rejoicing," then, serve as one cluster, suggesting obvious associations with joy and art, while "clash, opposing, crimson" clearly suggest strife. Similarly, "clash" contrasts with "music" and "peace" with "opposing."

Each of the "image centers" created by the end words plays on strong sensory description. The poem particularly exploits hearing, smell, and sight in its use of clanging armor and clashing spears, stinking and rotting peace, enflamed and bloody crimson. Yet, just as complex as the end-word structuring of the sestina form is the ironic use to which the image centers are put. "Music" is a good example. In this poem, "music" can mean the delightful songs sung by the jongleur, Papiols; the "frail" tunes of peace; or the sounds of battle. "Peace," too, holds this sort of ironic implication: For the "weak" and "lily-livered," peace means food, women, and wine; De Born, conversely, is only at peace when he is in the middle of combat. Thus, the major challenge of the sestina form—using each end word in a different sense with different associated imagery each time the word changes position—is clearly met in this poem.

Although the sestina is usually associated with Romance-language poetry of the Middle Ages, Pound here employs a kind of mock medieval English to place his poem in the English-language tradition. He does it in at least two ways: First, frequent alliteration, a major structural feature of Middle English poetry, is prominent in "Sestina: Altaforte"; second, archaic words are scattered throughout the work.

Stanza 1 offers a good example of Pound's use of alliteration and other sound repetitions. In line 1, for example, alliteration occurs in "this our South stinks peace" and in the repetition "all! All"; in line 3, "save/ swords,"; in line 4, "purple, opposing"; and in line 5, "broad fields beneath." Most readers will immediately note the use of archaic, Middle English words such as "vair" (the bluish-white color of squirrel's fur) in stanza 1, "destriers" (war-horses) in stanza 3, and "stour" (battle) in stanza 5. Finally, the syntax of the poem also mimics Middle English poetry. Reversal of parts of speech, for example, is common: "have I great rejoicing" in stanza 2 and "howl I my heart nigh mad" in stanza 1. In addition, a number of other archaic syntactic patterns appear, such as "Let's to music" in stanza 1 and "fierce thunders roar me their music" in stanza 2.

Themes and Meanings

The historically specific persona and setting, the medieval verse form, and the archaic word use of "Sestina: Altaforte" combine to suggest one of the poem's major themes: the culturally specific consciousness of a warrior during the Middle Ages. At this period in his poetic development, Pound was very much under the influence of the English poet Robert Browning, part of whose fame rests on his dramatic monologues, poems whose speaker is a real or fictional character usually drawn from past history. Pound was fascinated with this use of "personae" (the word originally meant "masks"), through which a poet could enter into a sensibility utterly different from his own: The challenge of creating another kind of awareness— remote in time and preoccupations from his own—excited him.

Indeed, De Born's personality, as the reader sees it in "Sestina: Altaforte" is in conflict with most modern assumptions about the value of peace over war, of nonviolence over violence. The poem turns ironically about the reversal the persona places on these assumptions: For him, war and death are paradoxically life-giving, and art and joy are to be found in the cries and noisy clamor of battle. Similarly, De Born's view of nature contrasts strongly with contemporary perceptions. The modern person, conditioned in part by the Romantics to see nature as benign and serene, may well be shocked by De Born's glorification of the violence of natural phenomena—the bloodiness of a sunrise or the way a storm "kills" a peaceful afternoon.

Ultimately, the irony in "Sestina: Altaforte" is twofold: first, there is the irony arising from the contrast between De Born's sensibility and that of the modern reader; second, there is the narrative irony existing between Pound's warlord persona and Pound himself.

The period during which this poem was written has often been viewed as a golden age in Europe, whose nations were then at the height of their imperial power. No significant conflict had disturbed European peace since the Franco-Prussian war of 1870, and no real continent-wide war had occurred since the battle of Waterloo in 1815. European commerce was thriving, and the general standard of living had never been higher. Curiously, though, many people, as De Born did, chafed at the complacency and dullness of this time of plenty; they longed for the "excitement" of struggle, which they would experience all too soon in the tragedy of World War I.

Thus, although "Sestina: Altaforte" concerns the warlike impatience of a petty ruler nearly eight centuries in the past, the sort of rage De Born felt over the stagnation of peace was beginning to rise to the surface in early twentieth century Europe. Pound captures this impatience while producing a masterful illusion of the past, both in the vivid re-creation of a medieval warrior and in the crafting of a difficult and archaic verse form.

John Steven Childs

THE SHIP OF DEATH

Author: D. H. Lawrence (1885-1930)
Type of poem: Lyric
First published: 1932, in *Last Poems*

The Poem

"The Ship of Death" is composed of 107 lines, divided into ten sections of varying lengths (section 4 has four lines, section 7 twenty-five lines). The title refers to the ancient burial practice of placing a model ship in the tomb with the corpse to carry the soul to heaven.

Section 1 describes the time of death as autumn, when apples fall and their seeds are dropped into the earth through the rotting fruit. Each person passes through such a period of autumn, as the person undergoes a separation of self from self. Each must prepare for such a separation. Thus, section 2 calls upon all ("you," the readers) to build a ship of death, because the season of frost has arrived and apples are ready to fall. The smell of death is in the air, and the soul cowers within the cold body.

Section 3 questions the success of suicide, refusing to believe that the murder of one's self could be rewarded with the desired tranquillity of death. Instead, section 4 asserts, one should rely upon one's experience of the peace that comes from "a strong heart." This is the kind of quiet that one hopes for, and it cannot be had through suicide.

The task of all is, therefore, to begin to prepare for the death that is a part of natural process, for the fall from life that is like the fall of the ripe apple in autumn. Each should build a ship of death for the long journey into "oblivion." Each can experience in the body the decline of nature as a bruising of being, as a passage of the soul from the weakening body. Time and space are experienced by the aging body as the buffeting of ocean waves against the beach; it is upon that limitless ocean, whose sources come from beyond time and space, that the ship of death will be launched.

The body breaks up and falls into pieces in section 6, where the soul discovers that it cannot find anything solid outside its body. The flood waters are death-waters, now within as well as without the body. The soul is increasingly frightened, huddling in terror as it waits the final annihilating waves of destruction.

"We are dying, we are dying," the poem says; since we are dying all the time, we can only resign ourselves to the inevitability of the end. We must help the soul by building a ship for it to cross the ocean of death; we must put aboard it the implements of life, "food/ and little dishes," for comfort of the frightened soul. One departs the body as a soul launched upon a ship that has no destiny, no charts to guide it, and no means to steer it upon the dark waters of death. In the deepening darkness, both the soul and the ship disappear as they drift without direction and fall into nothing, toward "nowhere."

Section 8 is a surrender, an absolute resignation to the disappearance of all: Both body and ship are "gone, entirely gone." The end has been reached, and the end "is oblivion." When all has sunk into nothing, something occurs. Section 9 is a break in the plane of oblivion, as "a thread" of light stretches itself out to make a horizon, to open a space for new consciousness. The stunned speaker is uncertain of what can be believed: "Is it illusion?" Then the thread of light "fumes" into a broader, dawn-like light. Suddenly, the ship is sighted, drifting beneath the gray light. Then the light turns yellow, and finally it is rose-colored; "The whole thing starts again."

The flooding waters of death subside to open section 10. A "frail soul," beaten and disoriented by the darksome voyage, leaves the ship and steps into a shell-like body waiting for its return. The ship returns upon the sea as the soul reenters its body. The soul now finds the peace of oblivion in its bodily being. This is what awaits the person who builds the ship of death, so each should begin to build what each will need to cross waters of death for the peace of oblivion.

Forms and Devices

"The Ship of Death" is an irregular form of lyric with elegiac material in free verse. Each section is made up of verses grouped into stanzalike units of independent clauses: These may be one line, or they may be as many as nine lines (as in section 7). The effect is a tone suggesting talk, solemn but intimate and ordinary. The intimacy is a product of bringing together the speaker and audience/readers at the opening of section 4: "O let us talk."

The main devices of this poem are symbolic images, literary allusions, and rhetorical questions. The poem moves in an undulating, shifting way from the declarative statements of section 1 to the interrogatives of 2, 3, and 4. Then there is an increase in the imperative, commanding tone: "Build then, . . . you must." With little exception, this is the tone sustained to the end, with its "oh build it!" The form of biblical prophecy or pastoral sermon helps shape the poem.

Literary allusions range from obvious to subtle, as Lawrence draws upon his rich literary heritage to help create the themes of his poem. The most obvious is in section 3, with its echoes of William Shakespeare's *Hamlet* (c. 1600-1601) "can a man his own quietus make/ with a bare bodkin?" Hamlet's soliloquy on suicide is invoked to put the issue of the poem on a line of courage that confronts death in a positive and heroic way. While this may be slightly ironic, indicating that modern souls are more timid than Hamlet, it still works to align the modern soul with the heroic Hamlet in a more subtle way. When Hamlet is sent to England, he makes a strange voyage by ship, from which he returns a changed person, resigned to providence. Lawrence's poem also aims for this. There are other, important allusions as well. The poem opens with strong references, through the imagery of the "falling fruit" of autumn, to John Keats's "To Autumn," as well as to Shakespeare's *King Lear* (c. 1605-1606), with its line, "the ripeness is all."

The imagery of falling fruit as a symbol for the fallen body, from which a "soul" exits like a seed from rotting pulp, is a way to keep the process of death and dying in a natural dimension; therefore, when the soul returns from its journey at the end, it is more credible, because the soul is like the seed which sprouts into new life after a period of germination in earth's darkness. The action of the fall is itself likened to a journey, and this is made to be a journey by water. References to the "ark" and "flood" make the journey an individual experience of the biblical narrative of Noah, so that the natural process is lifted into a spiritual and religious dimension as well.

Themes and Meanings

The meaning of "The Ship of Death" is religious, because it draws upon traditional beliefs to shape its expression. Invoking Hamlet's soliloquy puts the religious question of suicide in a Western, Judeo-Christian setting that rejects suicide. To allude to the building of the ark by Noah is to solicit the power of divine commandment for the preparation to die as a preparation to survive death; destruction is divinely determined, but obedience to God delivers one from the annihilation of that destruction.

There is ambiguity in the meaning of the ship as an ark, however, because there is quite clearly a connection between the "ship of death" and the model ships placed with corpses in the tombs of ancient Egyptians. This connection raises the possibility that the little ship may be less effective in its voyage than the story of Noah suggests. Those Egyptian ships have gone nowhere, have indeed sometimes lain ironically less preserved beside the better preserved bodies whose souls they were to protect.

Finally, "The Ship of Death" is less confidently a statement of certainty about religious hope for life eternal than it is about the stern necessity of psychological renewal in every person's natural life. Perhaps each night's sleep is a passage over the flood of death-darkness, so each morning is a survival of spirit from the death of the body in sleep's oblivion. More clearly, though subtly, the poem's meaning is limited to the search for self-identity: "to bid farewell/ to one's own self, and find an exit/ from the fallen self." This is a familiar theme of Lawrence's writing, in fiction as well as in poetry, and it produces a meaning of self-discovery through self-renewal in "The Ship of Death."

Richard D. McGhee

THE SIGNATURE OF ALL THINGS

Author: Kenneth Rexroth (1905-1982)
Type of poem: Lyric
First published: 1949, in *The Signature of All Things*

The Poem

"The Signature of All Things" is divided into three parts: The first comprises thirty-two lines; the second, twenty-five; and the third, twenty. The title of the poem derives from a book by the seventeenth century mystic Jakob Böhme, the reading of which initiates the poem. Written in the first person, the poem relates the visionary, intensely spiritual experience of the poet.

True to Böhme's teaching that the "outward visible world with all its beings is a signature, or figure, of the inward spiritual world," the poet begins with the image of his body "stretched bathed in the sun"; from his own physical being, the poet's awareness radiates to his surroundings, progressively more animate: water, laurel tree, and creatures.

These creatures perform the endless cycle of birth and death: The wren "broods in her moss-domed nest"; a newt "struggles with a white moth/ Drowning in the pool." Such observations lead the poet to recall his relationships, whether with humans— "those who have loved me" — or his natural environment—the "mountains I have climbed," the "seas I have swum in." These reminisces prove redemptive; his "sin and trouble fall away/ Like Christian's bundle." This reference to John Bunyan's *Pilgrim's Progress* (1678, 1684) reinforces the sense of the poet's life as a pilgrimage of love. Böhme, as the poet describes, "saw the world as streaming/ In the electrolysis of love." Electrolysis, a chemical transformation involving dynamic currents, can serve as a purification process.

The second part of the poem finds the recumbent poet now standing "at the wood's edge." Following the mystic way, he has emptied himself of all preconceptions: "Watching the darkness, listening/ To the stillness." His humility is rewarded; an owl— a symbol of wisdom— arrives and awakens him to a world brimming with light. He proceeds to an oak grove, formerly the site of an Indian village. There he comes upon a group of heifers, "Black and white, all lying down/ Quietly together." Opposites— life and death, black and white— resolve in a tranquil scene of fruitfulness and communion.

In the final part of the poem, the poet recovers a rotten log from the bottom of a pool. Once it dries in the sun for a month— a full cycle of the moon— he chops it for kindling. Emerging late that night, after reading "saints" and "philosophers" on "the destiney of man," the poet looks up at the "swaying island of stars," then down at his feet, where all about him are "scattered chips/ Of pale cold light" that are "alive." Witness to and finally active participant in the cycle of renewal, the poet forms the nexus of living worlds of light—experiencing his destiny.

Forms and Devices

In keeping with its sacramental vision, the poem abounds in natural imagery. Flora and fauna; elements of earth, air, fire, and water; senses of sight, sound, and smell—all direct the poet's inner journey toward the epiphany that climaxes the work. A visionary poet in the tradition of William Blake, Kenneth Rexroth has stated, "Poetry is vision, the pure act of sensual communion and contemplation."

Adhering to the doctrine of correspondences taught by the mystic Böhme, the poet evokes nature as emblematic of spiritual realities. The laurel tree symbolizes expiation and eternity as well as victory and triumph. The oak, rooted in the graves of Indians, connotes endurance; sacred to Zeus, it represents the essence of divine power. Such imagery infuses the poem with a sense of rebirth. The clearest metaphor of renewal is left for last: the rotten log that the poet transforms into kindling fuel.

The setting of July, the height of summer, implies growth and maturity. The poet, at "forty summers," is ripe for the mystical rebirth of his sensual awareness and creative power, which he experiences in the course of the poem. The context of these awakenings is described in the imagery of illumination: the owl's eyes "glow"; the meadow is "bright as snow"; creatures appear in the "blur of brightness" and "cobwebbed light"; scattered wood chips are "ingots/ Of quivering phosphorescence."

The poet conjures these sacramental images in familiar language. The unrhymed measured lines—ranging from eight syllables each in the first part of the poem to seven in the last two—convey the intimacy of conversation. Rexroth called this syllabic form "natural numbers," saying that it allowed him to emphasize the "natural cadences of speech."

Themes and Meanings

The central meaning of the poem, a celebration of personal transcendence, lies in spiritual illumination. Rexroth has said that "our experience of reality begins and ends in illumination."

Rexroth was a proponent of Personalism—identified with the work of Dylan Thomas and Walt Whitman, among others—which defines poetry as personal vision, communion, and communal sacrament. For the poet, meaning evolved from spiritual community, from Martin Buber's "I-Thou" communion. The poem's organic vision reconciles self and other, life and death in the eternal process of creation.

A student of Böhme, Rexroth took to heart the mystic's teaching that the light of divine love streams through the universe and that humankind is the signature of God in the world. In his introduction to the book for which "The Signature of All Things" is the title poem, Rexroth wrote: "These are simple, personal poems, as close as I can make them to integral experiences. Perhaps the integral person is more revolutionary than any program, party or social conflict."

With luminous faith, the poet sought to reassert the powers of spiritual communion against the anomie promoted by urbanization and industrialization in the twentieth century. As critic Morgan Gibson has commented, the experience of the "integral person" in communion is Adamic: The individual becomes universal, and the universal, paradisal. From his wide reading as well as his translation of foreign verse, Rexroth evidenced an aesthetic that transcended space and time. According to Victor Howes, in *The Christian Science Monitor*, Rexroth was looking for a "sort of day-to-day mysticism" — that is, a direct and universal one. As Rexroth himself put it, "that sense of exaltation, that feeling of being on the brink of the coming of the absolute, is really a habit of living."

Amy Adelstein

SIREN

Author: Christopher Okigbo (1932-1967)
Type of poem: Lyric
First published: 1964, in *Limits*; collected as "Siren Limits" in *Labyrinths, with Path of Thunder*, 1971

The Poem

The work of Christopher Okigbo, a Nigerian poet, is extremely difficult to approach, because it incorporates both the African and European traditions. This blending is evident in the imagery and allusions that rely interchangeably on the two heritages. It also distinguishes the technique, which not only reflects the indigenous literature and religious incantations of the Igbo people in Nigeria but includes as well the ritualistic language of Roman Catholicism and Western poets ranging from Gerard Manley Hopkins to T. S. Eliot.

The four numbered parts of "Siren" constitute what might be called Okigbo's artistic credo. Here the poet—noted for his reluctance to discuss his own work—is "Suddenly becoming talkative." Part 1 of "Siren" employs an essential ingredient of the Igbo religious ceremony, the incantation, as the poet invokes the goddess with her traditional trappings, "A tiger mask and nude spear." Having undergone his "cleansing" through this quasi-religious ceremony, he is ready to express his Africanness through poetry.

In the second part, Okigbo draws an elaborate metaphor in which he traces the development of a poet's career, starting as "a shrub among the poplars"—that is, an aspiring writer among those already established. He sees writers as "Horsemen of the apocalypse," which is a typical reaction in Africa where the writer considers himself and is considered by others to be the conscience and voice of a people battling to overcome the tragic aftermath of colonialism. Finally, he imagines fame displaying "its foliage" and hanging like "A green cloud" over the world.

The third part elaborates on the struggle of the artist, who creates in adverse circumstances amid "Banks of reed./ Mountains of broken bottles." The introduction of a line that will be repeated several times, "*& the mortar is not yet dry. . . . ,*" suggests the poet should not rush into the exercise of his craft until he is ready and until his audience is receptive: he must wait until the mortar, or the inspiration and receptiveness, has set firmly. Otherwise, "the voice fades . . ./ Not leaving a mark."

Okigbo often borrows lines from other poets, and such is the case with the refrain, "*& the mortar is not yet dry. . . .*" It comes from Canto 8 by Ezra Pound (1885-1972). The only change Okigbo made was to replace Pound's opening word "As" with "&." In its original context, the line stands as a warning to a painter not to paint the chapels until they are ready; as Pound says in the next line, "it w'd be merely work chucked away." Okigbo uses this quotation to clarify the stages of the poet's development and in so doing lends the rather mundane statement a fullness and richness lacking in its original presentation.

The account of the poet's plight continues in the fourth part, a series of abstract images representing the trials the artist faces in a hostile world. Once the difficulties have been overcome, though, the poet may be awakened from his dream of creativity and his "poem will be finished."

Forms and Devices

The lyricism, economy of expression, stark imagery, and emotional intensity of "Siren" draw not only from the indigenous forms of Igbo poetry but also from modernist European poetry, with which Okigbo was familiar. Such allusions as "weaverbird," "palm grove," "he-goat-on-heat," and "My lioness" are very African. At the same time, lines such as "So we must go,/ Wearing evemist against the shoulders," bring to mind the opening of T. S. Eliot's "The Love Song of J. Alfred Prufrock." Yet the poetry is not derivative; rather, it makes striking use for its own purposes of the poet's divided heritage by echoing African and European texts.

Some readers of Okigbo's work have observed that it does not really matter whether every line of the poems can be grasped intellectually and their exact meaning explained. The imagery, so much of it drawn from the African experience, both traditional and contemporary, may at times mystify the Western reader. Yet even when the density seems overwhelming, pure lyricism dominates and provides a poetic experience more emotional and aesthetic than cerebral. The fourth part of "Siren," for example, while undeniably obscure in its allusions and abbreviated expression, still brims with a poetic intensity that succeeds in itself.

A passage from the third part of "Siren," exemplifies Okigbo's technical virtuosity at its best. Five lines consist simply of "Hurry on down," each followed by an indented line; two of the lines describe actual places: the gate and the market. The other two admonitions to "Hurry on down" move from reality into "the wake of the dream"; this juxtaposition of the concrete and the abstract is a recurrent phenomenon in Okigbo's poetry. The final invitation to "Hurry on down" has as its destination the "rockpoint of CABLE." Cable Point is a real location in Nigeria, a sacred waterfront with a rocky promontory and the place where traditional religious pilgrimages end. The repetition and the rhythms established suggest the movement of a procession through the gate and the market; this section might well stand as a description of a pilgrimage. Then the glimmer of reality vanishes, as is always the case in Okigbo's poetry. And the pilgrimage becomes the poetic quest.

Another section in the third part shows how the poem gains emotional intensity through devices both dense and stark. Saying that the poet "must sing/ Tongue-tied without name or audience," Okigbo calls this moment "the crisis-point." Yet the voice survives and speaks, "Not thro' pores in the flesh/ but the soul's backbone." That metaphor, "the soul's backbone," so simple, yet so brimming with suggestiveness, is an altogether original way to describe the indefinable quality that directs the poetic process.

Although Okigbo expresses the fear at the end of the third part of "Siren" that his poetry, "Like a shadow," would fade, "Not leaving a mark," the misgiving was unfounded. His work is striking in its technique, both dense and spare, richly allusive, full of imagery coming "from the flag-pole of the heart." Admittedly, at times the very imagery that distinguishes the poetry sometimes distracts from its clear and concise meaning. Yet, like the oral African tradition from which Okigbo drew, a poem such as "Siren" more often sounds than means.

Themes and Meanings

Reared in the Catholicism brought to Africa by missionaries and educated in mission schools, Okigbo revolted against the imported theology and like a prodigal son returned to the religion of his ancestors. This rejection and return form the basis of much of his poetry, as does the plight of the artist caught in a chasm between two conflicting traditions, the indigenous and the borrowed. "Siren" gains resonance when read in the context of Okigbo's other poetry, but even alone it turns into an important document illustrating the way African poetry in English has usurped the colonial language and transformed it into that which is undeniably African.

On one level, "Siren" expresses Okigbo's dedication to the art of poetry. The poem's name, "Siren," suggests that he has no choice but to follow this path, for he has been bewitched. The title, drawing from Greek mythology, of course brings to mind those insidiously seductive creatures who by their singing lured mariners to destruction. Yet as Okigbo so often does with allusions, he reverse the destructive element of the Siren and turns her into the goddess of poetry whom he invokes in part 1. Thus the Siren of poetry, addressed as a kind of African goddess in spite of her Greek origins, retains the ability to bewitch and seduce, but sheds her pernicious qualities for creative ones.

On another level, "Siren" expresses the dilemma of many an African writer in English, not just that of Okigbo. After all, they are writing in the language of the former colonizer; and African writers and critics, well aware of this irony, often question how the African experience can be expressed in a borrowed language, especially that of a conqueror who had derided all things African. These writers also find themselves far from the "center" of English language literature, that is British and American writing. As Okigbo says they are "shrub[s] among the poplars." Who will listen to them or read them? Many of their countrymen do not know English, so the writers are sometimes accused of pandering to the West, where readers may think "the mortar is not yet dry" on what has come to be called "postcolonial literature." This writing from the former colonies, then, is at "the crisis-point" and may be in danger of "Not leaving a mark." Even as the poem concludes, Okigbo says "& *this poem will be finished*," thus implying that he — and the others — will continue the pursuit of the impossible, "To pull by the rope/ The big white elephant."

Robert Ross

THE SKATERS

Author: John Ashbery (1927-   )
Type of poem: Meditation
First published: 1964; collected in *Rivers and Mountains*, 1966

The Poem

The Skaters is an extensive meditation, its 739 lines divided into four sections of unequal lengths. The title, taken from the Giacomo Meyerbeer ballet *Les Patineurs*, introduces the controlling metaphor of the poem, figures gliding swiftly over opaque surfaces, and rightly suggests that the poem's technique will be one of actions rather than of statements and conclusions.

The poem is written in the first person, yet as with many of John Ashbery's poems, the identity of the speaker is in constant, restless metamorphosis. One can never at any moment claim to know exactly who the "I" is, and one must not assume that it is always the poet speaking as himself.

The Skaters is a poem of perceptions unrestricted by framing devices, and it presents the reader with an almost overwhelming panorama of details and incidents. It prefers experience to understanding and confounds any attempts to summarize it by ordinary means. As a meditation on the vast subject of uncertainty, that unseen region over whose mere surface the skaters move, it must be elusive in order to be true to its subject. Nevertheless, the intimacy and playfulness of its tone permit the reader, once the usual critical faculties are relaxed, to follow the poem through its distinctive movements into an understanding of its intentions.

Section 1 introduces the problem around which the poem conducts its meditations: How can one for certain assume that life is good when nothing in life is certain? This problem is embodied in the skaters whose "swift blades" glide gracefully but unknowingly, quickly but circuitously, leaving no permanent record of their passage behind them. The first section continues through many variations of this thematic imagery — "water surface ripples," "gestures half-sketched against woodsmoke," drifting balloons, soap bubbles — each of which intensifies the poet's awareness of his dilemma. If everything is merely transient, it is easy to conclude that "Everything is trash."

Section 2 describes the poet's attempts to escape his dilemma through numerous dreams in the form of imaginary voyages similar to those in Charles Baudelaire's "The Invitation to the Voyage" and Arthur Rimbaud's "The Drunken Boat." Being only imaginary, however, none of these voyages can ever be completed, so the speaker is thrown back upon his original problem, one which may now be thought of as a life of infinite departures and no arrivals.

Section 3 explores the harshness of reality after a long dream. The most naturalistic and autobiographical of the poem's sections (recalling details from the poet's childhood on a New York farm and from his years of voluntary exile in Paris), it discovers the one and only arrival of which the speaker can be certain: death. This certainty is quickly judged to be of little comfort and no practical use. Rejecting death, the speaker hurries to reaffirm dreaming as his "most important activity," his greatest freedom in an incomprehensible world.

In a parade of fragmentary scenarios, the final section reinforces the futility of attempting to contain reality with patterns and philosophies. Ashbery chooses to celebrate what he cannot refute: the arbitrariness of everything. The poem ends, therefore, with the constellations of Taurus, Leo, and Gemini rising in a "perfect order" which is neither astronomically nor astrologically valid, but which instead is the order of pure accident.

Forms and Devices

In a poem as turbulent and extensive as *The Skaters*, nearly all the devices of English poetry are employed, wholly or partially, literally or allusively, as the language of the work proliferates through the poet's various intentions. Indeed, it may well be said of Ashbery that he has constantly attempted to write a kind of poetry that cannot be captured by any conventional definition.

Still, there are clearly a number of key devices that propel *The Skaters* toward its thematic ends. Chief among these is the metaphor which gives the poem its title. A skater trusts his life to surfaces alone and so embraces in his activity the notion of experience without understanding, movement without depth. Were he to pause in his gliding, for reflection, he would fall and be none the wiser for having reflected. The skater accepts the circuitousness of his sport, not as a vapid sequence of repetitions, but as a series of infinitely unique variations on the theme of movement. Thus the skater is the perfect metaphorical representative of both the poem's rhetorical technique and of its closing affirmation.

The most memorable imagery in *The Skaters* serves to reinforce the effect of its principal metaphor. In nearly every passage, images of drift, of careless motion, appear. Balloons, soap bubbles, smoke, and sudden storms all arise in their turns and as quickly disappear, only to reappear at later moments, as if to proclaim the durability of their waywardness, the permanence of their transient natures.

Mirroring this waywardness at the level of language itself is Ashbery's propensity to combine vulgar phrases (such as "I'd like to bugger you" and "all your old suck-ass notions") with high poetic diction, passages of triviality ("Any more golfing hints, Charlie?") with those of profound seriousness. The effect is to make the poem's voice as elusive as its imagery and its central metaphor. The words of the poem are thus as restless as its subject matter and so emulate in verse the techniques of the American "action painters" (such as Jackson Pollock and Franz Kline), whose canvases Ashbery, himself a noted art critic, so fervently admires. As the action painters regard their pictures as pure surfaces across which paint is literally pushed and pulled by the various energies of the artist, so Ashbery thinks of his page as a white surface (like a frozen pond) over which his imagination crosses and re-crosses in the form of words. In literature, this method hearkens back to the aleatory (that is, intentionally accidental) devices of the French Surrealist movement founded by the poet/philosopher André Breton. Since *The Skaters* was written in Paris, Ashbery's affinity for Breton and his followers seems all the more serendipitous. Thus, one might say that all the devices of *The Skaters* work paradoxically to expose rather than to conceal their verbal trickery, just as it is the poem's paradoxical intention to celebrate intentionlessness.

Themes and Meanings

The Skaters unfolds its theme as a series of potential solutions to the problem of affirming life in the midst of countless uncertainties. Most philosophies console their adherents with at least the possibility of an absolute truth, a fixed point at the center of a changing world. Ashbery permits himself no such consolation, so he restlessly pursues the virtue of restlessness. The poem's very existence is the poem's theme (echoing the poet Archibald MacLeish's dictum that poems should not mean, but be), with the pursuit of affirmation substituting for affirmation itself.

Ashbery's theme has two distinct components. The first is essentially negative and expresses the futility of any search for certainty conducted among the chaotic surfaces of human life. The poem accumulates supporting evidence, not on behalf of Plato's harmonious world of eternal forms, but on behalf of the constant flux of Heraclitus, whose primary principle is expressed in the saying that no man steps into the same river twice. For the urban, twentieth century Ashbery (considered the chief figure of the New York School of poets), the ever-changing river becomes a city street: "We step out into the street, not realizing that the street is different." The world is entirely mutable; moreover, humans are not always even capable of perceiving its mutability. Such bleak considerations lead Ashbery to the expression of his theme's darkest component— "Only one thing exists: the fear of death." A person continues to live, not because any particular aspect of life is valuable or worthwhile, but because one would rather inhabit the unmeaning flux of being than achieve the fearful certainty of nonexistence.

Yet the lyrical profusion of *The Skaters* quickly evokes the brighter component of the poet's theme. There is, after all, a pleasure in uncertainty, the pleasure of anticipation, the ecstasy of the skater who seems to move effortlessly through an ever-accelerating panorama. While anticipation does not guarantee satisfaction, it does indeed vividly animate the days and years through which it transpires. If all experience is arbitrary, deprived of any ideal pattern, is there not possibly then a perfect arbitrariness, an accident entirely liberated from the disappointing constraints of hopeless intentionality? Thus Ashbery chooses to close *The Skaters* with those constellations rising in accordance with no mythological or scientific order whatsoever. One cannot fail to find certainty if one does not seek it, but instead rejoices in the infinite possibilities created by its absence. In the universe of *The Skaters*, the sheer abundance of dizzying perceptions available to anyone more than compensates for the poverty of human understanding. The meaning of life is in the mere living of it.

Donald Revell

SKETCH FOR AN AESTHETIC PROJECT

Author: Jay Wright (1935-   )
Type of poem: Narrative
First published: 1971, in *The Homecoming Singer*

The Poem

"Sketch for an Aesthetic Project" is a long narrative poem in four sections totaling ninety lines. Jay Wright employs the first-person voice to lend immediacy to the spontaneity of experience and thought. Three lines from Thomas Kinsella's "Nightwalker" introduce the poem: "I believe now that love is half persistence,/ A medium in which, from change to change,/ Understanding may be gathered." Wright's narrator achieves this understanding by equating aesthetics with the natural changes of love. The poem's first section contains three stanzas; the remaining three sections contain one stanza each.

In the first section's five-line stanza, the narrator describes his restlessness with his "stomp[ing] about these rooms in an old overcoat." Anxiety seldom compels him to leave his enclosure "even on sunny days," and his cold rooms suggest a dormant foundry.

One night, when he does leave, he finds emptiness, and this suggested locale corresponds to Wright's native Albuquerque, New Mexico, or the Mexico that he deeply enjoys. In the second and longest of this section's stanzas, the speaker discovers in the vacant environs a few persons, a burro, the sounds of his own footsteps, and the furtive "unthinking walkers" cursed by the arcane. The soul he hopes to meet "tugging a burro up the street/ loaded with wet wood" would be his alter ego, laden with fuel to ignite a beauteous aesthetic response, but this figure only beseeches him for alms. In this section, the poet establishes the searching artist who must tramp about in rain that soaks his sensibility and that, although he does not know it, becomes directly responsible for his sketch.

In his home place, the poet reconstructs his travels, "recalling the miracle of being there" — namely, in Harlem, New York — where he walked summers innocently while he breathed the city's smells, listened to its voices, and while his thoughts lingered on its religious and spiritual life, centered momentarily on the old deacon who is "a rabbi of the unscrupulous" to the women who watch him pass. The speaker identifies with this man who abides among the maddening voices of the people. Despite his physical distance from Harlem at this point in the poem, the aesthetic proximity unnerves him.

In section three, the narrator and "ingenuous sailors" experience the dullness of waiting near or on the sea. The speaker says, as if to himself, "Wake" to open the section to the artless but toiling sailors transporting their "bloody cargo" of slaves "up the shoreline." Keeping "a log for passage" enables him to record his emotional response to his project. The "parchments of blood" constituting this log happen to be "sunk where I cannot walk" because they are in his subconscious and racial memory. After the sailors have been "intensely buoyed by the sight of land/ and the fervent release of cankered bodies," the narrator remembers that even in the silence there prevails a "mythic shriek."

In the final and briefest section, the poet returns to the coldness, understanding the shriek as a metaphor for music. He realizes that his aesthetic solitude was an illusion, and that aesthetic beauty is undeniably alive and is "swift and mad as I am/ dark in its act/ [and] light" in the way it softens his irresolute notions about what an artist must do.

Forms and Devices

Because Jay Wright's poems are both deeply spiritual and profoundly experiential, his figurative language encompasses regions such as his native southwestern United States, Harlem, and other African-American communities, and the richness of their languages, idioms, and rhythms. Many of his poems reflect his appreciation of African culture and history and its dissemination in the western hemisphere, and his readers also encounter Mesoamerican allusions and images.

Wright's narrative technique utilizes subtle musical qualities. He quickly creates staccato effect in "Sketch for an Aesthetic Project" with *st* sounds, often referring to action, in section 1—"I stomp," "I step," "staggering," "streets," and "a dim-eyed student." He achieves a similar effect with "I clatter over cobbled streets. . . . I pretend not to be afraid of witches." The tensions that assist and sustain creativity are reflected in this section's hard consonants, but these hard sounds yield to softer sounds as the poem proceeds until they return in section three. The effective repetition of words and sounds, another musical quality, can be found in the phrase "only, perhaps" in line 8, restated in line 11 of the first section, and near the close of sections 1 and 3, where those whose presence the narrator needs would either "pluck my pity" or "pluck my bones."

The narrative style of section 2 is less figurative and more direct, its language denotative, although the poet finds vitality in the streets of Harlem. Yet Wright freely relies on hard verbs and active adverbs to heighten the subtheme of the suppression of ideas and actions. The narrator may walk his home streets, but he does not fear the witches who reside there "or any forces/ ground down under the years here,/ carping and praying under stones." These do not intimidate him. The burro tugged by one he hopes to meet carries a burden, and in front of the Harlem storefront church the speaker feels weighted down beneath the deacon's scrutinizing gaze, admitting that, later in the poem, he can neither "grovel under the deacon's eyes" nor remain on his stairs. These images culminate in his depiction of the reality of the sea upon which he cannot perform the miracle of walking.

In addition, the second section of the poem contains sibilant sounds, especially in the passage "I walk in summer, innocently,/ . . . down Seventh, . . ./ twisting." This sibilance continues into the third section, where Wright skillfully deploys *ss* words such as "blessed" and the "less" suffix.

Themes and Meanings

Cooped up in his rooms, the artist-narrator cannot create. He must depart to see emptiness, to remember a vibrant and colorful life, and to fashion his aesthetic from both conditions.

Aesthetics has to do with the artful and beautiful qualities of an artifact or an expression. The arts are characterized by intangibles that tend to defy descriptive analysis, and a precise meaning of aesthetics and aesthetic qualities may be relative to the individual artist and perceiver. Everyone, however, whether creative artist, inventor, layperson, or devotee, responds emotionally and intellectually to aesthetic qualities of harmony, symmetry, motion or rhythm, perception, sonority and tone, and the effects these and related elements have on the senses.

In "Sketch for an Aesthetic Project," Wright associates the restless search for the moment of creation with memory, history, and immediate reality. His speaker relates the total experience of intimate awareness about his surroundings, and this intellectual totality cannot be divorced from what he knows experientially. Wright does not quote Kinsella spuriously, for love is the principle of the artist's desire to create something beautiful. An artistic person cannot function without love, just as the tension love produces must be recognized as being stifled should he remain pensive in his cold rooms, avoiding the world outside.

The speaker loves his tranquil home and he loves Harlem. He comes to recognize and accept his ability to assimilate both places just as he can assimilate place and history. Slavers and "ingenuous slavers" can make no art; their anticipations of landfall are fruitless. Their cargo means more to him because he can connect the descendants of the cargo to something wonderful even if it is maddening. The sickly images of "cankered bodies" and the "bloody parchments" are the stuff of creation.

The music of the last section culminates the gathering process of his understanding, for the aesthetic gesture springs from those balances described by the "mythic shriek" of awareness, the "illusion of solitude," the "swift and mad," the dark and light. Wright has found that aesthetic principles make for a delicate balance of these images to one who resorts to understanding history, the spirituality offered by the mundane, and the divinely inspired perceptions of one's own self-worth.

Ron Welburn

SKUNK HOUR

Author: Robert Lowell (1917-1977)
Type of poem: Lyric
First published: 1958; collected in *Life Studies*, 1959

The Poem

"Skunk Hour" is written in free verse, but with a formal pattern of eight six-line stanzas (sestets) with a loosely regular rhyme scheme. The title suggests a particular hour in the day—the hour when skunks are likely to come out—and implies that this hour occurs on a regular basis. The title hints that time will be an important element in the poem.

Set in Maine, where Robert Lowell had a summer home, the poem begins by showing a series of events that denote a decaying society: The elderly heiress has bought up the houses facing hers and let them go to ruin; the millionaire has lost his money and auctioned off his yacht; the homosexual decorator has used the tools of fishing (net, cork, and awl) to brighten his shop. These events suggest that the human order has somehow gone wrong. They are narrated as one tells a story, in the third person. Although they are recounted in the present tense, in each case the action has already occurred.

Beginning with the fifth stanza, exactly halfway through the poem, the poet enters in the first person. (Lowell's biography almost insists that the speaker and the poet be considered identical.) He remembers (in the past tense) "one dark night" when he drove his "Tudor Ford" up the hill to watch for lovers in their cars. In the only metaphor of the poem, he describes the cars as though they were boats, lying together "hull to hull." He concludes, "My mind's not right." From this point on, the poet speaks from immediate experience, and it becomes increasingly clear that the external circumstances of the first four stanzas reflect the poet's vision of himself.

From stanza 6 on, the reader "overhears" the poet's thoughts, as in a more conventional lyric. The poet listens to a love song on the radio and feels himself to be loveless, tormented: "I myself am hell," he says, in a phrase layered with reference. At the same time that the poet speaks it in the present, its reference is to John Milton's Satan in *Paradise Lost* (1667), which, in turn, refers to Dante's *La divina commedia* (c. 1320; *The Divine Comedy*). In this way, Lowell places himself in a literary history.

The actual present moment of this poem does not occur until the seventh stanza, when the skunks march down Main Street. The poet feels almost invisible, standing on the back steps, lonely and isolated, watching a mother skunk and her kittens march past the Trinitarian church, past him, to the garbage pail. He sees their glinting eyes in the moonlight and knows that they see him. The mother skunk, intent on a cup of sour cream, does not do what skunks can do when they are threatened; she simply looks back to the food and drops her tail.

The poem ends with the skunk's refusal to react, which seems important. She "will not scare." It is as if Lowell, by allowing time to flow around him, finds in the one present moment some answer to his sense of failure and alienation. The outside world had reflected the inner hell, but, in this moment of stillness, when the tail is lowered, there is affirmation. Whether it is an affirmation that resolves the problem of identity and relationship to others, the reader cannot know.

Forms and Devices

In *Life Studies*, 1959, Lowell broke from the formal verse for which he was already famous to write in free-verse lines. "Skunk Hour" is its final poem, unfolding in a pattern that exhibits Lowell's sure sense of rhyme. A quick examination of each stanza reveals its particular variation. "Skunk Hour" is more a study in sound, however; with its dense, packed language, it is very difficult to read aloud. There is often evidence of an iambic beat, as though that were the ghost rhythm on which the poem was built. Examples of this rhythm are the moments when the speaker says "My mind's not right" and the final line "and will not scare."

Sound seems, somehow, to mirror meaning. The shift from a continuous past to an active present is marked by a shift of consonants. The early use of *l* sounds — the soothing sound of the past — changes, in the later stanzas, into a harsh, intense present dominated by *r* and *k* sounds. In addition, an urgency of accented syllables, or stresses, alters the tone of the poem as it moves into the present. "They march on their soles up Main Street:/ white stripes, moonstruck eyes' red fire" (with its many spondees) slows the voice for emphasis.

Shortly after seeing Allen Ginsberg read his poetry in San Francisco in March, 1957, Lowell began to feel that his own poems were stiff and humorless. In *Life Studies*, published two years later, he worked to make them clearer and more colloquial. "Skunk Hour" is dedicated to the poet Elizabeth Bishop, whose work Lowell greatly admired. Her poem "The Armadillo" served as a model; Lowell admired its straightforward images and its use of fact. The images in "Skunk Hour" reveal a new directness of his own. Even such a strange and visually uncertain image as "A red fox stain covers Blue Hill" refers, in actuality, to a particular fall color in a specific place. There is also a hint of violence in the use of the word "stain," a foreshadowing of his mental state. The effect of these specific details is one of intimacy, but not necessarily of coherence. The reader sees things as the poet apprehends them. With equal ease, one sees into the mind of the poet as one experiences, with him, a moment of extreme pain. Nothing is cushioned through metaphor; the poem is harsh in its honesty.

There are layers of time working within "Skunk Hour." "Century," "season," "now," "night," "hour" — time seems to condense as though it were working toward the final moment on the steps. Yet the hour occurs nightly, so it expands in the form of recurrence — the recurrence of a natural order suggested by the skunks themselves. Time is, in some sense, the very subject of the poem. In this way, the poem could be said to work on a metaphorical level, but it is clearly left up to the reader to decide the meaning.

Themes and Meanings

Robert Lowell's poems demonstrate the fusion of a personal and historical past. Time blurs, yet the stasis achieved only emphasizes loss and a sense of an irretrievable past. The poems move inward, deepening their colors. Each successive layer of time adds texture and insight.

As the culminating poem of *Life Studies*, "Skunk Hour" ends a book that traces the deterioration of Western civilization, the demise of Lowell's prominent American family, and the disintegration of the poet's sense of self. Questioning his own sanity, Lowell exhibits what has come to be known as the "confessional" stance. He allows the reader to act as the priest, hearing the confession. It must be cautioned that the reader is priest, not psychiatrist. The object of confession is absolution and a state of grace. In Lowell, there is a sense of the life examined, over and over, in search of salvation. Other confessional poets, such as John Berryman and Sylvia Plath, do not necessarily reveal such a desire for redemption, but Lowell's poems always seem to be striving for a moment of grace.

Seen in this light, the "chalk dry and spar spire" of the Trinitarian church can be seen to represent the failure of religion to offer twentieth century answers. In his essay "On 'Skunk Hour,' " in *The Collected Prose* (1987), Lowell himself declared, "My night is not gracious, but secular, puritan, and agnostic. An existentialist night." In this personal wasteland, Lowell laments that the social order has failed him, that he has failed himself. His own narrowed circumstances have been placed in history, set against the backdrop of the town and against the living memory of the dark night that occasioned the poet's malaise.

"Skunk Hour" might be simply another poem about humankind's inability to live within its own history, an alien creature on the earth. There is a moment, however, when the poem literally, stops and holds its pose for a moment before going on. The speaker holds his breath. The mother skunk drops her tail. This is the moment when she decides to live and let live, disdaining an entry into the human world. The skunks are seen with a mixture of awe and amusement. Lowell refuses to end the poem on a note of transcendence; a flat statement of fact will have to suffice. The affirmation is ambiguous at best.

"Skunk Hour" is a combination of two modes of perception—memory and attention. It is rooted in attention, in the perception of the moment, yet memory is the medium through which the present is seen. Thus it carries the present and past simultaneously. The poem's cumulative effect is a meshing of time; it comes back into phase with itself. The final synthesis comes from a fullness and complexity surrounding the lyric moment. The present hell is only understood through the past—the "dark night" that allowed the poet, and therefore the reader, to find a source of hope in the skunk's active presence in the night.

Judith Kitchen

THE SLATE ODE

Author: Osip Mandelstam (1891-1938)
Type of poem: Ode
First published: 1928, as "Grifel'naia oda," in *Stikhotvoreniya*; collected in
  Selected Poems, 1973

The Poem

"The Slate Ode," written in 1923, is one of Osip Mandelstam's longer poems, consisting of nine stanzas of regular iambic tetrameter. That is the traditional Russian odic meter, although Mandelstam chooses an eight-line stanza over the more typical ten-line stanza. Calling his work an ode, Mandelstam is associating himself with the archaizing drive among Russian post-Symbolists, since the use of generic labels such as "ode" or "elegy" as a way of marking meaningful distinctions had been in decline since the 1830's, along with the hierarchy of poetic forms which held for the eighteenth century.

The modernist revival of such forms as the ode is part of an attempt to model a continuous history in an age of war and revolution, an age in which, as Mandelstam once wrote, "the contemporary European has been evicted from his own biography." "The Slate Ode" not only revives an archaic genre but also alludes to a specific predecessor poem, "Reka vremen," ("The River of Time"), composed on a slate tablet by the great eighteenth century poet Gavrila Derzhavin just before his death in 1816.

Mandelstam's poem seems to take as its setting a starry night landscape, in which stone and water (the elements of "The Slate Ode" and "The River of Time") predominate. For several reasons, however, this landscape will not stabilize. First, one of its elements, a flinty path, is said to come from an old song, and "song," in Russian verse, is a synonym for "poem." Second, there are no identifiable references to location; instead, the linguistic quality of the setting is emphasized in this poem which speaks of "the speech of slate and air." Third, the components that might suggest a specific setting will not stay in their expected places: If the poem locates a slate-pencil drawing on the "layered rock of the clouds," the landscape motifs must be primarily figurative. In other words, the details are not occasioned by a particular place but point instead to the movement of the poet's consciousness.

The poet appears in the second stanza, contained within a "we" that is characterized by a sheepish somnolence. By contrast, nature, represented by geological motifs, is an active writer, whose rough draft, written with water on the earth's surface, is ripening. In the third stanza, this draft is figured as a precipitous, deeply etched, stony landscape, rendered metaphorically as a vision of steeply vertical cities.

The fourth and fifth stanzas emphasize time rather than space. It is night, the time of poetic creativity, and the transient impressions of the day are fading. The fifth stanza—the "hinge" of the poem—announces a condition of ripeness, which in the following two stanzas will be transfered from nature to the materials in the poetic imagination, that is, the fruit ripened to bursting is the poem ready to take shape. Only now, having achieved access to his creative resources, does the poet speak as an "I," the first-person singular appearing in stanza 6. In stanza 7, the voice of memory and of the poetic tradition brings understanding and directs the poet's hand in a transcription that is at once instantaneous and firm. (For Mandelstam, the poetic legacy is carried by the voice, because he believed that a poet's verses preserved his actual voice.)

As is typical for Mandelstam, the triumph of the creative process triggers reflections on the poet's self-definition, which is the theme of the eighth stanza. In the final stanza, which closely echoes the first, the poet claims his place within Russian poetry, declaring his intention to effect a junction between his own verse and the verse of his great predecessors.

Forms and Devices

One of the characteristic features of Mandelstam's writings is his refusal to accept the modern opposition between nature and culture. Instead, he sees them as continuous with each other; as he put it in the opening line of "Priroda—tot zhe Rim," a 1914 lyric (the first clause is also the title), "Nature is the same as Rome, and was reflected in it." All of "The Slate Ode" is built on a master metaphor that equates nature and culture, or the physical processes of nature and the work of the poet. All that is already contained in the poem's key word, "slate."

Besides being a synecdoche for Derzhavin's last poem, the motif of slate triggers the whole string of geological images on the one hand and the image of the writer's slate pencil, the emblem of his poetic activity, on the other. In an illustrative example of the fusion of culture and nature, the scratching of the poet's pencil becomes the "slate screech," and the pencil points mutate into the beaks of fledgling birds.

More generally, geological history, pictured as writing, is imbued with conscious intention, while poetry becomes a form of natural history, of attending to nature's writing. On an even more abstract plane, mind and earth become each other's analogues. For example, water flowing back to its underground sources is a metaphor for poetic resources which are not yet ready to emerge from the unconscious. By the same token, a vertiginous landscape prefigures the soaring of the poet's imagination.

Finally, the equation of geology with poetry in the poem's ruling metaphor is implicated in Mandelstam's revision of Derzhavin. "The River of Time" is a deeply pessimistic meditation, which asserts that historical memory and poetry alike are doomed to oblivion. By contrast, "The Slate Ode" implies that although the cultural record must contain its terrors and violent shifts, poetry, like the geological record, can preserve everything. For Mandelstam, the water does not destroy but rather writes.

Themes and Meanings

When it first appeared, Mandelstam's "Slate Ode" was attacked for its obscurity; in subsequent years, however, it has been considered one of his masterpieces. It dates from a time of transition, a period of intense poetic creativity that would be succeeded by five years in which Mandelstam would write no verse. The poem is part of a prolonged attempt at stocktaking, in which the poet must decide what legacy he will bring from his prerevolutionary Russian-Jewish past into his postrevolutionary identity as a contributor to Soviet Russian literature. Hence his acceptance (in stanza 8) of the synthetic identity of the "double-dealer, with a double soul" and his refusal of the organic identity, suggested by such traditional trades as that of the "mason," "roofer," or "boatman" (the Russian more commonly means "shipbuilder").

Mandelstam's list of trades is full of suggestiveness for the Russian reader; the young Peter the Great, for example, worked in a Dutch shipyard and became the "shipbuilder" of the Russian Navy. The term "mason," however, is more likely to trigger associations for the English-speaking reader, who may be aware of the conspiracy theories, which antidemocractic and anti-Semitic forces have revived, linking the Masonic movement and the Jews. In Mandelstam's Russian, the dual reference to the mason's trade and to freemasonry is stronger. Hence, one implication of the poet's self-definition is a rejection of anti-Semitic stereotypes.

Mandelstam's prose and verse alike in the early and mid-1920's are filled with eschatological forebodings. While Mandelstam never conclusively abandoned the faith in revolution acquired in his formative years, he was only too aware of the antihuman values which were taking shape in the Soviet Union. Generally contemptuous of the past, the emerging Soviet worldview seemed to threaten the highest values transmitted by Russian culture with annihilation. If he makes of his ode a dialogue with Derzhavin's deathbed verses, it is because Mandelstam feels the attraction of Derzhavin's final judgment on human effort.

For the rest of his career, Mandelstam's verse will struggle against the threat of being separated from its own wellsprings. In "The Slate Ode," as in much of Mandelstam's verse from this period on, a frequently elliptical poetic language will encrypt the past to preserve it for the future. Humble, everyday objects will become the cryptograms for encoding the cultural text. Whereas the young Mandelstam had confidently measured his own ambitions against the glory of a Gothic cathedral ("Notre Dame," 1912), in "The Slate Ode" he makes the fragile pencil, scratching away at its indelible record, the emblem of his poetic mission.

Charles Isenberg

THE SLEEPERS

Author: Walt Whitman (1819-1892)
Type of poem: Lyric
First published: 1855, untitled, in *Leaves of Grass*; as "Night Poem," in *Leaves of Grass*, 1856; as "Sleep-Chasings," in *Leaves of Grass*, 1860; as "The Sleepers," in *Leaves of Grass*, 1871

The Poem

In its final version, "The Sleepers" contains 184 lines, in free verse, divided into eight sections with varying numbers of lines. In the first section, the speaker overcomes initial disorientation by fixing his attention on the ordered arrangement of sleepers, from children in their cradles to a mother sleeping with her child "carefully wrapt." The poet embraces all in his vision, arranging them in pairs of opposites. He pauses to comfort the restless. He lies down with others, to become each and all; he enters their dreams and becomes "a dance" of vitality. He encounters strange, delightful companions who move with him, "a gay gang of blackguards." The poet-speaker becomes both beloved and lover at the end of the first section: He is the woman waiting in the dark, and he is the man who arrives to love; then he is confused between them, as he becomes the dark itself. Finally, he fades away with the dark.

The second section is a descent toward death. Here the speaker is first an old woman, then a "sleepless widow," and finally a shroud covering a corpse in its coffin, in its grave.

In the third section, the speaker bursts from the grave to watch a swimmer battling "swift-running eddies" of the sea. The poet helplessly calls out for the sea to cease its assault on the swimming man, but the scene ends with the drowning of the swimmer, whose body is dashed until his corpse is driven out of sight.

As if from the same beach as in section 3, the next section reports an account of a shipwreck. Here, the poet hears sounds of distress and cries of fear that diminish into nothingness. Again, the speaker feels the nightmare experience of helplessness as he runs back and forth on the beach in a futile effort to prevent the wreck. Bodies are washed ashore, and the poet helps carry them to a barn, where they are laid out in rows, like all the other sleepers of the vision.

The fifth section retains the beach location as the speaker assumes the posture of George Washington at the Battle of Brooklyn Heights, in which the general suffers for his dying soldiers. This dissolves into a later scene of Washington bidding his soldiers farewell at the end of the war.

Section 6 continues the historical retrospective, though here it is more personal; the poet identifies with his mother in one of her memories. The object of vision here is a beautiful "red squaw" who visited the homestead of the poet's mother; that woman, seen only once, has remained in the memory of mother to become the vision of the poet.

Section 7 initiates a series of "returns." The sleepers dream of their homes. In a context of autumnal harvest, the poet gathers in the dreams of his sleepers: Sailors dream of sailing home; exiles, of returning to their native lands; emigrants from Ireland, Holland, and numerous other European countries dream of returning whence they came. In the poet's vision, however, there is no difference between going out and coming in. All "are averaged now," with differences and degrees dissolved by "night and sleep" into the beauty of "peace." In this condition, the soul is released to "enclose the world" in an order promising perfection to all. Grotesque distortions of human form "wait" for the beauty promised by spirit: "the twisted skull waits, the watery or rotten blood waits."

The poem concludes with a grand procession of humanity, as the sleepers "flow hand in hand" even as they lie prone in sleep. Here, the poet envisions a spiritual transfiguration of individuals into a universal brotherhood, awakening to a new reality in their sleeping dreams. Men and women join hands forever, as do fathers and sons, mothers and daughters, old and young, masters and slaves. Bodies are transformed by spiritual awakening, as the poet himself returns, entrusting himself to the night, every night, to be its lover as well as its child.

Forms and Devices

Each section of "The Sleepers" contains a varying number of stanzas, or verse paragraphs, with varying numbers of lines of free verse. Each stanzaic unit is also a grammatical whole, a statement complete in itself, whose form generally extends a first line into longer and longer lines. This creates an impression of energetic progress, from line to line, stanza to stanza, section to section.

Although each line of verse is "free" (that is, unmeasured), it is not without form. The devices that give form to the poem are parallelism, repetition, and controlled point of view. The most emphatic is parallelism. There is a balancing of grammatical units, usually at the beginnings of lines, to create a "rhetorical rhyme." For example, in the first stanza of section 1, lines 2 through 5 are introduced with present participles: "Stepping," "Bending," "Wandering," and "Pausing." These create continuous action, present process. The second stanza of section 1 consists of two lines, each beginning with the same word, "How": a couplet of initial, exact rhyme. Stanzas 3 through 5 in section 1 are a series (a catalog) of phrases and clauses introduced by "The." These lines of noun phrases (third-person objects) are countered in later stanzas with parallel first-person openings: "I stand," "I pass," "I go," and so on. Parallelism occurs at the ends as well as at the beginnings of lines, through repetition of the same grammatical forms and, sometimes, the same word: "sleep" or "sleeps" ends eight lines between lines 15 and 25.

Images of movement abound in the poem, outward balancing inward movement: The speaker "steps" out to start the poem, "pierces the darkness," "descends," "turns," and finally "returns." This movement is governed by a controlling "I" as a central point of view, outside the vision at the same time it enters and moves through the vision. The final three stanzas of the poem appropriately turn around initial, parallel line openings on the word "I"; seven of the last eight lines begin this way, as if each line were a radius emanating from a central "I." The subject "I," however, does not finally dominate, and a sense of great egotism is avoided since the final word of the poem is "you."

Themes and Meanings

Although the poem took different titles over the years of its revisions (indicating that it resisted the final formulation that a title can impose), its settled title focuses upon the figures asleep in a night of the poet's dreaming. The poet-speaker is one of the sleepers, but he is also all of them at once in his "vision" of them asleep, of them awake, and of them dead and dying. He enters the dreams of sleepers to become the figures of their dreams, just as they are the figures of his dreams.

There are three points of view, perhaps four, in "The Sleepers." The subject of sleeping becomes a theme of interest because of these shifting points of view, as sleeping is turned from a literal into a metaphorical term: physical sleep (as death-in-life), with its resting physical energy, is transformed into the spiritual energy of life-in-death. The mode of this transformation is poetic vision, a power of imagination capable of penetrating all objects; it reshapes the grotesque, shapes the shapeless, and restores life to the lifeless.

The most self-conscious point of view is that of the poet-speaker, who announces his movements of consciousness; he is aware that he sleeps and dreams in his sleep. This speaking subject is like the subject of psychoanalysis, the one who reports a dream as a memory recollected from sleep. There is another, more constricted, speaker *within* the poet-as-speaker: one who moves within the dream, the representative of the dreamer. The poem presents a double subject, waking and dreaming speakers. The dreaming speaker also divides, first into two, and then into several others. The first division produces a dream figure who can move as a sleeping companion with all other sleepers in the dream; the second division occurs when the representative of the dreamer enters the dreams of others, to become an "other" and many "others." The outermost limit is reached in the blankness of death. Rebelling against this blankness, the multiple points of view reorganize to become one again at the end, and the cycle is poised to repeat itself.

The meaning that emerges from this plurality of points of view is that life is various but unified. The poet's vision comprehends differences as spiritual communion, and sleep is the vehicle for the visionary experience born of "mother" night. Capable of healing and renewal, the poet is godlike, and his poem is creative.

Richard D. McGhee

A SMELL OF CORDWOOD

Author: Pablo Neruda (Neftalí Ricardo Reyes Basoalto, 1904-1973)
Type of poem: Ode
First published: 1956, as "Oda al olor de la leña," in *Nuevas odas elementales*;
   collected in *Selected Poems of Pablo Neruda*, 1961

The Poem

"A Smell of Cordwood" is an ode (a song of praise) in seven stanzas; it is written in free verse. The title is significant in that it states the rather unusual subject matter being praised: the smell of ordinary wood.

The opening stanza begins abruptly, *in medias res* (in the middle of things). The speaker of the poem describes the feeling of the cold and starry night as it rushes in through the door of his home "on an ocean/ of galloping hooves." Night is personified as an invading presence.

In the next brief stanza, out of the darkness, "like a hand," comes "the savage/ aroma/ of wood on the woodpile." Like the night that invaded the speaker's domicile, the aroma of wood is humanized; it savagely assaults and overwhelms the speaker's senses.

The third stanza infuses the odor of the wood with life and form; it "lives/ like a tree." The odor is so palpable, so intense, in fact, that the poet, deliberately confusing the senses, calls it "visible." The stanza ends with another metaphor. The wood becomes so "alive" that it is as if it "pulsed like a tree."

When the speaker describes the odor as "Vesture/ made visible" in the next stanza (two lines), the metaphor in the preceding stanza is continued. This line is a play on the biblical phrase "and the Word was made flesh." Instead of the Word, however, the odor is made flesh. Moreover, the word "vesture" has a religious connotation of its own; it recalls the vestments of a priest. The next stanza is also two lines long: "A visible/ breaking of branches." The odor of the wood, then, becomes as "visible" a vestment of the tree as a broken branch.

In the sixth stanza, the speaker of the poem turns back and reenters the house. He notices in the distance the sparkle of particles in the sky. Yet the smell of wood overpowers all other senses and takes hold of the speaker's heart. The metaphors used to compare the seizure of the heart by the smell are that of a hand grasping at the heart, jasmine assaulting the senses, and, finally, "a memory cherished."

In the last stanza, the lengthiest, the speaker tries to describe the scent of the wood in negative terms. It is not, for example, "harrowing/ pine odor," or "slashed/ eucalyptus," or "like/ the green/ exhalation/ of arbors." It is something more obscure, more subtle. The speaker says that it is a fragrance that offers itself only once. It awaited the speaker there, that night, and "struck like a wave," then it disappeared into the speaker's blood or became part of him as he opened the door to the night.

Forms and Devices

Pablo Neruda's poetics in "A Smell of Cordwood," as well as throughout the three volumes translated as *The Elementary Odes of Pablo Neruda* (1961), strongly based on clarity and simplicity, is effectively portrayed by, and revealed through, the typographical medium employed. In the typographical arrangement of "A Smell of Cordwood," the separation of lines and the white spaces between words, as well as between stanzas, influence the meaning of the poem in the same way that silences and pauses form an integral part of a musical composition.

Neruda makes use of numerous lines in which only one word appears. This line division is clearly a great help to the unsophisticated reader of poetry, allowing him or her to concentrate on one or two words at a time, to grasp their meaning before continuing further. The simplified syntax of the Elementary Odes is particularly effective when Neruda's subject matter is a description of nature, as in this poem. In this case, the description, proceeding step by step and sense by sense, is reflected in the typography, in which each aspect of the scent of cordwood is expressed in isolation, as a single unit. Every line is a separate brushstroke contributing to the total effect, yet every line is also capable of existing as a discrete unit. Neruda's method in the odes has been likened to that of the finest nature artists. Vincent van Gogh, for example, used such simple brushstrokes and colors in his paintings.

In several of the Elementary Odes, the short line also functions in a way that makes it suggestive of the subject matter. In this poem about odor, for example, Neruda uses lines as short and concise as gusts of night air. The typography of the poem very simply creates a perfect blend of intention, form, and content. As a result of employing the short line, as well as the consequent break with the traditional effects of metrics, Neruda's odes are not only among his most easily accessible works but are also among his most translatable works.

Besides the language and syntax, the imagery of the poem is nearly always clear and unequivocal. Meaning is often literal. In the poem, Neruda sings the essential themes of humankind and exalts one element that makes up the material world in its individual form: the sense of smell. The poem is joyful, optimistic, and clear; the world represented is coherent, rational, and structured—in a word, realistic.

Themes and Meanings

An almost blind faith in the truth of the senses is one of the major themes of Neruda's poem. As is the case with most of the Elementary Odes, "A Smell of Cordwood" is a canticle of material passion to a simple sensuous experience in this world. In Neruda's instinctive materialism and ardent surrender to nature, the poet exhibits a new romanticism, intuitional and primitive, a weapon aimed at the idealism and intellectualism of the modernists. In this poem he sought above all things to communicate, to abandon whatever might obscure the understanding of his reader.

The truth of the senses, in the poem, is self-evident and needs no complex analysis or interpretation. The point of departure for the speaker's experience appears small, insignificant, and not fully poetic. Neruda, however, quickly establishes an emotional link with the scent of cordwood. The speaker sees each aspect of that night as a gift; Neruda's poetry is also a gift to a world that offers him beauty and life. Poetry, like the scent of pine, is a vehicle through which to give back to the world some of the beauty first given by the world to the poet's senses.

The emotional link that the poet establishes with the fragrance in "A Smell of Cordwood" is accomplished by reminding the reader what the speaker's impression was when he smelled the scent for the first time: "a fragrance/ that gives itself/ once, and once/ only." By indirectly likening the scent offered by the wood to the sensuality a woman might offer, Neruda adds a human dimension to a basic property of nature that it did not have before. Consequently, the reader is reminded of the link between the natural scent and nature of humankind. Linking that natural world with the human world, particularly at the end of the poem, when the speaker states that the fragrance became "lost" in his blood, Neruda underscores the fact that not only the fragrance but also the memory of the fragrance will live on in the speaker as well as in the reader of the poem.

Genevieve Slomski

SNAKE

Author: D. H. Lawrence (1885-1930)
Type of poem: Lyric
First published: 1921; collected in *Birds, Beasts and Flowers*, 1923

The Poem

"Snake" is a seventy-four-line free-verse poem divided into nineteen verse paragraphs (stanzas of unequal length). Like many modern lyrics, it incorporates a narrative element, recording the poet's encounter with a snake at his water-trough. Through this structure and carefully mobilized imagery, the poet reveals his conflicted, deepening consciousness, which moves from casual description to epiphanic confession. Written when D. H. Lawrence and his wife Frieda were living in Taormina, Sicily, in 1920-1921, the poem is derived from Lawrence's actual experience there. Its imagery and themes, however, are anticipated in the second section of his 1917 essay "The Reality of Peace."

The setting is a hot July day upon which the poet takes his pitcher to the water-trough, where a snake is drinking. The first five verse paragraphs establish the scene and provide the occasion for the poet's initial, sensual description of the snake. Domestic and exotic images are combined as the pajama-clad poet observes the snake "In the deep, strange-scented shade of the great dark carob-tree." Light and dark are contrasted in the snake's golden color and the surrounding gloom. The poet conjures the creature's snakiness with emphasis on his "straight mouth," "slack long body," and flickering, "two-forked tongue." He also compares the snake to domesticated farm animals ("drinking cattle") and to a human by referring to the snake as "someone" and describing him as musing. This imagery, which suggests an ascending hierarchy, anticipates the symbolic leaps later in the poem, when the poet compares the snake to a god, a king, and, finally, "one of the lords/ Of life."

The sixth verse paragraph introduces the poet's inner conflict, arising from his voice of education that instructs him to kill the "venomous" snake. The five ensuing ones trace the poet's intensifying crisis as voices challenge his manhood and courage as well as his instinctive admiration for the animal, which he feels has honored him by seeking his hospitality at the trough. He includes the reader in his dialectical self-scrutiny:

> Was it cowardice, that I dared not kill him?
> Was it perversity, that I longed to talk to him?
> Was it humility, to feel so honoured?

In verse paragraphs 12 through 14, the conflict is transposed outside the poet, when the speaker hurls a log in protest at the withdrawing snake. The concluding stanzas record the poet's fascination, regret, guilt, admiration, and pettiness, respectively. Lawrence's invocation of the albatross from Samuel Taylor Coleridge's "The Rime of the Ancient Mariner" underscores the poet's sense of sin and need for atonement. His use of the possessive "my" to refer to the otherworldly snake suggests that a profound transformation has occurred. Though banishing the creature by his "mean act," he claims it as his own. The implication is that were the snake to return, the poet would submit to its presence, its coming and going alike.

Forms and Devices

The free-verse form of "Snake," a form Lawrence champions in his essay "Poetry of the Present" (1918), facilitates his drive for knowledge through meditation and emotional perception. The long, unrhymed lines are written in straightforward, colloquial diction, inviting the reader to participate in the poet's experience. Divided into verse paragraphs, they approximate the quality of prose and, like the essays Lawrence was writing at about the same time, track a process of argument and self-discovery.

The lines conform at once to the physical and emotional experience of the poem, to the object of the long, slithering snake, and to the poet's fluid mind, which travels over experience, comprehending itself in the light of what it finds. Many free-verse conventions derived from Walt Whitman's poetry appear in Lawrence's poem: organic rhythm, parallel structure, and repetition. Yet the tone of the poem is personal in a way Whitman's poems are often not, and Lawrence deploys imagery more in the vein of the Imagists and the English Romantic poets.

In focusing on the snake, Lawrence recalls past literary texts, from *Genesis* to John Milton's *Paradise Lost* (1667, 1674), but Lawrence uses traditional imagery for his own ends. The serpent of eternity, the phallic god, the snake, usually a figure of evil, is a positive force here, while the poet has "something to expiate." Images of light and dark, often associated with virtue and sin respectively, are upended: "For in Sicily the black, black snakes are innocent, the gold are venomous." Even the black hole into which the snake retreats appears as an entrance to some desirable mystery. It is "the dark door of the secret earth," while the poet's "intense still noon" is, by contrast, a flood of missed opportunity and failure. In Lawrence's poem, the snake is a symbol for those elements associated with it: darkness, death, the underworld, and the erotic; the poet's ambivalent feelings are directed at those things as well.

Through Lawrence's particular turn of figures, he presents a central paradox in the poem. Contrary to what education dictates, the poisonous yellow snake is appealing. For all its reptilian features, it appears lordly, superior to man, not (as the customary view would have it) beneath him. Description becomes a means of perception as Lawrence transforms the snake from a creature that is obviously not human to one that is divine.

While the snake is clearly a metaphor, Lawrence attempts to depict the animal as it really is. He focuses on its concrete characteristics. In doing so, he manages to be personal, while keeping emotion in check, refuting the critic R. P. Blackmur's claim that Lawrence's use of expressive form excludes craft and control of imagery. The poignancy of the last four lines derives precisely from Lawrence's control throughout the poem and his ability to find imagery that does the emotional work of the poem—that presents, borrowing T. S. Eliot's phrase, an "objective correlative" for the feelings expressed.

Themes and Meanings

In "Snake," as in many of the poems in the collection *Birds, Beasts and Flowers* (1923), Lawrence explores the otherness of the creature world, defined chiefly by its purity and innocence in contrast to the corrupt human world. The poem is a subtle celebration of nature in the Wordsworthian tradition of nature poetry, wherein the ordinary becomes an occasion for celebration and revelation.

Lawrence's intense contemplation reveals what he shares with the snake (that creature state within himself) and what divides him from it—human consciousness. His imagery reflects the distinction he often makes between two modes of consciousness, that of intuition or instinct (the blood self) represented by the snake and that of intellect (the nerve/brain self) evident in humans. As he asserts in "Fantasia of the Unconscious" (1922), the snake's consciousness "is *only* dynamic, and noncerebral," while a person is composed of warring elements of instinct and willful intellect. In the poem, this conflict is dramatized first in the poet's instinctive attraction to the snake and the educated voice which tells him to destroy it, and again in his banishment of the snake and subsequent longing for its return.

The liabilities of human education is a recurring theme in Lawrence's work. In "Fantasia of the Unconscious," he argues that established ideas that do not square with a human being's "dynamic nature" arrest his individuality and damage his psyche. Clearly, in "Snake," the ideas fostered by education outside the poet impede his submission to the creature he admires.

Rather than deny instinct, Lawrence would strive for an acceptance of duality and polarity in the world as well as in himself. In "Snake," polarity and struggle are reflected in the contrasting juxtaposed imagery, the flux of conflicting feelings, and the ordinary diction with its mythic overtones. They find balance or resolution in the closing epiphany, in which Lawrence realizes artistically a need expressed philosophically in "The Reality of Peace": "I must humble myself before the abhorred serpent and give him his dues as he lifts his flattened head from the secret grass of my soul."

In the wake of Harold Bloom's *The Anxiety of Influence* (1973), it is tempting to read "Snake" as an expression of Lawrence's ambivalence toward his literary precursors (Thomas Hardy, William Wordsworth, and Milton, among others) and his anxiety over the problem of originality. How can any poet writing after William Shakespeare and Milton escape being derivative?

Such a reading is inspired by Lawrence's imagery, which posits the poet as a "second comer" to the trough, the snake which figures throughout literature, and the allusion to Coleridge at the end of a poem wherein the poet ostensibly disavows his education. Such a reading is valuable and justified inasmuch as Lawrence was steeped in literature of the past, and it adds a provocative dimension to the other themes and meanings of the poem.

Gardner McFall

SNAPSHOTS OF A DAUGHTER-IN-LAW

Author: Adrienne Rich (1929-   )
Type of poem: Dramatic monologue
First published: 1963, in *Snapshots of a Daughter-in-Law*

The Poem

"Snapshots of a Daughter-in-Law" is a ten-part poem, with each part composed of an uneven number of lines and stanzas. The speaker appears at first to address an older woman, probably the mother-in-law of the other, younger woman in the poem, a daughter-in-law. The two women are respectively "you" and "she," but neither of the two women "converses" with the speaker in the poem.

In each part, the speaker refers or alludes to a literary passage or phrase. The references provide her with a foundation for a philosophical discussion with the two women. Italicized phrases in the poem indicate the speaker's reference to another source, and at times she alters the original quotation. In part 3, for example, "*ma semblable, ma soeur*" is a variation of the phrase by the French poet Charles Baudelaire that reads, "mon semblable, mon frère." By changing *frère* (brother) to *soeur* (sister), the speaker emphasizes her discussion of womanhood.

Although the parts are numbered, the poem as a whole does not develop into a chronological narrative. The speaker structures her thoughts according to emotions or experiences. The first four parts of the poem set up the strained relationship between the two women in a series of "snapshots." The older woman, "once a belle in Shreveport," still dresses and plays the part of a Southern debutante. The speaker is critical of her fineries and accuses the older woman of a terrible sacrifice. The mother-in-law is now in the prime of her life, but because she chose superficial beauty over developing her intellectual skills, her mind is now "heavy with useless experience, rich/ with suspicion, rumor, fantasy."

In the third stanza of part 1, the daughter-in-law is characterized as "Nervy" and "glowering." She considers her mother-in-law's uselessness and, in the second part, the younger woman is caught in vignettes which reveal her dissatisfaction with domestic life. She hears voices or remembers something she had previously read; clearly she is struggling with what she thinks set against what she does as a dutiful daughter-in-law. In the next two parts, the speaker uses a kind of verbal camera to capture the two in snapshots which depict their conflict.

The next six parts are devoted to the thoughts roaring in the younger woman's mind. As the poem progresses, the reader begins to sense that the speaker and the young woman share an uncanny resemblance. In fact, toward the end of the poem, "you" and "I" become "we," and it is then obvious that all along the speaker has been criticizing her self.

Forms and Devices

The profusion of literary voices and the shifts in address between the speaker and the two women are confusing until the reader realizes that the speaker's perspectives are those of the daughter-in-law. The relationship that the speaker/daughter-in-law has with the older woman is riddled with their differences in attitude, values, and expectations.

The speaker is more comfortable speaking of the daughter-in-law—indeed, of herself—as a "she" rather than as "I" to gain psychological distance from the older woman, whose values she rejects. The younger woman's mind is fertile, though unexpressed, given the constraints of everyday life. Rather than have time to develop or write down her thoughts, she is seen making coffee or "dusting everything on the whatnot every day of life." The apparent frustration is revealed in the snapshots of her "Banging the coffee-pot into the sink" and sneaking moments to read while "waiting/ for the iron to heat," or "while the jellies boil and scum."

The poem is interspersed with the voices of learned men and women which the daughter-in-law might have encountered in those precious stolen moments of reading. The voices challenge the conventions—"*tempora and mores*" (times and customs)—of being a woman. The wisdom of thinkers such as the feminists Mary Wollstonecraft (part 7) and Simone de Beauvoir (part 10) as well as the poets Baudelaire (part 3) and Emily Dickinson (part 4) augment the speaker's own thoughts.

The literary allusions provide the speaker with authority as she criticizes the kind of lives women such as the mother-in-law lead. At the same time, the speaker does not yet know how to transform her knowledge into action. In part 5, she is seen shaving her legs as she ironically considers this female beauty ritual with others—"*Dulce ridens, dulce loquens*" (sweet laughter, sweet chatter).

The allusions authorize and justify the speaker's dissatisfaction, and they allow her to think beyond the everyday facts of existence. With them, she makes metaphors for her perceived entrapment, such as the image of the caged bird in parts 3, 4, and 6. By part 10, the speaker offers a snapshot of freedom: "Her mind full to the wind, I see her plunge/ breasted and glancing through the currents,/ taking the light upon her." Although the daughter-in-law's burden, or "her cargo," is never lightened, it has—through the inspiration of other voices—been "delivered/ [made] palpable/ ours."

Throughout the poem, the reader is led through the speaker's emotions and intellect. Because the speaker is actually addressing her own self in the role of a daughter-in-law, the poem's dramatic monologue is a kind of self-education as well. The poem is thus highly personal in the way it develops and in the choice of literary voices presented.

The poem's difficulty arises from the speaker's use of unfamiliar words and phrases. This strategy, however, is essential to the poem because it expresses and heightens the speaker's situation: She is an educated woman whose "*fertilisante douleur*" (enriching pain) is confinement to household chores. She will not simply accept the limitations of this domain; unfortunately, neither is she shown actively rebelling against her present condition. The voices painfully remind her that her life is unsatisfactory, but they stop short of prescribing a cure.

Nevertheless, while the poem seems to end on this discouraging note, the self-criticisms have been an educational process. The speaker has carefully scrutinized snapshots of herself. As she identifies the moments and causes of her dissatisfaction, the voices help her to enact a drama that makes it possible for the speaker to tell herself in the monologue that she must take action.

Themes and Meanings

Adrienne Rich wrote the poem over a period of two years when she herself was married to a Harvard economist and was a young mother with three children. Like the daughter-in-law in the poem, Rich lived within patriarchal structures that constrain a woman's intellect. In the early 1960's, white, middle-class, and educated women were expected to find men to marry and then be in the service of the American family. The speaker in the poem sees herself as a daughter-in-law, or as a person who exists in relation to other people and structures.

The conflict between the mother-in-law and the younger woman in the early part of the poem expresses the latter's desire to break from the confining conventions. They are "two handsome women, gripped in argument,/ each proud, acute, subtle" and "knowing themselves too well in one another" they provide the other with impetus to perceive differences in their entrapments: The mother-in-law's outworn beauty and the daughter-in-law's fertile intelligence are the main sources of their differences.

In part 6, the mother-in-law asks, "has Nature shown/ her household books to you, daughter-in-law,/ that her sons never saw?" The tone is contentious, but at heart, the older woman seems also to goad the younger woman onward in the latter's intellectual quest, as though to say, it may be too late for me, but not yet for you. By part 9, the speaker is aware that the disagreements between women are finally harmful to all women: "The argument *ad feminam*, all the old knives/ that have rusted in my back, I drive in yours" (from part 3) becomes a realization in part 9 that "Our blight has been our sinecure." The "our" is significant, since it signifies union rather than division. The "martyred ambition" of all women, then, becomes an important theme for the entire poem.

Significantly, the mother-in-law appears only in the first half of the poem, even though the break between the two remains ambiguous. Because the younger woman starts contemplating the literary voices rather than expending energy fighting with the mother-in-law, she embarks on a truly individual project. She demonstrates her emancipation in the second half of the poem by reflecting upon and questioning the value of the voices.

In this early poem, Rich was discovering the ways that women speak to each other and, most important, to themselves. "Snapshots of a Daughter-in-Law," with its suggestions of camera shots and shifts in focus, is mostly a poem of the young woman's mind. The speaker refers to herself as "she" to indicate the difficulty of perceiving herself as an autonomous individual.

The poem's tone is self-admonishing at times and, especially in the domestic snapshots of herself, the speaker is extremely critical. The portrait of the physical woman confined at home is not flattering: She is sullen, even vehement in her actions. The woman's strength resides in her mind and thoughts, where she rebukes the conventions and hears the orchestration of voices that signify a real need to further her intellectual growth.

Cynthia Wong

THE SNOWSTORM

Author: Marina Tsvetayeva (1892-1941)
Type of poem: Verse drama
First published: 1923, as *Metel*; in *Izbrannye proizvedeniya*, 1965

The Poem

    The Snowstorm is a short play that Marina Tsvetayeva subtitled "dramatic scenes in verse." It is the first of Tsvetayeva's dramatic works and was written in Moscow in December, 1918. Tsvetayeva's early dramatic works are written in a neoromantic style. Although Tsvetayeva is not generally considered as one of the Russian Symbolist writers, or as a member of any group of poets writing during what is known as the Silver Age of Russian poetry, this play is noticeably influenced by the Symbolists.

    The play takes place at an inn in Bohemia on New Year's Eve. A group of travelers is caught in a snowstorm. As is typical of a Symbolist play, the characters are types. They do not have individual identities, but instead represent a certain group of characteristics. An Innkeeper, a Huntsman, a Trader, an Old Woman, and a Lady in a Cape are gathered. The Old Woman is described as representing the essence of the eighteenth century. The Lady in the Cape remains aloof from the rest of the group, and her identity remains a mystery until near the end of the play. The three men seem merely to provide a backdrop of vulgarity to contrast with the action in the final scene. In that respect, they function as a chorus.

    After defending the Lady from the sarcastic comments of the three men, the Old Woman gives the Lady a diamond ring that was once given to her by the king. It is understood that she must have the ring, but no explanation is offered. When the ring is given, sleigh bells are heard. A Gentleman in a Cape appears who introduces himself as Prince of the Moon, Chevalier of the Rotonde, and Knight of the Rose.

    The Lady in the Cape turns out to be the Countess Lanska, who has suddenly realized that she no longer loves her husband and has set out in the snowstorm, not knowing quite why she did so. She talks to the Gentleman with great intimacy, feeling sure that she has met him before. The dialogue grows increasingly fantastic as the Gentleman confesses that they knew each other in a previous existence and that theirs is a preordained encounter. He puts a spell on her, forcing her to forget the encounter, and departs while she sleeps. He then disappears at the stroke of midnight, accompanied, once again, by the ringing of sleighbells.

    This drama in verse is not formally divided into acts, probably as a result of its brevity, but three scenes can be easily distinguished. The first scene consists of the arrival of the travelers at the inn and the ensuing conversation of the Trader, the Huntsman, and the Innkeeper. The second scene includes the soliloquy of the Old Woman and the cryptic exchange between the Old Woman and the Lady. The final scene is the mystical conversation that occurs between the Lady in the Cape and the mysterious Gentleman.

While the play does preserve the the the unities of time, place, and action thought to be essential to classical dramatic works, the plot, in the neoromantic vein of the Symbolists, is minimal. The action of the play gradually ascends from the vulgarity of the three men to the archaic speech of the Old Woman and finally to the mystical meeting of the Gentleman and the Lady. The action progresses from the real world to a world of higher forms.

Forms and Devices

In this drama, Tsvetayeva experiments with the elliptical style that is characteristic of her later verse. As in her lyrics, the verses begin in a regular metrical pattern and then gradually vary in rhythm. Tsvetayeva varies her style according to each character, although the style of writing remains essentially her own. In fact, Tsvetayeva is often noted for her ability to sustain different tones within the same collection of verse. In the first section of the play, the elliptical style lends a quality of colloquial speech to the opening conversation of the three men.

The exchange between the Lady and the Gentleman in the last section is modeled on Aleksandr Blok's style, as is Tsvetayeva's later "Verses to Blok." Repetition of the first word of the stanza is prominent in this section, lending an incantatory quality to the conversation. It is reminiscent of the singsong quality of a prayer. The speech of the Old Woman and the Gentleman is marked by archaisms and the longer lines characteristic of eighteenth century Russian versification. Although the repetitive patterning and archaisms are reminiscent of Blok, they are successfully assimilated into Tsvetayeva's lyric poetry. Tsvetayeva's later poetry is characterized by a mixture of colloquial and archaic diction. She also experimented with the repetition of sounds and roots of words in her mature verse as well as simply the repetition of certain words.

The similarities in the characterization of the Gentleman in the Cape and the Lady in the Cape are another significant aspect of Tsvetayeva's work as a whole. The main characters in her longer, epic poems often have qualities associated with the opposite sex; she often pairs male and female characters to represent two halves of the whole. This seems to be true of the Lady and Gentleman in *The Snowstorm*.

The play is couched in imagery typically found in Symbolist poetry. The most important of these images is the snowstorm itself. In the romantic tradition, the poet was considered to have a special bond with nature. Nature often reflected the inner world of the poet. In Symbolist verse, nature has a mystical function. It often creates a passageway to a spiritual realm. For the Russian Symbolists, this higher world was embodied in the form of a woman, the Divine Sophia.

Tsvetayeva, in her mature verse, tends to transform the external world into an inner reality. Images of nature are not very prominent in most of her poetry. In this particular work, however, she uses the image of the snowstorm in a way that is similar to that of the Symbolists. The snowstorm obscures everyday reality. By obscuring this world, it allows passage to a higher, but still mysterious, form of reality. Only a chosen few are able to catch a glimpse of it. The Lady in the Cape leaves the world of everyday reality — and her husband — in the storm and then passes into the magical world of the Gentleman in the Cape.

Themes and Meanings

The basic situation of the play is taken from the work of the Russian Symbolist poet Aleksandr Blok, whom Tsvetayeva greatly admired. In Blok's play *Neznakomka* (1906; mysterious woman), as in *The Snowstorm*, there is a mysterious bond between an astral being and a chosen mortal. The main character in Blok's play, however, is a poet who almost meets the embodiment of his own philosophical construction. Blok's play takes on a rather satirical tone. He pokes fun at images from his own poetry and ideas associated with the Symbolists.

Tsvetayeva's play, on the other hand, cannot be perceived as satirical in any way. Another significant difference lies in the fact that the genders of the protagonists are reversed in Tsvetayeva's play. The woman is mortal while the man is the being from another plane.

The play as a whole is a work in the tradition of Russian Symbolism. The concept of escaping from an unbearable present into the world of imagination is an idea taken from the Symbolist tradition. This concept is, however, central to Tsvetayeva's work. It seems that Tsvetayeva had a natural affinity for many of the concerns of the Russian Symbolists. Her feeling of alienation from Russian society and from the émigré society of Berlin and Paris bred a desire to escape from this world. Tsvetayeva escaped into the world of her poetic imagination.

The escapist tendency of the settings and treatments in her plays is prominent in her lyric output as well. In Tsvetayeva's work, there is an impulse toward a fixed world of peace and transcendence. *The Snowstorm* exhibits a fairy-tale quality with its fantastic plot and two-dimensional characters. Tsvetayeva was a master of transforming everyday reality into myth. In other poems, she often cast herself in the roles of literary or mythic personae, such as Phaedra or Ophelia.

There has been no known attempt to produce any of Tsvetayeva's verse dramas on stage. Tsvetayeva's dramatic works should really be considered poems in dramatic form rather than plays. Tsvetayeva had matured as a lyric poet at the time this first drama was written, but was just beginning to experiment in dramatic forms. While this short drama in verse is not a striking contribution to the development of Russian literature of the period, it remains a significant part of Marina Tsvetayeva's literary achievement.

Pamela Pavliscak

THE SOLDIER

Author: Rupert Brooke (1887-1915)
Type of poem: Sonnet
First published: 1915, in *1914 and Other Poems*

The Poem

"The Soldier" is a sonnet of two stanzas: an octet of eight lines and a sestet of six lines. It is the last in a series of five sonnets composed shortly after the outbreak of World War I. The poems are linked by theme as well as form; all reflect idealism and optimism in the face of war, expressing the idea of release through self-sacrifice that many experienced with the coming of that war. "The Soldier" is about the probable death of a soldier, but the poem has little to do with dying.

The first stanza establishes the situation. The first-person speaker requests that "If I should die, think only this of me:/ That there's some corner of a foreign field/ That is for ever England." Even in the war's earliest stages there was the realization that the battles would result in death for at least some of the combatants. The pain of dying or the physical degradation of death are totally absent, however; the references that follow are all to life. Brooke asserts that where his body is eventually buried, "a richer dust [will be] concealed." The dust of his body is richer than that surrounding it because he was a part of his country. The England that Brooke describes exhibits the characteristics of the rural countryside — in particular, a tranquil landscape like that of his native Cambridgeshire. The "English air," the flowers, rivers, roads, paths, and "suns of home" all define what the narrator claims that his country gave to and forged in him.

The second stanza assumes the speaker's death; however, death itself is absent: The conditional "if" of the first stanza has simply happened. As a result, the speaker has become transfigured: "this heart, all evil shed away,/ A pulse in the eternal mind." In his death, the narrator returns something of what England gave to him as he "gives somewhere back the thoughts by England given." The references are again to life, not death: "dreams happy as her day," "laughter," and "hearts at peace, under an English heaven."

The poem celebrates an idealized vision of pastoral England and the noble qualities of her inhabitants. Brooke's language emphasizes the universal, so that the England of the poem becomes every soldier's home, and the dead soldier is every Englishman. The tone is uplifting and idealistic but also self-sacrificial. There is a sense of romantic inevitability about the privilege and duty of dying for one's country. Feelings of patriotism and nationalism give nobility to that sacrifice, a sacrifice willingly crowned by death.

Forms and Devices

In "The Soldier," Brooke demonstrates his mastery of the sonnet, using the classic form to heighten the decorum and idealization conveyed by the poem. The long iambic pentameter lines and disciplined rhyme scheme enhance the poem's formal tone. Interestingly, Brooke uses the form originally borrowed from the Italian Renaissance poet Petrarch rather than the modified one popularized by William Shakespeare, who converted the octet and sestet of the Petrarchan sonnet into the three quatrains and couplet of the English sonnet. The advantage is that the Italian sonnet's sestet allows a more leisurely, fully developed concluding statement.

The imagery of the poem revolves around the generalities of the idealized English countryside. Brooke, in the first stanza, makes use of a litany of scenes from nature: "her flowers to love, her ways to roam,/ . . . breathing English air,/ Washed by the rivers, blest by suns of home." The images are almost placid in feeling, conveying a sense of Edenic escape. Brooke and many of his generation in the years before the war attempted to distance themselves from what they perceived as the corrupting influences of the too urban, modern world of early twentieth century Britain.

Brooke's rural images might also be seen as an intentional contrast to the horrors of modern warfare. Brooke had no experience in battle, but as a member of the upper-middle classes, acquainted with such politicians as Winston Churchill (then head of the Admiralty), he must have known the destruction that industry and technology would bring to the war. The rural images of a preindustrial England evoked in the poem may represent a deliberate denial of the barbed wire and machine guns of no-man's-land.

Brooke uses the melodic effects of assonance and alliteration throughout "The Soldier." He repeats the long *i* sound in "I" and "die" in the first line and the short *e* in "for ever England" in the third. Examples of alliteration are even more abundant, among them the repeated *f* in "foreign field," the play on "rich" and "richer" in the fourth line, the sonorous *b*, *s*, and *r* sounds of the seventh and eighth lines, and the *s*, *d*, *l*, and *h* sounds in the last three lines. He also reinforces his patriotic theme by repeating the words "England" and "English" on six occasions in the poem's fourteen lines.

Critics have also noted the use of what is sometimes called "high" diction by many writers in the late nineteenth and early twentieth centuries. Brooke's "The Soldier" exemplifies this choice of language. Rather than discussing dead bodies, he uses the word "dust"; instead of the battlefield or the front, "field" suffices; "heaven" is preferred to sky. Perhaps his most famous use of such diction comes from another of his poems, "The Dead," also printed in *1914 and Other Poems*: "the red/ Sweet wine of youth" becomes a euphemism for blood. This selection of alternative words reflects the revived interest in the chivalry of the Middle Ages which had become so common among the educated classes, again in reaction to the wrenching transformation caused by the industrial revolution.

Themes and Meanings

Brooke's "The Soldier" is one of the most often quoted of the many poems which were written during World War I, a war that affected a significant number of poets, particularly from Great Britain. Brooke's poems were among the first, but he was later joined by Edmund Blunden, Robert Graves, Siegfried Sassoon, Isaac Rosenberg, and Wilfred Owen. All responded to the challenge and trauma engendered by the "Great War," though in disparate ways.

"The Soldier" is less a war poem than an elegy on sacrifice. The subject is ostensibly war, and the speaker is a soldier, but there is nothing in the poem that suggests warfare as such. Instead, the poem justifies the soldier's willing sacrifice on "a foreign field," an explanation that has more to do with idealized concepts about oneself and one's country than the causes of war. There is nothing about the enemy or fighting, and only one direct reference to death, at the very beginning of the poem. Even this reference is softened by the qualifying "if," although the rest of the poem assumes that the speaker will indeed die.

What one should sacrifice himself for is his country, underscored by the constant use of "England" or "English" throughout the poem. This reflects the strong sense of nationalism endemic throughout Western civilization in the early twentieth century. As traditional religious feelings lost their impact upon some sections of society, nationalism became, for many, a new religion worthy of worship and commitment.

Yet "The Soldier" is a paean not to the England of Brooke's day so much as to the ideal of a pastoral England. This nostalgic vision excluded the present, in which factories and cities had become the norm. Brooke's poem is an elegy on nature and the transcendent values of the natural world, as manifested in the English landscape.

The poem is also about escape — not only from the ugly industrialism and urbanization which disgusted Brooke, but also from the frustrations of personal life. To die can be a release, and to die in a noble cause justifies the self's sacrifice. Brooke was not unique: Many in 1914 saw the war as a release from lives stultified by personal and societal obstacles.

Brooke's idealism did not long survive him. He enlisted in the military, but before he could see action in battle he died of infection in the spring of 1915. The war went on, and the number of deaths multiplied — there were sixty thousand British casualties, for example, at the first day of the Battle of the Somme in 1916. For other poets, the war lost its allure and death its nobility; in Wilfred Owen's "Dulce et Decorum Est," to die for one's country became an obscenity. In that context, Brooke's "The Soldier" appeared only naïve. His idealism was replaced by a world without ideals; his love of his English countryside gave way to a lost generation. Nevertheless, the search for transcendent meaning in life and the commitment to a noble cause have been recurring themes throughout human history; perhaps ultimately "The Soldier" is less a poem praising war and patriotism than it is a quest for personal identity.

Eugene Larson

SOMEWHERE I HAVE NEVER TRAVELLED, GLADLY BEYOND

Author: E. E. Cummings (1894-1962)
Type of poem: Lyric
First published: 1931, in *W* (ViVa)

The Poem

The poem "somewhere i have never travelled,gladly beyond" first appeared in E. E. Cummings' *W* (ViVa), a collection of seventy poems. It is poem 57 in a section often labeled "Poems in Praise of Love and Lovers." While the first thirty-five poems in the collection emphasize the author's low estimate of humans as social animals, the final half stresses a positive view of humankind based on individual love and on the bonding created by relationships.

The poem is an interior monologue using Cummings' lyric and mythic style. Using the Renaissance archetypes of gardens, flowers, and nature as symbols for his mistress and her laudable qualities, Cummings explores the essential rhythms and cycles of the natural world while drawing parallels to idyllic love.

The woman in the poem is thought to be Anne Barton, a witty, vivacious socialite who began an affair with Cummings in 1925. She was his second love, and she restored his liveliness of spirit after his disastrous affair with Elaine Thayer, a married woman who bore Cummings' first child. The poem begins with a travel/discovery image, as Cummings tries to explore the nature of his relationship with the woman. He is captivated by her but finds her very nearness disconcerting; it reveals what he is missing without her. Stanzas 2 and 3 picture Cummings as a flower, a reversal of the typical comparison of women to flowers; it also portrays the woman as spring and snow, natural and opposing elements. The opening and closing of the flower signify the power of the woman to control Cummings; her very touch opens his petals or closes the heart of his flower.

The woman's frailty, mentioned in stanza 1, is reiterated in stanza 4; paradoxically, it is the source of her power. This power is intense and compelling; it has the power to "render death and forever with each breathing" (line 16). Cummings' effort to understand the incomprehensible is stressed in the final stanza, but he is only able to say that the inexplicable exists in such depth that words cannot do it justice.

Though the poem is basically positive and consists of unabashed praise, several paradoxes seem to capture the problems of love as well. This portrait is at times disconcerting, for "beyond any experience" may suggest an inner stillness beyond reach that the poet can not obtain. A "remote voice" also implies the unpleasant possibility of loss; the "silence" may suggest either muffled suppression or quiet peace.

Finally, the touch imagery suggests not only physical contact but also an inability to comprehend or come to grips with a situation. Such a picture accurately paints the textures and color of love—it is both bane and blessing.

Forms and Devices

Cummings' "somewhere i have never travelled,gladly beyond" utilizes several experimental forms in order to transport the reader beyond the seen world into the unseen. The poem's synesthetic style is the most important innovation here; Cummings linguistically merges each of the five senses with traits that belong to another sense. The poem begins with sight (eyes) but also emphasizes sound (silence). The second, third, and fourth stanzas deal with the sense of touch and revolve around variations based on the words "closed" and "open." Yet the ability to feel is also strangely joined with the sight image of stanza 1 as the words "look," "colour," "petal," and "rose" in the middle stanza imply the necessity of vision.

The synesthesia repeats in stanza 5 as Cummings joins sound and sight in the words "the voice of your eyes." Smell is also implied in "deeper than all roses." The images culminate in touch, smell, sound, a visual image (having small hands), and the personification of rain.

Experiments with punctuation, capitalization, ellipsis, and fragmentation are also part of the uniqueness of the poem. For example, commas, semicolons, colons, and parentheses are present, while no periods are used. As a result, the reader slides effortlessly from idea to idea, and a simultaneousness of imagery is created.

Other poetic techniques employed by Cummings in the poem include oxymoron and simile. Oxymoron, the joining of opposites, is evident in "the power of your intense fragility" and "rendering death and forever with each breathing." Similes, comparisons using "like" or "as," are evident in the reference to the beloved as "Spring" or to himself as the heart of a flower. Personification is also used when Cummings gives human qualities to texture, flowers, and rain.

Another factor is Cummings' word choices, which suggest a linguistic joining of form and meaning. The complexity of the love relationship is expressed in monosyllabic words with ordinary suffixes. This joining is also evident in the meter of the poem, which appears to be a type of sprung-rhythm pentameter and suggests the flexibility of opening and closing stressed in stanzas 1 through 3. The perfect rhyme of the final stanza ("understands" and "hands") also seems to suggest the perfection of the relationship, a perfection that cannot be expressed in word meaning but may be captured in the word appearance, sound, and pacing provided by the author. As the imagery moves from spring to winter to spring again, it is evident that the author has utilized the seasons and the garden to integrate growth, birth, and dying as manifestations of love.

Themes and Meanings

The narrator of this love poem tries to express the inexpressible, to describe the intensity of his emotions. He finds himself unable to meet the challenge except in paradoxical words that simultaneously express his surprise and wonder at the mystery of love.

The narrator describes the love as similar to a foreign territory, an area never before explored; the effect of the journey is stunning, evoking a disorientation which

causes the senses to overlap. Yet at the same time he finds himself unable to delin-
eate the specific elements which attract him; instead, he explores the inexpressible
by saying that the sense of touch fails when objects are too near. Love can also bring
about a beautiful and sudden seclusion, with the individual shutting out other demands in favor of love; the speaker depicts such a closing by using the image of a
flower as it begins to close when it senses falling snow.

Cummings' descriptions of his beloved as having texture and color indicate her
depth of character, but they also, when combined with the word "countries" at the
end of line 15, suggest mapmaking and tie in with the poem's initial image of traveling. Just as explorers of new lands are awed by their initial discoveries, so the narrator reacts with surprise at the variety he finds in his lover, a woman who with her
very breathing destroys or breaks down the fear of death and eternity.

The narrator reiterates his inability to understand exactly what it is about the
beloved that possesses the power to open and close him. The image of the garden is
repeated, as the flower (rose) symbolizes both the narrator and his beloved, and the
powerful final line states the incomparable quality of love. No body and no thing
(lines 13 and 20) can truly attain the level of the narrator and his beloved. The rain,
nurturer of the symbolic garden, though it is important, pales in importance to the
small hands of the beloved, whose touch has moved the narrator to ecstasy, to a
height of emotion never before experienced.

The five senses, emphasized and raised by the association with love, are combined
with the traditional and archetypal symbols of a garden and flowers to serve as
symbols for wordlessness, for the inexpressible expressed and given life by the poet's
effort.

Michael J. Meyer

SOMNAMBULE BALLAD

Author: Federico García Lorca (1899-1936)
Type of poem: Lyric/ballad
First published: 1928, as "Romance sonámbulo," in *Romancero gitano*; collected in *Gypsy Ballads*, 1990

The Poem

Despite the poet's declaration that he himself did not know what was going on in the poem, "Somnambule Ballad," Federico García Lorca's supreme dream poem, readily yields most of its secrets to the patient reader. It narrates the plight of a wounded gypsy smuggler seeking refuge from the Guardia Civil (Civil Guards, the rural Spanish police force, at one time noted for its harshness) in the house where his sweetheart lived. Incantatory phrases, haunting images, and a confusion of the real and dream worlds form the background against which this ballad's action takes place.

A strong sense of Andalusia, a province in southern Spain, pervades the poem. Country houses there typically have verandas on their roofs to allow the inhabitants to appreciate the cool evening breezes, and a cistern or water tank can be found in most Andalusian patios.

The poem opens by invoking the allure of the color green, makes a reference to the smuggler's means of transport (ship and horse), and then describes a mysterious girl transfixed on a veranda. Her hair and eyes reflect the moonlight; while under its spell, she is surrounded by things that see her but that she herself cannot see. This is the first of many instances in which the characters in this dream ballad seem impotent, unable to move and to answer for themselves.

The narrator hears someone coming, and a dialogue occurs between two men — one of them the smuggler, the other his "compadre," who is possibly also the father of the bewitched girl on the veranda. The young and wounded smuggler wants to exchange his horse, saddle, and dagger for the domestic comforts of the compadre's house in order to die decently in a bed with fine linen instead of ignominiously by the side of the road. His friend, however, with the impotence common to dreams, and perhaps under the same spell as the green-haired girl on the veranda, says that he is no longer master of himself nor of his house; despite the smuggler's gaping wound, he cannot help.

The young man begs permission at least to climb to the veranda to see the girl. Leaving a trail of blood and tears, the two friends make their way to the roof. The smuggler cries out for the girl, and his friend retorts that for many a night, free of the moon's spell, with fresh face and black hair she waited for the young man.

In a sudden shift of scene, the narrator describes the girl as sustained on a shaft of moonlight as she rocks back and forth on the top of the cistern. The sound of the drunken Civil Guards beating on the door seals the young man's fate, and the poem closes with the lines with which it began.

Forms and Devices

García Lorca closely copied the classical Spanish ballad in both form and technique as he composed his modern versions. An indeterminate number of eight-syllable lines rhyming in assonance (vowels) in even-numbered lines is the set pattern for these lyrics. They also make use of dramatic dialogue and are given to exaggeration. Three hundred ladies-in-waiting accompany Roland's wife in the sixteenth century ballad "Doña Alda," and three hundred roses (splotches of blood) stain the smuggler's shirt in García Lorca's ballad. Spanish ballads frequently close on a note of impending doom: an unanswered question, an intruder knocking at the door. The listener or reader must supply the ominous details. García Lorca uses this device when he has the narrative line of the poem cease as the drunken Civil Guards pound on the door of the house where the smuggler has taken refuge. Part of the attraction of García Lorca's gypsy ballads is in their blend of a very traditional and popular form of literature with modernism.

The same mysterious, singsong lines open and close the poem. Green suggests nature, growth, and vegetation; it also introduces the color of the moon (the moon is made of green cheese, goes an old children's saying in English) that tinges the face of the gypsy girl. In Spanish, *verde* has an additional connotation of "off-color, dirty," a sexual association that no English translation can bring out. After the first two lines chant about the magic of the color green, they are followed by two lines that state simply the existence of objects of reality in their logical and natural surroundings: the ship on the sea, the horse on the mountain. Thus the poem at once establishes its characteristic play between dreams and reality.

García Lorca also makes use of images that have more prescribed meanings. Wounded in the mountain pass of Cabra and losing a considerable amount of blood, the smuggler speaks in metonymies. Horse, saddle, and dagger represent the active, adventurous, masculine life of the smuggler; house, mirror, blanket stand for the safe, domestic, and feminine aspects of shelter.

García Lorca is celebrated for his flair for metaphor, and this poem has many examples. When he writes that the fig tree rubs the wind with the sandpaper of its branches, he is employing one of his favorite devices: the reversal of normal roles. It would be natural for the wind to rustle against the harsh branches of the fig tree, not for the leaves to sand the wind. The metaphors often make extravagant or unusual associations. The outline of a mountain against the sky can be compared to the arched back of a cat, whose hairs stand on end like the century plant (agave). From the veranda, the tin plate lanterns turn into glass tambourines, whose sound (glare) clashes with the light of dawn.

Most of the metaphors present startling ways to look at the reality of nature. They are not only for decoration, however; they contribute to the theme. The gypsies are pursued by the forces of society (the Civil Guards), and whenever this takes place, elements of nature react in consternation: the wind blows, the mountain bristles, the moon intrudes.

Themes and Meanings

The gypsy population of Spain is concentrated in Andalusia. García Lorca grew up in Granada and knew well flamenco, the flamboyant music and dance of the gypsies. Living on the margin of Spanish society and often outside the law, the gypsies were looked upon with suspicion by the middle class and were persecuted by the infamous Civil Guards. In his earliest poetry (much of it still unpublished), García Lorca displayed a ready sympathy for the underdog. He found it easy to champion the gypsies in Spain and later the blacks in New York, and the enduring theme of his work is the evil of oppression in both its private and public forms.

From this web of social facts and personal interests grew the *Gypsy Ballads* (*Romancero gitano*). García Lorca proposed mythologizing the gypsies, turning them into subjects of poetry. In the ballads, he puts the gypsies on an equal footing with the forces of nature. They interact with the moon, wind, sun, stars, and ocean in one enlarged magical community. As in any community, friends and enemies vary. The sea can frown and olive trees grow pale as the gypsy girl Preciosa is pursued by the satyr wind in one of the famous ballads. Nearly all the gypsy ballads tell of an encounter between the idealized "natural" gypsies and the fierce forces of law and order. Such is clearly the case in "Somnambule Ballad," for in García Lorca's time, gypsies were often smugglers and it was the Civil Guard's business to catch them.

Much of the attraction of the "Somnambule Ballad" derives from its skillful handling of the dream atmosphere. Sigmund Freud said there are basically two kinds of dreams, wish-fulfillment dreams and anxiety dreams and García Lorca has managed to present both in a single poem. The opening lines sing of the desire for green, or for some kind of elemental force that can be love, sex, or nature and can permeate the world (the wind becomes green). The poem is framed by the narrator's deep desires. Within the body of the ballad, anxiety centers on the fate of the young man, his sweetheart (how did she die? did she throw herself into the cistern?), and the identity of the old man, all dramatized by the omnipotent and drunken Civil Guards.

Salvador Dalí, when he first heard García Lorca read the poem, is said to have remarked that there seemed to be a plot and yet there was not. In capturing so well this paradox of the dream state, García Lorca created an arresting poem.

Howard Young

SONG: TO CELIA

Author: Ben Jonson (1573?-1637)
Type of poem: Lyric
First published: 1616, in *The Forest*, part of *The Workes of Benjamin Jonson*

The Poem

"Song: To Celia" is a sixteen-line iambic poem written in four quatrains. The content of the poem divides after the second quatrain to form two octets representing two distinct scenes. The poem is the third of three songs addressed to Celia that are collected in *The Forest*. The other two, "Come my Celia" and "Kiss me, sweet," first appeared in Ben Jonson's play *Volpone* (1605).

"Song: To Celia" is Jonson's reworking of five different passages of prose from the Greek sophist writer Philostratus (third century A.D.). The lyric exists in several manuscript versions; Jonson reworked it until he hit upon what is generally considered his finest lyric, indeed one of the finest lyrics of the English Renaissance. In the eighteenth century, an anonymous composer set the poem to music, and it became a popular song.

The first half of the poem is a witty series of variations on the lover's pledge. Traditionally, a lover would toast his or her love and drink a glass of wine; here, the poet asks only for a pledge from Celia's eyes — a loving look — that he promises to return in kind. Even better, if she will "leave a kiss but in the cup" (that is, pledge a kiss), he will forget about wine. The pleasures of Celia's love are a more profound intoxication, a greater sensual delight, than alcohol.

The second quatrain starts more seriously. The poet claims his thirst is not physical, but that it arises from the soul, and that it can only be quenched with a "drink divine." This image flirts with the Christian concept of the "water of life" found in John 4:8-15, and it seems inappropriate in a sensual love lyric. The Christian sentiment, however, is undercut by the following reference to "Jove's nectar." Jove may be divine, but he is a pagan god who is known for his sensual, and specifically sexual, self-indulgence. Jonson claims that he would reject Jove's cup if he could drink from Celia's.

The second octet is a flashback. The poet had sent Celia a "rosy wreath" as a lover's token. He claims that he sent it not to honor her (obviously such a paltry, mortal token could not do justice to Celia's beauty), but in the hopes that the wreath would live forever in Celia's presence — she being a font of life, light, and joy.

The last quatrain tells of the poet's rejection. Celia sent the token back. The poet believes that she has breathed on the wreath and that her sweet smell still clings to it, but this is his fancy, his attempt to wring a compliment, and perhaps hope, out of his rejection. The poem ends on a slightly sad note as the poet tries to console himself, and perhaps even delude himself, regarding his rejection.

Forms and Devices

The lyric is dominated by two images: wine and the rosy wreath. The first octet offers a series of possible substitutions—love favors—that the poet is willing to accept in lieu of the traditional wine. Wine implies intoxication, the delirium of love, but also sensual gratification. The substitutes that the poet is willing to accept seem more ethereal: the glance, the kiss in a cup. Indeed, the wine itself becomes rarefied into Jove's nectar, a divine drink that reputedly had a rejuvenating effect— the same effect that Celia has on the poet.

The wreath dominates the second octet. It is a more concrete pledge than those requested in the first part of the poem, but it is rejected. The rose is the archetypal symbol of love in the English tradition. The wreath consists of a number of roses woven into a circle, which is itself a symbol of eternity. The eternal devotion that was the hallmark of the more spiritual love popularized by Petrarch is combined, then, with the sensual. While the circle may imply eternal love, the wreath's non-static quality is emphasized: "it grows, and smells." These flowers are still alive, growing as does the poet's love.

Finally, the wreath, an interweaving of flowers, stands for this poem itself, which is an ingenious interweaving of excerpts from the classical source. The weaving finds its analogue in the rhyme scheme of the poem. The short lines of both octets revolve on single rhymes and thus bind the poem together. The wreath itself has passed from the poet to the lover and back to the poet, describing in its movement a circle. It is the only physical thing that links the two, besides the poem itself.

This poem has a remarkably regular iambic meter that produces its lyrical quality. The only significant break in the rhythm is a caesura in the final line between "it-self" and "but." This pause draws attention to the final qualification in the poem. While the other qualifications undercut the ideal and metaphoric, this final quali-fication asserts the lover as an ideal who changes reality—she has altered the wreath. The caesura also lends emphasis to the concluding "but thee." The poem ends with the lover, a marked contrast from the beginning of the poem, which em-phasizes the poet.

Themes and Meanings

In this poem, as in most of his love poetry, Jonson reacts against the idealization of love, an idealization manifest in the imitation of Petrarchan conventions through-out the Renaissance literature. This poem highlights the realistic by juxtaposing it with the ideal, an ideal that is maintained by the poet's persona even as it is contra-dicted by his own words.

The qualification process takes several forms. First there is the juxtaposition of long and short lines. In the first stanza especially, the long lines tend to be meta-phorical and ideal, while the short lines, which usually start with a qualifying term such as "and," are more direct and concrete. The poem oscillates, then, between the ideal, or imagined, and the real.

This dialectic tension is manifested in the greater scale of the poem by the contrast between the first and second octet. The first octet depicts a scene set in the present. The poet is with his lover, and he begs a pledge that is both physical and spiritual. It is an ideal, if unconsummated, moment of love. The second octet, however, is set in the past. The poet is physically separated from his love, and his love token is rejected by her. The events that preceded the opening octet then were less than hopeful, but the poet persists in his idealization despite the rejection. The poem itself becomes an emblem of this fruitless drive toward the ideal; with its perfect iambs, it encapsulates and elevates what may be a failed relationship.

Finally, the poem contrasts the ideal and real by juxtaposing the physical and the spiritual. The poet's first request is for a loving glance. His second is for a kiss in a cup. He has moved from the realistic to the metaphoric. From here, the poet leaps to the thirst of the soul, the divine, the classical, and the impractical.

In the second octet when a physical token (a wreath) is sent to the lover, the poet assumes that she will have a supernatural effect on the object: It will live forever in her presence. The token, however, is returned, and so the poet is brought back to the realm of the physical. The poet, though, believes the wreath is now miraculously endowed. The physical and realistic—the wreath—combines with the spiritual and ideal—the infinite circle that it describes. So love continually combines the real and the ideal, the actual event and its glorification in art.

Paul Budra

A SONG FOR ST. CECILIA'S DAY

Author: John Dryden (1631-1700)
Type of poem: Ode
First published: 1687; collected in *Examen Poeticum*, 1693

The Poem

The first of John Dryden's two Saint Cecilia's Day odes, "A Song for St. Cecilia's Day," was written to commemorate November 22 as the day devoted to the patron saint of music. His second, *Alexander's Feast* (1697), a longer and more elaborate composition, appeared ten years later, near the end of Dryden's career. The practice of writing odes to commemorate St. Cecilia began in England in 1683, and Dryden was among the first poets to write at the invitation of a London musical society. Giovanni Battista Draghi's musical adaptation, the first of several for the poem, accompanied the initial publication. In form, it is an ode, consisting of seven stanzas and a grand concluding chorus, sixty-three lines in all.

The structure resembles the Horatian or Roman ode in its linear and logical development. Two general introductory stanzas are followed by five others, which identify and trace the effects of musical instruments, plus a concluding chorus. Yet the stanzas, unlike those of the Horatian ode, are irregular, employing a variety of meters and ranging in length from four to fifteen lines. Writing at a time when the classical ode was little understood, Dryden may have adapted this stanzaic irregularity from Pindar, whose Greek odes were highly esteemed.

The initial stanza opens the poem with the statement that creation, bringing order and harmony to chaotic matter, was accompanied by music. This vision of creation derives from Lucretius and Ovid, classical Roman poets whose works Dryden knew well. To stress the power of music, Dryden emphasizes the role of musical harmony in imparting order to the universe. The second stanza narrows the theme to the power of music in arousing human emotion, the poem's major theme. In the biblical account of the origin of music (Genesis 4:21), in which Jubal excited his hearers to wonder by blowing upon a sea shell, Dryden finds confirmation of the power of music over the emotions.

In stanzas 3 through 7, Dryden governs the structure by showing that each instrument arouses a particular human emotion in the hearer. These five stanzas, dealing with seven instruments, offer a basically chronological arrangement of instruments invented by man. Trumpets and drums arouse emotions associated with warfare, such as anger and courage. The flute and lute appeal to the soft emotions associated with romantic love, both its tenderness and its complaints of woe. Violins' sharp tones suggest the jealousy and pain of discordant love. Finally the organ, traditionally credited to St. Cecilia's invention, creates the sustained, majestic tones that inspire religious devotion.

Contrasting St. Cecilia with Orpheus, the legendary classical musician whose lyre moved trees to abandon their roots, the poem confers the greater power upon St.

Cecilia. For, while she played her organ, an angel appeared, thinking that the sounds came from heaven. She thus produced the closest approximation on earth to the heavenly music that Dryden celebrated in the first stanza.

In the final stanza, a "Grand Chorus," the poem envisions future heavenly music, when at the sound of the trumpet all shall gather on the final day. As music began the creation and sustained its harmony through the music of the moving spheres, so it will end it, and music will "untune the sky."

Forms and Devices

The ode form, permitting verses of varying lengths, enables Dryden to achieve a rich diversity of poetic effects. Varied rhyme schemes and intricate sound effects create the beat and cadence of musical passages. In the ode, he relies less heavily on schemes of repetition that are prominent in his heroic couplets, although, along with figures of speech, they do contribute as well to the poem's effects.

Just as the stanzas in the ode vary from four to fifteen lines, the lines vary from iambic trimeter to iambic pentameter, with a larger number of iambic tetrameter verses, permitting a complexity of metrical effects. The rhymes are similarly irregular and, therefore, form no pattern of inner consistency from stanza to stanza.

By the time he wrote the ode, Dryden was a master of sound effects beyond onomatopoeia, and the ode reflects his exquisite ear for poetic sounds. Onomatopoeic words such as "whisper'd," "clangor," and "thund'ring" have their texture enhanced by accompanying echoes and vigorous, direct meters: "The Trumpet's loud clangor/ Excites us to arms/ With shrill notes of anger,/ And mortal alarms." Short lines, forceful syllables—the final line shortened to five syllables—and a heavy reliance on the *s* sound heighten intensity. In stanza 7, contrasting Orpheus and St. Cecilia, the poem demonstrates how altering metrical form can create emphasis:

> Orpheus could lead the savage race;
> And trees unrooted left their place,
>   Sequacious of the lyre;
> But bright Cecilia rais'd the wonder high'r:
> When to her Organ vocal breath was giv'n,
> An angel heard, and straight appear'd,
>   Mistaking earth for heav'n.

Orpheus is accorded an iambic tetrameter line, largely regular and direct, but Dryden significantly emphasizes St. Cecilia by introducing her with an iambic pentameter line, made even more emphatic because it rhymes with a preceding trimeter.

The range of poetic sound effects can be studied by contrasting the abrupt staccato depiction of the drum, "The double double double beat/ Of the thund'ring Drum," to the extended majestic sounds used to describe the organ: "What human voice can reach,/ The sacred Organ's praise?/ Notes inspiring holy love."

In the first passage, alliteration, short vowels, onomatopoeia, and assonance create echoes of drumbeats. In the second, sonorants, long vowels, and assonance lengthen the sounds to mimic the elongated tones of the organ.

Although Dryden makes extensive use of simple repetition for rhythmic effects, he relies little on complex schemes of repetition, except for sound effects achieved through assonance, alliteration, and onomatopoeia. A notable exception occurs in the climactic conclusion: "The dead shall live, the living die,/ And Music shall untune the sky." In this passage, balance and alliteration combine with polyptoton (a type of word repetition) and paradox to produce highly memorable poetry. Figures of speech are also used sparingly in what is essentially a tour de force of sounds. Yet the metaphor "crumbling pageant" for the world in the chorus, and the personifications of instruments, endowing them with human power, enrich the imaginative texture of the ode.

Themes and Meanings

"A Song for St. Cecilia's Day" celebrates the power of music by drawing upon classical myths and Christian and Jewish sources and legends. The dominant theme is directly expressed in the line "What passion cannot Music raise and quell!" Its development associates specific passions with specific instruments. This theme is developed, however, within the larger context of the hexameral tradition which associates music with the creation and of the Christian eschatological tradition which associates the trumpet with Judgment Day and the crumbling of creation. The power of music to raise passions is developed in the middle five stanzas about how music from individual instruments raises emotions; only in the eschatological Grand Chorus does Dryden explore how music quells emotions.

The mythic figures mentioned in the poem contribute to the idea of music developing from humble origins after the fall of man. The sublime music of creation of the first stanza that regulates the spheres remains unheard by men after the Fall in the Garden of Eden. Instead, Jubal creates the first musical sounds by blowing upon a sea shell and, as Dryden's description indicates, fills his hearers with wonder. Orpheus, from Greek mythology, confirms the power of music by his appeal to the plant and animal kingdoms. Thereafter, music increases its power over human emotions, as more complex instruments are fashioned. Dryden's descriptions of drums and trumpets exciting war's valor and anger and of flutes, lutes, and violins exciting the pleasures and pains of love (stanzas 3 to 5) suggest the conflict between love and honor that wracks the heroes of his heroic plays. By giving the organ the final place in the development of the instruments he names, Dryden accords it—and its emotion, religious devotion—greatest power and dignity. The intimation that the organ was invented after the violin is incorrect, yet Dryden never questions the legend that St. Cecilia invented the instrument.

Contrasting Orpheus, whose lyre gave trees the ability to separate from their roots and to move to music, with St. Cecilia, who drew an angel to her sounding organ, takes Dryden to the origins of music. In Dryden's hierarchical arrangement of levels of being, the appeal to an angel's passion surpasses any appeal to elemental or human emotions.

Dryden's climactic sequence of instruments leads almost inexorably to the final eschatological vision of the trumpet that ends all creation and quells normal human emotion. The mythical music of the spheres, heard since creation only by the inhabitants of heaven and ever since denied to man, gives way to the sound of the trumpet. The sky itself is untuned by the final cataclysmic event, and afterward only heaven itself retains the harmony that had previously informed and regulated the creation.

Stanley Archer

SONG OF MYSELF

Author: Walt Whitman (1819-1892)
Type of poem: Epic
First published: 1855, untitled, in *Leaves of Grass*

The Poem

Begun as early as 1847, "Song of Myself" first appeared as one of the twelve untitled poems of the first edition of *Leaves of Grass* (1855). Regularly revised, it became "Poem of Walt Whitman, an American" in the second edition (1856) and "Walt Whitman" in the third through sixth editions (1860, 1867, 1871, and 1876). Not until the seventh edition of *Leaves of Grass*, published in 1881, did the poem undergo its final metamorphosis in name as well as form. The first and final versions of "Song of Myself" are virtually identical in subject, style, and even length (1,336 and 1,346 lines respectively). Phrasings occasionally differ, but never crucially so. ("I celebrate myself," the 1855 edition begins; "and sing myself," Whitman later added). The division of the free-flowing untitled poem into fifty-two numbered sections, like the addition and subsequent revision of the title, proves more significant, for this overt structuring appears to add a sense of order and progression that the poem originally seemed to lack. This is not to say that the 1855 text was formless, or that structure is something Whitman arbitrarily imposed. The numbering merely accents the organic principle from which the poem develops, for the poem's unity derives less from the numbering of its sections according to the yearly cycle of weeks than from the fusion of song and self.

Not identifying himself by name until section 24—and even then in half-biblical, half-comical fashion, as "Walt Whitman, a kosmos, of Manhattan the son" (in the 1855 edition, "Walt Whitman, an American, one of the roughs, a kosmos")—the thirty-seven-year-old narrator strikes a decidedly proud and personal pose and addresses the reader in a doubly direct manner. From the outset, he incorporates his listener/reader into the poem (as "you") and permits "nature" to speak "without check, with original energy," which is to say, free of the constraints of either poetic convention or social decorum. The freedom Whitman takes evidences itself not only in his language and intimate mode of address, but in his very posture as well. The poem presents not merely a mind thinking or a voice speaking, but an entire body reclining on the ground, leaning and loafing, "observing a spear of summer grass." Like Henry David Thoreau in *Walden: Or, Life in the Woods* (1854), Whitman situates himself and his poem outdoors and therefore outside convention and tradition; and, like Ralph Waldo Emerson in his essay *Nature* (1836), Whitman deliberately conflates natural world and poetical word, leaf of grass and *Leaves of Grass*. Radically democratic and explicitly (as well as metaphorically) sexual, "Song of Myself" goes well beyond even the extended bounds of Transcendentalist thought in its celebration of the relation between physical and spiritual, individual and universal.

The middle third of the poem extends still further the sexual union of self and other, body and soul. As earlier he had claimed to be able to "resist anything better than my own diversity," now it is sensuous contact of any kind that Whitman's "hankering, gross, mystical, nude" figure cannot resist. Taking Emerson's symbol of the "transparent eyeball" (from *Nature*) to the very frontiers of poetic expression, Whitman indulges in an orgy of seeing, hearing, and feeling (sections 25-28). The scene culminates in orgasmic release (section 29), and is in turn followed (section 30) by a postcoital peace that passeth understanding. The knowledge that "All truths wait in all things" leads to the poem's longest and most exuberant catalog (section 33). Paradoxically "afoot with my vision" and flying "those flights of the fluid and swallowing soul" (while rooted to the very spot where his song began, still leaning and loafing, still observing the same multi-meaninged leaf of grass), Whitman continues his transgression of all social, temporal, and spatial boundaries.

By line 798, however, the pace begins to slacken as Whitman identifies closely and narrowly with one segment of society only: the injured, the imprisoned, the enslaved, the despised. Whitman has become one of the "trippers and askers" that surrounded him earlier. Finding himself "on the verge of a usual mistake," he pulls back barely in time, resuming "the overstaid fraction," the individual I. Saved from torpor and despair, he rises from the dead, an American Christ, and rises from the recumbent position he has maintained, appearances to the contrary, throughout the poem, to proclaim his faith in himself and in all others, equally divine, and in a vaguely defined but enthusiastically embraced cosmic plan.

Declaring an end to his loitering and talking, he prepares to resume the role or guise he left off to become the chanter of this "Song of Myself." The poem's last eight sections are marked by the urgency of his departure: by last-minute preparations, last words of advice, and reluctance to leave at all until his listener, who is also his student and comrade, brother and sister, speaks his or her own word in response. Standing accused by the free-flying hawk, Whitman reluctantly but also joyously and certainly garrulously sounds the last words of his "barbaric yawp," continuing his "perpetual tramp," not so much departing the scene as dispersing himself into the elements themselves.

Forms and Devices

"Who troubles himself about his ornaments or fluency is lost," Whitman warned in the preface to the 1855 edition to *Leaves of Grass*. His admonition is, however, in a way misleading. While it accurately measures the great distance between his "barbaric yawp" and the conventionality that characterized the standard poetry of his day, Whitman's remark may lead readers to assume that "Song of Myself," or any Whitman poem, is somehow artless. Whitman divested himself of the "ornaments" and "fluency" of conventional verse in order to craft a poetry more natively American, not only in subject but also in style. He took upon himself the task of discovering a poetic form as raw, as free, as unfinished, as expansive, as experimental, and as full of promise as his Transcendentalist conception of his country. Unlike Henry Wadsworth Longfellow, he did not, except briefly, look back to the American past;

he looked instead to the present moment and to a projected future. Unlike his fellow Transcendentalist Thoreau, one of his earliest supporters, Whitman did not count a man rich in relation to the number of things he could do without. Whitman's "omnivorous lines" give the illusion of leaving nothing out, of being democratically all-inclusive, a strange mixture (as Emerson himself noted) of the *Bhagavad Gītā* and the *New York Herald*. The poem's democratic thrust is most obviously at work in Whitman's lengthy catalogs, and more subtly in the combining of these catalogs with passages of considerable narrative power and others of great lyrical intensity.

Free in form and epic in reach, "Song of Myself" creates a structure all its own based upon repetition of words, phrases, and parallel syntactical structures. At both the micro and macro levels, the poem develops its own cumulatively powerful rhythm of ebb and flow, absorption and release, stasis and motion, or, to borrow Whitman's own operatic conceit, aria and recitative. Singing, however, serves as only one of a multiplicity of metaphors at work in "Song of Myself," no more but also no less important than building, weaving, and sexual union. Each plays its pervasive but ultimately partial role in Whitman's drama of the emerging self.

The merging of self and other in terms of sympathetic identification serves to hold the poem's varied materials together in one organic, evolving whole. As important as this metaphorical merging is the emphasis the poem places on the "I" that emerges from the speaker's self-generating, self-projecting performance. The Whitmanian persona comes to embody the paradoxical process of becoming what he has always been and must be. Freeing himself from all poetic and social constraints, he becomes his own transgressive self: an Emersonian representative man, a Transcendentalist version of the typically American tall-tale hero, bragging for all mankind.

Themes and Meanings

Early in the poem, a child asks, "What is the grass?" Although he claims, or pretends, not to know the answer, the Whitmanian persona goes on to offer a number of surmises, each plausible, each partial. "Song of Myself" constitutes one such seemingly simple yet punningly enigmatic leaf of grass: a poem in a book, *Leaves of Grass*, that expands and changes shape over nine separate editions even as it remains in essence always the same. The poem is for the reader what the grass is for the child: a "uniform hieroglyphic" for which there is no single Rosetta Stone by which it may be deciphered, other than the faith that Whitman cheerfully and insistently proclaims. Its "barbaric yawp" opens itself to a variety of interpretative strategies but chiefly attests its own capacity to outstrip them all: "Do I contradict myself?/ Very well then I contradict myself,/ (I am large, I contain multitudes.)"

The self that Whitman sings and celebrates proves as much a "uniform hieroglyphic" as the grass: equally evocative, multiform, and full of contradictions. It is as much a physical presence as a projected (spiritual) possibility. It is Emerson's self-engendered, self-reliant man, one who exists not in Thoreauvian isolation but in "ensemble," speaking the word "en-masse." As self-appointed bard of democracy,

Whitman projects an "I" as expansive and diverse as the country itself, in a poetic form and language as experimental and new as the nation and its democratic political system.

Even as it overtly and enthusiastically expresses Whitman's faith in cosmic evolution and therefore in the essential indivisibility of Emersonian self-reliance and Over-Soul, "Song of Myself" also expresses in the very stridency of its affirmation a division deep within the poem's prototypical "self," within the poet himself (psychologically considered), and within the country (both socially and politically). It offers a Transcendentalist solution to the crisis of union that, only five years after the poem made its first appearance, would lead to civil war. "Song of Myself" presents, therefore, a complex set of variations on the theme sounded in more narrowly political terms in Abraham Lincoln's famous 1858 "A House Divided" speech. The poem did not resolve the national debate, nor did it bring about the Transcendentalist democracy Whitman envisioned— nor, apparently, did it ease the psychosexual divisions within Whitman's own psyche. Those failures, however, must be measured against the greatness of a work generally regarded not only as its author's most ambitious but also as one of American literature's most representative.

Robert A. Morace

THE SONG OF THE HAPPY SHEPHERD

Author: William Butler Yeats (1865-1939)
Type of poem: Pastoral/meditation
First published: 1885, as "An Epilogue to 'The Island of Statues' and 'The Seeker' "

The Poem

"The Song of the Happy Shepherd" is actually a theme poem, a declaration of poetic independence. It appears at the beginning of his first volume, and William Butler Yeats intended it as a manifesto—a statement of his poetic creed and a guide to the kind of poetry he was writing and would write. In it, he established his relationship to the poetry of the past and asserted that the role of poetry would have to change in the modern world. He stated that poetry would have to become more divorced from the things of the world, closer to the truths of the heart, more a law to itself.

The poem is divided into three unequal parts. Yeats begins by establishing the persona of the happy shepherd, following the ancient convention of the pastoral, centered on the country singer who comments from his innocent vantage point on the ways of the world. Yet almost at once he breaks from that convention by chanting, "The woods of Arcady are dead,/ And over is their antique joy." Arcady was the classical location of the pastoral. This shepherd is asserting that the old vision no longer holds, that the old kind of poetry has failed. Having given up on dreams, the world now demands "Grey Truth"—the dingy matter of the daily newspaper. The shepherd derides the attention given to "the many changing things," concluding instead that only words can confer value and permanence. Even the kings of the past now litter the trash containers of history, lucky to be recalled by words. Moreover, the discoveries of science suggest that all the things of this world may be little more than temporary accidents.

The second section begins by repeating this conclusion: History records only "dusty deeds"; truth is an illusion. Pursuit of truth can only force one to escape in dreams. The only real truths are personal. Scientists, for example, have deadened themselves to produce "cold star-bane"—dead figures and facts about dead things. It would be far better to fashion lovely bodies out of words, as singing into an echoing shell may recombine the original sounds into a higher music. Songs also fade away, but they die in beauty and remain beautiful in death.

In the third section, the shepherd takes his leave to follow on his singing way. He is called to tread the wood region of fable and romance, never far off for an Irish poet. This region of the old earth is still haunted by creatures of fancy, the forces he must immortalize in song. These are the "songs of old earth's dreamy youth," now inaccessible from routine daily life. That proves the necessity of poetry today, for it alone preserves the way into faerie, more important now than ever before.

Forms and Devices

"The Song of the Happy Shepherd" is composed in three sections of alternately rhymed iambic tetrameter—a somewhat flexible pattern first used in English by John Milton and freely imitated thereafter. Yeats develops his topics in a relatively straightforward way, employing few exotic or difficult figures, although some of the diction is ambiguous and some syntax gnarled. The principal device is simple: repetition of phrase and verbal pattern.

The first section, of twenty-one lines, establishes the situation and background by means of allusion. "Woods of Arcady" refers to the groves of Attic Greece, supposedly frequented by the first generations of poets in Western civilization. Then appear two lines that work on several levels simultaneously: "Of old the world on dreaming fed;/ Grey Truth is now her painted toy." The persona states that dreams sustained the world formerly, implying that they can do so no longer; the world has grown estranged from dreams. Now, in place of that wholesome food, she diverts herself with painted toys—baubles so empty in themselves that they have to be tricked out with paint to attract any interest. The best that can be done with current truth is to daub it with gray; it is too ambiguous to be either black or white. This kind of degeneration exhibits itself in all aspects of modern life: the restlessness and inattentiveness, the sickness of the children, even the dreariness of the dancing. Chronos—the spirit of time—sings now a "cracked tune," suggesting the corruption of civilization, the running down of time. In this context, only words—paradoxically—have substance, though on an earth that itself may be only "a sudden flaming word" that substance may be slight.

The second section of twenty-three lines weaves itself around the recurrent phrase "this is also sooth." By "sooth," Yeats means more than an old poetic synonym for truth, which in any case he has just discarded as a norm. As in the compound "soothsayer," "sooth" connotes the kind of truth hidden to most observers but of enduring moment—perhaps what he refers to later as the truth of the heart. The word also homonymically conjures up "soothe"—suggesting the kind of truth that alone consoles, that eases the pain otherwise generated by life. This section contains the key to the only solace now viable, something more also than the mere dreams to which that relentless pursuit of facile, mechanical truth will drive human beings.

Two specific images form the poles of this section. One is the "cold star-bane" of the "starry men." This difficult phrase is a Yeats coinage. By analogy with wolf-bane, it is the kind of lore that can be used to banish the stars. Thus it is the kind of knowledge that becomes a substitute for the thing itself, that drives the real presence away. It is star-bane because it diminishes the wonder of the stars by dwindling them to gray facts. The second image is of the "twisted, echo-harboring shell" which replaces the words of a simple story and transfixes them in beauty. That is the material instrument which makes music of human speech, the song which preserves the truths of the heart and soothes the soul.

The final section recapitulates the first two, again ending with the refrain on "sooth," but the techniques of this section are different. Here, Yeats arranges a cascade of images to illustrate heart truths: "a grave/ Where daffodil and lily wave"; a "hapless fawn/ Buried under the sleepy ground." These ingredients are those of the faerie land of the imagination, accessible only by turning one's back on the world of fact. In this way, man can keep in touch with the essential world of "earth's dreamy youth."

Themes and Meanings

Though called a "song," this poem is far from lyrical, and this discrepancy marks its first break with the past. The implication is that the old kind of song no longer works; it lacks currency. The poem's title also establishes the persona of the happy shepherd, suggesting with apparent inconsistency a link with the ancient tradition of pastoral poetry, which was centered in the fictitious invention of a timeless landscape populated with innocent sheep and blissful shepherds whose simple singing became poetry. Curiously, in both the original Greek and Roman versions of this convention, and in its Renaissance revival, the pastoral world is considered a refuge from and an antitype to the political world of influence and inside trading. Thus it can be used as a basis for social critique. By similarly withdrawing his happy shepherd, Yeats creates a persona removed from the world and privileged to comment on it.

That is exactly what his happy shepherd does. He begins by lamenting the fate of the woods of Arcady, because that is an image not only of his real home but also of a parallel universe necessary for the spiritual health of modern man. Having rejected that parallel universe, man today has nothing with which to nourish his soul in this world of gray fact. Mankind diverts itself with illusions, but evidences of spiritual decay abound in so-called civilization. The shepherd proclaims that in this materialistic jungle, only words offer certitude and value, for they alone provide access to the eternally green and eternally fertile world of "earth's dreamy youth." Words alone open gates to dreams.

The shepherd also announces a counter theme: However seductive the world of fact, recorded in history and analyzed by science, it is ultimately empty, because it does not sustain the spirit. The greatest of kings, including those who derided words — as Pontius Pilate joked about truth — are now reduced to words fumbled by schoolboys. Moreover, the earth and its fabled history occupy but a moment on a cosmic timetable. The old theory of auromancy, or sound magic, held that words preceded and created things, which means that even the world was once only a momentary word in the mouth of the Creator: In the beginning was the Word, as the Gospel of John presents it.

In such a situation only eternal words, the words that attach to dreams, are worth cherishing and preserving. That becomes the shepherd's third theme. These words are those of life, which connect modern imaginative consciousness with the mythic past of the planet and early man. The spirit of man cannot survive, the shepherd argues, without the solace provided by song, by words turning themselves to music through the agency of the poet. The kind of instinctive faith possible in the past is no longer available. Lacking that, people find refuge increasingly rare. The shepherd offers the help of dreamsong.

The final theme offers the possibility even of transcending or accepting death. The last stanza resembles John Milton's elegy "Lycidas" (1637) closely enough to constitute an allusion. In both, the shepherd leaves the scene, vowing to keep alive the memory of one untimely dead. In both cases, the song helps conjure up again the image of the departed, depicting him as once more transfigured by and enshrined in the song of the dream.

James Livingston

THE SONG OF THE POORLY LOVED

Author: Guillaume Apollinaire (Guillaume Albert Wladimir Alexandre
Apollinaire de Kostrowitzky, 1880-1918)
Type of poem: Lyric
First published: 1909, as "La Chanson du Mal-Aimé"; revised in *Alcools*, 1913;
collected in *Selected Writings*, 1950

The Poem

"The Song of the Poorly Loved" consists of fifty-nine stanzas, each five lines long. It is divided into seven sections, three of which have their own titles. Guillaume Apollinaire assembled it, probably in 1904, from poems and fragments he had written at various times over the previous few years.

The initial motivation for the poem came from Apollinaire's own life: In Germany, he had met and fallen in love with a young Englishwoman named Annie Playden. He visited her twice in London with intentions to marry her, but she emigrated to America. The poem opens in misty London, where Apollinaire was rebuffed by Annie in November, 1903, and closes the following June in Paris, where he returned with all hope lost in May, 1904. As the comparison between his love and the phoenix in the five-line epigraph indicates, the poem revolves around Apollinaire's efforts to resurrect his life after this unhappy love affair.

The long first section begins with a nightmarish episode in London. The poet is confronted by two figures who resemble his beloved and remind him of the transitory nature of love. He compares the mistreatment he has suffered to various fictional and historical examples of fidelity. Contemplation of his memories and regrets brings him to the nostalgic recollection of the heyday of his love. This he depicts in the three-stanza second section, which he calls an "Aubade" (a traditional form of morning love song).

In the third section, the poet is in Paris, reflecting on the death of love and on his inability to put his unhappy experience behind him. In pondering his faithfulness, he once again compares himself to a legendary paradigm of fidelity, this time the Zaporogian Cossacks of the Ukraine. Asked by the Turkish sultan to join his army, these Christian warriors of the seventeenth century are said to have rejected the invitation to betray their faith in a violently worded letter. In the three-stanza fourth section, the poet composes his version of the Cossacks' insulting and obscene reply.

In the first stanzas of the long fifth section, the poet returns to his own very mixed feelings about his beloved, expressing bitter disdain, then enduring commitment. Wondering what it will take to make him happy, the poet examines grief and unhappiness, both in relation to his own experience and in general. In thinking about his memories, he addresses his shadow—an image of his past, which will always follow him. Then he describes the transition from winter to spring, and this change signals the beginning of a more positive and productive attitude toward his past.

It seems as if the poet cannot completely come to terms with the pain of his unhappy love affair until he has somehow exorcised his melancholy, and this is apparently what he accomplishes in the sixth section. "The Seven Swords" is the most obscure part of this difficult poem: It has been interpreted in many different ways, none of which can claim to be definitive. Most significant, however, is the conclusion, namely the poet's claim that he never knew the beloved.

Consequently, in the eleven-stanza seventh section, the poet writes about fortune and fate with a new detachment. He tells of the mad Bavarian king, Ludwig II, who committed suicide—a reaction to unhappiness that the poet no longer feels inclined to emulate. Instead, he turns to Paris, seeing the modern city with a new responsiveness. The poem closes with a confident assertion of the poet's creative ability: Rather than feeling alienated from the city around him as he mourns his lost love, he is now sure that he can draw inspiration from both the present and the past.

Forms and Devices

Probably the most striking formal feature of "The Song of the Poorly Loved" is the enormous variety of tone and mood. Apollinaire borrows techniques from the poetic practice of both the recent and the distant past and adds his own inventions to create an original and quintessentially modern work.

In many passages, Apollinaire's writing owes much to the French Symbolist poets who were his illustrious predecessors. The description of the poet's melancholic state of mind in stanzas 9 through 11 employs images and formulations similar to those used by Charles Baudelaire in his "Spleen" poems. The complex syntax of stanza 13 is reminiscent of the work of Stéphane Mallarmé. Yet Apollinaire constantly disrupts this Symbolist tone by employing surprisingly crude language; the lyrical evocation of spring in stanzas 38 and 39, for example, is followed by the use of *cul* ("ass") as a simile.

The range of language in "The Song of the Poorly Loved" is such that scatological words rub shoulders with extremely erudite allusions. Most readers will need to research such esoteric terms as "argyraspids"; and they may look in vain, since Apollinaire liked to coin his own neologisms.

Another aspect of the poem's variety is the constantly shifting perspective. Even within a single section, the poet's point of view may change from impassioned lover to dispassionate narrator to reflective commentator. All of the wide-ranging stylistic variation is carried out with great panache and considerable humor.

"The Song of the Poorly Loved" has earned a reputation as a breathtakingly ambitious yet brilliantly executed poem because Apollinaire succeeds in uniting all these elements. He does so partly by means of the narrative of the poet's quest, to which the poem always returns in spite of the long detours it takes. Additonally, the whole poem is written in stanzas of five eight-syllable lines, and in French the same rhyme scheme is retained throughout. This meter not only provides consistency, but also invests the poem with a compelling rhythm that, like the narrative thread, drives the poem forward.

Finally, Apollinaire uses two recurring stanzas to bind the poem together further.

Stanza 13, which expresses the poet's aspirations toward something higher, symbolized by the Milky Way, is repeated as stanzas 27 and 49. The insertion of these five lines at three different turning points means that they serve as a measure of the poet's progress toward that higher realm. The final stanza of the poem first occurs in the third section, and this repetition also highlights the development of the poet's state of mind. The first time, it reads as a despondent expression of regret, but at the end it resounds as a triumphant assertion of confidence.

The modernity of the poem resides in Apollinaire's synthesis of so many disparate elements. Modernist literature is characterized by the lack of a stable center, of any reliable continuity; here the poet repeatedly disorients the reader by jumping from one mood and from one story to another. The order in which the poem proceeds is not dictated by conventional notions of time or logic. The technique of depicting the same event from several angles is related directly to the innovations of cubist painting (Apollinaire was an influential supporter of such contemporary artists as Pablo Picasso and Georges Braque). While the whole poem is unified by the voice of the "poorly loved," that aspect also reflects a very modern outlook: The poet's self is not depicted as a single, coherent entity, but rather as a succession of states of mind.

Themes and Meanings

While "The Song of the Poorly Loved" began as the expression of a young man's unhappy experience as a lover, the poem it grew into is primarily about a young man's sense of vocation as a poet. This is Apollinaire's main concern in this poem: how to turn one's past and present life into a source of creativity.

The past upon which the poet draws consists of his own personal experience, the literary forms and techniques of the centuries of poets who preceded him, and the vast range of his historical and cultural heritage. At first, the poet employs examples from the past to illuminate his own experience, but in doing so he remains too immersed in personal emotions. What he strives for and eventually finds is a way to use all of the past, including his own, as material for creative expression.

Apollinaire invests the poet with an analogous relationship with the present. Initially, the modern urban environment oppresses him, whereas what he seeks is a means to take advantage of it artistically. The poet demonstrates his progress toward this goal through the contrast between the London of the opening and the Paris of the close; by the end he is able to look Paris in the face and recognize both its sadness and its beauty.

A key metaphor for poetic creativity, established immediately by the title and epigraph, is the act of singing. At first it appears as if the poet will be singing about love, but in fact he will ultimately be singing about singing, that is, about the creative process. The "Aubade" is an example of simply singing about love, and the gently self-mocking tone in which the poet writes reflects his dissatisfaction with such modesty. The final stanza describes the true poet, one gifted and ambitious enough to make poetry out of any kind of experience.

"The Song of the Poorly Loved" also embodies a particular approach toward language and its possibilities. The linguistic variety that characterizes the poem in general, and especially the range of the language, constitutes a statement on Apollinaire's part about how poets may use words. By combining the most familiar and the most strange, the oldest and the newest, the poet can reenliven language, recognizing its past without being restricted by it.

Overall, the poem is about the quest for a means to transform experience into art, and it represents Apollinaire's own fulfillment of that quest. All seven sections are about experience turned into artistic form, but the final parts are the most original, because the poet has discovered his own voice. However one chooses to interpret the "The Seven Swords," it is, like the closing stanzas about Paris, an emphatic statement of the poet's individualistic response to the inspiration of his past and his present.

Neil Blackadder

A SONG ON THE END OF THE WORLD

Author: Czesław Miłosz (1911-   )
Type of poem: Meditation
First published: 1945, as "Piosenka o Końcu świata," in *Ocalenie*; collected in
  The Collected Poems, 1931-1987, 1988

The Poem

Divided into four stanzas, this twenty-six-line poem with its portentous title turns out to be wryly quiet, an ironic contrast to the dramatic events some have expected would accompany the end of the world. Concentrating on a description of vivid yet commonplace, daily realities, Czesław Miłosz fashions a deliberately simple, naive narrative of events.

The first stanza is devoted to descriptions of what might be called miniature worlds: "a bee circles a clover," describing quite literally the circumference of its world. Similarly, the fisherman mending a "glimmering net," "happy porpoises" jumping in the sea, the young sparrows playing about the rainspout, and the "gold-skinned" snake each express a world or a dimension of the world "on the day the world ends." There is a willed quality to this catalog of activities, a denial of change that is most explicit in the poet's insistence on the snake's color, which is "as it should always be."

The second stanza shifts to an emphasis on collective and individual human activity—women walking through the fields "under their umbrellas," a drunk growing sleepy "at the edge of a lawn," vegetable peddlers shouting in the street—while off in the distance can be seen a "yellow-sailed boat." Rather than the end of the world, again announced in the first line of the stanza, the descriptions seem to emphasize its continuity—like the "voice of a violin lasts in the air."

The third stanza takes up the disappointment of those who had assumed the world would end violently, with "signs and archangels' trumps." There is no unusual noise, no disruption of the common pattern of the earth. As long as nature and the elements continue in their course, as long as rosy babies are born, it is hard to believe that the world is ending now.

In the fourth stanza, a single witness, busy at his work but with the insight of a prophet, "binds his tomatoes" and repeats to himself twice that "there will be no other end of the world." The implication seems to be that the world will not end in some remarkable event but will complete itself in the same manner as the old man who is busy binding the tomatoes, or the bee circling the flower, or the fisherman mending his net. And again, the repetition of the last lines suggests a determination to celebrate the rudimentary values of labor and persistence that has no time for profound thoughts on the end of the world.

Forms and Devices

The strength of the poem inheres in the unity and pattern of its imagery. Images of light, for example, suffuse the poem with radiance. Often associated with a feeling of hopefulness, these images seemed to contradict the announced subject of the poem. In the fisherman's "glimmering net," the "gold-skinned snake," the "yellow-sailed boat," and references to the sun and moon, to lightning and "a starry night," give the poem a strong tension, a counterforce to the gloomy announcement that this is the day the world will end.

At the same time, the evocation of sounds accompanies the light imagery, especially in the second stanza's description of the vegetable peddlers shouting in the street and violin's voice lasting in the air. These are sounds that have an end, no matter what their length, and lead into "a starry night," or the end of day.

The poet's use of imagery and sound, then, seems paradoxical, evocative of both the beginning and end of the natural and human cycles. The cycle of day and night, of sounds and sights, seems reassuring and yet leads to the figure of the "white-haired old man" and to his enigmatic statement that "There will be no other end of the world," implying that the world is already at an end. Does his white hair imply he is wise? Certainly the suggestion that he "would be a prophet" adds support to the idea that his point of view speaks for the poet's.

The old man's words provoke questions: Are the things of the world the very "signs" of its end? Is this how the old man interprets things, suggesting that the world ends in the very process of renewing itself, of binding itself up, of completing a cycle? The repetitiveness of his statement seems to mirror the repetitiveness of the world that must come to its own conclusion, as he comes to his own.

The poet's aim apparently is to make one see every day as a portent of the world's ending, as the old man does, and see it only in the images, in the scenes described, not in arguments or spectacles of the world's end, or in some special announcement, a trumpeting of the end. The shift to the present tense in the poem's last two lines emphasizes that there can be no more ending to the world than there is in the poem's present.

Themes and Meanings

At the end of the poem, Miłosz appends a place and date: "Warsaw, 1944." At this time, the Nazis were destroying the Polish city — literally leveling it to the ground, so that it might have seemed as though the world were coming to an end. The poem contains no direct reference to this event or to the war. Indeed, it is astonishingly tranquil, and its evocation of nature is beautiful. The closing lines have a remarkable force considering how Warsaw was coming to its end.

It is as if the poet took the major event of his time, the devastation of Poland and of much of Europe, and decided to dwell on the universal patterns of nature and of human labor and not on the immediate evidence before his eyes. He does not forget his time and place — indeed, he carefully notes them at the end of the poem — but he superimposes on his present a vision of the nature of things, of the old man's steady work and the knowledge of the world he repeats to himself, of the bees, porpoises, sparrows, vegetable peddlers, and so on that bring the world to quite a different end from the one the Nazis believed they were achieving.

In an interview, the poet has acknowledged that he was describing an ideal world, that his poem was a deliberate exercise in naïveté akin to William Blake's great poem "Song of Innocence." Miłosz wanted to capture in poetry an undefiled world as a counterweight to the horror of war. Even though his conception was artificial, it had a therapeutic value and an ironic thrust, showing that the poet could still imagine an ordered, aesthetically pleasing existence no matter how grim the reality of Warsaw's destruction actually became.

Very much a poem about how to relate to the world, it is, paradoxically, an expression of hope, for the world does not end in bombing and killing, or in "lightning and thunder," but in an old man's words, indefatigable and indomitable, as he tends his plants and finds his rootedness in the world. There is no other way to conceive of the ending of the world, in other words, except in his terms, and in the poem's attentiveness to the world's life, which is honored in and for itself, and as an extension of the poet's imagination.

There is no forcing of a point, no world order or philosophy imposed on the structure of the poem. Indeed, the poem rejects people's preconceptions of the way the world will end; it rejects, in total, any interpretation imposed on the evidence of the world it presents. In this respect, the old man's words are the wisdom of age, of the absence of ideology; his thoughts seem to arise out of the imagery of the world and prompt a return to a reading of that imagery and an enjoyment of the poem that is an end in itself.

Carl Rollyson

SONNET 1

Author: Elizabeth Barrett Browning (1806-1861)
Type of poem: Sonnet
First published: 1850, in *Sonnets from the Portuguese*, part of *Poems*

The Poem

Although Elizabeth Barrett Browning called her famous sonnet sequence *Sonnets from the Portuguese*, in order to suggest that the poems were translations, in actuality she wrote them all herself. The forty-four poems describe the development of the love between Elizabeth Barrett, an invalid almost forty years of age, and the vital, energetic poet, Robert Browning, who was six years younger than she. Written during their courtship, the collection was not published until after Elizabeth and Robert had eloped, been married, and had a son.

All the *Sonnets from the Portuguese* are written in the form of a conventional Italian, or Petrarchan, sonnet—that is, a fourteen-line iambic pentameter poem with a prescribed rhyme scheme. Italian sonnets fall into two parts, an eight-line octave followed by a six-line sestet. This first sonnet varies from the pattern only slightly: The octave has been slightly expanded to eight and one-half lines, while the sestet, necessarily, is only five and one-half. The differentiation between octave and sestet is important, because generally in an Italian sonnet the movement to the second part of the poem is marked by a distinct shift or development in thought.

In this poem, the octave itself is based on a contrast. At one time, the poet says, she had thought about the way in which the Greek poet Theocritus had described life. To him, each year was precious, with its own gift; however, at the time when she was musing about Theocritus, the poet herself saw life very differently. To her, it was uniformly sad. Her years had been dark, not bright, and the recollection of them brought her only tears.

At that point, the poet recalls, she became aware of a presence behind her. This spirit seized her by the hair, taking control of her. In accordance with her melancholy view of life, she thought that it was Death which had come for her. To her amazement, however, the spirit identified itself as Love.

Thus the poem concludes with the word which states the theme of the entire sonnet sequence. It is the love of Robert Browning for her, and her love for him, which is to transform Elizabeth Barrett's life, which is to make her sing as rhapsodically as Theocritus.

Forms and Devices

Elizabeth Barrett Browning writes in a fairly simple, straightforward style. Yet the simplicity is as deceptive as that of the American poets Emily Dickinson and Robert Frost; through the skillful use of various poetic devices, Barrett Browning achieves her artistic purposes.

One of these devices, which is important in this first sonnet of the sequence, is that of repetition, which can be used to emphasize and to amplify physical or psychological description. In this sonnet, for example, "the sweet years" of which Theocritus wrote are further defined in the parenthetical phrase that follows, "the dear and wished-for years." By repeating the word "years" and altering the adjectives, that second phrase not only emphasizes the delight Theocritus found in life but also adds further meaning: Instead of merely bringing momentary pleasure, every period in the present creates the expectation of future pleasure.

That amplification is even more important as the octave proceeds into the description of the poet's own contrasting view of life. The seventh line closely parallels the second in form; it also begins with "sweet," as applied to years. In this case, however, "sweet" is united with "sad"; the implication is that the years were filled with disappointments and losses, with frustrated yearnings for a joy which could only be imagined, indeed, with the kinds of emotions the poet herself experienced after the deaths of her brothers and after her own seemingly permanent confinement to her couch and her bed. The simple combination of "sweet" and "sad" thus has an important effect. Still paralleling the second line, the seventh proceeds to a phrase that further explains the poet's viewpoint, "the melancholy years." Although there is no explicit statement as to the future, no "dreaded years" to match the earlier "wished-for years," the principle established in the first quatrain must still apply in the second. The nature of the present suggests the shape of the future, and if each year in the future is to be as unhappy as each year in the present, there is certainly nothing to look forward to, nothing to wish for. In the octave the contrast between the two viewpoints has been stressed both by repetition within each of these lines and by the similarity between the lines.

At the end of the octave, Barrett Browning uses repetition to establish her own hopelessness and to prepare for the unexpectedness of the event which she describes in the sestet. This segment of the poem is dominated by another poetic device, personification, a device already used effectively in the octave. The years are personified in the octave, probably as some kind of Greek supernatural beings. They have presents in their hands, at least for Theocritus. The personfication continues into the description of the poet's life. Each of her years has cast "a shadow" on her; since only a substantial being can produce a shadow, once again the poet is personifying an abstraction.

While personification is important as ornamentation in the octave, it is crucial in the sestet. Although they were inexorable, the years had not used physical compulsion but had operated at some distance; however, Love is personified as something forceful and compelling. The spirit materializes, pulls the poet by the hair, questions her, and identifies itself. The voice speaks "in mastery"; there can be no argument with Love, only acquiescence. The joy that came from acquiescence will be described in the sonnets that follow.

Themes and Meanings
There are several levels of meaning in the first of the *Sonnets from the Portuguese*.

First, the conflict that was settled with the writing of this sonnet is that between death and life. The sad, hopeless existence of the poet, a kind of death that evidently made her willing to submit to actual physical death, was defeated when she was happily conquered by love.

A second theme is that of time. If one is happy, the human power of recollecting and anticipating produces a triple pleasure; while enjoying the present, one recalls past happiness and looks for more happiness in the future. For the poet, however, both past and present are unhappy, and therefore the future can only be dreaded. This theme fuses with the first, for with such expectations, most people would indeed welcome death, as the poet seems to do.

A third theme is suggested in this important introductory sonnet, a theme that will be further developed as the sequence continues. This is the issue of sovereignty, implied in the forceful posture of personified Love and stated explicitly with the words "in mastery." It might appear that in the final lines, the figure that seizes the poet is in fact Robert Browning, capturing his beloved in the time-tested masculine fashion. Certainly Robert would never literally have seized the delicate Elizabeth by the hair, but the lines could be interpreted as implying that he imposed his will upon hers.

Such an interpretation would not be consistent with what is known about the relationship between the two poets. It was Elizabeth Barrett's poetry that first interested Robert Browning in her, and throughout their courtship and their marriage, both poets continued to work on their writing, encouraging each other in a very modern kind of partnership. As the critic Helen Cooper points out, the allusion in these lines is to the *Iliad* (c. 800 B.C.), where the goddess Athena pulls back Achilles, holding him by the hair so that he will not get into a fight. Certainly in Barrett Browning's poem, it is a divinity, not a human being, that has intervened in her life. The happy result, indicated by the description of the divinity's reply as "silver," is made clear in the rest of this sequence of love poems.

Rosemary M. Canfield Reisman

SONNET 6

Author: Elizabeth Barrett Browning (1806-1861)
Type of poem: Sonnet
First published: 1850, in *Sonnets from the Portuguese*, part of *Poems*

The Poem

Although the speaker in the poem is not identified as a woman, the poem reads better if one assumes that a woman is speaking. The conflict expressed in the opening two lines gains power if the speaker is seen as a woman fighting for her independence from a man, as well as a lover struggling to be free of her lover's dominating influence. It also helps to remember that in the background are two real-life lovers: An invalid (Elizabeth Barrett) is writing a series of sonnets to a lover (Robert Browning) whom her tyrannical father has forbidden her to see. This much biographical information, if not essential to an understanding of the poem, greatly enhances one's appreciation of it and makes the beginning of the sonnet clearer and the poet's conflict more poignant.

The poem opens abruptly with a command—"Go from me"—followed by a seeming retraction ("Yet I feel . . .") that introduces the poet's conflict. She appears not to want her lover to go, but he must, for reasons left unexplained. The peremptory nature of the command makes his leaving seem imperative and the fact of his going final. His going will give her strength to "stand"—or will she rise because she is alarmed by his leaving, as if to stop him? The second line takes back the suggestion in the first line that his leaving will make her somehow strong and independent—when he is gone, she will live in his shadow.

Continuing into line 3 and further, the poet reveals an even closer bond between herself and her lover: She will never again direct the "uses" of her soul without an awareness of him. His influence will be felt as far within her own being as she herself can go. Inwardly in this way and outwardly ("nor lift my hand . . . in the sunshine"), she will always have a "sense" of his intimate presence, evident in a "touch upon the palm." Broadening her vision to include the great distance "Doom" places between them, she asserts that even then they will share the same heart. In line 10 she returns to her own inner and outer life, saying that both her actions and her dreams will include him. The two lovers will be as indistinguishable as the taste of the wine is from that of the grapes (lines 10-12). Finally, when the poet seeks God's assistance for herself, the lover's name is heard, and God sees in the poet's eyes the tears of both lovers. Her poem begins with an imperative, the necessary parting of two lovers; it then explains the extent to which their lives shall henceforth be intertwined, touching on the serenity of their union. It ends on an expression of grief mingled with a sublime sense that their union shall be seen by God himself.

Forms and Devices

The poem employs the rhyme scheme of the Petrarchan (or Italian) sonnet, rhyming *abba, abba, cdc, cdc*, and uses the conventional iambic pentameter line, varying the placement of the stresses in some of the lines. Line 1, for example, begins on a stressed syllable ("Go") instead of an unstressed syllable, as the regular lines do. Instead of pausing where the rhyme pattern marks a quatrain, octave, or tercet, as in the Petrarchan sonnet structure, Barrett Browning pauses within the lines. The first heavy pause occurs not half way into line 1 (after "me"). The argument continues without a heavy pause to the end of line 7 ("forbore—"), and comes to an end stop just after the mid point in line 8 ("palm."). Another end stop occurs after "double" (line 10) and another after "grapes" (line 12). The effect of this patterning is to draw attention subtly away from the conventional rhyme pattern and pauses. By continuing her thought through the conventional pause points, she erases the seams of the sonnet structure in favor of the continuity of thought.

In line 1, enjambment—running the meaning from one line to the next around the line end—is used to reinforce thought. The reader comes to "stand," turns to line 2, and reads "Henceforward," reinforcing the image conveyed by "stand." In line 2, the poet's forceful response to her lover's departure is heavily qualified by "in thy shadow," which seems to reduce the poet to her lover's influence ("shadow"). The pause is followed immediately by "Nevermore," which is stressed twice (on "Never" and on "more") and is further emphasized by being placed at the end of the line. "Henceforward," at the beginning of line 2, is subtly contradicted by "Nevermore" at the end of the line.

In line 3, enjambment makes "Nevermore/ Alone" read almost like a single phrase, "Nevermore Alone," but because a slight pause occurs at the end of every line, the two words are actually read as two separate words, both individually qualifying Barrett Browning's assertion that she shall "Henceforward" be in her lover's shadow. The poet's conflict is thus emphasized by punctuation, placement, and metric peculiarities.

This way of proceeding, first suggesting an independent and solitary existence without her lover, then qualifying it with expressions of dependence and helplessness, comes to a major turning point in lines 7 and 8, which conclude just short of the sonnet's conventional octave. These two lines serve as a fulcrum in the poet's argument, giving the sonnet a balance dictated by the poet's feelings and ideas rather than by convention. Significantly, from line 8 to the end of the poem, the tone shifts from an inner conflict to self-confidence, culminating in line 12, where the poet declares an intention to "sue/ God for myself." At the same time, the yes-and-no conflict that characterizes the first eight lines subsides.

The imagery of the poem also reflects the poet's conflict. Images of strength are qualified by images that seem at first to weaken them but actually strengthen them. In line 1, "stand" suggests strength and independence, but it is qualified by "shadow," which suggests dependence. Addressing the "door" of her "individual life," the poet goes no further than the "threshold," suggesting hesitancy. Capable of action, she lifts her "hand," which might suggest an image of a feeble gesture were it not for "Serenely" (line 6) immediately following, which evokes the image of spiritual strength and grace. Even the tears in the final line suggest both grief and joy simultaneously.

Themes and Meanings

In this sonnet, the reader is in the world of profound feelings in the presence of spirit, although the physical world is not ignored. Indeed, it is used to convey the poet's feelings and inner states. She sees aspects of the physical world as an expression of the spiritual or abstract realm within her own being. The "threshold" of her "individual life" is a metaphorical expression of her inner state, though "sunshine" (line 6) moves thought into the physical realm despite its symbolic value. In subsequent lines, "palm," "land," "heart," "grapes," "eyes," and "tears" all refer to physical things, but their meanings in the poem relate to and reflect spiritual and emotional qualities. In them, her thoughts and feelings are embodied. What they represent, in the poem, explains how the poet sees her condition, herself, and her feelings.

As early as line 2, Barrett Browning suggests that she will be incapacitated by her lover's departure—she cannot act "Without the sense of . . ./ Thy touch upon the palm." Rather than rendering her helpless, however, her denial of his presence ("that which I forbore") will leave a "sense" of him with her, his "touch upon the palm." This image deftly suggests a strengthening, but his presence—no more than a "sense" and "touch"—nevertheless increases her, both spiritually and physically. Separation has taught her that she is both weakened by her lover's absence and strengthened by it, but only if she can see beyond the merely physical aspects of her life—"The widest land/ Doom takes to part us," for example. Seeing no further than the "hand" or the "palm" is to miss the highest meaning of their existence, and the purer realm of spirit. The poet makes her metaphors transpose physical into spiritual reality, where "thy heart in mine" can be and where "pulses" can "beat double."

Ordinary union pales before the union she feels and envisions; it is as real yet as rarefied as the taste of the grape in the wine, and the lovers are so commingled that in speaking her own name, God "hears that name of thine." The final line of the poem illustrates the poem's underlying paradox. Tears in the poet's eyes suggest grief, doubled because God will see both the poet's tears and her lover's, but in that union of grief (over their necessary parting) they will be united, and the tears may be seen as tears of joy and triumph. From their parting comes their ultimate oneness.

Bernard E. Morris

SONNET 7

Author: Elizabeth Barrett Browning (1806-1861)
Type of poem: Sonnet
First published: 1850, in *Sonnets from the Portuguese*, part of *Poems*

The Poem

Elizabeth Barrett Browning's audience probably understood the author of her son-nets to be a woman and probably read them as an expression of love from a woman to a man. It is known that before Elizabeth Barrett met her future husband, her health was very delicate and that it improved after their marriage. This much bio-graphical information is useful, for it heightens the experience of the poem, espe-cially since the sonnet deals with the poet herself nearly having died; knowing that two real-life lovers stand behind the poem increases its emotional impact.

The poem opens with the poet declaring that she sees the world differently since she "heard the footsteps" of her lover's "soul" beside her. Adding "I think" (line 1) to this declaration, however, suggests the poet's uncertainty as to the world-encompassing nature of the change. Her lover's footsteps moved between her and death (lines 3-7). She implies that her lover somehow saved her from "obvious death" and, in addition, taught her "the whole/ Of life in a new rhythm" (lines 6-7). Her recovery has given her new life and enough spirit to be glad ("fain") to drink the cup of sorrow or destiny ("dole"), which God "gave for baptism." She would even praise its sweetness, she says, addressing her lover, with him nearby.

The first six-and-a-half lines of the poem explain Barrett Browning's recovery from near death, a recovery of both life and spirit, because her lover brought love into her life. In line 7, the poet shifts from the past to the present—now she is ready to face life with him. The last five lines of the poem look around and ahead, explain-ing that further changes have followed from this revelation: "The names of country, heaven" are now changed. By implication, heaven is where her lover is or will be, "there or here." The "lute and song" the poet hears and "loved yesterday" are now valued only because her lover's name is in harmony with them.

Though addressed directly in line 9 ("Sweet"), the lover remains little more than a hidden reference, "footsteps" in line 2 and a "name" in the last line. Nevertheless, his presence has profoundly transformed her life— "all the world" and "the whole of life" have been affected by him, as well as her outlook and spirit, even her musi-cal preferences. Still, he remains a shadowy figure, one who provided or inspired the "love" (line 6) that snatched the poet from the brink of death and taught her a new vision of life. The purpose of the poem, it seems, is to acknowledge the lover's influence and to indicate its extent, which has saved her life and changed the way she sees the world and "life."

Forms and Devices

The poem follows the structure of the Petrarchan (or Italian) sonnet by rhyming *abba, abba, cdc, cdc,* and it uses the conventional iambic pentameter line, varying the placement of the stresses in lines 6 through 8 and again in line 10. More important, Barrett Browning does not follow the conventional pattern of pauses—at the end of the first and second quatrains, for example (to establish the octave). Nor does the poem use pauses to divide the last six lines into the conventional set of two tercets. Instead, the pauses occur within the lines and are indicated by commas, ellipses (line 12), and the period (line 7). Only lines 9, 11, and 14 end with a heavy pause (a semicolon or period).

The effect of this pause patterning is to pace the argument unconventionally, using light pauses (the comma and line ends) to give emphasis and structure to the argument. Enjambment—running the meaning from one line to the next around the line end—is used to de-emphasize the rhymes in favor of the continuity of thought. Though the poem, with few heavy pauses, has a light touch, it tends to break up its argument into discrete parcels, as though the poet were not entirely sure of herself. Diffidence is hinted at in the "I think" of the first line, and line 3 (which contains four commas) breaks into a tripping rhythm, as if to convey how the "footsteps" moved "as they stole."

The use of commas enables the poet to give some of her words double meanings. In lines 9 and 10, for example, placing commas around "Sweet" and "heaven" respectively suggests more than one reading. Though obviously an address, "Sweet" could be read as a complement of "sweetness," reinforcing that sentiment. In line 10, however, the commas render "country" and "heaven" both apposite and complementary, though the sense of the line makes them coordinate ideas. Indeed, coordination plays a large role in the last six lines of the sonnet, whereas subordination dominates the first eight lines. This structural peculiarity corresponds to a shift in the argument from an emphasis on the past to the present and future and suggests that the poet regards the past in terms of unequal measures and the present and future in terms of spiritual and emotional equality.

Barrett Browning makes some use of repetition and wordplay to reinforce her sentiments and subtly to lighten the subject of the poem. Opening with a reference to the "face" of the world and imaging "footsteps" stealing ("as they stole") in the shadowy world of the spirit and death soften the impact of the subject on the reader. When the poet says that she "thought to sink," one might remember the hesitancy of "I think" in line 1 and not feel directly confronted by the "dreadful" (line 4) subject being reviewed. The poet seems to want to move still further from this dolorous realm by repeating "sweetness, Sweet," mentioning the "singing angels," and even using words such as "fain" and "anear" to reflect the "new rhythm" she has been taught. Although one is certainly not in fairy land, echoes of it pervade the poem.

Themes and Meanings

It may not be too farfetched to suggest that the poem's meaning includes a trip from the "brink of obvious death" to the brink of heaven, a trip more than hinted at in the final lines, with their "lute and song" and "singing angels." A change indeed has taken place, physically (the poet was apparently at death's door), emotionally (the entire sonnet, while acknowledging the grimmer aspects of existence, seems to want to leave those thoughts and celebrate the poet's recovery and rapturous new state), and spiritually. Though a physical recovery is suggested, the poem deals with events occurring in the soul or suggests the spiritual realm: the "outer brink," "love," "the whole of life in a new rhythm," "cup of dole," and so on. This dualism is clearly evident in line 10, where "country, heaven" are juxtaposed to suggest their interchangeability, at least in the poet's mind.

The poet's confidence with regard to her own physical and mental state seems to increase from the first line to the last. The focus certainly shifts from "The face of all the world" to a spiritual realm filled with angelic singing. Between those two realms, the poet declares that her love has taught her a "new rhythm" and a new way of hearing the music "loved yesterday." The poem develops an argument that mounts from earth to heaven, reflecting the poet's own rise from the brink of death to a place where she views "heaven" and hears the notes of an angelic song. Between these two realms—and on the way from the one to the other—the poet would drink. Her sonnet balances on that point midway between her start and her destination. At the center of the poem, the principal elements of the poet's vision blend metaphorically: Sorrow ("cup of dole") is turned by love into "sweetness." The drink, the act of drinking, and the sweetness that is discovered are all metaphorical embodiments that express the poet's spiritual salvation.

Appropriately, Barrett Browning follows her libation with song, as the second half of the poem indicates. Elevation of spirit is reflected in a shift not only from the physical to the heavenly realm but also in the meaning of "Move" (line 3) and "moves" (line 14). In the first reference, the lover is simply walking, "oh, still, beside me," stealing as he goes along. In the last line, however, the lover is moving in time with the "lute and song . . . loved yesterday." Deftly the poet has told her reader that love has saved her life and lifted her spirit into the heavenly realm; at the same time, it has made her lover's name musical as it "moves right in what they say." She has been caught up not only into love but into its music as well, a music that runs through all life.

Bernard E. Morris

SONNET 14

Author: Elizabeth Barrett Browning (1806-1861)
Type of poem: Sonnet
First published: 1850, in *Sonnets from the Portuguese*, part of *Poems*

The Poem

Elizabeth Barrett Browning did not title the forty-four individual poems in the *Sonnets from the Portuguese*; however, the first phrase of the first line of Sonnet 14, "If thou must love me," serves as a kind of title. As such, it indicates immediately that the sonnet will be framed as an argument, using an "if . . . then" structure. Moreover, the word "must" hints that the poem will be more complex than a straightforward question about whether the lover being addressed indeed loves the poem's speaker.

The sonnet begins with the poet talking directly to her lover. She says to him that if he must love her, he should love her only for the sake of love and for no other reason. She says "only" to emphasize that feeling to the utmost. She says not to love her for the cheer of her smile, nor for beauty or the singular nature of her countenance. He should not love her for her voice or for what she says, nor for a special frame of mind that "falls in well" with his. Do not love me for any of these reasons, she tells him, because they could all change over time — or his perceptions of them could change — and the love they have may therefore wither. She adds, do not love her because she needs to be loved and relies on the comfort and support he provides her. She says, love her for "love's sake." Love her because of love and because of the eternal quality of love on Earth.

Taken out of the context of the other sonnets in *Sonnets from the Portuguese*, the idea of loving for only the idea of love itself seems to be confusingly circular. Yet the reader does come away with a strong sense of the fear of loss that underlies the poem. Barrett Browning married the dashing but somewhat footloose Robert Browning in 1846; for doing so, her father disowned her — for the rest of his life, he would not even communicate with his daughter. Furthermore, her brother had died in a boating accident in 1840. It is understandable that she would yearn for permanence and would worry about the loss of Browning's love after the losses and separations in her life.

Forms and Devices

What comes to mind immediately when reading Sonnet 14, "If thou must love me," is the point of view. Sonnets are traditionally given to a perspective of the poet addressing another person, a "you." The point of view is first-person singular, but its direction is entirely pointed at the other person — in this case, as in many, a lover. The reader is left out; that is, the speaker does not speak for the reader's emotions in particular, nor does the reader, in particular, feel something in common with the "you." Instead, one watches the psychological and emotional action unfold as one would watch a drama unfold. In *Sonnets from the Portuguese*, the drama is contained in a series or a sequence of sonnets that tells of the relationship between a man and a woman from the woman's point of view.

Sonnet sequences had traditionally been written by men, who placed their beloveds on a pedestal. The sonnets written by fourteenth century Italian poet Petrarch to Laura epitomize these works. Here the situation is reversed, and a reading of the entire sequence allows the reader to consider this issue more fully. The point of view is one to another, woman to man—and the reader is simply the audience, watching. The effect is to present the actors in their emotional pitches.

The principal device of the poem is the contrast between reasons people fall in love, stay in love, or fall out of love with the utmost reason for being in love—love itself. Barrett Browning arranges the poem in a structure that emphasizes this contrast. For example, the poem's frame is marked by the repetition of the phrase, "for love's sake." When one reads the phrase the second time, in the penultimate line of the poem, it is backed up by the argument Barrett Browning has made to her lover— an argument that readers have bought into by virtue of their role in the audience. The argument is, in a nutshell, that earthly desires for such things as beauty and lack of conflict should not override the eternal nature of love. She pleads with her lover to love her because love is eternal—hence, their love will be eternal.

Themes and Meanings

The main theme of Sonnet 14 is the eternal nature of love. It is not eternal, says the poet, if one lover loves the other for earthly, temporal reasons. These reasons she details in lines 3-12. Earthly reasons fade, as do human beings. Love itself does not fade and die, she states. Therefore, her lover should love her, if he must love her, for the sake of love only.

A crucial distinction here is the word "must." It is this word that casts the poem in the direction it ascends—toward "eternity." For example, if the poem had begun "If thou love me," one would find a different theme altogether. The poem would be about whether the lover truly loves. His love would be called into question, no doubt, even before the poet were to plead for a certain kind of love.

"Must," however, implies that the lover already loves the poet but that he does not have to. The "must" also suggests a different kind of vulnerability on the poet's part. Fate has a role here; she recognizes that if her lover "must" love her, if it is fated in the manner of a "must," then she wants him to love her for "love's sake only." She wants the love to be lifted out of the realm of human passion into the realm of eternal, heavenly passion. One thinks of the ending of the *Sonnets from the Portuguese*'s most famous poem, number 43 ("How do I love thee? Let me count the ways") that ends, "I shall but better love thee after death." The poet sees that if he must love her, it must be a love of eternal power.

This energy, then, becomes the power on which the love rests and through which it exists. To say the least, Barrett Browning has high expectations of her love. If she loses the love, she wants to lose for no less a reason than that the love could not attend to itself on its own course. It would fail because the lovers loved for less than ideal reasons — that is, for earthly and temporal reasons.

David Biespiel

SONNET 35

Author: Elizabeth Barrett Browning (1806-1861)
Type of poem: Sonnet
First published: 1850, in *Sonnets from the Portuguese*, part of *Poems*

The Poem

Sonnet 35, also known by its first six words, "If I leave all for thee," is written in rhymed iambic pentameter lines. The poem, written in the first person, is spoken not to the reader but to the poet's lover. The experience is universal: One lover addresses another. The energy of that address is also universal; it is fevered and intense. The reader watches, as an audience might watch a drama unfold. The sonnet is soliloquy-like, a monologue set apart from the action of stage and drama surrounding it.

The poem begins with the speaker, a woman, asking her lover whether he will make an equal "exchange." The items include nothing less than "all" of her love for all of his. There is a sense of extremes in this opening moment, and the reader senses a tone of desperation on the speaker's part. Something is awry. Her lover seems distant somehow, or she has lost something. The reader cannot be sure. Next she asks herself whether she would "miss" the quotidian of her life, whether the daily, temporal, and basically general talk, the "common" kiss, would be missed. She asks whether her lover could "fill that place" that she would have to give up for him.

The speaker has apparently lost something or someone, and she is deeply concerned about whether her lover can fill the absence. The poet is in grief, she says plainly: "I have grieved so I am hard to love." In this poem, unlike others in the *Sonnets from the Portuguese* sonnet sequence, the poet is preoccupied by something as earthly as death. Still, she wants the man to love her despite her grief. She asks him to open his heart to her, to provide his love for her (in exchange for her love for him) while she is mourning the loss she has suffered. In the final line, she compares herself to a dove who needs another to enfold her, to bring peace of mind to her.

In the summary of this sonnet, one sees that the poet is vulnerable and that the man, her lover, is beseeched to aid her, to bring her back into a less grieving state of mind. Knowing that to leave "all" for her lover is to be vulnerable, she began the poem by asking if he would do the same for her. At the end, she asks for him to take her anyway, so the question at the beginning becomes rhetorical.

It is almost impossible not to think of the courtship of Elizabeth Barrett and Robert Browning when reading the *Sonnets from the Portuguese*. The two poets met in 1845 and were married in September, 1846. Although they had fallen passionately in love, Barrett knew that if she were to marry Browning, her father would be upset, even furious (he suspected Robert Browning of planning to live on her money). The idea of leaving "all" for love was, therefore, a very real prospect. Indeed, her father did disinherit her. The Brownings traveled to Italy, and Elizabeth never saw her father again.

The grief she describes in the sonnet may also refer to (or at least have been inspired by) a particular event in her life. Her brother Edward had died in a boating accident for which she felt partially responsible. Barrett had gone to the English resort town of Torquay, in 1838, hoping that the climate would give some relief for the persistent cough she was suffering. Her brother visited her there but planned to return to London; she persuaded him to stay. When he drowned in the summer of 1840, she was overwhelmed by feelings of grief and guilt. One cannot help but wonder whether the sonnet's "dead eyes too tender to know change" were those of Edward.

Forms and Devices

The traditional sonnet structure is often called an argument. One often sees two or three variations or aspects of the argument, then a turn to a conclusion. For example, an unrequited love poem might run something like the following: Your eyes are dark as a river, your teeth are shiny as stones, your smile is like a waterfall; but you left me and I am drowning in the current of pain you have made. Three points are followed by a turn in emotion and direction.

Sonnet 35 presents an unusual argument. In fact, it is less an argument than an emotional imploring. The form follows the form described above, generally, but with these important differences. First, the poet addresses not only her lover but also herself. The effect of this device is to emphasize the indecisiveness the poet is experiencing. She wants to trade all of her love for all of her lover's love, but she is not so sure of her own end of the bargain. Second, she seems not entirely sure that her lover can fulfill his side of the bargain: "wilt thou fill that place . . .?" The indecision increases; by line 8, the argument is plagued by doubt. What might have appeared to be a series of rock-solid points are thrown into disarray; emotion is overtaking reason.

Third, Barrett Browning introduces her own preoccupation: grief. These lines appear to be the most interesting, most startling, and most memorable of the poem. She reveals that because she herself has grieved, she is "hard to love." She recognizes that it is harder, perhaps, for him to exchange all of his love for her, since her love is more complex. Yet, she pleads, "love me—wilt thou?" Here is the turn in the emotional argument, if one can call it an argument. She seems to capitulate to him, saying that she will give all of her love regardless of what he may do.

Themes and Meanings

Elizabeth Barrett Browning, as the speaker of this poem, is troubled, and her indecision and her "grief" are the paths down which one might look to discover some of the meanings of the sonnet. She appears to be asking her lover not only to conquer love—hers and his—but also to conquer her grief, because she cannot rid herself of a sorrow. For her to have feelings of both grief—which is "love and grief beside" — and love is to complicate the emotion her lover may have for her: Does he want to try to win her love, which is complicated by the utmost sorrow in human emotion? Although she hopes that they might "exchange," she realizes that the deal is loaded and that she represents the worse end of the deal.

Thus, a theme of the sonnet is the complexity of human emotion. When one enters into a love relationship, one brings into it all of one's past experiences (all of one's baggage, as the saying goes) and one deposits them on the doorstep of the new lover. Even if one does not consciously bring the baggage to bear, it follows. One can never escape one's past—or, in the case of Sonnet 35, one's grief. The lover, if he or she chooses, may search through these bags for old bones and ghosts—and may find some. A lover may reveal what is inside and then ask: Can you love me anyway? Can you open your "heart wide"? One's past emotions become complicated in new ones; one begins to experience oneself and one's life as small and fleeting, like a dove, the final image of the poem.

Another theme in this poem is the nature of the relationship between man and woman, and it reflects the traditional view of the protecting nature of a man over his lover. The woman wants to have an emotionally equal relationship. She states this in the first two lines of the poem, but something intercedes. She begins to feel that she may have overstepped—that she is to blame. On the one hand, one may take this to mean that she recognizes her vulnerability. On the other, through a more feminist approach, one may see that she feels imprisoned by her past and believes that she has no alternative but to give herself over to her man. Readers will have to draw their own conclusions.

Nevertheless, the poet desires her lover to take her, baggage and all, and she is willing to give "all for thee" without hearing whether he will reciprocate. What the reader sees, then, is a poet in the throes of turmoil, in a poem that enacts the nature of that turmoil.

David Biespiel

SONNET 43

Author: Elizabeth Barrett Browning (1806-1861)
Type of poem: Sonnet
First published: 1850, in *Sonnets from the Portuguese*, part of *Poems*

The Poem

All the forty-four poems in Elizabeth Barrett Browning's sonnet sequence *Sonnets from the Portuguese* were written during the period of courtship that preceded her marriage to Robert Browning. As a whole, *Sonnets from the Portuguese* is considered one of the finest poetic sequences in literature. It is Sonnet 43, however, often titled "How do I love thee?" from its memorable first words, which is the best-known of the collection; indeed, it is one of the most-quoted love poems in English literature.

Sonnet 43 is an Italian sonnet, a fourteen-line iambic pentameter poem written in a specific rhyme scheme. The first line of the poem asks a question; the other thirteen lines answer it. The question is simply, "How do I love thee?" The answer involves seven different aspects of love, all of which are part of Elizabeth's feeling for Robert, and the projection of an eighth, eternal love in the future.

As the poem proceeds, each variation on the theme of love is introduced with the words "I love thee." In the octave (the first eight lines), the poem speaks of the spiritual side of her love, which aspires toward God; then she mentions its earthly aspect, the love that enriches daily life. More briefly, she mentions the fact that her love is given freely, almost as if it were prompted by the conscience, and that it is pure, in other words, selfless, like the action of a humble man unwilling to accept praise.

In the sestet (the final six lines), the poet looks at her love in three more ways. First, she explains that this love makes use of the emotions once spent on grief or on religious faith. From this mention of faith, she proceeds to a slightly different idea: that in loving Browning, she has rediscovered a love like that she once felt for the saints of religion. Finally, she explains that her love is all-encompassing, involving her entire life, including moments of unhappiness as well as happiness; that her love is as much a part of her as breathing, that is, the very act of living. In conclusion, the poet asserts that, God willing, this love can even transcend death and continue in the next world.

In most sonnets, there are eight or twelve lines stating a question, a conflict, a problem, or a possibility. In the final six lines, or sometimes in a final couplet, the question is answered, the conflict resolved, the problem solved, or the possibility denied or extended in some way. This sonnet is unusual in that the question is stated in the first line, and the rest of the poem is made up simply of various answers to that question. Even the last line and a half, which could be said to provide some kind of resolution, is really only another answer to the original question, which might be restated as "What are the various ways in which love affects the lover?"

Forms and Devices

It is a mark of Barrett Browning's skill that the repetition of the phrase "I love thee"—nine times in a poem only fourteen lines long—simply serves to make the poem more effective. The phrase is first used in the question; then, when the poet sets out to "count the ways," she keeps score by introducing each new idea with exactly the same words. Certainly the repeated phrase is more than a marker; it emphasizes the fact she is stating—that indeed she loves the man to whom the poem is addressed. The repetition is also realistic; at least in the early stages of the emotion, most people who are in love have a tendency to reiterate the declaration frequently. The fact that the poem is structured around the repetition of the phrase "I love thee" is, therefore, one source of its effectiveness.

In addition to carefully crafted phrases, most poems as popular as this sonnet have striking images. One thinks of the description of the snow, even the sound of the horse's bells, in Robert Frost's "Stopping by Woods on a Snowy Evening," or of the moonlit beach, the lights of the French shore, and the final dramatic reference to armed conflict in Matthew Arnold's "Dover Beach." In contrast, "How do I love thee?" has almost no descriptions. The only real images in the poem are the mention of light in the sixth line and the reference to "breath,/ Smiles, tears" in the thirteenth. One might include the rather vague stretching of the soul described at the beginning of the sonnet.

Instead of relying on sensuous imagery, Barrett Browning describes the abstraction, love, by means of other abstractions. For example, love is compared to that expansion of the soul in search of "the ends of Being" (or the meaning of the world) and of "ideal Grace" (evidently the grace of God). Similarly, the similes in lines 8 and 9 involve movement toward or away from two other abstractions, "Right" and "Praise." The later references to "griefs" and "faith," even to "lost saints," are all made without an imagistic context. Because of this lack of images, the almost incantatory repetition of the simple phrase "I love thee" becomes even more important; it helps the reader proceed through the abstractions, just as the word-pictures created by images do in other poems.

It also should be pointed out that metrically this poem is extremely regular. There are few variations from the iambic pattern. Instead, the sonnet proceeds in a quiet and stately manner that seems almost to deny, or at least to suggest a different definition of, the "passion" the poet stresses in the ninth line. Only with the three stressed syllables near the end of the sonnet, "breath,/ Smiles, tears" does the speaker reveal the depths of the emotion so reasonably described; immediately thereafter, she returns to her dignified iambics for the conclusion of the poem. In interpreting the poem, one must look carefully at the point where the metrical pattern breaks; it seems likely that it will be the thematic center of the sonnet.

Themes and Meanings

As a complete sequence, *Sonnets from the Portuguese* describes the development of Elizabeth Barrett's love for Robert Browning. As the forty-third poem in a sequence of forty-four, "How do I love thee?" describes a fully realized love. Earlier poems often had mentioned the past, when the poet did not dream that such happiness would ever be hers. In this poem, she defines her present happiness by explaining how her love incorporates and transcends her past spiritual and emotional experiences.

For example, Barrett Browning speaks of her love as being the striving of her soul for the divine, for the purposes of life and for that "Grace" that is the gift of God. Similarly, the seventh and eighth lines suggest that her love is like the spiritual quests for morality ("Right") and for humility ("Praise"). Her love has brought her back to the kind of innocent faith she knew in her childhood, but seemingly had lost. All these descriptions indicate that the kind of love Elizabeth now feels for Robert is akin to the love that enables a human being to love God and to experience God's love in return.

Earlier poems in the sequence had referred to the unhappiness and despair of the years before Elizabeth met Robert. In this sonnet, the poet triumphantly announces that her love has redeemed those years. For example, the capacity for intensity that she developed in past sorrows now can be utilized, instead, in the joy of her love. Similarly, the capacity for belief that she developed in her youth now can be exercised in the complete faith that provides the security of love.

Even though in Sonnet 43 many references stress the spiritual, the poet also makes it clear that the relationship is solidly based on earthly needs. In the temporal world, day alternates with night ("sun and candlelight"), happiness with unhappiness ("Smiles, tears"). Barrett Browning does not expect a heaven on Earth; all she needs is the presence of the beloved during the changes that define life in this world. Finally, she emphasizes her awareness of the final change: that from life to death. In the final lines, the heavenly and the earthly, the spiritual and the temporal are united. The rhyme words are significant. With the help of God, the lovers will proceed together from a last "breath" into a new life and an even more devoted love "after death."

Barrett Browning's description of a love that thus encompasses past, present, and future has appealed to both men and women for almost a century and a half. Recent feminist critics have pointed out another significance of the sequence, and especially of the later poems within it, such as this. From the Renaissance on, sonnets have been used by men for the expression of their own emotions, first for love-complaints and later for expressions of friendship, anger, and religious uncertainties. In *Sonnets from the Portuguese*, a woman poet expressed her love for a man in her own unmistakably feminine voice. Sonnet 43 focuses on Elizabeth, not on Robert; it is the revelation of a woman's own heart and soul, fortunately inspired by a man who was worthy of her.

Rosemary M. Canfield Reisman

SONNET XXVII

Author: Pablo Neruda (Neftalí Ricardo Reyes Basoalto, 1904-1973)
Type of poem: Sonnet
First published: 1960, as "Sonnet XXVII" in *Cien sonetos de amor*; collected in
  One Hundred Love Sonnets, 1986

The Poem

Although Pablo Neruda calls the fourteen-line poems in the volume *One Hundred Love Sonnets* sonnets, he uses the traditional sonnet form in widely different ways— from a virtual free-verse order within the framework of a sonnet (as in "Sonnet XXVII") to the more conventionally strict forms; a sonnet is traditionally a lyric poem of fourteen lines, highly arbitrary in form, and adhering to one or another of several set rhyme conventions.

In the first stanza of "Sonnet XXVII," the speaker of the poem addresses his beloved. Opening the stanza with the word "naked," the speaker compares the simple lines of his beloved's naked body to the simplicity of one of her hands. He goes on to describe her body with the following adjectives: "smooth, earthy, small, transparent, round." Continuing the description, the speaker, in the final line of the stanza, in an apparent contradiction to the roundness emphasized earlier, compares his beloved's body to a slender grain of wheat, conjuring up images of another image of earthiness.

The second stanza begins also with the word "naked." The speaker continues to use metaphorical language to express his emotional response to his beloved's body. The first metaphor of the stanza declares that the woman's body is "blue as a night in Cuba." Metaphors of earthiness introduced in stanza 1 are continued in the next line: "you have vines and stars in your hair." The beloved's naked body is also compared to the sacredness of a beautiful summer day; it is "spacious and yellow/ as summer in a golden church."

The third stanza, like the previous two, opens with the word "naked." The lover likens his beloved's naked body to one of her fingernails. Her body is "tiny," "curved, subtle, rosy." It is only tiny, however, at night; at daybreak, her body retreats to a different place, to an "underground world."

The final stanza describes this underground world as "a long tunnel of clothing and chores." In the daylight hours, the beloved's body loses its brilliant light: It dons clothing, loses its earthiness; that is, it "drops its leaves." The delicate, almost magical shape and form of the woman's body at night becomes transformed, by daylight, into something more mundane. Her body is now merely a "naked hand again."

Forms and Devices

Although the volume *One Hundred Love Sonnets* was dedicated to Neruda's third wife (the greatest love of his life, Matilde Urrutia) as an affirmation of his love for her, it is not only to her that Neruda sings in these sonnets but also to the things that make up his life with her. Neruda's love for Matilde fuses in these sonnets with his love of nature.

The subject of "Sonnet XXVII" is woman in nature, cosmic woman, woman surrounded by the force and attributes of nature. Neruda as a nature poet is essentially an observer of his surroundings as well as his own emotional attachment to those surroundings. The inner world of his own psyche is often described in terms of the external world of nature and matter; it is formed and expressed through images and metaphors taken, in a process of synthesis, from the poet's external environment. In this way, Neruda is both a modern poet of nature and a poet of the human condition.

The basic images of "Sonnet XXVII" equate the beloved's body with some aspect of the natural world. In the process of linking woman to nature, Neruda's metaphors "explode" the human body, subject it to a peculiar tension, and extend it. For example, the unexpected imagery in the first stanza describes the beloved's naked body as having "moon-lines, apple-pathways." The poet describes the roundness of the woman's body by comparing its shape with that of objects in nature; it is also as slender as "a naked grain of wheat."

The poet builds a bridge between the human body and the universe; the woman's body is felt to be an important part of the cosmos. The beloved is a being endowed with supernatural powers; she has "vines and stars in . . . [her] hair." The beloved is, in this line, literally part of the earth, part of the universe from which she has come. Her sexuality transcends her individual nature, and the relationship between the speaker and his beloved transcends two individual people. The relationship becomes laden with philosophical consequences.

Woman's sexuality is described not only through nature imagery but also in quasi-religious metaphors. In the second stanza of the poem, the beloved's body is described as "spacious and yellow/ as summer in a golden church." In these lines, sexuality, nature, and religion fuse. The color of the woman's body and its spaciousness trigger a memory in the mind of the speaker: being inside a vast church on a golden summer day. The woman's body is described not only lovingly but also with reverence and awe by the speaker.

Themes and Meanings

In Neruda's earlier love poetry, *Viente poemas de amor y una cancion desesperada* (1924; *Twenty Love Poems and a Song of Despair*, 1969), love is described as both a joyous and a perilous experience. There is often a shadow lurking in the background, an indefinable threat, a romantic foreboding. In the mature Neruda of *One Hundred Love Sonnets*, however, there is only one tone; it is pure joy, sensuality, union, ecstasy, and triumph that inspire these poems. Love, Neruda seems now to say, can be explored in all of its enchantment without the fear of suddenly losing it.

The major themes of "Sonnet XXVII" are love, passion, and eroticism—but, as previously mentioned, always linked with nature. Neruda's relationship with nature is essentially sexual. Sex, for Neruda, is a way of entering the world, of conquering and being conquered by the world. It is a path to knowledge.

The poem is dominated by a purely erotic tone. Although it is the beloved's body that is glorified in this poem, the speaker's love transcends the body. He is unwavering in his devotion, and a sense of contentment and peace permeates the poem.

The speaker sees his beloved as part of two worlds: the world of night and the world of day. The woman is both day and night, as she is both round and slender (in the first stanza). The two colors used to describe the beloved's body in the second stanza are blue ("blue as a night in Cuba") and yellow ("yellow/ as a summer in a golden church"); thus, she is both darkness and light. The woman's body is described as a world in itself, as well as being part of the world of nature.

The final stanza describes the "underworld" to which the beloved descends after the night is over. There is a sense of regret in the speaker's tone when he must let her go and cross over into that world. This underworld is not, however, a place of darkness and death. In Neruda's poem, the underworld to which the woman returns is a place crowded with daylight and practicality. The woman emerges from the glorious and erotic night, her "clear light dims," and this extraordinary mortal resumes the tasks of an ordinary woman once again.

Genevieve Slomski

SONNET 18

Author: William Shakespeare (1564-1616)
Type of poem: Sonnet
First published: 1609, in *Sonnets*

The Poem

This fourteen-line poem begins with a straightforward question in the first person, addressed to the object of the poet's attention: "Shall I compare thee to a summer's day?" After a direct answer, "Thou art more lovely and more temperate," the next seven lines of the poem develop the comparison with a series of objections to a summer day.

William Shakespeare develops the "temperate" elements of his comparison first, leaving the "lovely" qualities for later consideration. His first criticism of summer is that in May rough winds shake the "darling" buds. This objection might seem trivial until one remembers that the poet is invoking a sense of the harmony implicit in classical concepts of order and form which writers of the Renaissance emulated. His use of the term "darling" extends the harmonious concept to include the vision of an orderly universe embracing its creations and processes with affection.

Such terms apply only to the ideal universe, however. In nature's corrupt state, after Adam's fall, all sublunary (earthly) forms and events fail to adhere to their primal harmony. Hence, rough winds shake the May buds and, as the next line indicates, summer is too short. Sometimes the sun is too hot; at other times the day becomes cloudy.

In lines 7 and 8, the poet summarizes his objections to the summer day by asserting that everything that is fair will be "untrimmed," either by chance or by a natural process. The most obvious meaning here is that everything that summer produces will become less beautiful over time. The word "fair," however, seems to mean more than merely beautiful to the eye and, like the words "lovely" and "darling," comprehends all desirable qualities. Here, too, the poet invokes the concept of sublunary corruption. Although he is apparently still discussing the disadvantages of a summer's day when compared to the person he is addressing, he is at the same time creating a transition to the next section of the poem by introducing the second element of his comparison, that comprehended in the word "lovely."

The last six lines of the sonnet detail the advantages of the person addressed, indicating no diminution in the durability or fairness of that individual. The reason lies in the "eternal lines to time" that Shakespeare creates in his sonnet, knowing that the poem in which the person is memorialized will last through all time.

Although in the concluding couplet Shakespeare gives a direct statement of the theme, he uses the pronoun "this" to carry the weight of meaning and gives no verbal referent to the pronoun. Yet in making the poem itself the referent, the poet creates the object that will transmit the immortality of its subject to eternity.

Form and Devices

This poem is a sonnet, a poem consisting of fourteen lines in iambic pentameter, a form created by Petrarch, an Italian poet of the fourteenth century. A Petrarchan sonnet usually contains eight lines sketching a situation (the octave) and six lines applying it (the sestet). The form was modified by Sir Thomas Wyatt and Henry Howard, earl of Surrey, appearing in poetic anthologies during the mid-sixteenth century. They and other poets created the English sonnet, consisting of three quatrains followed by a couplet, rhyming *abab, cdcd, efef, gg*. In this form, the eight-six division is occasionally maintained, as in Sonnet 18, but the concluding couplet summarizes the theme.

The sonnets of Shakespeare, taken as a whole, may be said to form a sonnet sequence: a series of sonnets, usually addressed to a woman for whom the poet has conceived a passion. From Petrarch's time on, the conventions of the lover's complaint pervade the imagery of these sequences, but their originality of imagery and conceit generally transcends the limitations of the troubadour traditions from which they derive. The women of these sequences have themselves become widely known: Petrarch's Laura, Sir Philip Sidney's Stella (Penelope Devereux), and Edmund Spenser's Elizabeth Boyle have achieved the kind of immortality that Shakespeare's Sonnet 18 contemplates.

It is thus ironic that the object of Shakespeare's own sequence should be unknown. The poems themselves range over many topics, including the beauty and desirability of marriage for a young man, a love triangle, a "dark lady," and several philosophical and moral problems. They form a unique source of speculation on Shakespeare's life in addition to being poems of great power.

In Sonnet 18, Shakespeare sets up his comparison by rhetorically introducing the basis for a simile that will underlie the structure of the whole poem: the comparison between the person who is the object of the poet's attention and a summer's day. The first image, of rough winds shaking May's buds, is stated directly. In the next line, however, the poet uses the metaphor of summer's lease being too short, aptly indicating the transitory nature of a season and, by extension, a year, and a life.

The use of metonymy in "eye of heaven" (the sun) illustrates the power of that device: The eye is usually thought of as the agency for perception and character; here the central focus of the sky seems central to the concept of nature itself. Personification of this eye enhances the subject of the poem as a whole, for dimming his gold complexion implies hiding the beauty of the individual whom the poet addresses — something the poet intends to prevent.

The personification of death in line 11 curiously treats the word "shade," often used to describe those who have died. Here it seems to signify, instead, the atmosphere of death — the shadow that hovers over those who come within its influence, which the poet's lines are about to dispel.

Themes and Meanings

As in his plays, Shakespeare's sonnet introduces several themes reflecting Renaissance thought. The most important of those here is the belief that everything under the moon was corrupted by Adam's fall from grace. Thus, although the sun (the "eye of heaven") moved in an uncorrupted sphere above the moon, the earthly influence upon its shining could make it either too hot (line 5) or too hazy (line 6). A corollary of this fall was the consequent mutability of the sublunary creation. For Shakespeare the change was not lateral; rather, it involved a progressive degeneration of beauty, created by chance or by the influence of time on nature (lines 7, 8).

In Shakespeare's Sonnet 18, one may thus discern Renaissance beliefs about nature. One can also see remnants of medieval thinking. This combination appears most obviously in the poet's treatment of the Ovidian tradition. The Middle Ages had interpreted Ovid (43 B.C.-A.D. 17) as a moral poet whose *Metamorphoses* (c. A.D. 8) contained a cosmology based on Greek and Roman myths. The Renaissance, on the other hand, saw him as an erotic poet whose *Amores* (c. 20 B.C.; *Loves*) and *Ars Amatoria* (c. 2 B.C.; *Art of Love*) provided the model for Petrarch and later sonneteers.

In Sonnet 18 one finds both the moral and erotic suggested in the words "lovely," "darling," and "fair." Emphasis on the physical beauty of the person addressed is tempered by hints that this beauty outshines that of the natural universe itself; through the poet's lines, it becomes one with Plato's eternal forms. Missing from this sonnet, however, is that part of the Petrarchan tradition that sees the lover complaining of his mistress' rejection and displaying his own despair or resolution resulting from it. In its place one finds the central theme of mutability, the imperfection and impermanence of the sublunary world, infusing the first eight lines and providing the foil for the rest of the poem.

In contrast to the mutability theme, the concluding sestet proclaims Shakespeare's art as the antidote to time and change. The poet's consciousness of his own genius, although placed here within a tradition maintained by several of his predecessors, transcends the limitations of the fallen world. *Ars longa, vita breve* (art is long, life is brief) becomes the underlying theme, arrayed in Shakespeare's unique and comprehensive poetic language.

Russell Lord

SONNET 19

Author: William Shakespeare (1564-1616)
Type of poem: Sonnet
First published: 1609, in *Sonnets*

The Poem

William Shakespeare's Sonnet 19 is a traditional English sonnet (traditional because Shakespeare made it so), consisting of a single stanza of fourteen lines, rhymed according to a standard format. Like the other 153 sonnets by Shakespeare, Sonnet 19 has no title.

In the first quatrain, the poet addresses time as a devourer, handing out a series of defiant invitations to time to perform its most destructive acts. First, time is instructed to "blunt" the "lion's paws," which gives the reader an image of enormous strength reduced to impotence. In line 2, the poet moves from the particular to the general, invoking time as a bully who forces the earth, seen as the universal mother, to consume all her beloved offspring. Line 3 echoes line 1. It gives another image of the strongest of nature's creatures, this time the tiger, reduced to weakness. Time, seen as a fierce aggressor, will pluck out its teeth. No gentle decline into age here. In line 4, the poet moves to the mythological realm. He tells time to wreak its havoc by burning the "long-lived phoenix." The phoenix was a mythical bird that supposedly lived for five hundred years (or a thousand years, according to some versions) before being consumed in fire. The phoenix was also said to rise from its own ashes, but that is not a meaning that the poet chooses to develop here. The final phrase in the line, "in her blood," is a hunting term that refers to an animal in the full vigor of life.

The second quatrain begins with a fifth invitation to time, couched in general rather than specific terms: "Make glad and sorry seasons as thou fleet'st." This takes the invocation of time's destructive power to a more refined level, because it alludes to the human emotional response to the hurried passage of time: Seasons of gladness and seasons of sorrow form part of an ever-recurring cycle. Lines 6 and 7 seem to continue the poet's willingness to allow time full sway to do whatever it wants wherever it chooses.

In line 8, however, the argument begins to turn. Having built up a considerable sense of momentum, the poet checks it by announcing that there is one limit he wishes to place on time. It transpires that all the concessions the poet has made to time in lines 1 through 7 are one side of a bargain the poet wishes to strike. The terms are now forcefully announced, as the poet attempts to establish his authority over time. He forbids time, with its "antique pen," to make furrows on the brow of his beloved. The friend must be allowed to go through life untouched ("untainted") by the passage of time. Anything less would be a crime, because the lover is an exceptional being who must represent to future ages the pattern of true beauty — an eternal beauty that stands outside the domain of time.

In the final couplet, however, the poet seems to acknowledge the futility of his demand, yet he remains defiant. In spite of the wrongs that time inflicts, the poet's friend will forever remain young because he will live in the poet's verse.

Forms and Devices

The sonnet is a highly concentrated work of art in which the poet must develop and resolve his theme within the strict confines of the sonnet form. Sonnet 19, like all Shakespeare's sonnets, follows a standard pattern. It consists of three quatrains and a concluding couplet, and it follows the rhyme scheme *abab*, *cdcd*, *efef*, *gg*.

The meaning of the sonnet is reinforced by the variations Shakespeare makes in the meter. This takes the form of a subtle counterpoint between the regular metrical base, which is iambic pentameter, and the spoken rhythm—what one actually hears when the sonnet is read. For example, in the first quatrain, the theme of the destructiveness of time is brought out more forcefully by a series of metrical inversions.

In the third foot in the first line ("blunt thou"), a trochee is substituted for an iamb, resulting in a strong stress falling on the first syllable. This gives "blunt" a much stronger impact than it would otherwise have, especially as the rest of the line follows a regular iambic rhythm. In line two, the last foot is a spondee rather than an iamb, resulting in two heavy stresses on "sweet brood." The emphasis on the "sweetness of what time destroys" makes the work of time seem even more harsh. Line 3 is a very irregular line, echoing the turbulence of the sense. There is a metrical inversion in the first foot (it is trochaic, not iambic) that serves to highlight the word "Pluck." This recalls, through assonance, the "blunt" of line 1. Both of these are forceful words that express the way in which time assaults the natural world. The second foot of line 3 is a spondee, and the assonance contained in "keen teeth" adds to its prominent impact in the line. The fourth foot of this line is also a spondee, making the "fierce tiger" very fierce indeed. Line 3 in particular, with its high number of stressed syllables, brings out the idea of time as an aggressive, fearsome warrior going to battle against all living things.

The meter of the second quatrain is more regular than the first. The speedy passage of the end of line 5 ("as thou fleet'st") echoes the sense, and this is emphasized again by the heavy stress on "swift" in line 6. In the third quatrain, the turbulent rhythm and harsh consonants of the earlier part of the sonnet vanish as the poet turns his attention to the friend. The smooth and regular iambic rhythm of line 12, for example, "For beauty's pattern to succeeding men," suggests the perfection of the friend.

Time makes a forceful reappearance in the first line of the couplet, with the spondee, "old Time," prominently positioned immediately before the caesura. This makes the triumph of the last line, in which the poet obtains his victory through the power of his pen (a contrast to the seemingly all-powerful "antique pen" of time), all the more striking and effective.

Themes and Meanings

In this sonnet, the poet faces up to one of the most fundamental facts of human existence: the transience of all things, even those of greatest power and beauty, and including those most loved. In seizing on this theme, Shakespeare echoed a passage from Ovid's *Metamorphoses* (c. A.D. 8), a source he turned to often: "Time, the devourer, and the jealous years that pass, destroy all things and, nibbling them away, consume them gradually in a lingering death."

The conflict between beauty and time, and the anguish of the lover who fears the touch of time on his beloved, is a major theme of the whole sonnet sequence. In sonnet 16, for example, the friend is reproved for not making sufficient effort to "Make war upon this bloody tyrant Time." In sonnets 1 through 17, the poet proposes a solution. He enjoins his friend to marry and produce progeny, so that he will live again through his offspring. Sonnet 12 states that nothing can stand against time "save breed." In Sonnet 19, however, this solution is implicitly abandoned because all of earth's "sweet brood" will be devoured by time. Here "brood" recalls the "breed" of sonnet 12, but the significance of the term has altered completely.

The battle against time is made more intense in this sonnet by the absolute value that the poet attaches to the friend. He is the very archetype of beauty, "beauty's pattern to succeeding men." Such an ideal view of the lover is repeated at other points in the sonnet sequence. Sonnet 106 states that all the beauty of past ages was only a prefiguring of what the friend now embodies. In Sonnet 14, the poet claims that the most fundamental values in existence are bound up in the life of his friend, and cannot endure after his demise. Sonnet 104 reveals that future ages will not be able to produce anything to match the beauty the friend embodies. It might perhaps be said that the poet sees in the friend what William Blake would later describe as the "Divine Vision." This presence of an absolute, transcendental element in the relative world of time and change fuels the dramatic tension that gives Sonnet 19, and others, a stark and poignant power.

Bryan Aubrey

SONNET 30

Author: William Shakespeare (1564-1616)
Type of poem: Sonnet
First published: 1609, in *Sonnets*

The Poem

The opening lines of William Shakespeare's thirtieth sonnet ("When to the sessions of sweet silent thought") evoke the picture of a man sweetly and silently reminiscing, living once again the pleasant (or "sweet") experiences of his past. The situation, however, soon shifts from silence to a sigh and from pleasantries to a lament for projects never completed, desires never fulfilled. The angst of this cannot be confined to the past but bursts into the poet's present consciousness. He suffers intense nostalgic pain for the wasted time that can no longer be reclaimed. Old woes are reborn, exacerbating a fresh hurt.

The second quatrain of the sonnet expands this idea, but the pain is heightened as the author thinks of the people who will never again come into his life. This brings tears into the eyes, as once again the pain of loss is relived. The vanished sights lamented are the faces of friends who have disappeared into death and the emptiness of love that is no more, but also suggested are places, possessions, and events that can never be re-experienced.

The third quatrain adds little new content, but increases the weight and significance of the poem's central idea: The act of remembrance recalls old griefs into the present where they become as painful in their rebirth as they were the first time they were experienced. It is as if the persona of the poem were caught in a psychological trap from which there is no escape and in which his mind, as if dragging chains, moves "heavily from woe to woe," unable to escape from the images that repeat "the sad account of fore-bemoaned moan." Though the account has been paid up in the past, the debt of pain is reopened and he must pay the entire amount again.

After twelve lines of bewailing the symptoms of the persona's condition, the final couplet of the sonnet moves abruptly to the solution. The cure is carefully coordinated with the disease, for just as the patient's woes were initiated by remembering the past, so are they dissipated by the thought of his current "dear friend," which restores all the lamented losses and ends all the reborn sorrows.

Forms and Devices

This sonnet is an "English," or "Shakespearean" sonnet—that is, it is composed of three quatrains and a couplet of iambic pentameter, rhymed *abab, cdcd, efef, gg*. What is different about the structure of this sonnet is that there is far less development from quatrain to quatrain than is usual for the overall collection. Shakespeare most often develops his sonnets by moving his argument in three quite distinct steps to its concluding couplet, or by developing three quite different images to be tied neatly together in the closing lines. This sonnet, however, has far more repetition than differentiation from quatrain to quatrain. The differences are subtle: The quatrains quietly move from wailing to weeping to grieving, a progression that is hardly noticed.

What makes this one of Shakespeare's most loved sonnets is not its structure but its music, achieved in part through the rhymes, but even more distinctively through the repetition of consonant sounds. In the first quatrain of the sonnet there are no less than twelve sibilant sounds, which, rather than hissing, evoke the music of the wind. The sound is repeated in the last line of the sonnet, surely an intended recapitulation to increase the feeling of completion. The fourth line of the poem introduces a series of alliterated *w* sounds: "And with old woes new wail my dear Time's waste." These sounds introduce the rhythm of wailing, which is repeated in line 7, "And weep afresh love's . . . woe," and again in line 10, "from woe to woe." Repeated liquid sounds in line 7 add a languid sound to the line — "love's long since canceled woe" — and repeated *m*'s add both softness and length to lines 8 and 11: "And moan th' expense of many," and "fore-bemoaned moan." A lengthening of sound comes in the repetition of *fr*'s in "friends" and "afresh" in lines 6 and 7. The poem's alliteration enhances the meaning of the text and emphasizes both the standard iambic pulse and the variations from this standard in lines 1, 6 and 7.

Another device evident in this poem is what seems to be a calculated use of ambiguity. In the first line, the word "sessions" denotes a meeting of a legal court, but in context it also suggests a mere period of time. Thus "thought" could represent the judge presiding over the session or merely describe the activity of a designated period of time. Again the persona, the "I" of the poem, could be the judge, summoning his remembrances to stand trial. In the fourth line, the word "new" could be an adjective modifying "woes," which were once old and have now become new, or it could act as an adverb modifying "wail." It is not beyond possibility that "my dear" could be a noun of address, since the final couplet makes it clear that the sonnet was addressed to a "dear friend," though it seems more probable that "dear" is an adjective modifying either "time" or "waste."

"Time's waste" could be read as either the person having wasted his time or (more likely) as time, the destroyer, having laid waste to items and qualities of ultimate value to him. "Expense" in line 8 could be read in its most usual modern sense as cost, the money spent, or simply as loss: something that is spent is gone. "Foregone" in the ninth line probably means simply past, as having gone before, but could also carry the connotation of "given up," or "taken for granted." In the tenth line, "tell" could mean to relate, but more likely has the older meaning of "count" or "tally." "Account" could mean a mere story, a financial account, or the final accounting at the last judgment. This accumulation of ambiguity engages the reader's mind, focusing it on the form and keeping it from wandering; it also enriches the poem by suggesting alternative readings.

The dominant metaphor of the poem is the comparison of a period of reminiscing to the session of a court of law, but even so it is not meticulously carried out in the nature of an Elizabethan conceit. Words such as "canceled," "expense," "grievances," "account," and "losses . . . restored" may suggest court language, but the idea is not worked into the syntax. Other uses of figurative language enriching the poem are an eye "drowned" in tears, friends "hidden" in night, a woe "canceled" as if it were a debt, and an "account" of moans that needs to be settled.

Themes and Meanings

Shakespeare's Sonnet 30 is a beloved, often-remembered, often-quoted poem simply because it is an exquisite description of the pain of nostalgia, an experience which is common to most of humankind. The human psyche does not want to let go of the experiences of its past, even when that experience was exceedingly painful, or perhaps especially because it was painful, since somehow the hurt has increased the meaning of the moment. It certainly has increased its intensity. The release which dissipates such remembered pain is also a welcome experience, and the reader of Shakespeare's sonnet experiences that release as the tension built up in the first twelve lines of the poem disappears in the recollection of a current, fulfilling friendship.

The poem is meaningful also because of its inclusion in the most famous collection of sonnets in the English language, if not in any language. Though almost no scholars believe that Shakespeare himself was responsible for the order in which the sonnets were printed, this poem does belong to the early group which were addressed to a young man. It also has a close relationship with the sonnet immediately preceding it and the one that follows, pointing to the probability that these were written together. Sonnet 29 has the same thought progression as 30, as the poet laments the fact that Fortune has not been kind to him and wishes that he might change places with anyone a bit higher on her wheel. When the thought of his friend intrudes on this mediation, however, all is made right: The lark announces day, the earth sings, and he would change places with no one. Sonnet 31 is largely an explanation of the thirtieth. "Losses are restored" because those whom the author "supposed dead," whom he "thought buried," are alive in his friend, who contains all of their virtues. The friend is the grave containing all of their lives, "Hung with the trophies of my lovers gone,/ Who all their parts of me to thee did give." In this realization, the poet discovers a new, integrated personality, for what he used to find by dividing his love among many, he now finds in only one person who contains in himself all of those who have gone before. Though Shakespeare's Sonnet 30 stands alone, perfect in its own merits, that unity is more fully appreciated in the context of its neighbors.

Howard C. Adams

SONNET 60

Author: William Shakespeare (1564-1616)
Type of poem: Sonnet
First published: 1609, in *Sonnets*

The Poem

Sonnet 60, like all sonnets, is a fourteen-line poem of one stanza, rhymed according to a traditional scheme. The sonnet is one of 154 untitled sonnets by William Shakespeare, each of which adheres to the form of what is referred to as the English, or Shakespearean, sonnet.

The first quatrain consists of an extended simile, comparing the passage of human life to the onward movement of waves rushing to the seashore. Each wave pushes the one in front of it, and is in turn pushed by the one that follows it. Each following the other in close succession, the waves struggle forward.

The second quatrain introduces a new thought, more directly relating the passage of time to human life. The newborn baby, once it has seen the vast light of day, quickly begins to crawl. This is the first stage in its growth to manhood. Once the human being is "crowned," however—that is, attains in adulthood its full stature as a royal king, the summit of the natural order—he is not allowed to rest and enjoy his status. The heavenly bodies, which have ruled his destiny since the day he was born, conspire against him to extinguish his glory. The same process that resulted in the gift of birth and growth is now responsible for change and decay.

The third quatrain develops the idea of time as destroyer, highlighting three lethal actions that time performs. First, time tears. It "doth transfix the flourish set on youth," which means that it pierces through the attractive outward appearance, the flower, of youth. Second, time imprints itself; it creates furrows ("delves the parallels") in the brow of the beautiful. Third, time is all-devouring. It consumes the most valuable and most prized things that nature produces. Nothing at all can stand against time, whose scythe will mow down everything.

It seems inevitable that time will be victorious, but in the final couplet the poet attempts to salvage what he can. He believes that at least one thing can survive the onslaught of time. In future times, his verse will "stand," if all else has fallen. At the same time, the poet reveals what has prompted his meditation on the destructive nature of time: his love for the youthful beauty of his friend. The poet's verse will always ring out in praise of this beauty, in spite of the devastation wrought by the "cruel hand" of time.

Forms and Devices

The frequent occurrence of *s* sounds in the first two lines (on no fewer than seven occasions) suggests the sound of the incoming waves as they break on the shore. The final two *s* sounds, in "minutes hasten," are placed closer together than the others, and this suggests the increasing speed and urgency of the passage of time.

The second quatrain is remarkable because it fuses three distinct sets of images: child, sun, and king. "Nativity" is at once the birth of a child and the rising of the morning sun. The child that "Crawls to maturity" is also the ascending sun, and "crowned" suggests at once a king and the sun at its zenith in the sky. This thought would have come easily to an Elizabethan mind, at home with the idea of an intricate set of correspondences between the microcosmic world of man and the macrocosmic heavens. The same image occurs in Sonnet 33, and Shakespeare's play, *Richard II* (c. 1595-1596).

At this point of maximum strength and power, the man-king-sun faces an assault on his position, as "Crookéd eclipses 'gainst his glory fight." "Crookéd" suggests the plotting of rivals to usurp his crown; "eclipses" is an astrological reference, suggesting an unfavorable aspect in the heavens that will bring about the inevitable downfall of the man-king, as well as ensuring the downward passage of the sun as it loses its glory over the western horizon. "Crawls" (line 6) and "Crookéd" (line 7) are given added emphasis by the trochee at the beginning of each line and by alliteration, which also links them both to "crowned" at the end of line 6. The rising and falling rhythm of the final line of this quatrain, "And time that gave, doth now his gift confound," sums up the idea conveyed in the first three lines.

The third quatrain is introduced by a trochee, "Time doth," which gives notice that time is to be the direct subject of this part of the sonnet. Another trochee in the first foot of line 11 emphasizes the consuming aspect of time, and Shakespeare again makes use of a trochaic foot, "Praising," in the first foot of the second line of the couplet. This paves the way for the defiant flourish with which the sonnet ends. The fact that the phrase "Praising thy worth" is followed by a caesura slows the line down and leaves this phrase echoing in the reader's mind, a magnificent counterpoint to the "cruel hand" of time that the sonnet has labored to convey. Labored is the appropriate word here, since the struggle of all sublunary things depicted in this sonnet is hard and unrelenting. Images of struggle begin in the first quatrain, as the waves "toil" and "contend" with each other. The slow struggle of the man upward is suggested by the caesura placed after "Crawls to maturity," and this struggle lasts far longer than his brief moment of glory, which dissolves after another fight.

Themes and Meanings

This sonnet is closely related to sonnets 63 through 65, and many others in the sonnet sequence, which also bemoan the inexorable advance of time and pose the question: How can beauty survive, given that all created things are transient and travel their allotted course to death? The theme of these sonnets was in part inspired by a passage from Ovid's *Metamorphoses* (c. A.D. 8): "The baby, first born into the light of day, lies weak and helpless: after that he crawls on all fours, moving his limbs as animals do, and gradually, on legs as yet trembling and unsteady, stands upright, supporting himself by some convenient prop. Then he becomes strong and swift of foot, passing through the stage of youth till, having lived through the years of middle age also, he slips down the incline of old age, towards life's setting. Age undermines and destroys the strength of former years." This passage gave Shakespeare the image of "Nativity, once in the main of light,/ Crawls to maturity," and the passage that follows in Ovid, "Helen weeps . . . when she sees herself in the glass, wrinkled with age," may have suggested to Shakespeare the image of "delves the parallels in beauty's brow."

Shakespeare is not content to leave the world, or his friend, to mutability. The attempt in this sonnet to immortalize the friend through the poet's verse is also a theme of many other Shakespearean sonnets, including numbers 19, 55, 63, 65, 100, 101, and 107. Some readers may find the resolution of the problem, which is accomplished in the final two lines of the poem, unsatisfactory. How can the hope expressed in the couplet somehow outweigh the remorseless pressure that has been built up in the first twelve lines? It might be argued that a poem about a beautiful person now dead is a poor substitute for the presence of the living person. The same argument might be applied to the solution proposed in sonnets 1 through 17, that the friend should marry and produce offspring, and thereby achieve a kind of immortality, but it should be pointed out that these are secular poems. The poet refuses to take refuge in any belief system that will soften or remove the effect of mutability. In this sonnet, as in others, there is no Christian heaven in which the lovers can look forward to another meeting, and the thought is not Neoplatonic; the friend is not described as a shadow or reflection of an eternal form, existing in an ideal world not subject to change. On the contrary, in this sonnet the human and the natural worlds are inextricably intertwined; the images of the devastating effects of time can be applied equally to both human and nonhuman realms. The poet thus works towards his triumph, limited though it may be, entirely in the terms that the natural order offers.

Bryan Aubrey

SONNET 65

Author: William Shakespeare (1564-1616)
Type of poem: Sonnet
First published: 1609, in *Sonnets*

The Poem

The opening quatrain of William Shakespeare's Sonnet 65 asks how beauty can resist that power in nature which destroys brass, stone, earth, and the sea, since beauty is less durable and powerful than any of those. The earth and sea together cannot withstand death, the dismal ("sad") state that overpowers everything in nature. In the third line, mortality becomes "this rage" — a violent anger, even a kind of madness, that opposes a most fragile supplicant, beauty. If the earth itself is no match for this force, beauty seems to have no hope of lasting, since its strength is no more than a flower's.

The second quatrain repeats the opening question, beauty now characterized by another of nature's insubstantial and temporary forms, "summer's honey breath," which the poet sees as the victim of an assault by a "wreckful siege" in the form of "battering days." The "earth" alluded to in the opening line is represented here as "rocks impregnable," and brass has been replaced by "gates of steel." Neither of these substantial forms can withstand time's battering and corrosive force. Though asking a question, the speaker implies that any resistance to time is doomed and, further, that natural things are in constant battle with a force that nothing survives, least of all something as evanescent as summer's breath.

The third quatrain begins with an expostulation that expresses the poet's feelings as he confronts the prospect of time's onslaught: "O fearful meditation!" Even flight is futile, for beauty, now represented as a jewel, cannot escape being encased finally and forever in "Time's chest." Time is then characterized as the swift runner whose foot cannot be held back. No outside force — no "hand" — can or will reach out and rescue beauty from time's onward thrust. At the close of the third quatrain, beauty is not only a doomed supplicant but also a helpless victim of time's plundering. At this point, the poet appears to have accepted the inevitable annihilation of beauty by time's relentless onslaught.

The final couplet offers hope, however — the written word. Mere ink, imbued with the poet's love, offers the only defense against Time's annihilating power, for the poet's words have the miraculous ability to reflect beauty's splendor in a timeless state.

Forms and Devices

The sonnet's fourteen lines form three quatrains and a concluding couplet, rhyming *abab, cdcd, efef, gg*. Known as the Shakespearean (or English) sonnet, this arrangement differs from the Italian (or Petrarchan) sonnet in adopting a different rhyme scheme and dividing the sestet (the final six lines) into a quatrain and couplet. The third quatrain addresses the poem's subject somewhat differently from the first two quatrains (which correspond to the octave of the Italian sonnet), and the couplet offers a final comment on, or a summary of, the foregoing argument. A typical line consists of five stresses, or ten syllables, called iambic pentameter: "Since bráss, nor stóne, nor eárth, nor boúndless séa." An extra syllable is occasionally added to the line, as in lines 2, 4, and 10. Within this highly patterned world, Sonnet 65 achieves myriad effects.

Wordplay creates much of the poem's irony by combining multiple meanings into one word. The "sad" in line 2 characterizes the personified "mortality," sad because it is his duty to destroy things; at the same time, "sad" expresses the poet's own feelings regarding this destructive force. In the third line, "this rage" ironically plays on the idea that mortality, usually thought of as a dormant state, is a violent passion, even a madness. Shakespeare twists the traditional conventions by assigning such a passion, not to the lover, but to the force that destroys beauty. Irony is implicit, too, in the reference to "boundless sea," which is nevertheless "bound" by "mortality." Though the tone of the sonnet may not be entirely serious— Shakespeare seems close to mocking the tradition of the forlorn lover in the line, "O fearful meditation! where, alack"—any playful spirit the poem may have is sobered by the ominous nature of the subject.

The poem's principal imagery focuses on the various forms given the chief antagonists, "Time" and beauty, though beauty is depicted in images that suggest insubstantial form (a mere "plea" and "summer's honey breath"), a passive hardness ("jewel"), and a helpless victim (Time's "spoil"). Time is personified variously, too, as a force that "decays," keeps jewelry in a chest, has a swift foot, and plunders his victims. When the poem wants to suggest the delicate, impermanent nature of beauty, imagery is deft—"flower . . . summer's honey breath." When it wants images of strength, it is prolific—"wreckful siege . . . battering days . . . rocks impregnable . . . gates of steel."

Numerous sound effects underscore the poem's doleful tone. Repetition of words (such as "nor" and "O" and structures—the five questions, for example—suggests the relentless assault of "this rage" as well as the urgency of the speaker's mingled hope and fear. Apt alliteration—"steel so strong" and "none, unless"—and vowel sounds reinforce the meaning. The sound of "brass" and "stone" suggests more durable qualities than those of a flower and honey breath, and the phrases "rocks impregnable" and "gates of steel" sound "harder" than the more mellifluous sounds of "miracle have might" and "my love."

Themes and Meanings

Shakespeare's central theme is the opposition between the transitory, delicate nature of beauty and the devastating effect on beauty of mortality and its principal instrument, time. The opening questions seem rhetorical, indirectly arguing the poet's conviction that beauty is no match for aging and death. The final two lines dispel the gloomy predictions implicit in the questions, however, by pointing to the power of the written word to sustain its subject—in this case, beauty. As the poem advances through the first two quatrains, the changes in the images of time suggest an increase in the implacable strength of time, which only "o'er-sways" in the second line but turns to a "rage" and then a "wreckful siege of battering days" attacking such impressive things as "rocks impregnable" and "gates of steel."

The final two lines, by opposing "black ink" with the light which the poet's love emits, leave the reader with the central conflict of the poet's vision: light (beauty) is opposed by darkness (black ink), and therefore utter annihilation. The balancing imagery of the final line suggests a resolution to this conflict and so ends the poem on a bright note, literally on the word "bright" itself: The poet's love, expressed in this written sonnet, is the one force that can successfully oppose time and death. The word "still" in the last line introduces a paradox. If "my love" is "still," meaning lifeless, it cannot "shine," yet it does, or might; if it is indeed motionless, it cannot "still" be shining, yet it may, in "black ink," and in that form, it can forever oppose the destructive motion implicit in the phrase "this rage." The poet's skill is the only force that can reverse the effects of aging and stop time's forward motion, which carries all things to their death. The poet's hand becomes the "strong hand" (line 12) that can indeed hold time's "swift foot back." The surprise is that the strength is not physical but poetic.

A more subtle surprise is that, while appearing to address what male lovers are expected to address, a beautiful woman, Shakespeare here focuses on beauty, perhaps in keeping with the poem's general air of indirection—rhetorical questions develop the poet's subject all the way to the final couplet in place of direct argument. The poem seems to suggest that to be any more direct, by addressing his beloved directly, he would "expose" her to time's onslaught. By remaining as "hidden" and insubstantial as "Time's best jewel," the object of his love may be saved. If the "black ink" of his poem draws a curtain of darkness before the face of his beloved, her beauty may nevertheless shine through the love that the poem expresses.

In keeping with the delicate indirection of the poem, the poet makes only slight references to the sexual aspect of his love, principally in the third quatrain, where "impregnable" subtly suggests where the poet's mind is going—time is a ravager of beautiful women, one way or another. Hints of ravishment continue as the poet references "gates of steel" and concludes in his using "spoil" (plundering) that beauty cannot "forbid."

The structure of the final line reflects brilliantly the poem's resolution, the inky blackness of annihilating time at one end of the line and, at the other, the redemptive light of the poet's love. Between these two states is the poet's "love," the fulcrum that forever separates and balances them.

Bernard E. Morris

SONNET 73

Author: William Shakespeare (1564-1616)
Type of poem: Sonnet
First published: 1609, in *Sonnets*

The Poem

This fourteen-line poem, which is divided into three distinct quatrains (four-line stanzas) followed by a couplet (two lines), is addressed to the poet's lover and comments on the approach of old age in the speaker. As in all the Shakespearian sonnets, the voice is that of the poet. The lover has sometimes been interpreted as the unknown "Mr. W. H." to whom the first quarto edition was dedicated, but Samuel Taylor Coleridge surmised that the lover must be a woman.

The poet opens by stating that his lover must behold him at the time of life corresponding to late autumn, when almost no leaves remain on the trees and the birds have flown south. The poet's calling attention to his old age might seem incongruous, since many lovers might try to hide the fact from their companions. Yet, in this relationship, William Shakespeare not only is being forthright but also seems to be seeking the sympathy of his dear friend.

In the second quatrain, the image shifts from the time of year to the time of day. He chooses twilight, the period between sunset and darkness, to reflect his state. "Twi" originally meant "half," so "half-light" signifies a period of diminished abilities and activities, again calling for the sympathy and understanding of the poet's friend. The second half of the quatrain brings forth more forcibly the associations of darkness with death and emphasizes the immanence of that mortal state in the poet's life.

The third quatrain moves from the world of seasons and time to the more restricted compass of natural phenomena—the way a fire burns itself to ashes and then is smothered by those ashes. As the magnitude of the image decreases, the force of its message concentrates, concluding with the very picture of a deathbed.

The concluding couplet sums up the purpose of Shakespeare's revelation of his decreasing powers: to request that his friend love more strongly because of the short time left to the poet. Critics have been concerned with the word "leave" in the last line, since it might be thought to indicate that the lover is the one to depart. Some have even commented that "lose" might better convey the idea. Certainly the death of the poet would cause a separation to occur, however, and the lover would have to "leave" him.

Forms and Devices

This poem, a sonnet, consists of fourteen lines of iambic pentameter. The form, which was created by Petrarch, an Italian poet of the fourteenth century, usually consisted of eight lines sketching a situation (octave) and six lines applying it (sestet). The form was modified by Sir Thomas Wyatt and Henry Howard, earl of Surrey. They and other poets created the English sonnet, which consists of three quatrains followed by a couplet, rhyming *abab*, *cdcd*, *efef*, *gg*. In this form, adopted by Shakespeare and frequently called by his name, the couplet summarizes the theme.

Shakespeare's sonnets range over many topics, including the beauty of a young man, the desirability of his marriage, a love triangle, a dark lady, and several philosophical and moral concerns. In addition to their poetic power, they remain a unique source of biographical speculation.

Sonnet 73 contains three distinct metaphors for the poet's progressive aging. The first of these is the implied comparison between his state and the time of year when a few yellow leaves, or none at all, remain on boughs shaking in the cold winds, deserted by the birds that usually inhabit them. One might be tempted to compare this directly with graying and loss of hair, but it is more probably to be taken generally as a reference to the aging process. William Empson has pointed out manifold connotations of the "bare ruined choirs" in his *Seven Types of Ambiguity* (1930), evoking images of ruined monastery choir stalls made of wood and infused with the atmosphere of stained glass and choirboy charm, showing how that richness is unified by the way that the poet's subject relates to his narcissistic affection.

The second quatrain moves from the time of year to the time of day. Again there is a metaphor: The poet's likeness is that of a day fading in the west after sunset. Instead of the yellow of the first quatrain, there is the black of night's approach, a more sinister prospect. There follows a personification within the metaphor, naming night as death's second self, in essence creating a new metaphor within the first as it envisions night, which "seals up all in rest." The word "seals" suggests the permanent closing of a coffin lid, providing a finality that is only slightly relieved by the knowledge that the reader is actually seeing not death, but night. Some critics have suggested that the word "seals" suggests the "seeling" of the eyes of a falcon or hawk, a process of sewing the eyes of the bird so that it would obey the falconer's instructions more exactly. This suggests an even more forcible entry of death into the metaphor.

Structurally, this concept would close the octave of a Petrarchan sonnet, and although the English sonnet has ostensibly eliminated the eight-six division, the vestiges of a division remain, since the poet moves from his year-day metaphors to another kind of figure in his next quatrain. Here, the metaphor involves a complex process rather than a simple period of time. The afterglow of a fire gradually being choked by the ashes of its earlier burning becomes the description of Shakespeare's aging. The ashes of the fire's earlier combustion are the poet's own youthful dissipation, hinting an extravagance of which we know nothing biographically except the metaphorical statement made here. Although there is no specific color named, one senses the red of a glowing fire, enhancing the yellow and black of the previous descriptions. The concluding couplet moves from metaphor to direct statement, summarizing the purpose of the poet in revealing so frankly his approaching old age. After the richness of the preceding lines, it might appear almost anticlimactic, yet it is important to the structure of the form, lending finality to the whole.

Themes and Meanings

As do his plays, Shakespeare's sonnets introduce themes reflecting Renaissance thought. In order to understand them, one must realize what the term "Renaissance" implies. The word was introduced into art criticism by John Ruskin in *The Stones of Venice* (1851-1853), when he referred to a return to "pagan systems" in Italian painting and architecture during the fourteenth century. Essayist Walter Pater extended the meaning of the term to include all phases of intellectual life. Scholars have associated with the Renaissance such phenomena as Neoplatonism, humanism, and classicism. Recently, they have also deduced that medieval traditions were not utterly displaced; there was no sharp dividing line.

Perhaps the most obvious theme in Sonnet 73 is that of mutability, deriving from Greek and Roman philosophers, but strained through the theological thinkers of the Middle Ages and modified during the Renaissance. Basically, it describes all "sublunary" phenomena (those beneath the moon, thus corrupted) as subject to change. Thus they lack the permanence both of biblical perfection and of Platonic ideals.

In this sonnet, Shakespeare's consciousness of himself and of his beloved friend remains rooted in mortality and mutability. Unlike the idealized relationship portrayed in earlier sonnets, here there is a strong consciousness of the changes that old age brings to the poet and to his relationships with others. Here is resignation in the face of the inevitability of death and his permanent separation from his beloved. Time becomes omnipotent. It controls all natural processes, and no expedient of art can resist it. The most one can do is to express a heightened affection for one who is soon to pass away.

If one examines the consistency with which Shakespeare has joined his three sets of images, one may glimpse something of the coherence created by the poet's genius. The words "bare ruined choirs" of the first quatrain are strengthened in the second into the words "Death's second self." In the third, what was previously merely a metaphor for sleep has become metaphorically a deathbed. The concluding couplet may be considered a further step still, since it translates metaphorical references to death into personal ones referring to the poet's own approaching end.

It has been shown that the poet uses a variety of colors within the quatrains of this sonnet: yellow, black, and red (glowing). These colors have suggested to other poets images of death and pestilence. Shakespeare uses them to describe metaphorically his approaching old age. Thus he maintains the theme of inevitable change and sublunary corruption throughout.

Russell Lord

SONNET 76

Author: William Shakespeare (1564-1616)
Type of poem: Sonnet
First published: 1609, in *Sonnets*

The Poem

The first quatrain of the sonnet consists of two questions that address a supposed problem with William Shakespeare's own verse — its utter conventionality, barrenness of thought, and monotony (it is "far from variation"). A more ambitious or imaginative lover, he says, would express himself with variety and surprise ("quick change"). The second question implies that, in keeping with the fashion ("the time"), the poet should employ better "methods" and new "compounds." Besides being destitute of invention, it seems that he lacks a pleasing spirit of adventure. The second quatrain questions the poet's motives or common sense in writing verses that are "ever the same" and have a familiar appearance ("noted weed"), since it can easily be known who wrote them and where they were sent ("did proceed"). In matters of love, the implication is, discretion is the soul of wit.

Having presented one side of love's coin in the first eight lines of the sonnet, the poet turns the coin over in the third quatrain, answering the implied charge of triteness and lack of imagination. Actually, he argues, by writing always of one subject, "you and love," he is being clever; instead of wasting his effort by trying always to invent new words, he devotes his "best" to simply dressing up the old and thereby finding continued use in what has already been used. Expressing his love in verse is in fact like spending money, and words are like coins. His subject, "you and love," enables him to give familiar words new meaning, to reuse those that have been used before. The benefits of this kind of recycling are too obvious to argue: less effort, less waste, greater efficiency.

Lest his beloved not be convinced by this curious way of looking at his verse, Shakespeare in his final couplet points out that his method is the very principle upon which the sun operates, returning again and again, ever the same yet always new. What better model can a poet have than the sun itself? His verse repeats what has already been written, or spoken, but like the sun, it brings with it a new look, the difference being the poet's "love."

Forms and Devices

Unlike the Italian (or Petrarchan) sonnet, the Shakespearean (or English) sonnet is divided into three quatrains and a couplet, rhyming *abab*, *cdcd*, *efef*, *gg*. The first two quatrains introduce and develop the subject of the poem to the end of the eighth line, where a pause occurs. The third quatrain addresses the subject from a somewhat different perspective, concluding the poet's argument in line 12. The couplet sums up the foregoing argument or, as in Sonnet 76, delivers a final statement that clenches the matter.

Each line of the sonnet regularly consists of five stresses, or ten syllables, called iambic pentameter. In Sonnet 76, lines 1, 3, 5, 8, and 12 are irregular. All these lines except line 1 combine iamb feet (in which the stress falls on the second syllable) with trochees, two-syllable feet whose stresses fall on the first syllable of each foot: "Whý with the tíme do Í not glánce asíde," for example. The last four syllables in the first line vary the conventional line even further, placing the stresses and unstressed syllables in pairs (illustrated here within brackets): so bár[ren of néw príde]." These variations subtly contradict the poet's conceding that his verse is conventional.

Structurally, the poem develops as an argument. The first eight lines challenge the poet with three questions, which he answers in the third quatrain and final couplet with a witty rejoinder that demonstrates his skills as a noteworthy opponent. Within this debatelike format, Shakespeare's logic weaves a paradox, which ironically displays those very qualities and skills that the questions imply he lacks. His verse is deficient in "new-found methods" and "compounds strange," yet his poem is a compound of wit, logic, and sophisticated argument: By writing always of his "love" and "dressing old words new," the poet transforms old coin into new and in that way gives his "love" permanent currency ("still telling"). While seeming to admit his artistic failings through the first twelve lines, the poet's conceit—that writing and loving are like reusing the same words and spending money—cleverly demonstrates those skills he appears to admit not having.

The poem's rich wordplay is evident in simple puns, such as the use of "time" (line 3) to mean poetic meter and the time in which the poet lives; the double meaning of "O, know" (line 9); and the more subtle play on seed in "proceed" (line 8). Its more important role is developing at least three arguments simultaneously by playing on the various meanings of spending, telling, inventing, and arguing.

This wordplay is evident in how the poet suggests various roles for himself. As an actor, he might perform a "quick change" (line 2), develop a new style of acting ("new-found methods"), or stay with the familiar mode and dress ("noted weed"), performing his "best" by "dressing" old words in new ways. In this conceit, he ironically hints that his words are nothing more than memorized speech and that he is "acting" the part of the lover, ending with the ambiguous compliment of repeating ("telling") again and again "what is told (line 14)."

As a dealer in coin, on the other hand, he might make "quick change" or deal in new "compounds" (metals or coinages); his words, being coins (punning further on the notion that words are coined), reflect the value of his name, and he spends the word-coins that have been spent before (line 12). Finally, as the poet-logician, he debates the question of his method with a skillfully reasoned argument: His "love" and the words in which he expresses it are the same "coin" that he counts out and spends, making new currency out of the old or, like the sun, returning always the same but always new.

Themes and Meanings

The principal metaphor of the sonnet equates words with coins that the poet counts out, or spends, as he writes verse. Line 2 suggests that the poet's verse is unacceptable as currency, "far from . . . quick change." In line seven, "tell" plays on the idea of counting out the poet's name as if it were coin. The metaphor of spending continues in line 12 and concludes in the last line, where the twin actions of counting out ("telling") and being spent ("told") are brought together. Because "telling" also means revealing, the poet conducts a simultaneous argument, that to write verse is to reveal his love to the world, and he ends with a pun on "told," which conflates these two meanings and conclusively demonstrates the poet's skill in both writing and "spending," for he brings his argument to a close at the very point where it and his love are "told" — summed up, counted out, and revealed.

The idea that lovers should not let others know their secret runs through the puns already mentioned, especially the use of "tell," which suggests revealing a secret and hints at verbal indiscretion. The last line plays on this notion by asserting that the poet's "love," represented by this poem, continues to reveal publicly — so long as it is read — the fact of his love and its valued substance, which is already reckoned and revealed ("told"). If his verse is as repetitious as the sun, it is also as visible as the sun.

A third argument is evident from the first line, where "pride" suggests an animal in heat. This idea is continued in the reference to "birth" (line 8) and to spending and being spent (line 12), giving "new and old" (line 13) the additional meaning of generation. From old words come new life, as the old generation procreates the new.

The theme of the old producing the new unifies the various arguments of the poem. As an actor, Shakespeare is challenged to invent new "methods" instead of keeping "invention in a noted weed" that is "ever the same." His "best," however, is to dress "old words new." As a dealer in "coin," he is perhaps expected to make "quick change," seek "new-found methods" and "compounds strange" so as to avoid having "every word . . . tell" his name — that is, reveal its commonplace value. The third quatrain asserts the poet's superior value, the ability to spend "again what is already spent." Writing verse confers upon him a power, like the sun's, of continuously returning, by being read again and again, each time his verse shedding upon the world the brilliant light of his "love." The old generates new life by simply returning (being read or "told" again). The act of writing verse goes beyond even the procreative act, however, for the old is not replaced by the new; rather, the old and the new unite forever in the poem, which is "still" reckoning and revealing what has already been revealed and reckoned.

Bernard E. Morris

SONNET 87

Author: William Shakespeare (1564-1616)
Type of poem: Sonnet
First published: 1609, in *Sonnets*

The Poem

The sonnet opens with William Shakespeare bidding a farewell to his beloved. The lady is too "dear" for the poet to have, he says; he does not deserve her, so his right of ownership reverts to her. The first four lines establish the "legal" justification for his giving up possession: the "charter of thy worth," a contract which grants its owner the right to be released of any "bonds" should the holder be found unworthy of maintaining possession of the property.

This legality established, the poet in the second quatrain argues the basis of his decision. The lady herself has granted him possession on the assumption that he was worthy of such a gift, yet he does not deserve "this fair gift," and according to a legally binding contractual agreement, he therefore must relinquish possession; his right ("patent") is hereby being returned ("back again is swerving").

The first eight lines of the poem soberly lay the legal foundation of the poet's ruling. The case is unarguable, since the "law" is clear on the matter of granting patents of ownership. Once the case has been decided, the poet pauses and, in the third quatrain, turns to events leading up to his decision. Originally, the lady — "fair" (line 7) probably refers to female beauty — gave herself to the poet because she was ignorant of her own value, or she overestimated the poet himself. As a result, her "great gift," increasing because of the misunderstanding ("misprision"), returns to the owner herself now that better judgment has been achieved. The final couplet appears to end the poem on self-effacement. The poet now realizes that he has been living a dream that both flatters and deludes him, for only while sleeping is he a king deserving of such a gift (or made a king by the gift); awake, he discovers the dream to be a delusion and finds that he is not a king — "no such matter."

Forms and Devices

The sonnet's fourteen lines form three quatrains and a concluding couplet, rhyming *abab*, *cdcd*, *efef*, *gg*. In lines 1 and 3, "possessing" and "releasing" appear to be "near" rhymes, and "wanting" and "granting" (lines 5 and 7), sight rhymes. A typical Shakespearean sonnet line consists of five stressed and five unstressed syllables, called iambic pentameter. The first two quatrains, corresponding to the octave of the Italian sonnet, develop the poem's argument from one perspective. Whereas the Italian sonnet ends with a set of six lines, a sestet, Shakespeare divides his final six lines into a quatrain and a couplet. The third quatrain addresses the poem's subject differently from the previous two quatrains, and the couplet makes some kind of summary statement about the whole argument.

Sonnet 87 is unusual in that all but two of the lines (2 and 4) are irregular, containing an extra unstressed syllable at the end of the line. All but two of those syllables are "-ing," the other two being "-er." This attention-getting feature makes the reader wonder what the poet is up to. The "falling" syllable at the end of the line tends to weaken the effect of the rhyme, and collectively these rhymes may hint at a similar "weakness" on the part of the poet, either in his resolve or in his attitude toward his subject and himself. Perhaps the diffusion of structural force reflects a corresponding diffusion of spiritual force. The extra syllable may also reflect a corresponding "looseness" or excess in other areas of the poet's character and behavior.

By ending ten out of fourteen lines with the present progressive (such as "possessing," "releasing," "granting," "deserving"), Shakespeare focuses attention on the presentness of his actions. Though the poem speaks of past actions, the rhymes emphasize the ongoing nature of the poet's state of mind. The poet has given up possession of his "fair gift," but his feelings and thoughts continue to be occupied by the "matter" at hand. The opening— "Farewell!"— focuses attention immediately on the present moment and sets up the "logic" of the progressive verb forms. In this way, the poet's structural peculiarities reflect, even underscore, not only his state of mind but also the principal ideas of his poem.

Typically, wordplay informs the sonnet throughout and enables the poet to develop multiple meanings simultaneously. For example, "bonds" (line 4) refers to the bonds of love and friendship as well as to legal documents. The lover's "how do I hold thee" refers to a physical act, but in figurative terms, legal possession is meant. Line 8 plays on the idea that a "patent" gives one a license to sell or manufacture something, but used in conjunction with "swerving," it has moral overtones while describing the course of a metaphorical ship.

Three principal metaphors control the contents of the poem. One is evident in the idea of the woman being a ship that has come to the poet's port and now is being returned to its own port ("back again is swerving" and "Comes home again"). The second metaphor is that of legal proceedings having to do with ownership, estimates, patents, charters, bonds, and so on. The poem becomes a courtroom where possession is returned to its owner once "judgment" (line 12) has been made. This perspective is reinforced by such words as "misprision," which is a legal term that means a wrong action or omission, specifically the failure of an official to do his duty, and "matter," which refers to something to be tried or proved. The third metaphor develops the idea that the lover "possesses" his beloved sexually, and if "this fair gift" (line 7) refers to her virginity, Shakespeare's argument is ironic, for one cannot return such a gift.

The puns and metaphors give the sonnet an air of a legal proceeding that on the surface seems playful, the poet cleverly displaying his verbal skills and wit. Upon closer scrutiny, however, the poem reveals something other than a flattering display of the poet's feelings for the person he addresses.

Themes and Meanings

The central focus of the poem is on the idea that in romantic and legal affairs alike, possession is granted upon a certain understanding of a thing's, or person's, value. The poet appears to be confessing that he is not good enough for the woman, and the sense of disappointment that pervades the poem from beginning to end appears to express the poet's sad discovery that he must give up possession of his "fair gift" according to the stipulations of his patent. Self-discovery and self-sacrifice are implicit, and they conclude with the poet's final stipulation — that he is in fact no "king," but far from it.

A darker side develops under the surface of this two-faced poem, however; the poet may be announcing to the lady that he is sending her away because she has lost value. In this light, the tone of the poem is sharpened to a cynical edge — now that the poet has "had" the woman (line 13), her value is depreciated, and she must be returned. The matter is clear, and she "like enough" knows her "estimate" now that she has been possessed: She has given herself to a man too freely, without justification ("The cause of this fair gift in me is wanting"), so possession is forfeited. Indeed, he may not even want her now.

If one accepts the assumption that the "patent" guaranteed him a virgin or an unpregnant woman, his possessing her (sexually) has voided the contract. The statement "thy worth gives thee releasing" ironically refers to the woman's present condition, now debased because of her "misprision." The phrase "upon misprision growing" hints at a "mistake" that resulted in the woman's pregnancy — "swerving" in line 8 reinforces the idea that the lady has gone off course morally or otherwise. The poet's discovery that, awake, "no such matter" exists could therefore refer to his profound disappointment in finding that she is neither a "dream" nor "matter" fit for a king.

Couching his thoughts in legal terms may hint at the poet's underlying intent to pass judgment on the woman for her mistake, void their agreement, and send her packing. Shakespeare is careful to make clear who is responsible — she is the one who granted him possession of herself in the first place (line 5); "Thyself thou gavest," he repeats (line 9), and she is guilty of poor judgment, which "better judgment" (line 12) must correct. He hints that the better judgment is his, and in the final two lines he suggests that all these errors have been occurring while he was asleep. The "dream" follows his having "had" the lady, and awaking and judging the matter, he sees her and the situation for what they are, not at all a dream. On sober judgment, he ends where he begins: "Farewell!" This reading turns the poet's self-sacrifice into a cynical legal rescue.

Bernard E. Morris

SONNET 91

Author: William Shakespeare (1564-1616)
Type of poem: Sonnet
First published: 1609, in *Sonnets*

The Poem

Sonnet 91 by William Shakespeare is a relaxed work when compared to its predecessor, Sonnet 90 ("Then hate me when thou wilt, if ever, now"). The initial quatrain of Sonnet 91 is clear; it remarks that there are those who glory in birth, skill, wealth, strength, and worldly possessions.

The poet is establishing in the first quatrain a platform from which he will depart. The seemingly sardonic nature of this introduction becomes clear with the reference in line 3 to the "new-fangled ill"—a description of clothes that are fashionable but ugly. The unattractiveness of material possessions serves as a metaphor that is related to the implicit ugliness of the other attributes mentioned. The second quatrain begins by excusing the vanities of those who prize the attributes listed in the first quatrain. The narrator simply says that each person's "humor"—personality or temperament—finds some joy that it particularly prizes. The quatrain ends, however, with the speaker turning to his own preferences. He interjects that none of those individual tastes suit him. Further, he states, he is able to do them all one better in "one general best."

That "general best" is named in the first line of the third quatrain, where the narrator identifies it as the love of the woman he loves. He then explicitly states that his love means more to him than high birth, skill, and material wealth or possessions. This idea separates him from those mentioned in the first quatrain, for he has put his love above all else. The narrator, however, omits a comparison with the strength that is prized by some in the first quatrain.

In the final couplet, Sonnet 91 abruptly assumes a paradoxical tone. The apparent adulation of the previous quatrain gives way to the narrator's recognition of the power that his lover holds over him and of the vulnerable, if not tenuous, position in which he has placed himself. The narrator admits that this love makes him "wretched" in one respect: He recognizes that his lover can take from him what he desires most—she herself. The end result of such an action would leave him even more wretched.

The departure in the last couplet from the initial quatrains illustrates the irony of love: One is wretched while in love and one is wretched when love has ended. The other attributes first mentioned and then disregarded by the narrator are all elements in which the possessors have some kind of control; they are all theirs to lose and cannot be taken from them. All those attributes either must be relinquished by neglect or bad decisions or must be willingly released. This is not the case with love. The final couplet of Sonnet 91 illustrates the vulnerability of one who succumbs to love. Once this has occurred, the lover is at the mercy of his beloved; it is the one whom he adores who holds his happiness. The narrator fears that he may one day lose the one thing he holds dearest.

Forms and Devices

The poem's form is that of a conventional Elizabethan sonnet. Each of its fourteen lines contains ten syllables. The poem consists of three distinct quatrains; the first two are complete sentences, and the third is directly linked to the concluding couplet. It begins with a series of images highlighted by the cadence which is produced by Shakespeare's steady use of anaphora in the first quatrain.

The extensive repetition of "some" (seven times in four lines) stresses the idea which will be refuted by the following two quatrains and couplet. This technique strongly links the lines of the initial quatrain. When this link is broken in the second and third quatrains, the isolation of the narrator is raised to a peak that climaxes in the final couplet.

The anaphora also seems to debase those who are primarily interested in things other than love. This attitude produces a certain irony in the poem's shift to the singular in the second and third quatrains, where an image of superiority is produced. The narrator, who seems to be deriding those who care so much for items and ideas which cannot reciprocate their affection, actually appears pompous by placing himself above the others.

This technique also produces an oxymoron which is as startling as it is ironic. Love should not be a wretched affair, yet the psychological realism of this emotion is often just that. Love does cause pain and concern as well as a feeling of contentedness. The usual practice of the sonneteer was to glorify love; the heights of this devotion could reach nearly absurd proportions. Shakespeare chooses to vary from this technique, and the result is a shocking revelation which clearly illustrates the point.

Shakespeare's use of surprise or negation in the closing couplet further elaborates the nakedness a lover feels when he expounds his feelings for his beloved. The effect elicited by this negative couplet is a stark contrast to the usual pouring out of love and devotion found in the sonnets of Petrarch and others. It is the very twist of this conclusion that ties the sonnet into an organic whole and makes the poem so effective. All the attributes mentioned in the initial quatrain parallel the emotions of the final quatrains and couplet.

As different as this conclusion may be, Sonnet 91 retains many of the elements which are traditionally included in the genre. The anaphora of the initial quatrain gives way to the expected love analogy. Certainly the narrator adores and idolizes his beloved. The explication of such emotions is the normal function of the sonnet form. It is the irony of the poem's shift in the closing couplet that differentiates it from more traditional sonnets.

Themes and Meanings

Shakespeare's Sonnet 91 exemplifies how vulnerable lovers become when they put their love above all else. He has slightly altered the traditional Elizabethan sonnet from a form which glorifies love to one which exposes it as a deeply disturbing emotional experience. While countless Elizabethan poets employed the traditional techniques of composing sonnets, Shakespeare uses his control of language and images to twist the form and create an unusual and moving piece.

The pining and lamentation for lost or unrequited love, a theme prevalent in many traditional sonnets, is replaced by a psychological examination of the process of love. Further, Shakespeare has developed the first quatrain in such a way that it heightens the poem's surprise conclusion. This technique depends on several items, which the poem fails to explore, to present this viewpoint. Shakespeare never clearly produces facts that any of the scenarios noted in the first quatrain are to be shamed as excessive or covetous. Indeed, many of the traits are honorable: One's name is one's identity, for example, and it is paramount that artists be skilled. In retrospect, the elements listed in the initial quatrain are normal characteristics of life.

People become admired for certain values and scorned for others. Yet, in any society, high values are placed upon birth, wit, wealth, beauty, and material possessions. Those items do not seem to fit in a love poem, however, except to serve as grounds above which love can be elevated. Thus, it is expected that once those attributes are mentioned, they will be acknowledged as foolish, and the author will demonstrate that love is much better.

Shakespeare does follow this to a point, but then he breaks from tradition. The narrator claims that he is better off than others because he has obtained love. Yet love is not a measurable attribute; one may determine another's "worth" in terms of name, artistic ability, and sporting prowess, the elements mentioned in the opening quatrain and downplayed in the third. Moreover, love can be more decimating than those others when it is lost.

This raises the question of the value of love, which is answered by Shakespeare's omission of strength from the characteristics downplayed in the third quatrain. It is the strength of the feelings between the two lovers that creates both the thrill and the torment of love. The energy that exists between lovers clearly surpasses the power which comes from one's social standing, vocation, and sporting ability. It is love that bridges the gap between these characteristics, for it does not care about their value. Sonnet 91 demonstrates Shakespeare's superb ability to stray from the normal path and manipulate the language to express deep emotion in a way which ironically heightens the psychological trauma of love.

R. T. Lambdin

SONNET 94

Author: William Shakespeare (1564-1616)
Type of poem: Sonnet
First published: 1609, in *Sonnets*

The Poem

Sonnet 94 is a typical English or Shakespearean sonnet: fourteen lines of iambic pentameter rhymed *abab*, *cdcd*, *efef*, *gg*. This rhyme scheme effectively divides the poem into three quatrains and a closing couplet, unlike the Italian or Petrarchan sonnet, which tends to be structured as an octave and sestet. In Sonnet 94, William Shakespeare's first-person voice of the lover extols the virtue of stoic restraint and suggests that acting on emotions corrupts the natural nobility of a person's character and, thus, compromises identity itself.

The first line opens the poem with a subject and a restrictive clause that describes the stoic character: Such persons have the power to act, to hurt others, but refuse to do so. The next three lines of the quatrain elaborate on this quality through a series of restrictive clauses: Though such persons may seem to threaten to act, they do not; they move others to act but are themselves unmoved, show little emotion, and restrain themselves from temptation.

Having defined the subject with these restrictive clauses, this rather long opening sentence finally arrives at the verb in line 5: "do inherit." Persons who can exercise such restraint are the proper recipients of grace (divine assistance or protection) and, in turn, protect the earthly manifestations of grace ("nature's riches") from waste. Those who can restrain their emotions and actions, moreover, are in control of their own identities—that is, they are not fickle or quick to change but constant. Such persons truly may be said to follow the advice voiced by Polonius in *Hamlet* (c. 1600-1601): "To thine own self be true." Others, the poem continues, rightly must be subservient to the virtues kept alive by such stoic characters.

In line 9, the formal "turn" in the sonnet, the poem shifts to a new conceit, that of the "summer's flower" as a metaphor for human identity. Though as an individual one recognizes one's value to oneself as self-evident in the fact of one's existence, one's life also has a value to the age and community in which one flourishes: The flowers of summer are "sweet" to the summer itself and contribute to making the summer the pleasant season it is. The speaker adds, however, that if that flower allows itself to be corrupted, then the value of that flower's identity—not simply to itself, but to its community as well—becomes lost, and, in that event, even weeds seem more dignified.

The couplet reiterates this point: Virtue may be corrupted by actions—"Sweetest things turn sourest by their deeds"—and such corrupted virtue is far more damaging to a community than the baseness and vices of individuals—"weeds"—who had no potential for beauty and virtue in the first place.

Forms and Devices

The most striking device in the opening five lines of Sonnet 94 is the repeated use of the word "do" in the sense of "perform" ("do none," line 1); as an intensifier ("do show," line 2); in both senses ("do not do," line 2); and finally, again, as an intensifier to emphasize the verb ("do inherit," line 5). Although the poem is about persons who restrain their actions, this repetition of the most basic word for performing an action, "to do," suggests that actions are being performed. In fact, though, if one looks at the grammar of this first sentence, one sees that all but one of these instances of the word are contained within restrictive clauses, and the main verb of the subject "they" is restrained, as it were, until the second quatrain: "do inherit" in line 5. The sentence thus echoes the sense that the "thing they most do show," like the appearance of grammatical action in "do," is restrained. When one does get to that main verb, moreover, it is a verb not of doing but of receiving, of inheriting.

The poem introduces its most significant metaphor in the second quatrain. The speaker compares this stoicism to legal inheritance and ownership of land, land that is then cultivated and made productive. Ownership of land was, in the sixteenth century, a traditional privilege of the nobility, although this rapidly was changing as members of the mercantile middle class accumulated more and more wealth. In lines 7 and 8, this metaphor depicts the relationship between the stoic personality and others in terms of social rank: The former is a lord for whom others are but servants. (It should be noted, however, that both types are, in effect, "stewards," with some serving the stoic's "excellence" and the stoic himself serving to protect "nature's riches."

The third quatrain makes a surprising leap from these images of land and social rank to the image of the summer flower. The suddenness of this shift from one image to another seemingly unrelated one is characteristic of Shakespeare's methods in the sonnets. It is also perhaps one reason that his contemporary, Ben Jonson, said of Shakespeare, *sufflaminandus erat* (that he needed to put on the brakes, to restrain his free ways with the language). One need not share, however, in Jonson's criticism of his illustrious friend. Instead, one should see this leap as a device that, like metaphor itself, leads one to new and surprising perspectives on its subject.

The natural beauty of the flower is also responsible to its environs, as the stoic is to nature's riches and as others are to the stoic himself. Additionally, its natural beauty, like the nobility of the stoic, can be so corrupted by "deeds" that it becomes inferior to those of less beauty or those of lower social rank—"weeds." The final rhyme of these two words, "deeds" and "weeds," makes emphatic the connection between unrestrained action and the corruption of personal identity and social responsibility.

Themes and Meanings

Shakespeare viewed nature in terms of its benefits to human society. On its own, nature produces wild, unweeded, overgrown fields and woods that neither please the aesthetic sense nor feed a community as effectively as the gardens and crops produced by horticulture, by "art." Nature, therefore, must be nurtured by human industry in order to be beneficial to society. In his poetry, too, Shakespeare's images of nature do not focus on the natural environment in its own right, but have ulterior poetic motives that refer the reader to human experience.

In one of his last plays, *The Tempest* (1611), Shakespeare uses gardening and careful husbandry as metaphors for political and romantic relationships: Friendship and marriage are means of nurturing natural sexual desires into a morally productive relationship; charity, forgiveness, and restraint are means of nurturing desires for political power and possession into an ethical and productive political state. In this play, too, the reader sees noble characters who, because they are unwilling to restrain their greed for power, seem less noble than their social inferiors who "seek for grace." These are the themes of Sonnet 94.

Nobility, as a political status, was passed through inheritance; its attendant personal virtues of honor, strength, and moral rectitude were, it was thought, genetic, passed through the blood. What Shakespeare suggests here is that true nobility is neither inherited nor inherent, but achieved. Political power that is beneficial to others is achieved by first having power over oneself, having the power to hurt, but having the restraint not to exercise such power.

Humans must first and foremost be "lords and owners of our faces." Conversely, if society is to be mutually beneficial, that responsibility for having control over one's own identity is not solely a responsibility to oneself, but also a responsibility to those with whom one lives. The flower produced by summer gives summer its character and has the potential, if corrupted, to make summer seem rank with decay rather than, as it should be, redolent of birth, growth, and life.

James Hale

SONNET 106

Author: William Shakespeare (1564-1616)
Type of poem: Sonnet
First published: 1609, in *Sonnets*

The Poem

In William Shakespeare's Sonnet 106, the speaker calls upon the glories of the past to illustrate the present. He perceives that the beauty of his lover has been prophesied by the pens of past authors who are now long dead. The initial quatrain establishes the tone as one of courtly elegance. The references to "chronicles," "ladies," and "knights" all recall the glorified stereotypical image of a time long past, when a knight was obligated by the chivalric code to behave bravely in the battlefield and solicitously in the community.

This highly elevated rhetoric establishes the mood of Sonnet 106, yet the elegance seemingly gives way to irony in the juxtaposition of adjectives in line 4: "Ladies dead and lovely knights." The "beauty" of line 2 has been usurped by the truth of mutability: The ladies are literally dead; they live only as images created by the words of the old rhymes. Further, it seems that the adjectives describing the ladies and the knights have been willingly transposed. The common conception of the lady or mistress in the old poetry was of a fair and lovely creature of inspiration; it was the valiant knights who died for her.

The introductory octave continues with a shift in the second quatrain, where the narrator personifies beauty in the form of a coat of arms which accentuates the erotic images of his love's finest attributes: foot, lip, eye, and brow. These common physical, and even sexual, images initiate a change from the spiritual to the physical. The second quatrain concludes with a vivid image: The narrator visualizes that the earlier poets would have expressed just such a beauty as his love. Thus the initial octave establishes the background from which the sestet will depart.

The sestet begins, in the third quatrain, by connecting the past with the present: The praises of the poets from an earlier age become actual prophecies. The narrator perceives that futuristic visions of his beloved provided the impetus for the old poets' works; however, this idea is quickly amended. Even though those authors were guided by divine inspiration, they were still unable to praise or describe the beauty of the narrator's lover adequately.

The concluding couplet emphasizes the futility of such an effort in the composition of love poems. It is clear that the authors of the past, now long dead, have transmitted their words along to the authors of the present. Yet their adoration remains an enigma; it is impossible for an author to describe his love truly by using mere words.

Forms and Devices

Sonnet 106 conforms to the Elizabethan fourteen-line stanzaic form. Each of the lines contains ten syllables, and the poem consists of two sentences. The first encompasses the initial octave, and the second, the final sestet. This form is similar to Shakespeare's Sonnets 32 and 47. The initial octave may be broken into two distinct quatrains. The first initiates the work with a "when" clause that, while syntactically logical, cannot stand alone.

The second quatrain counters the first with a "then" clause. Through this syntactical convention, logic is used first to divide and then to unite the initial octave. The final sestet similarly depends upon its syntactical sequence first to answer, then to expand upon, the logic conceived in the initial octave. Despite its unification, the sestet is composed of both a distinct quatrain and a concluding couplet.

The quatrain of the sestet begins a new sentence that remarks on the evidence put forward in the preceding sentence. It states that despite the worthy stature of the poets who composed the earlier works, their attempts at prophecy fall short: They were incapable of capturing the beauty of the narrator's beloved in words. The main point of the work, however, is the narrator's own seeming inability to put his love's beauty into words.

The sonnet uses alliteration, particularly of the *s* sound, throughout the poem. Shakespeare also creates effects by expanding or contracting the number of syllables that appear between certain repeated sounds. In the couplet, for example, a pulsating alliteration emphasizes the poem's conclusion; the "praise" of line 14 represents a compression of the *pr* and *ay* sounds previously heard in the "present days" of line 11. There is also an expanding alliterative pattern in the placement of *b* and *pr* sounds. In line 9, the pattern begins with "but prophecies." The sound is stretched in line 13 — "behold the present" — and stretched even further in the final line: "but lack tongues to praise."

Sonnet 106 exhibits Shakespeare's uncanny ability to manipulate language into poetic form; the poem is not as simple and straightforward as it may appear. In line 3, the narrator refers to the "beautiful old rhyme" of bygone days, yet he is speaking a poem that both echoes and modifies those old rhymes, a poem that will one day take its place in the canon to which they belong.

Themes and Meanings

Sonnet 106 is in many ways a typical love poem filled with conventional techniques. While it does not offer significant insight into the many mysteries of the sonnets, it does provide a glimpse of an idea far too often overlooked in much criticism — that Shakespeare and other Elizabethan writers depended upon the authors of the past. It is often perceived that the literary works of Renaissance England rely solely upon the classical traditions or spring from an author's sudden burst of inspiration. Sonnet 106 proves that is not true, for it clearly displays Shakespeare's debt to medieval authors and their works.

Shakespeare was influenced by the work of Geoffrey Chaucer, whose "The Knight's Tale" from *The Canterbury Tales* (1387-1400) is a major source for the plot of *A Midsummer Night's Dream* (c. 1595-1596). While Shakespeare somewhat alters the myth surrounding the marriage of Hippolyta and Theseus, the Chaucerian influence is abundant. This type of borrowing is continued in Sonnet 106. In this poem, Shakespeare clearly reminds readers of his debt to the older works. He also shows an understanding of the themes of many of the ancient texts: ladies, knights, courtly love, and chivalry.

It is clear that perceiving beauty is one thing, while putting those visualizations into words is quite another. Thus, ironically, the narrator fails miserably in his quest—yet he is also successful to some degree. Despite his omission of any physical description, he has captured at least a part of his love's essence, and he is honoring her with a poem. Like the women who were glorified in literature long before her, she, too, has been given eternal life.

Sonnet 106 also has a consciousness of the theme implicit in the phrase "this our time" (line 10). The sonnet constantly reinforces the idea that what lovers can do is mandated by their particular era; what has previously occurred affects them, so they cannot ignore the past. Yet, after their death, they are doomed to become faint images for other authors to wonder about. At best, they can attempt an understanding of the ideals and the images of their present. This theme, introduced in Sonnet 106, is furthered in the more famous Sonnet 107 ("Not mine own fears, nor the prophetic soul"). The message of Sonnet 106 is clear, and its technique is conventional. It is of particular value because it shows an aspect of Shakespeare's work that is too often overlooked: its debt to medieval authors.

R. T. Lambdin

SONNET 116

Author: William Shakespeare (1564-1616)
Type of poem: Sonnet
First published: 1609, in *Sonnets*

The Poem

Sonnet 116 is generally considered one of the finest love poems ever written. In this sonnet, William Shakespeare raised the theme of romantic love to the status of high philosophy. At a time when love between man and woman was not often recognized as essentially other than a form of family obligation, Shakespeare spiritualized it as the motivator of the highest level of human action. Love of that kind has since become the most sought-after human experience.

The poem is a regular English sonnet of fourteen lines arranged in three quatrains and a concluding couplet. It begins by using the language of the Book of Common Prayer marriage service to make an explicit equation of love and marriage. It not only suggests that marriage is the proper end of love, but it also goes beyond to make love a necessary prerequisite. The quatrain continues by describing the essential constituents of the kind of love that qualifies. Such love does not change under changing circumstances; in fact, constancy is its first element. It continues even when unreciprocated or betrayed. Further, true love does not depend on the presence of the beloved, but actually increases during absence.

The second quatrain uses a series of metaphors to flesh out the character of proper love. Its constancy is such that it not only endures threats but actually strengthens in adversity. Its attractive power secures the beloved from wandering, and it sets a standard for all other lovers. Although conspicuous and easily identifiable, its value is inestimable. Aspects of it can be measured, and many of its properties are tangible, but it resides in another dimension, unassessable by normal instruments in space and time.

The third quatrain considers the constancy of true love under the threats of time and aging. It declares that love is unaffected by time. To begin with, love far transcends such mundane physical characteristics as size, appearance, condition, and shape. For that reason, it ignores physical changes caused by age or health. It defies time and everything in its power, including death. True love operates in the realm of eternity. Not even death can part true lovers; their union endures forever. Because love has the capacity to raise human action to this exalted state, it alone enables humans to transcend temporal limitations. Humankind becomes godlike through love.

The sonnet ends with a simple couplet which transfers the focus from the ethereal region of eternal, transcendent love to the routine present of the poet-speaker. He merely observes that if he is ever proved wrong, then no man has ever loved. It seems a trivial conclusion, until one recognizes that this is exactly the feeling that allows men and women to continue to fall in love and to endow that feeling with meaning.

Forms and Devices

In spite of being one of the world's most celebrated short poems, Sonnet 116 uses a rather simple array of poetic devices. They include special diction, allusion, metaphor, and paradox. All work together to reinforce the central theme.

Shakespeare establishes the context early with his famous phrase "the marriage of true minds," a phrase which does more than is commonly recognized. The figure of speech suggests that true marriage is a union of minds rather than merely a license for the coupling of bodies. Shakespeare implies that true love proceeds from and unites minds on the highest level of human activity, that it is inherently mental and spiritual. From the beginning, real love transcends the sensual-physical. Moreover, the very highest level is reserved to "true" minds. By this he means lovers who have "plighted troth," in the phrasing of the marriage service—that is, exchanged vows to be true to each other. This reinforces the spirituality of loving, giving it religious overtones. The words "marriage" and "impediments" also allude to the language of the service, accentuating the sacred nature of love.

Shakespeare then deliberately repeats phrases to show that this kind of love is more than mere reciprocation. Love cannot be simply returning what is given, like an exchange of gifts. It has to be a simple, disinterested, one-sided offering, unrelated to any possible compensation. He follows this with a series of positive and negative metaphors to illustrate the full dimensions of love. It is first "an ever-fixéd mark/ That looks on tempests and is never shaken." This famous figure has not been completely explained, although the general idea is clear. Love is equated with some kind of navigating device so securely mounted that it remains functional in hurricanes. It then becomes not a device but a reference point, a "star," of universal recognition but speculative in its composition; significantly, it is beyond human ken.

In "Love's not Time's fool," Shakespeare moves on to yet another metaphorical level. To begin with, love cannot be made into a fool by the transformations of time; it operates beyond and outside it, hence cannot be subject to it. This is so although time controls those qualities which are popularly thought to evoke love—physical attractions. Shakespeare conjures up the image of the Grim Reaper with his "bending sickle," only to assert that love is not within his "compass"—which denotes both grip and reckoning and sweep of blade. Love cannot be fathomed by time or its extreme instrument, death. Love "bears it out"—perseveres in adversity—to the "edge of doom"—that is, beyond the grave and the worst phase of time's decay.

The final device is a conundrum in logic. It establishes an alternative—"If this be error"—then disproves it. What remains, and remains valid, is the other. It also bears a double edge. If this demonstration is wrong, Shakespeare says, "I never writ," which is an obvious contradiction. The only possible conclusion is that it is not wrong. He proceeds then to a corollary, "nor no man ever loved," which is as false as the previous statement.

Themes and Meanings

In this sonnet, the theme is the poem. Shakespeare presents an argument, forcing the double conclusion that love transcends normal human measures and that it represents the highest level of human activity. Yet, as a famous love poem, it is highly unusual: It is not a declaration of love but a definition and demonstration. It still accomplishes the object of a love poem, however, because the inspirer of this statement could not possibly be flattered more effectively.

Sonnet 116 develops the theme of the eternity of true love through an elaborate and intricate cascade of images. Shakespeare first states that love is essentially a mental relationship; the central property of love is truth—that is, fidelity—and fidelity proceeds from and is anchored in the mind. The objective tone and impersonal language of the opening reinforce this theme. This kind of love is as far removed from the level of mere sensation as any human activity could be. Like all ideal forms, it operates on the level of abstract intellect, or of soul. Hence it is immune to the physical, emotional, or behavioral "impediments" that threaten lesser loves. It is a love that fuses spirits intuitively related to each other.

The poem proceeds to catalog a number of specific impediments. The first involves reciprocation. Does true love persist in the face of rejection or loss of affection? Absolutely, even though those might be sufficient grounds for calling off a wedding. True love endures even the absence of the beloved: not that the heart grows fonder in such a case, as in the cliché, but that it operates independently of physical reminders. Such love stabilizes itself, as if possessing an instinctive self-righting mechanism. Shakespeare himself uses this kind of gyroscopic and autopilot imagery; like the navigational devices to which he alludes, true love serves as a standard for others, maintains its course under stress, and guarantees security against storm and turmoil.

This imagery duplicates the sequence of promises exchanged by true lovers in the marriage service that Shakespeare quotes in the opening of the poem. True love vows constancy regardless of better, worse, richer, poorer, sickness, health—all the vagaries of life and change. The simple series, however, seems to minimize the intensity of love necessary to do this. On the contrary, love is absolutely secure against external assault. In particular, it holds firm against the ravages of time. Since the poem begins by dissociating love from the limits of time, this should not be surprising, especially since the marriage service insists on the possibility of love surviving time and its consequence, change. So strong is the popular belief that love is rooted in physical attractiveness, however, that the poem is forced to repudiate this explicitly. It does it in the starkest way imaginable, by personifying time as the Grim Reaper and by bringing that specter directly before the eyes of the lover. This happens; the threat is real, but the true lover can face down even death.

The marriage service does that also, by asking the thinking lover to promise fidelity "until death do us part." Shakespeare's poem uses imagery to give form to this belief that true love has to be stronger than death, set as a seal upon the lover's heart.

James Livingston

SONNET 129

Author: William Shakespeare (1564-1616)
Type of poem: Sonnet
First published: 1609, in *Sonnets*

The Poem

Sonnet 129 is a typical Shakespearean sonnet in form, written in iambic pentameter with twelve lines rhymed *abab*, *cdcd*, *efef*, and a closing couplet rhymed *gg*. Unlike the majority of William Shakespeare's sonnets, however, it is not addressed to a particular individual but is directed to an audience, as a sermon is.

The first line is the only one that presents any difficulty in interpretation. Shakespeare sometimes compressed a large meaning into few words, creating an impressionistic effect. Although this opening line appears a bit garbled, it is easy enough to understand and well suited to the mood of the poem. It creates the impression of a mind overwhelmed by a whirlwind of bitter reflections.

He is obviously talking about sexual lust. The first line states that lust is shameful and spiritually debilitating. The rest of the poem simply expands upon this idea. The torrent of adjectives and short descriptive phrases that follows suggests the different ways in which sexual lust can lead to tragic outcomes. The reader may evoke specific illustrations from personal experience or from the world's literature which, from the Bible and Greek mythology to modern novels such as Vladimir Nabokov's *Lolita* (1955), is full of warnings against lust.

Each word or phrase in the opening lines suggests different scenarios. For example, the word "perjur'd" suggests the lies men tell women, the most common being "I love you" and "I want to marry you." Lust drives people to say many things they do not mean. The word "perjur'd" also suggests the humiliating experience of having to lie to the fiancé or spouse of one's lover, who might even be a personal friend.

The word "bloody" suggests even more serious outcomes of sexual lust. The outraged husband who discovers his wife in bed with another man may murder her, or him, or both. Lust also may lead to bloody abortions and suicides. "Full of blame" suggests the painful aftermath of many affairs based not on love but on lust. The woman blames the man for deceiving her; he blames her for leading him on, for allowing herself to become pregnant, or for confessing her adultery to her husband. "Full of blame" in Shakespeare's time probably suggested the great danger of contracting syphilis or gonorrhea, and in recent times it suggests the modern plague of acquired immune deficiency syndrome (AIDS).

The closing couplet of the sonnet alights gracefully, with the juxtaposition of "well knows" and "knows well." The tone is like the calm after a storm. It is not a happy conclusion but a truthful one. Humanity repeats the same mistakes generation after generation. Sexual passion is hard to control and leads to much of the tragedy that human beings experience.

Forms and Devices

There are two important things to notice about the structure of this sonnet. One is that, except for the closing couplet, it consists of a single run-on sentence. The other is that it is built around a single simile, which takes up the seventh and eighth lines. The effect of crowding most of the poem into a single outburst is to leave the reader with a feeling of agitation mirroring the conflicting emotions that accompany sexual lust. Run-on sentences are often the targets of English teachers' red pencils, but at times such sentences can be extremely effective.

Shakespeare often filled his sonnets with metaphors and similes, as he did in his famous Sonnet 73, in which he compares his time of life to winter, to sunset, and to a dying fire. In other sonnets, however, he deliberately avoids metaphors and similes in order to obtain the maximum effect from a single striking image. This is the case in another of Shakespeare's most famous sonnets, Sonnet 29, which begins, "When in disgrace with fortune and men's eyes." After complaining at length about his miserable condition, the speaker changes his tone entirely and says that, should he happen to remember the friendship of the person he is addressing, his state, "Like to the lark at break of day arising/ From sullen earth, sings hymns at heaven's gate." These are two of the most beautiful lines in English poetry, and they are more effective because they are not competing with any other imagery in the sonnet.

In Sonnet 129, the dominant image is contained in the lines

> Past reason hated, as a swallowed bait
> On purpose laid to make the taker mad.

After this—but without starting a new sentence—the poet launches into another tirade, echoing the word "Mad" at the beginning of the next line and rhyming it with "Had" at the beginning of the line after that. These devices arouse apprehension because it seems as if the speaker may actually be starting to rave.

People do not set out poisoned bait to kill human beings. The kind of bait Shakespeare is referring to is commonly used to kill rats: They are driven mad with thirst or pain and run out of the house to die. One of the reasons the image is so striking is that it implicitly compares people motivated by uncontrolled lust to the lowest, most detested animals. Sonnet 129 is unlike most of Shakespeare's other sonnets and in fact unlike most other Elizabethan sonnets, which are typically full of references to love, the moon, the stars, and other pleasant things. This strange sonnet on lust has a modern, experimental quality to it which foreshadows the cacophony and deliberately shocking ugliness of much twentieth century art.

Themes and Meanings

Shakespeare was not a deeply religious man. The moralistic tone of this poem seems so out of character that one distinguished Shakespearean scholar, A. L. Rowse, suggested that Shakespeare did not intend it to be taken seriously but wrote the sonnet as a sort of private joke for his circle of friends; yet its emotional effect is so powerful that it is hard to believe that Shakespeare was not writing with true feeling. It has also been suggested that Shakespeare wrote the sonnet after discovering that he had contracted syphilis from a liaison with a prostitute—or possibly from the mysterious "Dark Lady" mentioned in some of his other sonnets.

The theme is simple and clear. The poet is preaching a brief sermon on the dangers of sexual lust. These dangers have been a subject of literature since the stories of Samson and Delilah and of David and Bathsheba, recorded in the Old Testament. The Trojan War, which led to the destruction of a whole civilization and was described in both Homer's *Iliad* (c. 800 B.C.) and Vergil's *Aeneid* (c. 29-19 B.C.), was reputedly caused by Paris' lust for Helen, the wife of Menelaus. In Shakespeare's own long poem *The Rape of Lucrece* (1594), the story is told of how the Etruscan rulers came to be driven out of Rome because of Sextus Tarquinius' rape of Lucrece and her subsequent suicide.

In Leo Tolstoy's novel *Anna Karenina* (1875-1877; English translation, 1886), the heroine throws herself under the wheels of a locomotive after she has left her husband and children and ultimately finds herself deserted by her faithless lover. In Henrik Ibsen's play *Gengangere* (1881; *Ghosts*, 1885), a promising young man dies because he inherited syphilis from his profligate father. In Anton Chekhov's best short story, "Dama s sobachkoi" (1899; "The Lady with the Dog," 1917), an adulterous relationship leads to endless mental torture for both parties involved. In Theodore Dreiser's novel *An American Tragedy* (1925), lust leads to murder and death in the electric chair.

As Shakespeare wrote, the world well knows that sexual intercourse without love is often a grave disappointment and can lead to torment in a wide variety of forms. Unfortunately, many people have to learn this truth by bitter experience.

Finally, a political statement might be read into this sonnet. The fact that it departs from the norm and is not pretty and soothing might be taken to indicate a view that art should serve a higher purpose than merely helping the genteel elite to pass their leisure hours. Its denunciation of sexual lust might be read as an indictment of the aristocracy, whose favorite pastime, as shown by so many of the songs, poems, and paintings of the period, was playing at the game of love. Thus, it might be seen as foreshadowing views that led to the English Civil War which began only twenty-six years after Shakespeare's death and changed the course of history.

Bill Delaney

SONNET 130

Author: William Shakespeare (1564-1616)
Type of poem: Sonnet
First published: 1609, in *Sonnets*

The Poem

Sonnet 130 is a blazon, a lyric poem cataloging the physical characteristics and virtues of the beloved, in typical English or Shakespearean sonnet form—three quatrains and a couplet in iambic pentameter rhymed *abab*, *cdcd*, *efef*, *gg*. The first-person voice of the poem should be understood as that of a dramatic persona; even if William Shakespeare means it to represent himself, he nevertheless has to create a distinct personality in the language, and from this distance, the reader has no way of knowing how accurately this might describe the man. The speaker describes his beloved in comparison, or rather in contrast, to natural phenomena. In the love poem tradition, as it emerged in English poetry in imitation of the sonnets of fourteenth century Italian poet Petrarch, poets often compare their beloveds to the elements of nature. In this sonnet, Shakespeare takes the opposite tack by describing his beloved as "nothing like" the beautiful productions of nature or art.

Her eyes, the poet begins, do not shine like the sun; nor are her lips as red as coral. When compared to the whiteness of snow, his beloved's breasts seem "dun," a dull gray. The "wires" of line 4 refer to gold spun into golden thread, and his beloved's hair, if the metaphoric description of hairs as golden wires is valid, can only be seen as black, or tarnished beyond all recognition.

The damasked roses of the fifth line are variegated roses of red and white, and such, the poet continues, cannot be seen in his woman's face. Perfume, too, is an inaccurate simile for his lover's breath, since most perfumes are more pleasing. The word "reeks" in line 8 simply means "breathes forth" in Elizabethan English, although our modern sense of the word as denoting an offensive smell certainly emphasizes Shakespeare's point of contrast.

At the ninth-line "turn"—the formal point at which sonnets typically introduce an antithesis or redirect their focus—the speaker continues in the same vein, noting how music has a more pleasing sound than his lover's voice, though he also introduces an important point: None of these contrasts is to suggest that he finds his beloved any less pleasing. He loves her voice, as he does her other characteristics, but honestly he must acknowledge that music is, objectively speaking, more pleasing to the senses.

Lines 11 and 12 dismiss conventional descriptions of women as goddesslike. Who among mortal men has ever witnessed a goddess in order to make such similes in the first place? All this lover knows is what he sees, and his mistress is, like him, quite earthly and earthbound, walking on the ground.

The sonnet's couplet then explicates the point of the above contrasts. The lover's objective comparisons of his beloved with nature and human artifacts of perfume and music, however unfavorable to the woman, do not change his subjective perception of her: She is as rare as any of those women whom poets describe with comparisons that exaggerate, and thus belie, human beauty.

Forms and Devices

The effect of the formal division of the Shakespearean sonnet, the four quatrains and closing couplet, is to pile up examples of a single idea—that the beloved's beauty is really not comparable to the productions of nature and human art—so that by line 12, the reader wonders if there is anything at all about the woman that can be seen objectively as beautiful. The last two lines then provide a memorable explication of that idea: Objectivity and actual beauty are really no concern of the lover. While lines 11 and 12 dismiss comparisons to heavenly beauty as meaningless— mortals have no experience of the metaphysical world on which to base such similes— Shakespeare uses the mild expletive "by heaven" in line 13 to suggest in contrast that the impassioned subjectivity of the lover is itself metaphysical in origin, a kind of grace.

The speaker's attitude in this poem is strikingly antimetaphoric, and lines 3 and 4 subject two conventional metaphors to examination by deductive logic. Line 3 begins with a premise, "If snow be white," and concludes that the woman's breasts are "dun." In technical terms, the rhetorical device employed here is an "enthymeme," a syllogism in which one of the terms is left out and must be inferred by the reader. One may reconstruct the full syllogism thus: Snow is white; my lover's breasts are dull gray; therefore, my lover's breasts are not like snow. Since snow is in fact white, one can concur with the conclusion's logic and deny the validity of the simile "women's breasts are white like snow." Line 4 offers another enthymeme beginning with the premise "If hairs be wires" and concluding that the woman's hair is black, or tarnished, wire. The full syllogism here would read: Hairs are golden wires; my lover's hairs are black; therefore, my lover's hairs must be tarnished.

The conclusion follows logically, but the metaphoric premise is untrue: Hairs are not wires, and if the woman is judged on the basis of this premise, one can only conclude by denigrating the woman's physical characteristics as sullied examples of an ideal: tarnished gold. This is what Shakespeare means by "false compare"— unjust comparisons that not only ignore the possibility that the woman may be beautiful in her own right, but also miss the value of the beloved in the eyes of her lover: To him, she is, if not golden, at least as "rare." That the poet has his persona subject love and beauty to deductive logic at all tells the reader something important about the lover's attitude and about the overall meaning of the poem.

Themes and Meanings

The ostensible subject of this sonnet is the so-called dark lady of the later sonnets, a woman with whom the speaker of the poems is having a passionate sexual affair. The first 126 sonnets are addressed to a man, in whom the speaker denies having sexual interest. (See Sonnet 20, where the speaker notes that the male beloved has "one thing to my purpose nothing.") These sonnets to and about the man attempt to consider the dimensions of platonic love, "the marriage of true minds" (Sonnet 116), without the compromising motive of sexual desire. In contrast, the sonnets addressed to the dark lady suggest that once sex enters into the relationship, the possibility of achieving a higher, platonic love is virtually lost. Indeed, the speaker and the dark lady engage in quite a sordid affair.

Although the poem focuses on this woman, its main subject is perception itself and the methods by which poets represent love. Poets often concern themselves with the nature of their art and, in creating new ways of seeing human experience, question the validity of the poetic conventions of their predecessors. This poem prompts some very fundamental questions about poetic devices. What does metaphor actually tell about the objects on which it focuses? If poetry attempts to bring one closer to what is true in the human experience, why is it that most poetic conventions are falsehoods? Love is not a rose, beloveds are not heavenly goddesses, lovers do not die from being rejected by their beloveds. As the character Rosalind, in Shakespeare's play, *As You Like It* (c. 1599-1600), remarks in response to the "poetic" language of her lover: "men have died from time to time, and worms have eaten them, but not for love."

In Sonnet 18, when the poet asks of the male beloved, "Shall I compare thee to a summer's day?" the answer — no — calls attention to the inadequacy of conventional metaphors and similes to describe accurately not the beloved, but the subjective nature of love. In the case of Sonnet 18, however, such comparisons are insufficient, the lover suggests, because they are not superlative enough. Here, he suggests the opposite: They are too superlative to give a realistic picture of his beloved. Such metaphors and similes are, after all, mere lies — poetic lies, perhaps, but lies nevertheless. Although clearly in love with the woman, this lover seems poignantly aware of the way she really looks, beyond his love-inspired subjectivity.

Sonnet 130 provides logic instead of metaphor, objectivity instead of hyperbole. In one very important sense, this focus on actual physical appearance seems appropriate to the affair between the speaker and the dark lady: Throughout the sonnets that represent this affair, Shakespeare continually stresses the point that their relationship is based primarily, almost exclusively, on physical appearance and physical attraction — on what Sonnet 129 calls "lust in action."

James Hale

SORDELLO

Author: Robert Browning (1812-1889)
Type of poem: Narrative
First published: 1840; revised and collected in *The Poetical Works of Robert Browning*, 1863, 1868, 1888

The Poem

Sordello is commonly described as the least comprehensible poem written in the English language. Its publication caused the author unending troubles with the critics of his day. Robert Browning wrote it between the years 1833 and 1840; he apparently wrote four different versions, each with a somewhat different purpose in mind. The version most often read today is a poem of 5,982 lines in iambic pentameter, rhyming in couplets, and including running titles that summarize the action.

Browning's historical sources for the story appear to have been Dante's *Purgatorio* and the *Biographie Universelle* (a popular nineteenth century biographical dictionary) that was in his father's library. Sordello was a Mantuan poet and warrior of the early thirteenth century, and thirty-four of his poems in the Provençal language are extant. His age at the time of his death remains uncertain (some historical accounts describe him as middle-aged, others as old), but Browning chose to have his character die at the age of thirty.

Other characters who figure in the drama include the Lady Palma; the minstrel Eglamor, whose place at court Sordello tries to usurp; the Ghibelline leaders Taurello Salinguerra and Ecelin; Ecelin's wife Adelaide; the literary critic Naddo; and Palma's fiancé, the Guelf Count Richard of St. Boniface.

Before the actual story gets under way, in book 1 Browning introduces a speaker who promises to tell the story but who first paints an elaborate picture of a street scene in Verona in the twelfth century. He explains the history of the political battles between the Guelfs (supporters of popular liberation headed by Pope Henricus III and affiliated with the Este family) and the Ghibelline aristocracy (Frederick II and the barons of the Austro-German empire). He also apologizes for not using his usual dramatic monologue narrative technique and discusses Dante, who was Browning's principal source for the story. Around line 400 he finally introduces Sordello.

The rest of book 1 shows the young Sordello in the town of Goito in the domain of the tyrant Ecelin, aspiring to become a great poet. As though he is naïvely fitting himself to some classical pattern, he finds himself ready, at the end of the canto, to fall in love.

In book 2, in order to win the love of the Lady Palma, Sordello pits himself against Eglamor in a poetry contest. When Sordello wins, Eglamor dies of grief. This convinces the younger man that he is himself quite talented, and he briefly experiences a sense of victory. Eglamor's death over such a defeat, however, convinces Sordello that this more experienced minstrel, like many others, had been writing poetry strictly for popularity, and that Sordello's victory is, therefore, hollow. He decides to attempt the writing of a poetry that will be more subjective yet clearly directed to the ennoblement of humanity. The critic Naddo ridicules the young poet and suggests that the world does not need more half-baked philosophers, especially among writers of poetry. Disheartened but not defeated, Sordello leaves the court of Taurello Salinguerra.

In book 3, Sordello first spends a year alone, recouping his energy and idealism. Then Naddo recalls him to court and asks him to write a public poem celebrating the impending marriage of Palma to Count Richard of St. Boniface, which would secure peace between the Ghibellines and the Guelfs. Sordello, however, professes his own love for Palma. She discovers the secret of Sordello's birth but does not reveal the truth to him. She professes her love for him. Following her suggestion, the two move to Ferrara and become politically active in support of the Kaiser. Salinguerra helps them. Sordello's musings prompt the narrator to digress from the story and discuss the role of the poet in society, with some reference to his or her affiliation not only with the socially prominent but also with the suffering poor.

Book 4 seems principally a further exposition of the twelfth century history of the conflict between the Guelfs and Ghibellines, but it focuses particularly on the psychology and history of Salinguerra. His service of Ecelin is discussed. The reader learns that Adelaide, Ecelin's wife, revealed to her husband that Salinguerra was, in fact, Sordello's father. Discovering this, Ecelin had retired from the world and entered a monastery at Oliero, announcing, at the same time, the proposed marriage between Count Richard and Palma (mentioned above). Salinguerra had been in Naples, preparing to depart on a crusade with Emperor Frederick II, and he hurried back to Ferrara when he heard what Ecelin had done. Count Richard attacks him, but is imprisoned. This leads Sordello to condemn both parties in his heart. He asks whether solidarity between individuals of all classes might be more important than loyalty to any party.

Though he does not align himself specifically with the Guelfs, in book 5 Sordello embraces the democratic cause of the people and intercedes with Salinguerra, encouraging the leader to use his great power to help the poor of northern Italy. Salinguerra scorns the advice and tires of the long speech, but he offers to abdicate in favor of the idealistic poet. At that point Palma reveals that Salinguerra is Sordello's father. The poet is now left with a crucial ethical dilemma: Can he enforce his ideals by assuming the power of a tyrant?

Somewhat shorter than the others, book 6 reveals that Sordello died at the end of the former book, unable to resolve the conflict with which he is there presented: He is a Ghibelline ruler by birth, but a Guelf democrat by instinct. Before his death, he crushes Salinguerra's badge beneath his feet. Beyond this brief exposition, book 6 is a discussion of the question of Sordello's successes and failures as both a poet and a leader. Much of the answer, the narrator suggests, must await the next life. There is, therefore, little sense of closure at the end of the poem.

Forms and Devices

Structurally, *Sordello* is organized into two halves, the first dealing more or less with the young man's development as a poet, the second half with his development as a politician. Temporally, however, the poetic development lasts for more than thirty years, and the political for only three days. The first three books, therefore, are something of a digression from the action promised in the opening. This combination of anticipation and discontinuity becomes a persistent—and initially annoying—device that thematically stitches the poem together while appearing structurally to tear it apart.

Unlike Browning's other distinctive poems, which are, in most cases, dramatic monologues, this early effort is narrative. That description can be misleading, however, since the poem does not set out, in simple expository form, the story of a particular Mantuan poet. Alfred, Lord Tennyson wryly noted that the poem begins with the line, "Who will, may hear Sordello's story told," and ends with the line, "Who would has heard Sordello's story told," but both statements, in his opinion, were lies. Anyone approaching the poem without some idea of the story will be quickly frustrated by the extensive digressions from the plot and the juxtaposed sequence of incident.

This latter device, in fact, is not far from the *progression d'effet* later used by the modern novelist Ford Madox Ford in his novel *The Good Soldier* (1915). It may at first appear that Browning's narrator is suddenly remembering an important detail that had slipped his mind. This can disconcert the reader, who expects a more obvious competence in straightforward storytelling, but it is Browning's attempt to force reassessments of events and to make any one view of history seem relative. As noted in the next section, this formal device mirrors one of the poem's themes. Digression, while potentially frustrating, should therefore be viewed as an essential device in Browning's decision to step back from the onrush of heroes and villains. He wants a psychological portrayal of the artistic temperament and its development and must, therefore, show reflective activity as it happens.

The use of ellipsis, the breaking off in the middle of sentences, further slows the action; this, coupled with the complexity and length of some other sentences, the extensive use of enjambment and strong caesuras, have led critics to suggest that some of the poem's difficulties and stylistic variety are the result of transforming an early version of the poem in blank verse into one in rhymed couplets. This reference to the earlier versions of the poem (there were three before the final one) helps explain the frequent confusion over whose consciousness is being depicted—Sordello's, the narrator's, or Browning's. The dreamlike atmosphere of the narration that results, joined to the rather esoteric historical knowledge demanded of the reader over such a lengthy poem, discourages many potential readers.

Despite these challenges, though, as the Victorian Edmund Gosse noted, the poem has "passages of melody and insight, fresh enough, surprising enough to form the whole stock-in-trade of a respectable poet." An effect Browning seems to desire in his use of colloquial diction and parenthetical expressions, one that he perfected later, is the sound of ordinary language despite the metrical straitjacket. The delineation of character that Browning would later perfect is certainly here in much of *Sordello*, as is the energetic description of locale. This "word-painting," Browning's great success at visualizing his events, would have been particularly appealing to his contemporaries—those, that is, who could get through the dense and allusive narration (another Victorian, Jane Carlyle, said she had read the poem cover to cover and could not decide whether Sordello was a person, a book, or a town; yet another, Douglas Jerrold, feared as he read it that he had lost his mind).

This reference to mind is actually of the greatest significance, since the greatest formal success of the poem is its early, pre-twentieth century experimentation with the representation of consciousness. The poetic devices that caused such confusion in the Victorian period and that continue to distress the casual reader are not far short of the fixation on the portrayal of mental states found in the works of James Joyce or Joseph Conrad.

Themes and Meanings

Sordello invites a political interpretation, since it is so heavily involved in the politics of the twelfth century. Viewed allegorically, it can be described as Browning's critique of the bourgeois class in England that considered itself liberal in its republican sentiments, while maintaining a political alliance with the aristocracy. In a note to a friend, however, Browning protested that the historical setting of Sordello was somewhat arbitrary and was simply a backdrop to a more immediate drama that was not notably political: "The historical decoration was purposely of no more importance than a background requires; and my stress lay on the incidents in the development of a soul." Though the setting is medieval, the ideas being discussed are very much of the nineteenth century, and they are more psychological than political.

To his interest in portraying a young poet's consciousness, Browning added the Victorian preoccupation with duty. On the one hand, therefore, he follows the Romantic tradition of examining degrees of poetic inspiration in the types of poetry one may be called upon to write. On the other hand, considering the Romantic tradition of the isolation of the artist from society, Browning's spokesman becomes increasingly and emotionally preoccupied with the question of the role of a poet or of any artist in the political world.

Sordello, like the earlier *Paracelsus* (1835), offers Browning an opportunity to mull over the sort of poetry that he wants to craft and to confront the possibility that the higher the poetic aspiration, the greater the chance not only of perceived failure among his contemporaries, but also of genuine failure in the eyes of history. In book 1, he discusses two approaches to poetry. The first is a validation of the world and its manners, and the artistry that results from such an attitude is an imitation of that world. The second approach, the less popular path, seeks instead to better the world and to do so in an original and possibly misunderstood manner. Such an approach leads to a poetry that challenges the reader far more than may be welcomed.

Especially in book 5, Sordello discusses three types of poets, each important in his or her own way. First there appear epic poets who use individuals as allegorical representations of good and evil, and thereby teach a moral lesson. Then there are dramatic poets, who drop allegory for greater realistic representation; the moral judgment of the actions of their characters is left up to the reader. The third sort, the synthesist, deals with interior action and uses the physical only so far as necessary. Such a poet is a "Maker-see," and, as in the case of Sordello's homiletic intervention with Salinguerra, seeks to awaken others to their responsibilities to the rest of the world.

Briefly put, the question that Sordello comes gradually to ask is this: Beyond the personal satisfaction of successfully wooing a beautiful maiden or the acclaim attendant upon the success of a popular public poet, what sort of impact can and should a poet have in the rough world of wars, economics, and vengeance?

In this early poem the question of love, here the love of the Lady Palma, does not receive the complex psychological treatment that it does in later Browning poems. Already contained in *Sordello*, however, and blossoming into full flower in such later poems as "Andrea del Sarto," is the ancillary question of the inevitability, and possible benefit, of human fallibility in any committed activity in the world. For Browning, to have loved and lost seems, in some sense, even better than to have loved and *not* lost, and in *Sordello* there is already a clear preference of imperfection over perfection.

Sordello's sudden death in the midst of his crisis of conscience, and on the verge of what might have been a great political success, leads to a question that was already assuming great importance in Browning's mind. Beyond one's possible role as a poet, what would constitute a "successful" life? For someone such as Sordello, Browning's narrator suggests, success cannot take the form of political power. It must derive from the ethical force that leads others to act in responsible and generous ways. The true leader, as Sordello in some sense is, therefore serves as a prophet.

Especially if he is a poet, his real task is to embody a new consciousness, a new idea, that will someday take root in those more politically powerful; they, in turn, will change governments and all social structures that enslave. For the Browning of *Sordello*, therefore, the successful poet is not necessarily the one whose poetry is immediately accessible, beautiful, or even didactic. Sordello helped others see the conflict not only between Guelfs and Ghibellines but within each individual as well. That job accomplished, his brief life was a success.

John C. Hawley

SORTING, WRAPPING, PACKING, STUFFING

Author: James Schuyler (1923-1991)
Type of poem: Lyric
First published: 1969, in *Freely Espousing*

The Poem

"Sorting, wrapping, packing, stuffing" is a poem in free verse, its sixty-five lines divided into seven stanzas of varying lengths. The title strongly suggests the poem's method and tone by signifying busy activity, the four consecutive participles accumulating into a sense of hurry and culminating in a sense of fullness. The poem is written in the first person, yet the role of this person is not so much to reveal his character or emotions as to be the instigator and then the witness of the poem's events. He appears to the reader more as a performer than as a speaker.

"Sorting, wrapping, packing, stuffing" begins with a disorderly catalog of tacky domestic trivia, such as "dirty socks in dirty sneakers." The atmosphere is one of carelessness and transience; then this atmosphere is startlingly transformed by the ringing of a "great bronze bell." The sound elevates the tone of the poem to one of importance, of some unnamed crisis in which the soiled ephemera of the opening lines must be reassessed and sorted out. This emergency surprises the speaker in the midst of his own domestic trivia, just as he is making some instant coffee and a sandwich. Suddenly he is compelled to judge and to rank his belongings, to choose from among them those he will rescue from the still unnamed crisis. The madcap pressure of his situation is epitomized by what is apparently his most prized possession, "a blue fire escape": How can such an object be packed and, itself a means of rescue, be rescued? This pressure prompts the speaker to make avowals that are simultaneously tongue-in-cheek and profound, avowals that express the impregnability of the human heart even as they attest its ordinary materiality: "All there is/ is blood and thump."

Offering no transition, the speaker announces that it is now the next day and that the fire escape has somehow been successfully packed. There is no diminution of the crisis, however, because every next day is still a today, and every future eventually becomes a critical present, an ordinary but strident domestic situation of weeds and weather. The speaker considers the conventional escape of a trip to Florida, but chooses to remain in his city, there to dwell among the unexotic but irrepressible details of the life he apparently knows so well. This decision seems to elevate the status of everything in sight to a stellar level, and the speaker's life comes "unpacked," illuminated, as though his rubbish were the Milky Way or the northern lights.

This transformation is celebrated by a hurried sequence of nonsense exclamations punctuated by promises of further revelations. Abashed by the chaos, the speaker quickly calls a halt to the sequence, declaring that the "time is getting out of hand," a phrase that, in this case, is literally true. The poem concludes as it began, with a catalog, this time of imaginary books whose comic titles suggest the reconciliation of seriousness and absurdity, of imaginary and ordinary life, a reconciliation that, it is now obvious, has been the poem's purpose all along and that is affirmed by the closing words' declaration that "the world will fit."

Forms and Devices

A founder of the New York school of poetry (along with John Ashbery, Kenneth Koch, and Barbara Guest), James Schuyler expertly employs the most characteristic technique of that group: a verbal equivalent of the methods of such painters as Jackson Pollock and Franz Kline. As these painters treat their canvases as fields across which the paints move nonrepresentationally in unpremeditated patterns, so does Schuyler treat his page as a white expanse over which his words are free to group and regroup without being restricted to any conventional narrative or expressive plan. Schuyler trusts that words, having definitions, can never become meaningless, and so he literally finds his meaning in the actions of language—the sorting, wrapping, packing, stuffing of his title, for example. Schuyler desires for his words the freedom of stars, which can be imagined in countless changeable variations called constellations. This is perhaps the reason that his blue fire escape becomes a Milky Way when it is unpacked.

Schuyler's action technique does not signal a complete divorce from conventional poetic devices; it is instead a reanimation of those devices. Chief among these in "Sorting, wrapping, packing, stuffing" is the key metaphor of the "blue fire escape." Like Schuyler's words, it seems at first to be an object of use reduced to nonsense. What possible point is there in painting a fire escape blue? How could it get into someone's eye, much less be removed therefrom by a druggist? Most tellingly, how could it be packed and carried off in an emergency, only to be unpacked somewhere else? The answers to these questions provide much of the poem's meaning and prove that Schuyler's nonsense is really the elevation of the mundane to the level of true metaphor, since here a usually unregarded means of exit is transformed, by the poet's affectionate attention, into an entrance into new worlds of perception and understanding.

Schuyler's other principal poetic devices all participate in this process of transformation. The catalog was originally a convention of epic poetry, as in the catalog of ships found near the beginning of Homer's *Iliad* (c. 800 B.C.). Schuyler employs catalogs, such as the one that opens "Sorting, packing, wrapping, stuffing," in order to constellate ordinary or absurd articles into sudden clusters of meaning invested with the kind of dignity that accompanies meaning. His catalogs are more than lists; they are challenges to one's perception of one's own individual methods of sorting and categorizing in the creation of meaning, just as, upon viewing a Jackson Pollock painting, one is challenged to perceive a pattern in seemingly accidental drips and swirls of paint. In a similar device, Schuyler embeds these catalogs within the larger context of a continuously shifting poetic tone and vocabulary. His unexplained transitions from narrative to declamatory to nonsense language and then back again charge his poem's atmosphere with a busy energy that compels readers to keep their eyes constantly moving forward, their interpretive faculties constantly revising and so enlarging their understanding of the poem.

Themes and Meanings

As do all of Schuyler's best poems, "Sorting, wrapping, packing, stuffing" radiates an unselfconscious love for the world and all its minutiae. Its uniquely energized way of paying attention to its subject matter advocates the dignity of mere being. Schuyler's voice is one that rejoices in the transitory nature of things, the inevitable, unpredictable differences between one day and the next that so many other poets lament. Appearing frivolous at first, Schuyler's poems turn out to be meticulously, movingly faithful life studies of our extraordinary ordinary lives, studies in which it is a joy simply to say the names of things out loud.

For Schuyler, the acts of seeing and imagining are simultaneous, virtually identical in their purpose of recognizing the dignity of things and nature, recognizing, in keeping with this poem's title, that each object—stone or weed or article of soiled clothing—is a thing unto itself, larger in its reality than any abstract category in which we might wish to wrap and pack it. The stuff of life is just that—stuff. This stuff cannot be estranged from the human heart (itself a mundane reality of "blood and thump"), which so fervently and so mysteriously cherishes it. All dwell together in a time that is eternally the present. Schuyler rejects both nostalgia and anticipation as attitudes that subordinate the world to fixed interpretations, rejects them in favor of celebration, finding in those things that others commonly ignore—the fire escape that may be a galaxy, the "brown bat" droppings that may be a source of light and warmth—the literal material of the marvelous. In this eternal present, it is abject folly to seek to flee time and change as one might flee a New York winter by vacationing in Florida. Time and change accompany everyone everywhere, and so it is far better freely to accept and to choose change, as Schuyler chooses to "slip into this Ice Age remnant granite boulder," one of the many left behind by the glaciers in what is now New York's Central Park.

From the perspective that Schuyler's poem recommends, there can be no contradictions, no mutually exclusive options, for such things arise only from abstract principles of logic. Just as any two words may be typed beside each other, so any two objects may combine to form new landscapes of new meanings. This is the theme of Schuyler's closing booklist. "*The Great Divorce Has Been Annulled*" celebrates the end of paralyzing distinctions and definitions that shrink the world, a world that Schuyler's poem believes to be a perfect fit.

Donald Revell

SPARROW HILLS

Author: Boris Pasternak (1890-1960)
Type of poem: Lyric
First published: 1922, as "Vorob'evy gory," in *Sestra moia zhizn*; collected in
  Selected Poems, 1982

The Poem

"Sparrow Hills" is a lyric poem consisting of five stanzas of conventional quatrains, with the regular rhyming scheme *abab*. The title refers to a hilly section of Moscow situated on a bend of the Moscow River. At the time of the writing of this poem (1917), Sparrow Hills was an area on the edge of Moscow, but now it is completely inside the city limits, near Moscow University. The poem is written in the first person, with Boris Pasternak addressing directly either the reader or himself, now describing the scenery, now expressing his thoughts and feelings or giving a friendly suggestion, even a warning. The poem is set in the summer, which is especially luxuriant in both the open and the wooded countryside. The persona begins by exhorting the unknown listener or reader to submit himself to the charms of nature, to let his breast be kissed as if "under a tap," for the summer will not always be so gallant and one will not be able to dance to accordion music night after night.

In stanza 2, the poet suddenly switches to musing about old age, saying that he has heard all kinds of terrible prophecies about it—"no face in the grass,/ No heart in the ponds, no God in the trees." There will be nothing in old age to inspire one toward the stars. After he has conditioned the reader with this mild warning, in the third stanza the poet exhorts him all the more to liven up and partake of this beauty. "Where are your eyes?" he asks goodnaturedly. The poet's goal seems to be to convince his reader to look around and to realize that the world is at the high noon of its development and that clouds, heat, woodpeckers, pine needles, and pinecones can all inspire elevated thoughts and gentle feelings.

In the fourth stanza, the poet reinforces the pastoral charm of the scenery. The rails of the streetcars end here simply because they can go no farther, for beyond that line is a holiday atmosphere; the glade rolls on, grass hugging the branches.

In the final stanza, the poet allows nature itself to tell the reader that the world is always this accessible—one need merely ask the thicket, the fields, and the clouds pouring down transfigured light on the people in their summer clothes. The poem ends on a very positive, invigorating note, just as it has begun. Its message has been delivered, and the reader's prospects of heeding it are hoped to be improved.

Forms and Devices

In a poem centered almost entirely on nature, it is not surprising that "Sparrow Hills" abounds in nature images, representing the main device used here by Pasternak. The images are reinforced by metaphors carefully selected to fit the atmosphere of the poem.

It is also not surprising that, since the poem takes place in the summer heat, most of the images should be connected with water as the source of the most satisfying relief. In the very first line, Pasternak uses the metaphor of a breast being soothed by the kisses of invisible rain, as if under a tap. Further images centering on the refreshing effect of water follow. When the poet exhorts the soul to come to life, he wants it to bubble up in foam, and when clouds, woodpeckers, pine needles, and pinecones are called on to display their "Sunday best," they cluster in fleecy sprays, inspiring creative thoughts. In the final verse, the poet also hails the soothing power of water in the form of light that descends from the clouds like vapor.

Auditory images are also abundant, as if to underscore the teeming, seething nature of a hot summer. The summer "bubbles up," everything is astir, and the thoughts evoked by the summer scenery are effervescent. The sound images complement the sight images and vice versa.

Other images deal with spatial delineation between the two worlds — that of the city and that of nature. As revealed in the first three stanzas, the poet emphasizes through water images the beneficial aspects of nature providing relief in the summer heat. Next, he turns to the city by way of the metaphor of the rails stopping at the foot of Sparrow Hills. There is no place for them beyond that point. From there on, it is the pines, the clearings, the holiday spirit as expressed metaphorically by the word "Sunday."

By constantly shifting his focus between nature and humankind and by combining complementary images and metaphors, Pasternak achieves a certain unity of purpose and creates a compact, well-defined poem.

Themes and Meanings

"Sparrow Hills" is a lyric apotheosis of the beauties of nature. Pasternak wrote numerous poems extolling nature, including the other poems in the same collection *Sestra moia zhizn* (*My Sister, Life*, 1959), but this poem is among his best, if not the best, in that respect. Some of his most powerful images are to be found in "Sparrow Hills."

For Pasternak, nature represents the best things that life has to offer. It has a soothing and healing power that is there for the taking. Even the frightening specter of approaching old age cannot diminish the beneficial power of nature, as illustrated by the poet's dismissal of the "terrible prophecies" concerning old age. All one has to do is to be attentive to the signals coming from nature, and the vital forces in man will be released.

Yet Pasternak is not merely praising the beauties of nature. He is also warning humankind not to be so blind, as, for example, when he asks rhetorically, "Where are your eyes?" The veiled warning of the potential for incalculable loss is contained in the final stanza, where he bestows on nature the power to light up the whole world (metaphorized by "noon"), all holidays ("Whitsunday"), and all motion ("walks"), all of which can be lost if humankind is indifferent or abusive. Life has always been like that, and nothing will ever change it. The woods know it, the clearings know it, the clouds know it—only human beings seem to be blind to it. They can ignore nature, however, only at their own risk: the risk of the loss of vital energy and of the very reason for their existence.

In reality, the poet is addressing himself, hinting at his own negligence of the vital link with nature. As a creative artist, he can gain much more than others from an intense commitment to all reality, when, in the words of Rimvydas Silbajoris, the heat of the poet's passion melts down the barriers between different categories of phenomena. Therefore, nature, as the depository of these phenomena, represents the best source of creative power, and thus the summer heat and the heat of creation are used by Pasternak as similes.

"Sparrow Hills" was written in the summer of 1917, a few months before the October revolution. Although Pasternak probably was not predicting it, the disintegration of the country and of the fabric of Russian life was already in progress, having started with World War I and continued with the revolution of February, 1917. People were in danger of losing their spiritual compass and of forgetting the basic values that had nourished them so far. Until then, the Russians had been known to be in uncommonly close contact with nature, especially because the vast majority of them lived in rural areas. Seen from that perspective, "Sparrow Hills" seems to express the poet's plea to his countrymen—and to himself—to revert to communing with nature, as they had done for centuries.

Seen within the entire opus of Pasternak, especially when complemented by the poems of *Doctor Zhivago*, in which nature also plays a decisive role, "Sparrow Hills" fits into the large mosaic of Pasternak's poetry as a shining and important tessera.

Vasa D. Mihailovich

THE SPIRIT OF THE AGE

Author: Friedrich Hölderlin (1770-1843)
Type of poem: Ode
First published: 1800, as "Der Zeitgeist"; in *Friedrich Hölderlin's sämmtliche Werke*, 1846; collected in *Poems and Fragments*, 1967

The Poem

"The Spirit of the Age" is a short ode of twenty lines. An ode is a poetic form derived from a Greek model (ode means "song" in Greek); it was often used by the Romantic poets for lyric poetry of high seriousness. Friedrich Hölderlin called this poem a "tragic ode," meaning that it combined the lyricism (or personal tone) of the ode with the heroic or fateful tone of the tragedy.

The title of this poem might be better translated as "The God of Time," for "Zeitgeist" — literally, "time-god" or "time-spirit" — means here both the élan (mood or spirit) of a time period, such as William Hazlitt was later to describe in a work by that title (1824), and a sort of divinity that Hölderlin invokes.

The poem contains five stanzas of four lines each, with no rhyme scheme. The meter is irregular (a mixture of iambs and dactyls) but somewhat consistent: In each stanza but one (the fourth), the first two lines have five feet and end with a stressed, "masculine" syllable, and the last two lines have four feet and end with an unstressed, "feminine" syllable.

The first stanza is an invocation of the god of time, who is, the poet says, "above my head." This god seems rather frightening and threatening, like the "dark clouds" in which he dwells. The same mood is continued in the second stanza, where the poet describes being tempted to ignore this god by pretending to be still a boy, innocent and unknowing, and by looking at the ground and into a cave, involved in earthly things, away from the god above. He calls the god "the all-shattering," he who shakes and convulses everything.

By the third stanza, there is a sudden reconciliation of opposites and a resignation to the rule of this god. Twice the god of time is called not "the shatterer" but, simply and naïvely, "Father." No longer wishing to avoid seeing him, the narrator now asks for his own eyes to be opened. By accepting the god, the narrator becomes truly innocent, not through ignorance, but through open-eyed, knowledgeable faith.

In the fourth stanza, where the rhythm varies slightly from that of the rest of the poem, there is a shift to natural imagery; the maturation of the narrator is compared to the ripening of grapes to make wine, and the movement of the god is compared to a "mild spring air" in which "[mortal] men" are "wandering/ In orchards calmly." This stanza flows directly into the fifth stanza without a sentence break, but there is nevertheless another sudden shift here: The mood returns to that of the beginning of the poem, but with an important difference. Now the "Shaker" is seen as a teacher of the young, as one who teaches the old to be wise, representing a threat only to those who are "evil" or "bad."

Forms and Devices

Although the poem is written in the first person, there is an aesthetic distance between the poet Hölderlin and the narrator of the poem. This means that the poem has an impersonal, universal quality to it rather than the ambience of a highly personal experience. Even in the first line, there is an air of generality or of repeated, lasting experience, not of a one-time occurrence: "Too long above my head you have governed there."

In fact, the narrator does not appear in the last two stanzas, where the god who is addressed is described in terms of his effect on "us," "youths," and "older men"— generalized terms—not on the "I" of the beginning. Throughout the poem, there is more emphasis on the "you" to whom the poem or invocation is addressed than on the "I" who relates or prays. This structure is appropriate to both the form of the poem as a "tragic ode" and the meanings of the poem. A tragic mood must have universal—not merely individual—validity, and the meanings of this poem, as will be demonstrated, have to do with the significance of the self in terms of the whole society.

The original Greek ode (the Pindaric ode), upon which this poem is loosely based, consisted of three sections: a strophe, an antistrophe, and an epode. Since music, poetry, and dance were united in Greek art, these poems were chanted and danced by a chorus, which moved up one side of the stage for the strophe, down the other side for the antistrophe, and remained standing for the epode. This structure still exists (if only abstractly) in "The Spirit of the Age": The first two stanzas manifest strife and conflict; the third and fourth stanzas show a growth and change in attitude, and then a vision of one's being within the universal context of the natural world; and the final stanza returns to the original conception of the god, but with a vision that looks toward the future and an understanding of the significance of the threatening god.

Several sets of opposites work within the poem to show the original lack of unity of the poetic voice. The god in the clouds "above my head" is contrasted with the "ground" and the "deep cave" on which the narrator at first wishes to concentrate. Such a contrast of the spiritual and religious with the physical and earthly is common in Western poetry. Another contrast is that of original blindness with open-eyed recognition.

This leads to a slightly more confusing contrast in the poem: that between youth and age. At first, boyhood seems to represent ignorance, for the narrator wishes, wrongly, one may assume, to return to boyish naïvete. Shortly thereafter, he refers to himself as "stupid" ("Poor craven") in this context. Yet the reader then sees that youth can also be viewed as a time of potentiality, of grapes not yet ripe, of wisdom not yet attained. Since the poet now addresses the god as "father," one can see that it is not childlikeness that is criticized here, but willful ignorance. Like William Wordsworth in his famous poem "Ode: Intimations of Immortality" (1807), Hölderlin calls for a return to youthful innocence insofar as this means a turning away from worldly concerns and from what Wordsworth termed "the light of common day" — human reason and reasonableness, the petty mundane things that make one forget one's immortality and divine nature. Neither Romantic poet desires an abdication of responsibility or a return to childish dependence, but rather a movement toward a new, more highly developed state in which child*like* (not child*ish*) awareness is mingled with adult consciousness to create a better world.

Themes and Meanings

Hölderlin's background in the Pietistic religion of the eighteenth century, which stressed a personal, mystical, self-observing religious experience, is very evident in his poetry. Yet he was later to adopt the pantheistic beliefs of the followers of the philosopher Baruch Spinoza, and his poetry cannot be understood fully without reference to this theory.

Hölderlin felt that God manifested himself in all natural phenomena, a system of belief that did not necessarily contradict orthodox Christianity but did alter some of its doctrines. In "The Spirit of the Age," the god that is invoked is not really the Christian God, but something more like the Greek divinities that inhabited all of nature. Thus the poem under discussion mingles a pantheistic conception with traditional Christian imagery.

The god in the clouds of stanza 1 clearly evokes the brooding spirit who moves over the waters in Genesis. This god, like the Christian God, is a "father" who teaches (stanza 4) and who puts the spirit of life into mortal man (stanza 3). The image of ripening grapes recalls the wine of the Christian Last Supper; for Hölderlin, however, wine meant more than this. In his poem "Bread and Wine" (1807), a clear reference to the Last Supper, Hölderlin mixes in imagery of the Dionysian "drunkenness" (Dionysus was the Greco-Roman god of the grape harvest and wine) that he associated with the "drunkenness" or loss of purely rational capabilities of poetic inspiration. This poem, too, is an appeal to the gods of poetic, not religious, inspiration.

All this is not to say that Hölderlin was completely abstract and cut off from the historical occurrences of his times. The poem's final stanza reworks the Christian parable of the separation of the sheep from the goats, making it clear that the gods punish only those who are "evil" and therefore deserving of punishment. For Hölderlin, this had a very real significance. In a time when his country was under the rule of people he thought were tyrants (the nobility) and was threatened by attack from abroad (by Napoleon), political right-mindedness was of extreme importance. Hölderlin wanted a democratic government, which he thought could be effected through poetry. By achieving a unity with nature, such as can be seen in this poem, a new level of consciousness could be reached. By contemplating the divinity with open eyes instead of concentrating on worldly affairs, humans could return to a natural state, a "Oneness" with the universe, from which they have "fallen" (again, the concept is Christian) as a result of limited knowledge and vision. Although this attitude must certainly seem very naïve and even ignorant in the twentieth century, for the Romantics it represented a radically new way of perceiving man's place in the universe. It is in part because of their vision that humanity now has the luxury of considering it outmoded and wrong.

Laura Martin

SPOON RIVER ANTHOLOGY

Author: Edgar Lee Masters (1868-1950)
Type of poem: Poetic sequence
First published: 1915

The Poem

Spoon River Anthology is a book-length collection of 243 free verse epitaphs, in which the citizens buried in the graveyard of a fictional Midwestern town (Spoon River) talk about their lives, their failures, their loves, their philosophies, their triumphs, their conflicts, their secrets, and their crimes. Edgar Lee Masters published many of these pieces in *Reedy's Mirror* under the pseudonym Webster Ford (for whom Masters composed the epitaph that concludes *Spoon River Anthology*) during 1914; with encouragement, however, Masters collected his pieces, introduced them with the lyric "The Hill," concluded them with "The Spooniad," and published them as a book under his own name in 1915. The epitaphs, most of which are spoken in the first person by those buried in the Spoon River graveyard, range from five lines in length ("Alexander Throckmorton") to forty-five lines ("Caroline Branson"). Many of the lives and stories in the collection are related and intertwined, and to read the entire *Spoon River Anthology* is to experience a panoramic view of human existence and experience, a view filtered through the perspective of a small American town.

Masters' choice of title reveals much about his attitude toward his subject and about his stylistic approach to that subject. The word "anthology" is from the Greek, meaning a collection of epigrams. Masters knew Greek, and in selecting this title, he calls our attention to the epigrammatic form—a style of poetry that traditionally is pointed, brief, focused, sometimes a bit cynical, and always enlightening and wise. Even when the inhabitants of Spoon River do not display deep insight, these epigrams still cause the reader to think over what has been said, to reflect on it, and to come away enlightened.

The collection begins with a table of contents, which lists the poems in alphabetical order. Since most titles are simply the names of the persons under consideration, the table of contents has the effect of reducing the inhabitants of the Spoon River graveyard to a list of meaningless names. Reading the list— "Ballard, John; Barker, Amanda; Barrett, Pauline; Bartlett, Ezra; Bateson, Marie"—is like encountering a faceless crowd. The artistry of the *Spoon River Anthology* becomes clear when one begins reading the epigrams themselves, for each person emerges as a unique individual, a strong personality.

The first poem in the collection, "The Hill," is not one of the epitaphs but rather represents an example of the *ubi sunt* theme in poetry, through which the lost things of the past are lamented. *Ubi sunt* is Latin for "where are," and in this poem, Masters asks "Where are Elmer, Herman, Bert, Tom and Charley,/ . . . Where are Ella, Kate, Mag, Lizzie and Edith?" His answer is that all "are sleeping on the hill" in the graveyard. "The Hill" sets the tone for the rest of the volume, for—despite some moments of satisfaction, pleasure, and triumph—most of the monologues in *Spoon River Anthology* are somber.

The first epigram in the collection is "Hod Putt," and this short piece offers the voice of a man tried and hanged for murder. Hod Putt tells the reader that he lies "close to the grave/ Of Old Bill Piersol,/ Who grew rich trading with the Indians." As Piersol grows rich through manipulation of the law, Hod Putt becomes angrier and angrier, finally resorting to armed robbery, killing his victim. There is a note of ironic triumph in the poem, however, for Hod Putt concludes, "Now we who took the bankrupt law in our respective ways/ Sleep peacefully side by side." "Ollie McGee" and "Fletcher McGee" present two different sides of a troubled marriage. The relationship between the two sounds emotionally murderous, for Ollie McGee claims, "That is my husband who, by secret cruelty/ Never to be told, robbed me of my youth and my beauty," while Fletcher McGee says, "she died and haunted me,/ And hunted me for life." Typically, readers never discover what actually went on between these two, but it is clear that they destroyed each other.

"Robert Fulton Tanner" presents one of Masters' most dreary depictions of the universe, for Tanner claims that "A man can never avenge himself/ On the monstrous ogre Life." Man is rendered, in Tanner's view, little more than a rat in a trap, and all life does is "stare with his burning eyes at you,/ And scowl and laugh, and mock and curse you,/ . . . Until your misery bores him." The situation for women is equally cheerless in Spoon River. Daisy Fraser, the town prostitute, asserts that while she may be scorned and reviled, at least she contributes "ten dollars and costs/ To the school fund of Spoon River" each time she is brought before Justice Arnett. She sets herself in sharp contrast to the town fathers (the editor, the judge, the minister), who—she claims—are immoral and corrupt. The plight of Minerva Jones, "the village poetess," is hopeless in a more dramatic way. Jeered at by the "Yahoos" in the town, she is raped by "Butch" Weldy, who "Captured me after a brutal hunt." From her grave she implores someone to gather her verses into a book. She laments, "I thirsted so for love!/ I hungered so for life!"

The love that might come of a comfortable marriage is described by Trainor, the druggist, who asks, "who can tell/ How men and women will interact/ On each other, or what children will result?" Observing the families of Spoon River, Trainor says, "I Trainor, the druggist, a mixer of chemicals,/ Killed while making an experiment,/ Lived unwedded." Looking at "Amanda Barker," one can see why marriage seems unsavory in Spoon River. Amanda says, in eight short lines, that her husband Henry "got me with child,/ Knowing that I could not bring forth life/ Without losing my own." She asserts that Henry did not love her "with a husband's love" but rather killed her to "gratify his hatred."

Other noteworthy pieces from this collection include "Reuben Pantier" and "Emily Sparks." Emily Sparks is the town schoolteacher, who has great hopes for "The boy I loved best of all in the school"; she is "the teacher, the old maid, the virgin heart," but she does express some positive feeling about the young man of whom she dreams. Unfortunately, it is probably Reuben Pantier she thinks about, and he—as his poem reveals—has been driven from town for being involved with the milliner's daughter. In France, he has taken up with other women and corrupted himself with alcohol: "I passed through every peril known/ Of wine and women and joy of life." Sadly, but sweetly, he remembers Miss Emily Sparks and cries for her, saying, "I owe whatever I was in life/ To your hope that would not give me up,/ To your love that saw me still as good."

The collection concludes with "The Spooniad," a "fragment" of an epic planned by one of the residents of Spoon River, Jonathan Swift Somers. This rather long, blank-verse piece, which presents the events of Spoon River in a mock-heroic fashion, is meant to mimic the form of such great epics as Homer's *Iliad* (c. 800 B.C.) and *Odyssey* (c. 800 B.C.). In effect, this section rounds out the entire work, since it presents the inhabitants of Spoon River as living human beings, interacting with one another rather than speaking somewhat somberly from the grave.

Forms and Devices

Spoon River Anthology had a heavy impact on the reading public of early twentieth century America; it provoked anger, wonder, disgust, puzzlement, and admiration. The work was translated into many other languages, performed as an opera, and enjoyed a long popularity; it has, moreover, been adapted for many theatrical presentations over the years. What compelled the early readers of this work, though, was the question of its genre—was it poetry, fiction, drama, essay? The pieces in *Spoon River Anthology* did not look or sound like poems. They were written in free verse, having no rhymes or metrical patterns. They did not even seem to use imagery or metaphor heavily. In fact, the language was considered by some to be simply flat, careless, ugly, and uninteresting—certainly unpoetic.

The strength and poetry of these pieces derive from another source; it is their psychological insight, their social awareness, their range in perspective, and their philosophical questioning that make them great. These short monologues, presented in the natural speech of small-town Americans, reveal human passions with such openness and honesty that they were like a splash of cold water in the face of American propriety. Each is quick and pointed, but each is deadly accurate in its rendering of human emotions, human tragedy, human conflict, and human yearnings.

The organization of *Spoon River Anthology* conveys a sense of modernity and fragmentation that one might find more characteristic of T. S. Eliot than of Edgar Lee Masters. Each epitaph is locked solidly into the point of view, the perspective, of the person who speaks it. Many of these individuals are clearly misguided, even criminal, often vicious. The fact that cross-references exist, that the same story is heard from several different perspectives, that many voices speak, gives a more complete picture of one American community. Although none of the citizens of Spoon River can speak for all of Spoon River, their voices taken as a choir offer a rich and fascinating picture of that imaginary town.

It is important to note the realism of the work since that realism was one aspect of

Spoon River Anthology that many early readers found offensive. Masters is straight-forward in dealing with many unsavory subjects—rape, abortion, murder, child abuse, suicide, thievery, and many less lurid events. In fact, there is almost something matter-of-fact about the way some of these people speak of the most horrible aspects of their lives. The unswerving determination Masters brings to bear on his subjects, his refusal to blush before an unpleasant issue, his grasp of the psychological realities of human emotions—these factors turn the brief narrative portraits into poetry. Their honesty and unswerving clarity of vision make them art.

Finally, in considering the morality or vision of *Spoon River Anthology*, it is necessary to note that each poem concludes, if not with a distinct moral lesson, at least with some moment of insight for the reader. In fact, Masters is quite concerned that his audience be involved in these brief encounters, for many of the pieces refer to or imply an audience—sometimes a traveler, sometimes the town itself, sometimes a passerby. This person or this group is invited by the speaker to consider the facts, to consider the consequences, to learn from what has happened. Some speakers even offer warnings to the audience. Moreover, the entire shape of the book encourages a more positive reading than might be apparent initially. While early portraits are those of misfits and outsiders, sinners and cynics, later portraits present more philosophical speakers, people who wonder about life, who consider larger issues, who themselves enjoy moments of insight along with eternities of pain.

Themes and Meanings

To understand fully what Masters hoped to achieve in *Spoon River Anthology*, it is important always to keep one fact in mind: The people speaking are dead. Masters did not offer a picture of a town full of living people, so the careful reader must ask: Why not? Why must these people speak to us from the grave? What does Masters hope to accomplish with this technique? The first answer must have something to do with the liberty the dead have in addressing the living. These people are no longer members of a community in which they must preserve a facade, please a parent, or impress an employer. They have nothing to lose by their honesty. Many upright people in Spoon River admit to having had affairs (Sarah Brown, Willard Fluke, and Doc Hill), to having participated in illegal and immoral acts (the town marshal), to having practiced deception and fraud (Dr. Siegrfied [*sic*] Iseman), and to engaging in secret and shameful corruption (Deacon Taylor is a prohibitionist who dies of alcohol-induced cirrhosis of the liver). Death frees them to show the reader the reality of their lives and their emotions. With this freedom, the audience is granted a visceral and moving portrait of how members of the human family can and do treat one another, how they really behave, what truly motivates them.

The fact that all the speakers in *Spoon River Anthology* are dead leads one to consider Masters' thematic preoccupation. There are several positive and strong declarations in this collection. Lucinda Matlock, for example, describes her life as full and lusty, claiming that "Life is too strong" for most people; "It takes life to love Life." Even the village atheist is filled with spiritual energy: "Coughing myself to death/ I read the *Upanishads* and the poetry of Jesus./ And they lighted a torch of hope and intuition." Despite these declarations, however, Masters seems to emphasize the vanity of human aspirations. No matter who people are, no matter how great they feel themselves to be, they find themselves at the end of their lives, "sleeping on the hill"—beggars, thieves, judges, harlots, teachers, philosophers, visionaries, and cynics—all are brothers and sisters in death, all are dust in the end.

Masters' world view seems, then, heavily naturalistic—that is, characterized by a sense that one's fate is determined more by biology, material circumstance, external forces, than by human will or desire. Even when the inhabitants of Spoon River have strong desires (such as Harry Wilmans' naïve patriotic desire to go to Manila to fight for his country or Seth Compton's desire to provide books and knowledge for the residents of this town), they are destroyed by these desires. It is almost as if—in Masters' view—desire is destined to become disease or compulsion. Moreover, the citizens of Spoon River seem, frequently, to be slaves to their desires. Eugenia Todd compares human love and ambition to "an old tooth . . . a pain in the side, . . . or a malignant growth," implying that the souls' desires are nothing more than manifestations of some biology beyond conscious control; and Judge Selah Lively attributes his ambition to become a successful professional to the fact that he "stood just five feet two" and that people "jeered" at his size. The human spirit seems quite impoverished in Masters' view, and traditional religion offers little comfort. Henry Phipps tells the reader that he lived his whole life "made white/ With the paint of the Christian creed" only to lose all, ironically, by an act of God.

Even human love and the family seem hopeless. Herbert Marshall tells the reader that the tragedy of human life is that people must love, people need to love, but the ones who people love usually do not return the affection: "This is life's sorrow:/ That one can be happy only where two are;/ And that our hearts are drawn to stars/ Which want us not." In fact, there is one hopeless love after another in *Spoon River Anthology*. Pauline Barrett and her husband seek unsuccessfully to recover their affection when she is left "the shell of a woman after the surgeon's knife"; Julia Miller marries a man thirty-five years older than she to provide a father for her unborn baby but then kills herself and the child, longing for the baby's real father; Mabel Osborne laments the love she missed because no one saw her need: "I, who had happiness to share/ And longed to share your happiness;/ I who loved you, Spoon River,/ And craved your love,/ Withered before your eyes, Spoon River—/ Thirsting, thirsting." The family offers little comfort to these lonely, deserted people. Barry Holden attends the trial of Dr. Duval for the murder of Zora Clemens, and "It was clear he had got her in a family way/ And to let the child be born/ Would not do." Shaken, Barry Holden goes home to his wife and eight children: "And just as I entered there was my wife,/ Standing before me, big with child./ She started the talk of the mortgaged farm,/ And I killed her."

There is a deep and pervasive hopelessness in Edgar Lee Masters' *Spoon River Anthology*, one that fills the reader with an inexorable sadness for the human condition. Harold Arnett expresses this sadness when he thinks of his failures in Spoon

River and asks, "Of what use is it/ To rid one's self of the world,/ When no soul may ever escape the eternal destiny of life?" Perhaps it is simply this sadness which Masters evokes in the reader that will be salvation. Griffy the Cooper challenges readers by observing how little they know about the world and people around them: "The cooper should know about tubs./ But I learned about life as well,/ And you who loiter around these graves/ Think you know life." In one of the final epitaphs in the collection, "Jeremy Carlisle," Masters puts Griffy's words into perspective, showing that it is one's duty to try to know the people of one's community, to try to pierce the loneliness and lies and sadness that separate one person from another. Jeremy Carlisle addresses the reader directly, declaring, "Passer-by, sin beyond any sin/ Is the sin of blindness of souls to other souls./ And joy beyond any joy is the joy/ Of having the good in you seen, and seeing the good/ At the miraculous moment!" It is this blindness that *Spoon River Anthology* seeks to redress.

Kathleen Margaret Lant

SPRING RAIN

Author: Boris Pasternak (1890-1960)
Type of poem: Lyric
First published: 1922, as "Vesennii dozhd," in *Sestra moia zhizn*; collected in *My Sister, Life and Other Poems*, 1976

The Poem

"Spring Rain" is a short poem of twenty-four lines that are broken into six stanzas of four lines each. Set in the spring following the February beginning of the 1917 bloodless Russian Revolution, the poem is written as if the speaker were not a participant but simply a witness to the urban scene recorded. While there is no reference to an "I," the last line of stanza 6 contains the word "our," which by implication broadens the voice. In the quotation from Nikolaus Lenau's poem "Das Bild," the epigraph to *Sestra moia zhizn*, the volume in which "Spring Rain" first appeared, "my beloved girl" is named as someone who the poet wishes to draw into the experience of the poems. The "our" could be interpreted to mean the poet and the beloved girl of the epigraph.

From the beginning line, rain takes on properties beyond that of mere water falling from the sky. The speaker anthropomorphizes the downpour such that it first grins at a wildflower, then sobs, and then soaks things as diverse as the hard shine of vehicles and breeze-blown flora. In the last two lines of the stanza, the speaker sets the scene: The action is outside at night, near a theater where a crowd of people is being managed by a policeman.

The effects of the rain and the moonlight, the positive transforming powers, are described in the next two stanzas. Drops, called both "tears" and "damp diamonds," touch everything, including the people gathered, arousing joyfulness. Moonlight bathes the scene in white, capturing the drama of the historical moment in a plaster-like silhouette. A question begins the fourth stanza, and in its unfurling, the heightened emotion of the crowd finds expression. "The minister's" refers to Aleksandr Kerensky, who was the minister of justice in the government that was set up after the abdication of Czar Nicholas II. His charismatic address has melted the assemblage together in unity of spirit.

The series of denials that begin both stanza 5 and stanza 6 erases the scene's carefully constructed details in order to focus on two observations by the poem's speaker. What remains to look on is the momentousness of what has taken place to bring about the uproar. The speaker places the triumph of revolution in context by drawing an illustration from ancient Rome, suggesting the disparity between hopeless entrapment in the dark catacombs of the past and freedom of movement in the city's heart of public commerce in daylight. This is one measure of the feeling of liberation that is unleased by the ongoing revolution.

Yet the speaker does not restrict his elucidation to the boundaries of his country, for in stanza 6 he links the rain and the moon to the rest of Europe, intimating that what has begun in Russia will, like unstoppable tides, come to Europe's troubled shores as well. The fullest meaning of the rain as a symbol of the spiritual impetus and energy that the speaker finds in the revolutionary air is finally expressed with approval as the speaker makes the street outside the theater the "forum." He returns to his original anthropomorphism, describing the rain as "proud" of its Russian geography.

Forms and Devices

Boris Pasternak's poems contain many metaphors and metonymies. As a young man, Pasternak considered a career as a professional musician. He devoted more than six years to the study of composition but abandoned the pursuit when he became convinced that he lacked the required technical skill. The musical training greatly influenced his poems, however, and the artistry of sound design, as well as rhyme and meter, guided his word choice and resulted in intricate metaphoric and metonymic usage. "Spring Rain" falls among the group of poems in which the poet found parallels in nature to convey his theme and discovered an abundance of metaphors and metonymies to both strengthen the poem's form and add crisp originality to its imagery.

In stanza 2, first a simile—the raindrops as tears filling a throat—and then a metaphor—"damp diamonds" burning—is followed by the metonymy of "eyelids" to imply the congregation in the street.

The pallor cast by the moon is metaphorized, along with the moonlight-silhouetted urban scene, as a plaster sculpture in which the congregation in the street again is represented by metonymies. This time, there is a series: "queues, tossing dresses, . . . enraptured lips." The "fingertips" and "aortas and lips" of the next stanza, are also pieces representing wholes. The government minister has raised his hands in his moving oration and has unified the emotional and verbal response of the people.

The last two stanzas employ the device of negative parallelism, wherein the first two lines of both stanzas begin with a list of what is not to be considered from the scene previously presented. These stanzas also contain elaborate metaphors. In stanza 5, the description of finding a way out of catacombs is used as a metaphor for the atmosphere of the revolution, implying a turning from a past mired in persecution and secrecy toward a future filled with openness and public deeds.

The metaphoric pattern of stanza 6, the most interwoven, again suggests that the street in front of the theater is the "forum" of ancient Rome, thus bringing to the reader's mind that great empire and its epic magnitude. The rain, previously allowed human characteristics of mood and whim, is now metaphorized as "the surf of Europe's wavering night" that feels "proud of itself." A complex web of metaphors, as "wavering night" is a metaphor as well, stands for what Pasternak perceived as a healthy unrest calling the revolution to traditional European civilization as it did to Russia. The final words, "on our asphalt," display metonymy as well. "Our asphalt" broadens to mean all of Russia as the incubator of a dynamic revolutionary spirit.

With regard to structure, "Spring Rain" can be divided into two parts. The first three stanzas focus on the details of the scene, such as the rain, the flowers and trees, and the crowd. The following three stanzas turn from concrete detail to focus on the atmosphere of history in the making. The language of liquids, mostly water, permeates both halves, however, and acts as an artful unifier.

Rain sobs, soaks, and congregates in "puddles." It is like tears, and it is "damp diamonds." Clouds, themselves collections of moistness, feel a wet form of happiness. Hiding in "enraptured" is the sense of being carried away, or filled, both suggestive of liquid action. Further on, blood rushes "in a flood" just before a "blinding emergence," which can be seen as something akin to a flood. Lastly, the crowds "roar" precedes "surf," two words often connected by a sound link, and rain feels proud "on our asphalt," a metonymy which allows a characteristic of water to be part of the image, in the idea of the wetness that has covered the street.

Themes and Meanings

"Spring Rain" is a poem about dynamism and the energy that is formed by unifying individuals. Pasternak uses the atmosphere of liberation in the spring immediately following the first 1917 revolution in Russia as a vehicle to illustrate the exhilarating effect that such a cataclysmic, monumental event has on the collective human spirit. Electrified air, exuberant crowds, nature dazzled with wetness—all point toward a positive release of pent-up grievances which is created from hope for the future and the unifying glory of national pride.

The lightning-rod revolution, in combination with a summer love affair (with a woman never specifically identified), inspired Pasternak to capture the everyday events in a poetic history which became the cycle of poems called *Sestra moia zhizn*. Olga Andreyev Carlisle, in her prologue to the translation of this work, entitled *My Sister, Life and Other Poems* (1976), quotes Pasternak's remarks about the period forty years later:

> During the remarkable summer of 1917, in the interlude between the two revolutions, it appeared as if not only the people participated in the discourse, but together with them also the roads, the trees and the stars, the air, free and unlimited, carried this ardent enthusiasm through thousands of versts and seemed to be a person with a name, possessing clear sight and a soul.

"Spring Rain" is but one of fifty poems in a narrative cycle which celebrates the romance of life. In its entirety, the cycle is a discourse between the poet as character and the poet as author. "Policeman's Whistles," the companion to "Spring Rain" in the cycle, directly opposes the enthusiastic applause for revolution of "Spring Rain" and tells instead of the suffering and vulnerability of the individual striving for identity in the revolution's whirlwind of change.

Virginia Starrett

STANZAS FROM THE GRANDE CHARTREUSE

Author: Matthew Arnold (1822-1888)
Type of poem: Meditation
First published: 1855; collected in *New Poems*, 1867

The Poem

"Stanzas from the Grande Chartreuse" is a philosophical poem of thirty-five stanzas, each of which contains six lines of iambic tetrameter verse, rhyming *ababcc*. The poem is deeply personal, describing Matthew Arnold's own struggles to find a faith that would give his life meaning.

The poem begins as a narrative. The setting is a mule trail in the Alps, and the time is right before dark on a windy, rainy autumn day. Arnold, a guide, and an unnamed companion or companions are riding slowly up the trail toward the monastery of the Carthusians, who provide shelter and food to passing travelers such as those in Arnold's party.

In the next segment of the poem, Arnold describes the ascetic way of life inside the monastery. The monks devote themselves to prayer, to penitence, and to the study of religious texts. Their only "human" work is growing the plants from which they make their famous liqueur, chartreuse.

At the monastery, Arnold thinks about two faiths that he has rejected: the Christianity represented by the Carthusians and the rationalism that the teachers of his youth presented as a substitute. Believing in neither, Arnold can only suffer. Arnold then thinks of Romanticism, which seemed to offer a new faith. Three Romantic writers—the English poets George Gordon, Lord Byron, and Percy Bysshe Shelley, and the French author of the romance *Obermann* (1804), Étienne Pivert de Sénancour—are all mentioned as examples of Arnold's predecessors, who were willing to suffer to lead human beings to a better life but who left nothing but literary works describing their agonies.

In the final seven stanzas, Arnold defines his state of isolation and of intellectual uncertainty in dramatic terms. He and those who share his sense of alienation are compared to children who live in an abbey. Although they catch sight of passing soldiers, although they hear the sounds of revelry, they have been conditioned to live another kind of life. They cannot obey the calls to "action and pleasure"; they must remain in the cloister, to which they are accustomed.

Forms and Devices

Arnold had a gift for clarifying and dramatizing his often-complex ideas through the use of imagery and metaphor. The beginning of "Stanzas from the Grande Chartreuse" is an example of his technique. On one level, the description of the trail to the monastery captures the reader's attention. On another level, however, the images combine to suggest the poet-speaker's state of mind. The time of day and the season both conventionally symbolize the approach of death. Furthermore, the stream below sounds "strangled"; the mists that arise from it are "spectral," or ghostly. The frightening supernatural is further invoked by the description of the rapids below as a "cauldron." The "scars" on the rocks and the "ragged" trees add to the total picture of fearful desolation, a desolation that is less objective than subjective. This is nature as perceived by a troubled and apprehensive human being.

In the description of the monastery that follows, Arnold again selects images that will emphasize his own reactions. At first, the monastery looks like a "palace," and Arnold rejoices that "what we seek is here!" Literally, he means food and shelter, but more profoundly, his words suggest the faith for which he is searching. Even though the monastery is full of activity, however, the fact that its motivating force is dead, at least to the poet, is emphasized by references to silence, to cold, to the "ghostlike" monks, and to death. After the Mass, the monks bury their faces in their cowls; at night, they lie in the beds that will become their coffins. To the poet, as to his rational teachers, the monastery is in fact merely a "*living tomb.*"

Sometimes, instead of using clusters of images to dramatize his perceptions, Arnold explains his philosophical stance by the use of an extended metaphor. For example, he compares himself to a Greek, far north of his own land, looking at a marker in an ancient Germanic language, a marker that evidently is the remains of some long-vanished religion, such as that of the monks. The Greek remembers his own gods, as Arnold recalls the devotion of his rational teachers. To this Greek wanderer, however, those gods are in reality as nonexistent as the Germanic gods represented by the stone before him.

Similarly, in the final section of the poem, Arnold depends on a comparison to make his point. This extended simile is signaled by the opening words, "We are like children. . . ." The significance of the two groups who ride by is indicated in line 194: One represents "action," the other "pleasure." Both groups are on their way somewhere; both are purposeful, in pursuit of something. In contrast, the thoughtful "children" such as Arnold somehow lack the power to leave their refuge. Their alienation is suggested by the fact that they are "forgotten," that they remain "secret" and enclosed, among the graves of the dead, in a "desert" dominated by the dead. Only the candles on the altar give them a glimmer of hope.

Themes and Meanings

Explicitly and implicitly, in "Stanzas from the Grande Chartreuse" the poet has explained the predicament of a person with spiritual aspirations in the modern world. Even though he respects the faith of the Carthusians and, by extension, of other Christians, Arnold cannot embrace it. As his images of the monks and the monastery suggest, the poet believes that faith is dead.

On the other hand, while Arnold still respects the teachers of his youth, their rationalism has not given him a basis for living. Similarly, he cannot see any lasting benefit from the passion of the Romantics, whose descriptions of their own pain did not in any way lessen the pain of future generations.

Evidently, the poet believes that his world is given over to the pursuit of pleasure and of material progress. In ironic phrases, he praises the men of action, who dominate nature, who "triumph over time and space." Certainly, they are energetic, but as he politely rejects them, the poet is suggesting that all their pride and all their energy are purposeless and superficial.

Having rejected Christianity, rationalism, Romanticism, and materialism, Arnold seems to have very little left. He is in a kind of limbo, "Wandering between two worlds, one dead,/ The other powerless to be born." Yet, the poem is not totally pessimistic. One must recall the poet's identification with children in the imagined abbey, who "watch those yellow tapers shine,/ Emblems of hope over the grave."

One source of optimism is the future. Perhaps an age will come when humanity can be wise but not hard-hearted, happy but not dedicated to trivial pleasures. Evidently, most of the great intellectual leaders of Arnold's time placed their hope in such a future time. As the Greek hero Achilles retreated to his tent when he could not prevail against Agamemnon, these leaders have given up the fight; they "wait to see the future come."

There is another source of hope in Arnold's poem: the fact that there are still idealists in the world, people who yearn to believe. Above all, this is the significance of the final metaphor. Although the abbey is deserted, as long as the children of faith listen for "accents of another sphere," they may hope to be rewarded. As long as there is a saving remnant of would-be believers who continue to keep their vigil, there will be a chance for humanity and for a new faith to make life meaningful.

Rosemary M. Canfield Reisman

STATION ISLAND

Author: Seamus Heaney (1939-   )
Type of poem: Meditation
First published: 1984, in *Station Island*

The Poem

"Station Island" is a long meditation on Seamus Heaney's own poetry. The poem sets forth a series of encounters with "ghosts" or remembered figures, many of them from Heaney's own life, some from his reading. The poem takes its title and major setting from Station Island in County Donegal, a devotional shrine; the "stations" there are fixed locations of prayer. The poem is, briefly, a parallel to Dante's *Purgatorio* (c. 1320).

The "I" of the poem is Heaney himself. A few of the ghosts are identified by the text or by Heaney's notes. What is more important is what they say to the poet—the advice and counsel they give him about how to write and how not to "break covenants and fail obligations" to himself, to his art, and to his culture.

Part 1 seems to take place largely in memory. The boy Heaney, on his way to church, encounters an old man, breaking the Sabbath by collecting wood. It is Simon Sweeney, head of a family of tinkers who camped near Heaney's boyhood home. Heaney, hearing bell-notes which are both part of the remembered Sunday and part of the procession on Station Island, sees "a crowd of shawled women," who may very well be his fellow pilgrims. Like the poem itself, the crowd grows into a larger crowd of "half-remembered faces." Heaney sets out "to face into my station." Sweeney, however, is not done with him yet: "Stay clear of all processions" is his shouted advice—processions of religion, politics, and literary and cultural conformity.

Part 2 seems to occur on shore, before Heaney has taken the ferry ride to the island. Seated in his car, he is approached by an angry ghost, who proves to be the nineteenth century Irish novelist and folklorist William Carleton. Carleton was Catholic by birth but converted to the (Protestant) Church of Ireland. Much of his writing records the life of rural peasantry and the sectarian hostilities evident in it even more than a century ago. He is connected to Station Island by way of his first published work, "The Loch Derg Pilgrim," which describes his own visit to the shrine.

Heaney admits that he has read the "Pilgrim." Carleton, perhaps somehow having read Heaney's own accounts of the current sectarian violence in Ulster, is struck by the long persistence of such violence.

Heaney tries to reject the model of Carleton and goes on to suggest how close his own Derry upbringing imitates the peasant life observed and described by Carleton. It is another example of persistence, yet seemingly a less threatening one than the persistence of the Ribbonmen (Catholic nationalists) and "Orange bigots" (Protestants claiming a loyalty to England) whom Carleton notices. Carleton begins to show some of the self-doubt that will shortly overcome Heaney as well, condemning his conversion as the act of a "turncoat." He has been a man who followed Sweeney's advice and refused to follow the expected processions. A part of what Carleton goes on to advise— "Remember everything and keep your head"— is advice that Heaney seems long before to have followed. Maybe he acknowledges this in his enigmatic last message, a strange and not very pleasant metaphor for an art rooted, like Heaney's, in the details of a particular rural way of life.

Part 3 finds Heaney hearing in the devotions of the present a direct continuation of the religious devotions of his childhood. The ghost here is Heaney himself, as a child saying his prayers with the family and rather mischievously hiding in a large oak sideboard. There he finds the family's relics of a dead aunt.

Part 4 is built around renunciation, first as part of the present pilgrimage, second in the life of a young priest who became a missionary. Heaney's memory of the priest is ironic; he can recall how the priest became a kind of "holy mascot." The priest, in turn, accuses Heaney of a kind of a nostalgic return to the Catholic life within which he was reared. The priest wonders if Heaney is endeavoring to take "a last look" at the sources of his own life and mind or is only returning to the devotional habits of his childhood.

Part 5 may in part be a response, since it begins with "a last look" at his schooling in Anahorish school, and especially at Barney Murphy, a master there who taught Latin to Heaney. Murphy and another unnamed schoolmaster soon give way to two of Heaney's literary "masters," first the Ulster novelist and short story writer Michael McLaverty, and finally the loud voice of the poet Patrick Kavanagh. Kavanagh speaks rather dismissively of Heaney's accomplishment as a poet. Perhaps he represents that nagging voice which prompted Heaney to move from his basically lyric poems into longer ventures such as "Station Island" and *Sweeney Astray* (1983).

Part 6 seems to take its cue from Kavanagh's final rude and sarcastic remark about chasing women. Again Heaney looks back, into the world of adolescent lust and at an unnamed girl whom he pursued in those days. The present world of the pilgrimage interrupts this reflection and suggests other, more "literary" lines of thought—the pastoral verse of Horace, then the love poetry of Dante.

Part 7 forcefully interrupts the mood of revery; the ghost here is not some beautiful girl or the poet himself as a rather foolishly lovesick boy, but the victim of a sectarian killing. The poem offers a straightforward account of the murder of the ghost. In one sense, the poem is important for what it does not say. The victim, a small-town shopkeeper, was in fact the Catholic victim of a reprisal killing. The killers were off-duty Protestant policemen. The poem itself invokes no sectarian labels whatsoever; Heaney refuses to follow in that "procession" which is the self-generating cycle of sectarian victimization in his native Ulster. The encounter and the poem that records it cannot wholly escape politics or political commitments; confronted with the existence of such victims as this, Heaney feels guilt over his own, less direct part in the politics of civil rights in Northern Ireland. He asks forgiveness, but none is offered.

Part 8 finds the poet-pilgrim still on his rounds. There he encounters two ghosts from his own past, and the note of guilt deepens. The first ghost is that of one of Heaney's friends, an archaeologist who worked near Belfast. Heaney regrets now his inability to talk satisfactorily with the man during his final stay in the hospital. Again he can find no forgiveness. A second ghost appears, that of Heaney's cousin Colum McCartney, another victim of sectarian violence and the subject of the poem "The Strand at Lough Beg" in *Field Work* (1979).

McCartney, like many of the other ghosts, is angry; he does not find Heaney's having remade his death into poetry at all a consolation, and indeed rebukes him for his commitment to poetry rather than to the sectarian struggle which cost Mc-Cartney his life. Worse still, he says, "You confused evasion with artistic tact" — once again, he did not find the correct words, as he had not with his dying archae-ologist friend. The result was a "whitewash" job, prettifying the "ugliness" of the actual killing and hiding it behind "the lovely blinds of the *Purgatorio*." Part 9 hears another sectarian voice, that of an Irish Republican Army (IRA) hunger striker. The ghost drives Heaney all the way to "self-disgust" — the emotional low point of the poem — and prompts another apology for lack of full commitment. Heaney goes further: "I hate where I was born."

Yet as part 10 shows, he is not finished with his own past; more gently and lovingly, he recalls a mug used in his bathroom, once used as a prop by some trav-eling players near his childhood home. Part 11 again looks back, to an unnamed priest who urges Heaney to translate the Spanish mystic and poet Saint John of the Cross — perhaps as partial answer to the entrapment in the personal and cultural which Heaney seems to feel. The greater part of this section is in fact, just such a translation — of a poem explicitly about the "fountain" of faith and eternal life in God, but implicitly about the fountain of poetic inspiration.

In part 12, Heaney returns to the shore, but he is not done with ghosts quite yet. A final figure appears; it is James Joyce, who rebuffs the poet's effort to discuss his *A Portrait of the Artist as a Young Man* (1916). Joyce offers advice which echoes Sweeney's. Against Carleton's insistence that Heaney attend to and remember the details of Irish life, Joyce argues for a freer path. The poem as a whole thus ends with the notes of radical self-doubt and "Irishness" as an obligation rejected unequivocally.

Forms and Devices

The poem moves through a variety of forms. There is occasional rhyme and near rhyme in the five-line stanzas of part 1 and the quatrains of part 3 and part 10; there is a careful approximation of Dante's terza rima in the tercets of parts 2 and 12, and less elaborately in part 7. The translation from Saint John of the Cross in part 11 is in short rhymed stanzas with a refrain. Ironically, Colum McCartney rejects poetic elegance generally (part 8) in elaborately rhymed verse. Parts 5 and 6 are written in ten- or eleven-syllable free-verse lines.

The most evident and consistent device is the appearance of what Heaney calls

"Presences," which are in fact recollections and imaginations— "ghosts," but more accurately enactments of Heaney's own self-accusing voice.

Themes and Meanings

Several questions repeatedly arise in the poem, all of which bear directly upon the body of Heaney's own work. What relation should a poet and his work bear to the poet's own past? Can a poetry, like that of Heaney's mentor and friend Robert Lowell, which arises from intensely and often mysteriously personal experience, be satisfactory? The poem examines what relation a poet's work must bear to the (in Heaney's case, harsh) political realities of his culture. It asks how, if at all, a poet may respond to the chilling fact of death. The poem is a prolonged meditation on Heaney's commitments, especially to himself and to Ireland. He hears firmly given advice about going his own way and speaking in his own voice; but how, in practical terms, is such advice to be followed?

These questions often are cast in the language of obligation, which makes them particularly pressing in the tortured world of Ulster, where almost any speech is political. The poem's final advice seems to be in favor of an independence of voice and mood, but that is perhaps offset by a prevailing concern about failure.

John Hildebidle

THE STEEPLE-JACK

Author: Marianne Moore (1887-1972)
Type of poem: Lyric
First published: 1932; collected in *Selected Poems*, 1935; revised in *Collected Poems*, 1951; revised in *A Marianne Moore Reader*, 1961

The Poem

The six-line stanzas (thirteen in all) of "The Steeple-Jack" look oddly ragged at first glance, until one sees that each stanza's pattern is rigorously maintained throughout. Because the poem reads in straightforward sentences, the subject of the whole is easy to identify. A speaker with much information at his or her disposal is providing the reader with a description, full of out-of-the-way details, of a charming New England seaside town. Throughout the poem, the town is described as a peaceful, safe haven; the ocean's waves are "formal," and fishnets are "arranged" to dry. All sorts of people could find refuge here, from waifs to prisoners to presidents. Even a storm is no more dangerous than "whirlwind fife-and-drum" music.

In the course of praising the town as a place of unassuming beauty and inviting elegance, this speaker names three people who are, or would be, "at home" here, "each in his way": first, the German painter Albrecht Dürer, whose close-viewing artistic sensibilities were also Marianne Moore's; second, an out-of-town college student named Ambrose, who also likes to look at the town from a hillside perch; and third, the town's own steeplejack, C. J. Poole, who repairs the steeple on a local church—no doubt one of those picture-postcard churches North American readers associate with New England. Moore published a revised version of the poem in 1961, shortened to eight stanzas, in which the student appears only briefly and is not mentioned by name. The steeplejack has set out two signs in front of the church where he is working; one gives his name, and the other warns, "Danger." The steeplejack's precarious position high in the air provides the only note of tension in the poem, and it hints that—no matter how secure things may appear—there is no haven that is completely safe.

Forms and Devices

In "The Steeple-Jack," Moore uses an idiosyncratic meter that is typical of her verse—a meter that is neither counted in metrical feet nor grasped as "free verse," but rather consists of an exacting syllable count in each line. What the eye cannot see nor the ear hear is that there are exactly eleven syllables in the first line of every stanza. There are ten syllables in all the second lines, thirteen syllables in all third lines, and eight syllables in all lines 4 and 5. Most of her poetry uses this odd method, in which there is an apparently arbitrary syllable count from line to line of an opening stanza which is then rigidly adhered to in subsequent stanzas. This remarkable versification is a Marianne Moore invention; no one writing in English verse had used it before. Most readers do not ever discover it, and no reader, short of counting out the syllables and keeping a record, can grasp by ear the peculiar method. Her famous poem "Poetry" uses a line count of exactly, and preposterously, nineteen, nineteen, eleven, five, nine, and seventeen syllables, repeated five times. The poet must often go to great lengths to keep score. Many lines throughout Moore's opus end in mid-word or on a dangling "the." In "The Steeple-Jack," this delightful event occurs at the end of stanza 3.

Moore loved hiding form inside this mind-boggling tactic. One senses from the liveliness of her poems that Moore devised her method for the sheer fun of it, but in addition to such sport, Moore's use of hidden formal properties is related to several of her themes.

Themes and Meanings

One of Moore's themes in "The Steeple-Jack" is boldly stated early in the poem: "it is a privilege to see so/ much confusion" (lines 23-24). In listing the special features of the town, Moore has placed the banalities of lighthouse and town clock right alongside very painterly specifics, such as the exact names of the changing color of the sea. These two vantage points—the banal and the artistic—cannot be brought together easily without her medium: language. A faith in the aesthetics of odd and ironic juxtapositions places Moore squarely in the high modernist tradition of T. S. Eliot, Ezra Pound, and Wallace Stevens. The speaker, looking down on this tiny whaling town, loves employing, as richly as she can, her strange language palette. Poetry has a reality of sound all its own. On a stroll through this town, anyone might enjoy the flowers, but it is Moore's special privilege to bombard the ear and the language eye: "snap-dragon and salpiglossis." It is especially within her province to rhyme however she wishes, and she wishes to rhyme some very unlikely words, rhyming "diffident" with "serpent," and "fishing-twine" with "trumpet-vine." These kinds of rhymes are not for convenience; they make frames of reference collide. Such collisions are only possible through the poet's special language tools. Trust Moore to have learned how many whales have been said to have washed up in this town from time to time; she then gives the reader the pleasure of all eight whales at once—in a kind of surreal timeless image. This poem is as much about its own bravura as it is about the real town it describes. In fact, one purpose of the poem may be to help one question what is meant by a "real" place. Fundamentally, place is something larger than what can be noted as buildings and population.

Understanding this underlying theme and meaning—how poetry bountifully gathers reality in its own way—will help readers understand what happens when Moore finally arrives at the ostensible topic of the poem: There has been a steeple-jack on top of the church the whole time. Part of the poem's meaning is to disclose the steeplejack's odd connection to the "ring lizard" and "little newt/ with white pin-dots on black horizontal spaced/ out bands."

For one thing, ring lizards and newts and Mr. Poole provide an odd grouping which, in part, releases readers from stereotypes of comfortable New England towns with sugar-bowl-shaped summer houses and sugar-coated sentimentality.

Usually one does not think of waifs and stray animals as being tolerated easily in such a place. Moore would have readers see the postcard notions of New England as one frame of reference among many others that bring fresher vision. There is the vision of the painter, of the student, and of Mr. Poole—each removed and elevated. Mr. Poole is so high up he needs a sign to alert the ordinary passerby.

Once readers hear this urbane and amused tone in Moore, they are faced with exactly what makes her challenging and complicated. Her last odd gathering under the church portico, for example, of waifs, children, animals, and prisoners is made altogether lopsided by her fifth category in the list: presidents. Presumably, like everyone else, presidents may also find release from their normal frame of reference (other politicians who have moral agendas). Poetry is a "place" where one can travel, at least in the mind and soul, far beyond the ambitions and one-dimensional concerns of politics and business. There is a poetic sphere—a sphere of sight, sound, and accuracy—which has little to do with piety or judgment. The accuracy of the newt's markings and Mr. Poole's hand-painted signs provide a reader at times, if by no means always, with a larger truth from which one needs to be at some distance in order to see and enjoy. One must not presume that Moore, for her own convenience, has deliberately ignored small-town stuffiness or prejudices. Few have any illusions that the citizens of such towns actually permit waifs to stand on church doorsteps for long. Nothing is pat in Moore's thinking, either. Something above small-town mentality is more important and vital to the speaker—and to Ambrose, Dürer, and the steeplejack: elegance. Elegance is a key word and underlying theme of the poem.

One rarely knows how to account for elegance ("of which the source is not bravado," line 50). Moore suggests that true elegance eludes human strivings and pride. Elegance is achieved by a poetic ordering of the sort she has managed here, in which the world is not judged nor the hypocrisy in people proved. Moore's is the studious, meditative elegance achieved by disinterested love. Like Mr. Poole, she puts out her danger sign and then goes ahead and climbs that faulty steeple—always in need of repairs, yet always a symbol for humankind's highest spiritual transportation from one small frame of reference to another, larger one. From the top one will have, at the very least, a spectacular view and, at the very most, a new way of seeing and believing.

Beverly Coyle

STILL, CITIZEN SPARROW

Author: Richard Wilbur (1921-   )
Type of poem: Lyric
First published: 1950, in *Ceremony and Other Poems*

The Poem

Like many other poems in English, some of them quite famous, Richard Wilbur's "Still, Citizen Sparrow" takes as its subject, at least partially, a bird — in this case, a vulture. It does so, however, by addressing itself to another bird, a sparrow.

The use of the opening word, "Still," suggests that the reader is entering the poem at a point where the speaker has already been talking to the sparrow, in a way presumably sympathetic to that bird's belief that the vulture is an "unnatural" creature. This negative characterization is undoubtedly based, for the most part, on the vulture's habit of feeding on dead flesh, "carrion." The use of "Still," however, indicates that the speaker now wishes to qualify whatever he has conceded before the start of the poem proper. In fact, the poem will make a case for the vulture and his mode of existence. This view needs to be argued, not simply because the sparrow thinks otherwise, but also because many human beings share the sparrow's view, responding to this scavenger bird with revulsion, both because of its appearance (its bald head is registered here by the term "naked-headed") and the nature of its diet.

The vulture is presented as rising into the air, bearing the dead flesh he has seized. The initial part of his flight is seen as clumsy (he "lumbers"), but very quickly Wilbur creates an effect of contrast. Once the vulture has ascended to a very high point ("the tall/ Tip of the sky"), he appears to move with effortless ease (he "lie[s] cruising"). In fact, the poem makes an extremely positive judgment of the vulture, saying that there is no more beautiful bird in the sky. Part of the bird's appeal at this point in the poem (the second stanza) lies in its alertness, presumably with respect to detecting creatures who have died.

The vulture is seen as in some way supporting nature, and the sparrow is asked to forgive this scavenging bird, because it rids the earth of dead things. It thereby jeers at changeability ("mutability") by removing evidence of one of its chief manifestations, the change from life to death.

Having devoted half of "Still, Citizen Sparrow" to the vulture, Wilbur then uses the second half of the poem to give his version of a story found in the Bible. Because the inhabitants of earth were wicked, according to the Old Testament, God decided to destroy the world by causing a great flood. Humanity, however, was not to be entirely wiped out; it would survive in the form of Noah and his family. In order to withstand the Flood, Noah was directed by God to create a boat, an ark. According to legend, when the floodwaters subsided, Noah's ark came to rest on Mount Ararat.

The sparrow (along with the reader) is asked to "forget" Noah's activity in building the ark as well as his ability to look down on the drowned world. Rather than make a negative judgment of Noah, the sparrow is asked to empathize with the difficult position of the man, who had to live with the experience of seeing almost everything he knew brought to an end and who had to preside over the surviving small world of the ark and its inhabitants. The sparrow is told that, put in the same position, it would rather have died along with its world. Noah, however, chose to live and is to be seen as the father of humanity.

Forms and Devices

An "apostrophe" is a device often found in poetry. It is an address, usually of an elevated nature, to someone or something not literally present or, if present, not literally capable of hearing or understanding. Yet its use presumes, for the purposes of the poet, that the being or object addressed will hear and comprehend. The apostrophe constitutes a kind of theoretical communication with the reader of the poem; the ultimate audience of the apostrophe, the reader, overhears, so to speak, the words being uttered. "Still, Citizen Sparrow" falls into the category of apostrophe. What makes the employment of this device unusual here is that the apostrophe is not addressed to its initial central subject, the vulture, but is directed instead to another sort of bird, one of the most commonly seen, the sparrow. As such, Wilbur's poem contrasts with two famous works where the bird-subject is directly addressed: John Keats's "Ode to a Nightingale" and Percy Bysshe Shelley's "To a Skylark." In neither of these cases is the poet confronted with having to defend a bird commonly regarded with revulsion, as Wilbur is.

The sparrow is startlingly addressed as "citizen." This is one of several instances in the poem of a notable or unusual diction. Another example is the term "watchfuller," which is an invention, or coinage, on Wilbur's part, one that would seem to violate convention. He uses it instead of the "correct" form— "more watchful"— to dramatize the vulture's admirable alertness. Other examples of unusual diction are found in the phrases "frightfully free" (used to describe the vulture) and "bedlam hours" (used to describe the poem's second central subject, Noah, as he goes about building his ark). In the first case, a negative term is conjoined to a positive one, the freedom in question perhaps that of the vulture's being able to soar on the basis of feeding off the dead; in the second instance, a word most often used as a noun, "bedlam" (meaning a madhouse), is used as an adjective. Other phrases of note include "rotten office" and "carrion ballast." The first of these uses "office" in its sense of "duty" or "function," attaching to it the adjective "rotten," which can be seen as doing double service. It could constitute a pejorative comment on the vulture's function, as seen by the sparrow; it could also refer to the rotting meat the vulture is willing to consume. The term "ballast," which usually refers to heavy material placed in the bottom of a ship to give it stability, is here made to refer to the carrion the vulture eats and carries with him into the sky. It gives his flight a stable foundation.

Another device Wilbur uses is that of allusion— reference to well-known material drawn from history, literature, mythology, and the Bible. In this poem, the allusion is to the biblical story of Noah. Incorporating that story as he does, Wilbur is making use of yet another device: apparent discontinuity of subject matter. Without warning, the sparrow (and therefore the reader) is asked to shift focus from a scavenger bird to a biblical character. The reader may wonder what one thing has to do with the other, but the poet seems to be leaving it to the reader to close this apparent gap.

There is a notable use of sound patterning, particularly alliteration, in the poem. Alliteration is employed to intensify the effect of certain phrases, such as "the tall/ Tip," "frightfully free," "Devours death," and "mocks mutability."

Themes and Meanings

The unusual nature of the apostrophe in "Still, Citizen Sparrow," the poem's use of striking words and phrases, and its sudden switch of focus are all congruous with the unusual perspectives it is attempting to convey. Wilbur's poem is trying to shake up the sparrow's preconceptions and, ultimately, those of the reader as well.

The sparrow may be said to be a representative of the norm, an ordinary "citizen," having conventional responses both to the vulture and to the idea of cataclysmic destruction. This common bird is presumed to feel repugnance in both cases, being put off both by the vulture's feeding on what has died and by the prospect of surviving in a world where everything one has known has come to an end. The sparrow, according to the poem, would have been only too willing to die along with its world if it had been in Noah's place.

In the view of the poem, which modulates from making a positive aesthetic judgment of the vulture to a positive moral judgment of that bird as well as of Noah, both the scavenger and the biblical character are capable of confronting death and enabling life to continue — the link between the poem's seemingly unrelated subjects. The vulture participates in a physical cleansing of the earth, while Noah participated in a moral cleansing of the same. Neither of them is a "nice" figure. The bird eats rotting meat, while Noah agrees in effect to see his fellow humans killed without having to share their fate. Niceness is not a premium for the poem, however, although it may be for the sparrow, which is viewed as living at a relatively low level. Both the vulture and Noah are placed at a height, the elevated position being ultimately that of the hero, the unusual being, who can confront and absorb the awful, which is part of the necessary rigors of life. It is a difficult endeavor but one that is required if life is to continue. The hero may in some way be a repugnant figure, one who has to be forgiven, but he does what must be done, and in that sense humankind is indebted to him — "all men are Noah's sons."

Alan Holder

STILL TO BE NEAT

Author: Ben Jonson (1573?-1637)
Type of poem: Lyric
First published: pr. 1609, pb. 1616, in *Epicœne: Or, The Silent Woman*

The Poem

"Still to Be Neat" is a song sung by the character Clerimont in one of Ben Jonson's most successful and highly praised comedies, *Epicœne: Or, The Silent Woman*. Clerimont is a rowdy co-conspirator of Sir Dauphine Eugenie, a young man who is to inherit a fortune from his self-centered uncle, Morose. Morose, wishing to disinherit his nephew, marries Epicœne, a young woman whose future children, he plans, will receive his estate instead of Dauphine. At the end of the play, it transpires that Epicœne is actually a young man hired and trained by Dauphine for the role of wife to Morose.

The song is in two stanzas of six lines each. Like the plot of the play, it concerns appearances which can belie reality. The first stanza could be paraphrased as, "Lady, although because of cosmetics you are lovely on the surface, you may not be beautiful at all underneath." The second stanza says, "I prefer a woman whose surface is simple and unaffected, unadorned, but who is lovely within." One key to understanding the poem is to know that the word "still" here really means "always" and carries a concessive sense: "Still to be neat" could therefore be paraphrased, "Although you always appear neat." "Neat," "dressed," "powdered," and "perfumed" describe the cosmetic artifices employed by a woman in high society to make herself beautiful to the eyes of admiring, eligible men.

The "hid causes" of art could be either a natural, inner beauty or merely cunning strategies of self-adornment. Since the lady is always seen covered with powder, perfumed, and clothed in fancy, carefully arranged dress, it is to be presumed that she hesitates to show herself without the protecting artifice of cosmetics. Therefore, even though one has not discovered art's hid cause, one may conclude that it is not natural beauty, but cunning and conceit. She is not entirely as sweet as she appears; her beauty is hollow and not "sound."

"Give me a look, give me a face/ That makes simplicity a grace" is a sort of rationalist motto. It means that the singer prefers a woman whose face and figure ("look" may refer to how she looks overall) are pleasing in themselves. Simplicity is exactly the opposite of artifice and implies a lack of adornment. Grace is used in a double sense; it means "graceful," but it is also a word for "virtue," as in the cardinal virtues recommended by religion. So, just as simplicity — a sense of straightforwardness and lack of design, lack of a hidden agenda — is a moral virtue, so a simple face without makeup is graceful and lovely.

"Loosely flowing robes" are contrasted with clothes that are always ("still") "neat." The hair, rather than being powdered and piled up in a fashionable coiffure, should hang loose in "sweet neglect." "Adulteries," like most of the key terms in this song, also has two meanings: sexual dishonesty and adulteration. Literally, art or artifice in a woman's makeup is something unnecessarily added to her natural beauty—an adulteration of her physical virtues. If "art" here refers to the fine arts in general, then to use artistic devices to hide the fundamental situation is to make an adulteress of art. Although these "adulteries" of high fashion, makeup, and dress may attract a man's attention ("they strike mine eyes"), they do not win his heart.

Forms and Devices

Poems that express a sentiment, impression, or moment of contemplation are called lyrical, which opposes them to narrative poetry, which tells a story. This poem, however, is literally a lyric—that is, it is the words to a song. This must be remembered in considering the form of the poem. First, one should note that the lyric is performed by a fictional character and therefore is not directly the voice of the author. Clerimont sings this piece in the midst of a play about deceptive appearances when he has special knowledge that the object of the play's attention, Epicœne is not really a young girl at all, but a boy in disguise.

Lines which are broken in the middle by repetition alternate with lines which contain no caesura; the rhythm matches the structure of the melody. The second stanza repeats exactly the pattern of the first, with strong syntactic caesuras in lines 7, 9, and 12. In the first stanza, therefore, there is a special accent which picks up the words "neat," "dressed," "powdered," and "perfumed" and matches them with "not sweet" and "not sound." The same pattern occurs again in the second stanza: "look," "face," "flowing," and "free" match with "mine eyes" and "my heart." In the same way, "art's hid causes" and "adulteries of art" are parallel in the song pattern. Such resonances, repetitions, and echoes are characteristic of the genre of poetry called ballad or song. They occur naturally when words are well-matched with music. Merely to think both stanzaically and melodically will produce structures this strict.

What is peculiar to Jonson in this poem is the plainness and straightforwardness of the language—the seeming lack of metaphor or simile. "Still to Be Neat," like its theme of honesty and directness, seems to avoid the usual ornamental figures of speech and tropes that are the natural tools of poetry. Every word can be taken literally, as if this song were merely prose that happened to have a meter and rhyme. The simplicity, however, is itself a poetic effect, an artifice. Most of the key words invite a double reading—are, indeed, almost puns. For example, if the word "art" is taken to mean not "artifice" but the fine arts such as poetry, then "Still to Be Neat" could be read in a second way as a poem about the writing of poetry itself. Then the sartorial imagery becomes symbolism, not literal reference, and the word "adulteries" becomes a powerful statement about morality in aesthetics. "Eyes" become symbolic of superficial perceptions in which value and beauty are separated, whereas "heart" refers to a more authentic response, implying a more authentic poetry.

Themes and Meanings

Accepting this "symbolic" interpretation of "Still to Be Neat," this elegant little song becomes a typical statement of Ben Jonson's position on the nature of art and language. Jonson lived in a time when the natural philosophy of thinkers such as Francis Bacon and Thomas Hobbes, who were attempting to develop what would today be called a scientific view of reality, engaged in a critique of figural language. When poets employ symbolism and figures of speech to ornament the expression of their meaning, they are moving away from direct reference—from the clean and uncluttered literal designation which would be the ideal of the scientific revolution in the seventeenth century.

This distrust of linguistic embellishment, of poetic fancy and ornament, was based on a philosophy that placed nature before art. Western civilization's new-found confidence in its ability to know the natural world through direct observation and experimentation was replacing a medieval approach to nature as a sort of text written by God. Jonson seems to accept the change in values and tries to reflect it in the rhetoric of his poetry. As Arthur F. Marotti says in his article "All About Jonson's Poetry," "Jonson reveals an hostility to sensuous imagery as well as metaphoric inventiveness, which are to him impediments to communication, a disguising of subject matter he would like to represent in a more direct way."

Jonson's great comedies express the concept in the vaster field of general human morality. In his most famous comedies, *Volpone* (pr. 1606, pb. 1607), *Epicœne*, and *The Alchemist* (pr. 1610, pb. 1612), he represents gullible characters who are easily fooled by appearances and are at the mercy of scoundrels who take advantage of their uncritical acceptance of convincing language and their unpenetrating observational powers. His highly polished epigrams and eulogies often warn of art's ability to deceive. It is ironic that this poem, whose theme is a praise of directness and lack of artifice, makes full use of artistic indirection and double entendre to praise the same thing in poetry.

Robin Kornman

STOPPING BY WOODS ON A SNOWY EVENING

Author: Robert Frost (1874-1963)
Type of poem: Lyric
First published: 1923, in *New Hampshire: A Poem with Notes and Grace Notes*

The Poem

"Stopping by Woods on a Snowy Evening" is easily one of the most famous, as well as one of the most anthologized, of Robert Frost's poems. It consists of four quatrains that have the following rhyme scheme: *aaba, bbcb, ccdc, dddd*. The poem's central narrative is simple, and the scene is understated, even stark, bare of elaboration or detail. A traveler pauses late one snowy evening to admire the woods by which he passes. He reflects that the owner of the woods, who lives in the village, will not see him stopping to "watch his woods fill up with snow."

The speaker interrupts his reflections by imagining that his "little horse must think it queer" to stop without a farmhouse nearby on the "darkest evening of the year." In the third stanza, the speaker expands this conceit, suggesting that anxiety over the untoward action causes the horse to shake his harness bells "To ask if there is some mistake." Then, by way of contrast, the speaker notes that "the only other sound's the sweep/ Of easy wind and downy flake."

Something about the woods compels the speaker's interest, and by the poem's end, as most critics note, one has the sense that there is more to these woods than meets the eye. In the last verse, the speaker acknowledges that the "woods are lovely, dark and deep." He seems reluctant, however, to pursue this insight more deeply, since he immediately observes that he has "promises to keep,/ And miles to go before [he] sleep[s]." Nevertheless, the central focus of the poem is not the woods. Of more importance is the inward drama of the speaker as he reflects about and understands—or fails to understand—why he stops and why he finds the woods so captivating.

The poem ends, then, ambiguously. The reader learns very little about the speaker—either where he is coming from, where he is going, or why he stops. The speaker, however, does not permit himself to reflect too deeply about the occasion, either. One can only speculate, and this is perhaps the full intent of the poem's title: "Stopping by woods" is a gratuitous action, a grace note, an imaginative possibility. The reader, like the speaker, is always "stopping" by woods, and the reader, like the speaker, can choose to make the most of them or to go on.

Forms and Devices

Robert Frost wrote to Louis Untermeyer in 1923 that "Stopping by Woods on a Snowy Evening" would be his "best bid for remembrance." Frost's instincts were correct, but like Walt Whitman's famous "Captain, My Captain," Frost's poem is often remembered for all the wrong reasons. Part of its appeal, surely, is its simple and accessible narrative, which contains only sixteen words that are more than one syllable. In addition, Frost's end-stopped lines, accentuated by the insistent rhyme, make the poem easy to remember.

Frost, born in California, worked hard at developing the persona for which he is now mostly known—the farmer-poet from New England, the writer of Currier & Ives miniatures. "Stopping by Woods on a Snowy Evening" is Frost's most memorable "genre study" in his "New England" manner, though examination of the poem reveals nothing distinctively regional about it at all. Despite Frost's reputation as a regionalist, his lyrics are generally so underdescribed that they tend toward allegory or parable. "Stopping by Woods on a Snowy Evening" is an example of Frost's art in this respect: It gains its power by suggestion and implication, in its stark understatement, powerfully conveying a depth and fullness of human experience. It is, as Frost remarked, "loaded with ulteriority."

Criticism of the poem has generally treated it allegorically or biographically, and it is easy to see why. Like "The Road Not Taken," another frequently misread lyric, "Stopping by Woods on a Snowy Evening" is almost earnest in its simplicity, though close attention to the text shows it to be more crafty than at first it appears. For example, as is often the case in Frost's first-person lyrics, the speaker of the poem is not to be mistaken for the poet himself, nor is the "I" in a Frost lyric always credible or aware of the complexity of his reflections.

Thus in this poem, the speaker indicates that his horse thinks it "queer" for them to stop, though it is evident that whatever the horse may think or feel, it is the speaker who projects his own anxiety onto the horse. The poem is constructed as the speaker's reflections of the event, and the first line indicates the speaker's sense that the woods are owned. Thus, some nameless feeling of impropriety or perhaps social violation keeps him from his ease. Consequently, his abrupt dismissal of the wood's allure and his lofty response that he has "promises to keep," though idealistic and possibly true, sounds like a dodge. Mistaking the speaker for Frost himself, one could miss the author's implied criticism of the speaker's sentimentality—who avoids the issue of why he stops by taking refuge in rhetoric and cliché.

To read "Stopping by Woods on a Snowy Evening" as simply a story about a weary traveler longing for the comforts of home, or even to allegorize it as the journey of Everyman, is to miss the subtle qualities that identify it as a Frost lyric. For one thing, Frost balances the onward rhythmic pull of the verse against the obvious stasis of the poetic scene itself: The speaker never arrives, nor really leaves; he is simply always stopping. Frost also arranges the natural scene so as to heighten the drama of the encounter and to reveal its symbolic density. Finally, Frost's sense of dramatic and contextual irony undercut the simplicity of the narrative. After all, despite the speaker's confident assurance about where he is going and the miles he has yet to go, his restiveness (projected onto the horse) and the vagueness of the future "promises" he must keep reveal his assurance to be, in a word, a fiction. This is an important point for Frost. Frost celebrated the necessity of imaginative extravagance in human affairs, but he knew well enough that the imagination traps as well as frees.

Themes and Meanings

Whatever "Stopping by Woods on a Snowy Evening" means, it is evident that the poem makes meaning; it has suffered many designs upon it, and even Frost thought that critics had pressed it too much for meaning. Nevertheless, the poem contains tensions and oppositions that are characteristic of Frost's symbolic terrain in general and of his poetics as well.

The woods is a pervasive image in Frost's poetry, evident in his earliest poems as well as in his last. Dark and unowned, woods are a metaphor of life's wildness, and Frost contrasts them, generally, with places owned by human beings and made artful by their craft. Domesticated spaces such as pastures, clearings, even homes, show the presence of human beings; in these places they make themselves at home, spiritually and physically. In "The Constant Symbol," Frost observes that "strongly spent is synonymous with kept." The human spirit must risk and spend itself, paradoxically, in order to fulfill its nature.

Poets risk themselves and their skill as they create a poem out of the wildness of language. Consequently, readers of Frost's verse, like the speaker stopping to watch the woods fill with snow, find themselves in a typically Frostian place: The poem is a partly wild, partly domesticated place, demanding risk and commitment, involvement and acceptance. Poems, like woods, are lovely, dark, and deep, but only if one will risk entering them more deeply and will let them work upon the imagination.

"Stopping by Woods on a Snowy Evening," then, directs one's attention to that moment when one stops, or at least pauses, between two equally delicious possibilities, and this insistence upon human choice is characteristic of Frost. The "woods" that are "lovely, dark and deep" echo and suggest other sorts of "woods"— the "woulds," the limits, conventions, and oughts by which poets and readers alike live and write. Fenced around with social convention and imaginative need, facing wild woods and dark choices, one must balance and choose.

Frost commented that "Stopping by Woods on a Snowy Evening" is a "commitment to convention." It is also a commitment to risk and to extravagance, especially imaginative extravagance, in order to possess something aesthetically—the woods, for example—that one cannot possess or "own" in any other way. The poem is about patterns and predictability, about rhythms and the complex ways human beings respond to patterns. It contrasts the horse's habituated responses to the human, if less predictable, response of the speaker. The human being must be able to break conventions and rhythms as well as create them. The poem is, finally, about more abstract conventions and rhythms, those of knowledge and understanding, or those of history and the movement of time; it is about how one discovers beauty within these rhythms. It also is about smaller patterns— social manners and expectations, habits enforced by hunger and sleep. The poem is about the boundaries and limits within which human beings live and—Frost's denials to the contrary—the limits within which one must die.

Ed Ingebretsen

STRANGE FITS OF PASSION HAVE I KNOWN

Author: William Wordsworth (1770-1850)
Type of poem: Lyric
First published: 1800, in *Lyrical Ballads*, second edition

The Poem

"Strange Fits of Passion Have I Known" is one of six short lyrics generally classified as the "Lucy poems." William Wordsworth wrote all six between 1799 and 1801, and each speaks about a young woman or young girl who has died. (In "Lucy Gray," it is a young girl who has died; in others, including "Strange Fits of Passion Have I Known," Lucy is older and seems to be spoken of as a lover.) Whether Lucy represents a specific person in Wordsworth's life is not known; the poet's close friend Samuel Taylor Coleridge speculated that the poet may have been inspired to write these works when "in some gloomier moment he [Wordsworth] fancied the moment his sister might die" (David Perkins, *English Romantic Writers*, 1967). Since Wordsworth was very close to his sister Dorothy, this explanation is plausible, but it is not necessary to offer a biographical interpretation for any of the Lucy poems; they can all be read as explorations of the impact of loss on the speaker, an emotion both universal and particularly poignant.

In "Strange Fits of Passion Have I Known," the speaker describes a moonlight ride through the English countryside as he travels toward the home of his beloved Lucy. The "strange" fit of passion he wishes to explain to the reader is the rather ironic premonition of death he feels as he rides through the moonlight toward Lucy's cottage. In the opening stanza, the speaker takes the reader into his confidence ("I will dare to tell" of this experience, he notes in line 2); this story is not for everyone, he suggests, but "in the Lover's ear alone" (line 3) can he express his feelings.

The speaker's story is a simple one. At a time when the object of his love looked "Fresh as a rose in June" (line 6), he traverses the countryside toward her cottage. Over "paths so dear to me" (line 12) the speaker's horse carries him toward the object of his travels. All the while, the speaker himself keeps his eyes fixed on the moon, which lights his way as it descends from its point high in the sky, where it sits as the journey begins.

In every stanza except the first and last, the moon is mentioned specifically; in the fourth, fifth, and sixth stanzas, it is described as descending in the night sky, finally dropping behind the roof of Lucy's cottage as the speaker approaches. The passage of the moon in the night sky prompts the speaker to engage in a fantasy, one which he cannot explain logically but which grips him nevertheless. As he watches the moon pass out of sight behind Lucy's cottage, he experiences what he describes as a "fond and wayward" thought (line 25): "O mercy! . . ./ If Lucy should be dead!" (lines 27-28). On that strange, ironic note, seemingly out of context with the idyllic scene depicted throughout the first six stanzas, the poem ends. Unquestionably, this "strange fit"—the choice of words becomes clear to the sensitive reader in this final stanza—is prompted by the speaker's passion for his lover and has no basis in logic; it captures the feelings that often overwhelm one who is passionately devoted to another.

Forms and Devices

As he does with many of his early compositions, Wordsworth uses the ballad stanza form in "Strange Fits of Passion Have I Known" to achieve a note of rustic simplicity. His technique is deliberate and has a historical explanation: In the eighteenth century, most poets relied on elevated language and formal devices that reflected the influence of classical literature. Wordsworth and Coleridge made a conscious effort to transform poetry into something more simple and direct, in which human emotions could be expressed directly in language that all people would understand. Wordsworth states these principles in his famous Preface to the second edition of *Lyrical Ballads, with other poems* (1800); there, he describes poetry as "the spontaneous overflow of powerful feelings . . . recollected in tranquillity." A poet is not some seer invested with special divine powers; rather, Wordsworth says, he is "a man speaking to men."

"Strange Fits of Passion Have I Known," and all the Lucy poems, exemplify Wordsworth's premises about the nature of poetry. The language is direct and virtually free of literary tropes. The only simile the poet uses is the rather cliché "Fresh as a rose in June" (line 6), which he says describes the way Lucy looks to him every day. Even his use of adjectives and adverbs is limited. Only in characterizing the path of the moon in the night sky does Wordsworth attempt to suggest change and motion through choice of descriptors: that sphere is variously "sinking" (line 15), "descending" (line 20), and finally "bright" (line 24) as it drops out of sight behind Lucy's cottage. The result of such sparseness of verbal decoration, coupled with the sparseness of the ballad stanza itself (quatrains of alternating lines of four and three beats), focuses the reader's attention on the action in the poem. Much of that action is simple mental reverie, but the growing state of anxiety which the speaker feels as he approaches Lucy's cottage is made apparent to the reader through the simple language and rustic form of this ballad.

Themes and Meanings

"Strange Fits of Passion Have I Known" is one of several poems in which Wordsworth explores the experiences of solitude and loss. Personifying the idea of solitary beauty in the figure of his chief character, Lucy, the poet uses his reactions to the girl's growth in the country and her death to examine his own attitudes about the value of life and the importance of nature in shaping life.

The very simplicity of Lucy's life-style has strong appeal for Wordsworth. Looking back over almost two centuries of poetry shaped by Romantic ideas about the importance of nature and its prominent place as a counter to the evils of civilization, it may be hard to imagine the significance of Wordsworth's achievements in this and the other Lucy poems. Wordsworth's contemporary Francis Jeffrey, editor of the influential *Edinburgh Review*, thought that in "Strange Fits of Passion Have I Known" the poet was trying to handle the "copious subject" of "Love, and the fantasies of lovers" in "one single thought." It is "improbable," Jeffrey thought, that any reader would comprehend Wordsworth's meaning from such a simplistic endeavor (*Edinburgh Review*, 1808).

Such an opinion would hardly be considered tenable in the twentieth century. The tenets of Romantic poetry, which include a recognition of the power of unadorned speech, have gained considerable ascendancy in literary criticism, and twentieth century readers are much more likely than Jeffrey was to sympathize with Wordsworth's intent in this poem. The direct statements concerning the speaker's idle reverie have an immediacy of impact that makes the poet's central ideas easily understandable. This poem is about the simple joys of love and the intensity of feeling that one person can have for another; it emphasizes the tremendous sense of attachment such a feeling provokes. At the same time, the poem serves to remind readers of the tremendous sense of loss that follows the death of a beloved. Wordsworth has carefully woven into his lover's reverie the possibility of such impending doom through his consistent references to the descending moon; its path through the night sky serves as a symbol for the fading lover whose death is foreseen at the end of the poem.

It would be unwise to make too much of this single lyric, however; taken in the context of the series of Lucy poems, it serves to give readers a glimpse into the kind of simple but sincere passions that characterize the life of rustics, a group of people Wordsworth greatly admired. By extension, these passions are ones that Wordsworth attributes to all people of genuine sensibility. These passions are, in his opinion, what define individuals as truly human and what make life worth living.

Laurence W. Mazzeno

STRANGE MEETING

Author: Wilfred Owen (1893-1918)
Type of poem: Elegy
First published: 1919; collected in *Poems by Wilfred Owen*, 1920

The Poem

"Strange Meeting" is a short elegy lamenting a soldier-poet's participation in World War I, the most cataclysmic event that had occurred up until that period in recorded history. The poem is written in the first person; it can be safely assumed that Wilfred Owen and the narrator are the same person and that this is Owen's private journey into hell.

Drawing from many trips into the underworld by characters in earlier literature, Owen seems to escape the horrors of the battlefield; he enters a "profound dull tunnel" where the sounds and scenes of the war are not evident. Noticing that he is not alone, Owen probes one of the "sleepers," awakening one who seems to recognize him and bless him: "By his dead smile I knew we stood in Hell."

Entering into a discussion with the awakened sleeper, Owen informs him that there is no reason to mourn, since the guns and deaths from the battles above are divorced from their presence. The sleeper replies that even though this is true, he grieves over "the undone years,/ The hopelessness." The sleeper, too, had been a soldier-poet—in fact, he is Owen's alter ego, and he realizes the effect he might have had on society if he had not been killed but had been allowed to live and continue writing poetry.

The alter ego continues that World War I, considered at that time as the war to end all wars, is only the beginning of conflicts that will plague men for eternity. The calamity is that "Now men will go content with what we spoiled"; worse yet, if they do not accept conditions, they will simply go to war again, with nationalism dominating human progress. The only slight hope that the alter ego has is that the legacy left behind by the dead might be able to exert influence on the populace "with truths that lie too deep for taint." Leaders would therefore not be able to falsify the reality of war and would not be able to force war upon society.

The alter ego knows that the true duty of the soldier-poet is to inform the public, and he would have gladly given his all to accomplish this goal. Unfortunately for him (and society), he was killed before he was able to do this. Even if he had not been killed, he is afraid that his sensibilities would have been permanently warped by the horrors of war, because the "Foreheads of men have bled where no wounds were."

Owen's alter ego finally identifies himself, in the last five lines, as the man whom Owen had bayoneted to death the day before. Owen then realizes that he too is dead and is bonded with his alter ego, who closes with "Let us sleep now. . . ." Eternity then begins for Owen.

Forms and Devices

By looking formulaically at the structure of "Strange Meeting," one can look at the introduction, the body, and the epilogue separately and can trace the devices Owen uses to produce his desired effect.

In the three-line introduction, Owen draws extensively from the traditional dream-vision poetry of the Romantic period, but he also bases this descent on several incidents from his actual experiences. It has been recorded that Owen once spent more than fifty hours trapped in a caved-in dugout with his only companion a mutilated fellow officer. He also had an almost surrealistic experience when he was a young child with his family in a misty Irish woods; he was haunted in his dreams by both experiences. His preoccupation with the terror of being trapped underground or in a "profound tunnel" manifests itself in the entry into the netherworld of the poem.

In the body of the poem, antithesis is evident throughout. The newly initiated dead (Owen, even though he does not yet realize that he is dead) is rejoicing at being away from the horrors of the battlefield and questioning his alter ego about why he should mourn now that they are safe and "no blood reached there from the upper ground." The alter ego, conversely, is mourning the lost opportunities to influence society positively through poetic works and language that will educate the public about the futility and folly of war. No sacrifice would have been too great for the alter ego except that of dying and not fulfilling his duty as a poet. He says, "I would have poured my spirit without stint/ But not through wounds; not on the cess of war." Ironically, the price he had to pay was the only one he was unwilling to pay— death— and he mourns the pity in that.

The alter ego is also mourning the Pandora's box that he prophesies World War I has opened. Using the "tigress" as a metaphor for the world as a jungle and man as the relentless carnivore, the alter ego is imagining a world in which only the strong will survive, by subjugating the weak. He sees no hope for humankind, because the world and progress are retreating from aggression.

Antithesis is also highlighted in the closing lines as the alter ego addresses Owen by saying, "I am the enemy you killed, my friend." This juxtaposition of opposites, enemy and friend, transcends the animosity of nations and advocates the universal brotherhood of man. It is ironic that this brotherhood is only recognizable and reconcilable after death; on the battlefield Owen was so committed to killing his "enemy" that he had to frown in concentration to accomplish his task.

Themes and Meanings

The central theme in "Strange Meeting" is the futility and horror of modern war. There is no chivalry or honor, which the traditional poets found in war; instead, there is only suffering and death. Owen is attempting to inform the public of the horrors of trench war as seen by the common man in an effort to motivate this self-serving public into a front to force an end to World War I and to be aware enough not to allow another war to happen.

"Strange Meeting" was the end result of a metamorphosis undergone by Owen and other World War I soldier-poets. They went through many changes as their exposure to the war and trench life increased. Initially they wrote patriotic verse, designed to help build a united front opposing the aggressions of Germany. This quickly changed as they began to realize the grim realities and arbitrariness of war. As their frustrations grew, they lashed out at those they saw as either profiting from the war or misguidedly supporting it. Their final stage reflects the sadness and waste of any war at any time no matter what side the combatants and populace are on. Owen was no exception; "Strange Meeting" is perhaps his most poignant poem and strongest antiwar work, crowning his short list of achievements.

Owen is not only lamenting the terrors his generation must face; he is also sadly prophesying future conflicts between nations. He is attempting to show the public the waste such conflicts create, but he realizes the futility — no matter what the truth is nor how it is presented, there will always be those who will strive to go "Into vain citadels that are not walled." It will be the common man who will pay the ultimate price for the conquest of nations.

"Strange Meeting" is a moving elegy for the unknown dead of all nationalities who shared the suffering and deprivations for their nations and gave their lives in a conflict very few understood. War is nothing more than murder between strangers, and, modern technology raises it to new levels of proficiency. Owen and his alter ego — both soldier-poets, both dead — have concluded their journeys; they are now sleeping together as comrades, even though they were proclaimed enemies by the uniforms they wore. Those differences have been overcome by the universal brotherhood of man. As fellow poets, they know they have been cheated by death of the influence they may have provided. Owen can only hope that by showing their human bond amidst the horrors of war, he can exert some slight influence to urge the world to a warless future.

Stephen H. Crane

STUMBLE BETWEEN TWO STARS

Author: César Vallejo (1892-1938)
Type of poem: Meditation
First published: 1939, as "Traspié entre dos estrellas," in *Poemas humanos*;
  collected in *The Complete Posthumous Poetry*, 1978

The Poem

"Stumble Between Two Stars" is a short poem of forty-five lines divided into nine irregular paragraphs that range from eleven lines to one line in length. The title affects a reading of the poem since the word "stumble" is the only indication of movement in the poem. It is possible, but by no means certain, that César Vallejo intends to suggest that the meditation which follows is based upon observations made during a walk along city streets.

The poet's "stumble" consists primarily of observations and the emotional response that those observations provoke. Thus, in the first two stanzas, the poet turns his attention to "people so wretched" that they have lost their bodies, and by implication, perhaps their souls as well. The poet's description of them certainly echoes that of Dante's lost souls.

The second stanza continues the observation of these wretched people. The poet emphasizes their doomed condition. They were born to death; every hour of life is death. In their wretchedness, not even language is available to them, for their alphabet is frozen.

This wretchedness moves the poet to a cry of pity in the third stanza and begins the incantatory litany that comprises the bulk of the poem. In the next five stanzas, the poet delivers this litany in an almost hypnotic chant, as he calls up those who are "beloved" and details their characteristics. There is a decided echo of the biblical prophets in this chant, as the poet mixes the prophetic voice of vision with that of lamentation. That the biblical prophets were considered spokesmen for God is no doubt part of Vallejo's intention here: The poet is in essence the voice of God expressing both pity and tenderness toward the wretched. It is, nevertheless, an ironic God who speaks through the poet, and the tenderness affected offers rather cold comfort to the blighted souls accounted for in the litany.

It is certainly an odd collection of souls that the poet calls forth. Most seem to suffer an obvious physical poverty or torment or misery, such as hunger and thirst; others suffer more subtle spiritual or psychological ailments; and some suffer from what would appear to be relatively minor complaints. Regardless of the source of their woes, they all are demeaned in some way, reduced to an almost subhuman condition. The poet feels pity at the sight of them.

Forms and Devices

The logic of "Stumble Between Two Stars" is that of Surrealism. Therefore, in order to make sense of the poem, it is essential to understand some of the basic aspects of surreal metaphors. The Surrealist poet seeks to discover new realities by linking unusual or incompatible objects. Through swift association and arbitrary metaphors—the more arbitrary the better—a deeper reality can perhaps be glimpsed. Contradictions may be apparent in such linkages, but the Surrealist meaning resides precisely in those contradictions. Vallejo, for example, uses adjectives that are not usually associated with the nouns that they modify in his poems. It may not be normal to speak of people with "hair quantitative," but by connecting mathematics or statistics with the human body, Vallejo can make an unusual and subtle point: The wretched people, in this instance, are demeaned, treated in cold statistical terms. Perhaps, too, this concept of quantitative hair is meant to be connected to the biblical statement of Jesus that the hairs of one's head are numbered. Thus, the apparently arbitrary connection of adjective and noun—initially bizarre and esoteric—reveals many possible layers of meaning.

In 1926, Vallejo wrote two articles that urged poets to abandon the false, stylized poetry predominant at the time. In "Poesia Nueva" ("New Poetry") and "Contra el secreto profesional" ("Against the Professional Secret"), he called for poets to avoid simple mimicry of style and instead to embrace nontraditional techniques. In his own work, Vallejo met this call by inventing a unique poetic language that confronted the chaos in the world by approximating and reflecting it. One way in which this language reflected the chaos was by adopting the aesthetics of cubism. In art, Cubism was a movement led by Pablo Picasso and Georges Braque that broke an object into simple geometric shapes and re-presented various views of the object simultaneously. Similarly, Vallejo's poetry attempts the re-presentation and recomposition of not only particular images, but also of the language used to communicate that imagery.

In "Stumble Between Two Stars," for example, Vallejo creates new images by fragmenting familiar ones into parts. The result is a surrealist version of synecdoche and metonymy. These two rhetorical devices, by which parts become representative of the whole, are transformed by Vallejo's irrational vision. In presenting imagery, Vallejo consistently focuses on unusual aspects of the image—in this case of the many "beloved" people who are called forth. The aspects that Vallejo chooses are decidedly unusual. Vallejo concentrates on eccentric imagery in an attempt to parallel the ambiguity inherent in contemporary experience. The aesthetics of this poem thus mirrors the irrational world that the poet experiences. Through surrealist metaphor and the off-center use of synecdoche, he conveys in language the chaotic, bizarre, and often incomprehensible nature of life in his age.

Themes and Meanings

"Stumble Between Two Stars" expresses the sense of alienation and despair that distinguishes much of the great literature that came out of the Paris literary scene of the 1920's and 1930's. Vallejo spent the last fifteen years of his life (1923-1938) in Paris. Vallejo, however, lived a poverty-stricken, bohemian life, moving from hotel to hotel. His experience with poverty and his association with Marxist groups influenced his poetry. Thus, Vallejo, perhaps more than any other artist in Paris, was sensitive to the degradation of human life and the trauma of living a meaningless and gratuitous life on the fringe of society. Vallejo is truly the poet of the *Lumpenproletariat*.

His wretched people—and Vallejo includes himself among this group—are doomed from birth. These people are born in sarcophagi; they constantly suffer; they do not even have the recourse of language, for their alphabet is frozen. Although Vallejo seems to suggest initially that this wretched multitude is condemned to its own Dantesque circle of the Inferno, his incantation of pity for them does offer the hope of something better—purgatory at least, if not paradise. By calling them "beloved," Vallejo offers his own blessing and holds out some measure of hope, however small, for his fallen, weeping fellow wretches. The poet's litany calls to mind the Sermon on the Mount and the Beatitudes that Jesus recites in Matthew. It also brings to mind the chantlike tone of American poet Walt Whitman. The similarities between Vallejo and Whitman may at first seem tenuous, the former being the great bard of democracy, progress, and possibility, and the latter being the poet of personal anguish who wrote of those who suffered under the very forces that Whitman celebrated. On another level, each poet attempts to name the nameless, to identify the hidden, and to give voice to the voiceless.

It is difficult to supply a precise meaning for Vallejo's imagery, since the words in the text are not limited to the meanings that they have in everyday usage. Often, Vallejo simply plays with words and their sounds, and he ends up with phrases such as "the sanchez ears" in line 15. Such wordplay is lost in translation. It is not necessary to find a single correct meaning behind each metaphor or image in the poem, for a basic theme of Vallejo's work concerns one's inability to grasp fully whatever meaning does reside in the world around him or her. His poetry confronts the chaos of the world with a chaos of its own—a chaos of fragmented images and broken syntax. By detailing the drudgery, the poverty, and the physical misery that define human life, Vallejo voices the frustration that is inherent in the human condition. It is a world where hunger can only be satiated by thirst, that is, one deprivation replaced by another—and even that dubious solace often proves unavailable. The poet bemoans the fate of those who have no spiritual control, who have lost part of what defined them as individuals. They no longer remember childhood. They are deep in debt. They fall to the ground, neither dead nor alive, and are not even allowed the comfort of tears. "Stumble Between Two Stars" is a poem full of the anguish, compassion, and hope that Vallejo had for his fellow humans.

Stephen Benz

THE STURGEON

Author: Raymond Carver (1938-1988)
Type of poem: Lyric
First published: 1989, in *A New Path to the Waterfall*

The Poem

"The Sturgeon," written in free verse, consists of fifty-six lines, which are divided into five stanzas or verse paragraphs. The title bluntly states the apparent subject of the poem; as with other poem titles in this posthumous collection— "Wine," "Suspenders," "Lemonade," "Letter," and "Summer Fog," for example—Raymond Carver does not force the title to mean anything. It simply names the object on which Carver decides to focus the poem.

The poem is written in the first person, and the speaker is the poet himself reminiscing about his father and the stories his father told him. The poem begins, however, with an objective description of a sturgeon. Unlike some of the more embellished nature poems by Marianne Moore or Elizabeth Bishop, Carver baldly describes the fish's habitat, body, and habits: "the sturgeon is a bottom-feeder/ and can't see well." He continues, "The sturgeon/ lives alone . . . and takes/ 100 years getting around to its first mating." This is not a baroque style to say the least; Carver's words are as close to prose as poetry is likely to get.

The second stanza moves this description out of a timeless world into a specific moment in time with the description of a specific sturgeon. It seems the opening journalistic description was imitating or recalling "a sketch . . . of its biography" of a nine-hundred-pound sturgeon the author and his father saw "winched up in a corner/ of the Agricultural Exhibit Building." At this point, where the poem will lead can only be guessed.

The third stanza, as in the first, has the first-person persona removed from the description. Again, only the facts about the sturgeon are here: "The largest are netted/ in the Don River/ somewhere in Russia." The knowledge displayed about sturgeons is encyclopedic, and the style of the poem is reminiscent of the language of a common reference book. Carver has let the air out of the grand style of poetry writing.

The flat language is used to tell a tall story in the fourth stanza, in which the narrator and his father reappear. The reader discovers that apparently Carver is writing— "I am quoting"—from memory or from an imaginary recollection of the "particular specimen . . . killed in the exploratory dynamiting/ that went on in the summer of 1951," when Carver was twelve or thirteen. The poem picks up pace with the father's description of a hooked sturgeon that fights to a standstill a team of horses fastened to the line.

Carver, however, does not like pyrotechnics—he cuts the story short: "I don't remember much else—maybe it got away." All he can remember is his father beside him "staring up at that great dead fish,/ and that marvelous story of his, all/ surfacing, now and then." The concluding stanza does not resolve any of the principal questions a reader might have about the poem, but it does raise new ones about the importance of the story to Carver as a boy and as a man recollecting it and about what the poem says about the presence of memory in poetry. It is also interesting to consider whether William Wordsworth's definition of poetry fits here, for example, whether this poem is an instant of "emotion recollected in tranquillity" or whether Carver is trying something different.

Forms and Devices

Carver is known primarily as a brilliant short-story writer, although his poems are also well regarded by many. His poems owe much to the short-story genre, as is clearly evinced in "The Sturgeon." The poet uses a plain style, with descriptive details that shy away from metaphor or simile, and a narrative to hold the work together. Carver also takes Wordsworth's words about poetry quite literally: Wordsworth argued, in his 1800 preface to *Lyrical Ballads*, that poets should write in a "language really used by men" and that there should be no "essential difference between the language of prose and metrical composition." Carver seems intent on blurring whatever norms or conventions separate the two genres. This poem reads in places as if it were a reference work; his use of figurative language in the poem— "Mosslike feelers hang down over/ the slumbrous lips"—occurs in the section in which he is apparently quoting from an unnamed source rather than being "poetic."

One of the primary distinctions between a short story and this poem—besides the line breaks—is the fact that the narrator is Carver himself; this poem is not, he insists, fiction, although the fact that Carver cannot quite recall the events central to the poem slurs this distinction. The other central poetic technique used here is the juxtaposition of the simple, descriptive sections (parts 1 and 3) and the parts that are devoted to the capturing of memory (parts 2, 4, and 5). It is this juxtaposition that forces the reader to wonder about the point of joining together the story about the hanging fish, including "its biography—which my father read/ and then read aloud" and Carver's silence about his feelings for his father. The reader is left wondering whether this poem is about grief, and, if so, where the true emotion lies.

Themes and Meanings

In some ways, this poem resists interpretation. It seems to want to remain on the surface, on the level of description only. As with much minimalist fiction, however, there is a hint of another world beneath the poem's prosaic language. Perhaps in the same way that the sturgeon is brought up out of the depths and hung up to dry, this memory that Carver is dragging out of the subconscious is on display for all to see.

What makes this story/poem interesting is the narrator's inability to piece together the story entirely. Yes, he remembers chapter and verse descriptions of the huge fish, but he admits to only partial knowledge of the significance of the memory: "I don't remember much else—maybe it got away/ even then." The memories surface "now and then," and he cannot capture the past in its entirety; it is this honesty that is so winning in the poem. The reader believes a poet who admits fallibility. Also, the poem accrues some tension by this paralleling of encyclopedic fact and incomplete memories, if in fact anything happened—anything "significant"—when he actually stood with his father "staring up at that great dead fish."

Although the poem rejects the traditional devices of poetry—metrics, metaphors, images, or lush sounds—in some ways the poem can be seen as an old-fashioned allegory. The poet is similar to the team of horses in his father's story that is trying to drag the fish—or in the poet's case the memory—up to the surface, but the poet is not even sure who wins in this battle.

The poem does manage to capture a glimpse of a father-son relationship, one that Carver wrote about often in his essays and poems. The relationship is not a warm one or one in which great truths are passed from father to son; there exists one story about horses versus a fish that flashes in the poet's mind, but beyond that the reader is given a picture only of two males staring at a dead fish. The reader is left to decide whether the fish is emblematic of memory or the father in some way or whether the depths at which the fish lives are symbolic of the quiet, almost chilling depth of feeling—the unexpressed feeling—that exists between Carver and his father. It is not a poem that expresses itself; it is as reticent as some men are, as muted and oblique as some relationships between father and son.

Perhaps in Carver's inability to bring the memory of the fish into sharper focus for the reader, he is allowing a glimpse into the world of a man who, like the fish, "lives alone." The accumulation of factual information about the fish is one way to form a bridge of communication, but essentially the poem suggests that there is a central loneliness even in the most intimate relationships. The "marvelous story" of the father that surfaces in Carver's memory "now and then" is a gift that the poet cherishes, but the relationship itself seems as mysterious and strange as the sturgeon, "something left over from another world," now that the poet's father is dead. The poem does not wear its heart on its sleeve, but there is silent mourning in the recollection of what has been lost and perhaps of what was never quite there.

Kevin Boyle

A SUMMER NIGHT

Author: W. H. Auden (1907-1973)
Type of poem: Lyric
First published: 1934, untitled; collected as "A Summer Night 1933," in *Look, Stranger!*, 1936

The Poem

"A Summer Night" is a lyric of ninety-six lines, divided equally into sixteen stanzas (a later version has only twelve). On a June evening, the poet-speaker lies on the lawn, looking at the constellation Vega and aware of the moon beginning to rise. He feels fortunate to be here: a place and time of erotic happiness and fertile friendships. He is an equal lying here each evening with his friends; enchanted, each is called forth, as flowers are drawn by light into fullness of blossom.

These are experiences that will later be recalled when the friends are separated. These evenings, when beastly emotions are tame and there is no consciousness of death, will be important to remember when emotions may be violent and times are chaotic. There is one friend among these others whom the speaker regards as his beloved; their eyes exchange affection, and each is present for the other through the passing of each day.

The second phase of the poem (stanzas 6 through 12) begins when the poet becomes aware of outside pressures threatening to destroy his happiness. He considers the larger world, that part which lies under the light of the rising moon. There, many others in all their variety are also lying at rest. The moon, however, looks down impersonally upon all objects, not discriminating between "churches and power stations," not capable of enjoying the art that its light illuminates in the great galleries of Europe. Indeed, the moon is unable to respond to anything except gravity.

Somewhat like the moon itself, the poet and his friends look out from their island of happy contentment as if from a garden secure against the pains and sufferings that exist in the world. In their tranquillity of love, the friends do not know, and do not want to know, about the threats to Poland or anywhere else in the world. They do not want to think what might be in store for England; they indulge themselves as if on "picnics in the sun."

Inside the wall of their garden, the friends are protected from the sight of "gathering multitudes" whose physical distress is separated from the happy friends' metaphysical debates and limited charity. Even as he distinguishes his garden retreat from the world outside, the speaker is aware that he and his friends are nevertheless being driven down a path that they have not chosen. Their energies have been sapped, their contentment has drained them of the power to direct their own lives. They would give all they have enjoyed from their youthful past, if they could keep alive that happy contentment forever.

In the last phase of the poem, however, their tranquillity is broken by the force of events outside their happy garden. Each of them has been made small by the overpowering flood of violence, as if each had been a river dreaming of itself as the whole reality, when suddenly the great ocean overwhelmed all and revealed how inconsiderable each really is. Each is confronted by the great and horrifying fact of death as it crashes through the "dykes of our content." Still, even ocean floods eventually retreat. While mud yet covers the devastated landscape, some "shy green stalks" will peep through, as "stranded monsters gasping lie" scattered about the landscape. Sounds of rebuilding will disturb the monsters, but those sounds will join the sight of green wheat to promise renewal amid destruction.

The speaker imagines such a future ahead for him and his friends who lie outside this June evening. He resigns himself to loss of private happiness, accepting a future strength in the rebuilding that will come after violence. That future strength that will rise through the mud of political chaos will be the product of his own, and his friends', present happiness in love; it will be like the happy cry of a child through whom the "drowned voices of his parents rise/ In unlamenting song." That strength of a new civilization, like the art nourished by tradition, will be a calm after storm, a strength born of patience and loving forgiveness.

Forms and Devices

The short lines, repeated rhyme scheme, and brief stanzas of "A Summer Night" are appropriate for the meditative mood of carelessness that governs this poem. Despite the brief interruption of imagining apocalyptic events, the poem is a sustained reflection upon the virtues of friendship, simplicity, and provincial tranquillity. The lyric is therefore like the ode practiced by the Roman poet Horace (65-68 B.C.), who sang his songs of happiness in rural retreats to his farm, where he could put great historical events into controlled perspective. Such a lyric may therefore be called a Horatian ode, with its repeated brief stanzas moving through a landscape of tranquil emotion and considered thought.

The devices employed to move the poem in this way are shifts in meter to mark changes in feeling and perspective, variations in the rhymes, and links of sound by alliteration and assonance. The first stanza, to illustrate the shifts of meter, contains two strong pauses and one weak pause before stopping with the period at the end. The first strong pause, a semicolon, occurs at the end of a line, while the second occurs in the midst of a line. The second stanza offers one strong pause and four weak pauses to balance the rhythm of the first stanza. Within the simple and uniform stanzas, thus, are shifts of feeling conveyed by shifts of rhythm.

There are subtleties of rhyming to complicate the appearance of uniformity and simplicity of the *aabccb* scheme. Masculine rhymes (space/place) are varied with feminine ones (summer/newcomer) and mixed ones (bed/overhead). In addition, there are slant- or partial-rhymes (hiding/pleading, wretchedness/distress), which cause a wrenching of the feelings beneath the prevailing tranquillity. Finally, harmonies of sound within stanzas are made by echoing consonants and vowels: In the third stanza, the consonants of "equal" link "colleagues" and "calm," while the vowel of "with" links "in" and "sit"; the play of these links continues in "light" and "hiding," "light," "leaves," and "logic," and "leaves" and "pleading."

In addition, image as symbol is a major device in the poem's development. The image of the moon, which is barely noticed (by the poet's "feet") in the first stanza, becomes prominent in stanza 6, where a new phase of awareness begins and where the speaker's imagination is identified with the moon's light. Sunlight provides a balancing image, hinted at early as the power forcing flowers into blossom and late as the energy summoning wheat from the mud of devastation. Similar balancing of images, to create a rounded or symmetrical form to the poem as a whole, appears in the mention of "lion griefs" early and "tigress . . . motions" late, "forest of green" early and "shy green stalks" late.

Themes and Meanings

Such balancing of sounds and images expresses the meaning of the poem as a balancing of feeling against numbness, of love against hate, and peace against violence. The enchanting light of the moon reveals beauties it cannot appreciate, but it serves well as a vehicle for the poet's humanizing imagination: Everything is made equal by the moonlight, as in a political sense, all should be equal in the human community; but the humanizing of that light allows for political equality to support aesthetic quality and civilized values. The sun provides energy for life, but the imagination provides ethical direction for that life: "The murderer" can see himself "in his glass" by aid of the sun's light, but only an ethical imagination can "forgive the murderer in his glass."

Themes of love and friendship, retirement, nature, and nurture work together to create a harmony of balanced reconciliation between various forces of opposition. Love among friends provides a resource of strength to be drawn upon when hate threatens: Thus, civilization can survive violence on account of its base as communion (community). Retirement behind walls of security appears to be a retreat from reality, because it seems to exist at the expense of a world of suffering; however, it proves to be the source of emotional strength needed for rebuilding after the walls have been broken down. Nature is a calm source of life, even in the worst of times, although it cannot be the end (as either goal or threat) of life. For that, human imagination is required. Instincts (of hunger or sex) may be natural, but their satisfaction will need something more than nature.

Auden, in 1933, anticipated the terrors of World War II to come. He imagined the need to create sources of strength from which to draw in future need. His poem refuses to surrender loving human commitments in the face of threat and want.

Richard D. McGhee

SUMMER NIGHT

Author: Joy Harjo (1951-   )
Type of poem: Lyric
First published: 1986; collected in *In Mad Love and War*, 1990

The Poem

"Summer Night" is a thirty-five-line poem visually arrayed so that alternating lines dominate either the right- or left-hand side of the page. The poem, written in free verse, describes the persona's impressions of a balmy summer night spent waiting for a lover to come home. In an autobiographical piece, Joy Harjo wrote that she had wanted the poem to capture the feel of a humid Oklahoma night and the impressions of her family's home.

The narrative opens with a description of the nearly full moon and flowers. In the night, children can be heard playing; their parents' laughter and music can also be heard inside the house. The narrator observes this world, listening to its sounds and feeling its rhythms while she waits, once again, for someone to return home — something that apparently is a common occurrence.

Although the poem is not divided into stanzas, the beginning of line 17 marks a shift in perspective from the neighborhood and other people to focus on the emotions of the speaker. The narrator talks of loneliness and of what it feels like to be waiting in the dark on a humid, heavy summer night. Everyone else is sleeping, and it seems that they are all sleeping with someone: Even the night itself is cradled in the arms of day. The narrator sees herself as the only thing without a partner.

The poem's final section is marked by the unseen intrusion of the person she has been waiting for, a return heralded by the scent of a honeysuckle brushed by the person, whom Harjo describes as blooming out of night's darkness. The poem concludes, giving no indication of whether the reunion is pleasant or what problems cause this unnamed individual to be away so often — or even, precisely, who he or she is.

Forms and Devices

The arrangement of the alternating lines that dominate either the right- or left-hand side of the page is an important device for several reasons. To capture the languid rhythms of a humid night, Harjo spreads the words across the page so that they almost lazily descend down the page with blank spaces joining succeeding lines. This wispy visual form also makes the poem seem drowsy and heightens the feeling of warm oppressiveness that can occur on a hot, sticky midsummer's night. Harjo begins the poem by describing the "humid air sweet like melon," a heaviness that dominates most of the first fifteen lines of the poem. The open, alternating visual array also adds a drifting, floating aspect to the poem and helps to portray the wandering, semifocused attention of someone sitting in the dark listening to the night sounds and waiting. Finally by alternatively pushing the lines right and left,

Harjo builds tension, because this placement is unnatural or unfamiliar. The tension helps underscore the narrator's own subtly expressed tension gained from waiting for someone's return.

Not only does the poem's visual sprawl embody the tensions and laziness of the summer night, but it also makes a powerful nonverbal statement about the speaker's isolation. All lines in the poem—with the exception of one—follow the alternating pattern: After the narrator tells the reader that everyone has a partner with whom to sleep, the reader's attention is turned to the narrator's own isolation in line 28 ("Everyone except me"). This is the only line of the poem that is centered on the page. To further heighten the feeling of loneliness, Harjo has made the previous two lines very short, creating a visual blankness above line 28 so that it truly stands all alone.

Harjo is a blues fan and saxophone player; "Summer Night" re-creates some of the cadences of that music. The slow, languid musical rhythms of the lines drift from one topic to another in much the same way that blues spills from harmony to harmony. Harjo gives a bluesy rhythm to her poetry by making use of numerous sentence fragments, a technique that mirrors musical phrasing. Each fragment is the equivalent of a tone, and the combination of these fragments establishes much of the poem's feeling of languor, isolation, and loneliness—in other words, the blues. Harjo underscores this aspect of the poem by mentioning the "wornout records" of the children's parents in line 8 and by equating her own loneliness with "an ache that begins/ in the sound of an old blues song." Just as blues songs sing about people who have been abandoned and who are heartbroken, "Summer Night" works as a blues lament for an unfaithful lover.

"Summer Night" is a poem that circles back on itself: The poem opens with a description of the almost full moon hanging melonlike in the night sky above sleeping flowers. This leaves the reader with the unstated impression of a perfumed night. The poem then moves inward to more and more specific, personal references: first to the darkened neighborhood where only voices in the night can be distinguished, then to a family's home and the intimate sounds of music and laughter, and finally to the narrator's self, which Harjo equates to a darkened home with one light burning patiently through the night. From this point, the poem remains on the level of the abandoned individual and is concluded and moved full circle when the returning lover is described as a "flower of light," echoing the flower image of the poem's second and third lines.

Themes and Meanings

In "Summer Night," Harjo talks of loneliness and anticipation in such a way that the reader is lulled into this sadness by the sleepy rhythms and sprawled lines that propel attention into the middle of the poem and, metaphorically, into the speaker's darkest, most secret private places. It is in the middle of the poem that the speaker confesses her loneliness. Because she says that this waiting "happens all the time, waiting for you/ to come home," she reveals that the loneliness is deep and of long duration. This mood of waiting and watchfulness is intensified by the placement of line 16 ("to come home") on a separate line far to the right of the page.

Harjo calls the narrator's loneliness an "ache" that starts in a blues song. By mentioning this particular type of music, Harjo enables the reader to draw on all the associations that contribute to the power of the blues. Traditional blues is itself a cry for a lost love, a plea for a lover's return, a lament for ill treatment; "Summer Night" is Harjo's blues. In her essay from *I Tell You Now: Autobiographical Essays by Native American Writers* (1987), Harjo says that she wanted "to sustain a blues mood, pay homage to the blues . . ." and that she hears "the sound of a sensuous tenor saxophone beneath the whole poem." Thus, the theme of loneliness is reinforced and its poignancy heightened by the one-time mention of blues in line 18. The poem is a lament, the blues; it is a plea for reunion.

Metaphors also serve to intensify the emotion of "Summer Night." The narrator equates her feelings of loneliness with "a house where all the lights have gone out/ but one." By placing the words "but one" alone on a line at the far right-hand side of the page, Harjo reinforces this isolation. The loneliness—the light mentioned in line 20—burns through the night into the "blue smoke of dawn." The metaphor of smoke calls to mind a spent candle or a lantern guttering out, perhaps in the same fashion as the persona's hope for the absent lover's return.

The low ebb of the poem is the narrator imagining herself as the only person or thing alone—even the night's "sound of a thousand silences" has itself for company. The fact that the night sounds are now quiet implies that they are at rest, peaceful, satisfied. Only the narrator remains awake, watchful, and alone.

Despite the narrator's isolation, at this point the poem's mood grows more affirming: The perfume of a bruised honeysuckle literally sweetens the air; the lover has returned. The poem concludes with the lover radiating light, a light that blooms to fill the darkness. Although Harjo never alludes to why the two people have been separated, and there is no resolution of whatever conflicts caused one person to be absent for an entire night, the poem ends on a positive note; the night is now described as "miraculous."

Melissa E. Barth

SUMMER ORACLE

Author: Audre Lorde (1934-   )
Type of poem: Dramatic monologue
First published: 1976, in *Coal*

The Poem

An oracle is a prophecy or prediction of the future transmitted through a priest. Audre Lorde's "Summer Oracle" is a prophecy transmitted through the voice of an African-American lesbian poet. The poem is a prophetic meditation on the consequences of hopelessness. In the first stanza of this thirty-seven-line poem, the reader is given the world without hope: "Without expectation/ there is no end/ to the shocks of morning/ or even a small summer." At first it is difficult to grasp how the two basic and utterly unremarkable moments of beginning can be experienced as "shocks." Yet in the world of the hopeless, where the morning leads to the inevitable night and the summer to the inevitable winter, there can be no "expectations" of the sort that make morning and summer emblems of hope and transformation.

The oracular voice of the poet begins in the second stanza to characterize and prophesy the world without "expectations." What is described are expectations, but they are ones of fire and insurgency: "Now the image is fire/ blackening the vague lines/ into defiance across the city." The oracle has presented an image, a way to understand what had in the first stanza been merely undefined "shocks." "Defiance" defines the city, and the definition operates both in the sense that it gives meaning to the city and in the sense that it makes it visible. The sun, which had in the first stanza been a shocking reminder of a morning or a summer without expectations, has now become the "sun warming us in a cold country/ barren of symbols for love." Once the definition of violence and defiance has been given to the cold and barren city, it begins to be possible to imagine something else: It becomes possible to imagine love, or at least the symbols for love.

In the next and longest stanza of the poem, Lorde shifts from addressing a social audience to addressing a specific "you" (a member of the barren city now defined with the image of fire). The defining force of defiance is personified, or made into a humanlike actor in the oracle's vision. The earlier stanza had ended with a hope for "symbols of love," but this stanza proclaims that Lorde has "forsaken order" and instead imagines "you into fire/ untouchable in a magician's cloak."

With the introduction of the "magician's cloak," Lorde begins to link the world of the occult and the supernatural with the world of political transformation. The magician (who is also the force of defiance) is "covered with signs of destruction and birth." These are the ancient alchemical signs of the transmutation of base metal into gold, but they are also the revolutionary symbols of apocalyptic transformation: The destruction of the old is joined with the renewing force of birth. The cloak is "sewn with griffins and arrows and hammers and gold sixes." The griffin is a linking of the lion and the eagle; the "arrows and hammers" balance warfare and carpentry. Each emblem operates in two realms: the political and the supernatural.

The new force in history that Lorde has summoned can find no companionship among other ancient magicians and warlocks. Since a warlock is a male witch, the force of history is marked with the signification of the male gender. The new force is not adorned as was the old one: "no gourds ring your sack/ no spells bring forth peace."

The poet who speaks with divine inspiration has brought the "image of fire" into being and has given it the trappings of prophecy, numerology, and alchemy. She has also created the image for destruction and rebirth. The abstract symbols on the cloak do not take into account the real, practical, and human concerns of summer: "I am still fruitless and hungry." The individual human needs are not met. She is "fruitless." Even the fruit is fruitless: "peaches are flinty and juiceless/ and cry sour worms."

The final two stanzas bracketing the long central section return the reader to the poetic fact that "The image is fire." Now one is able to understand more fully specifically what (apart from being a force of defiance and an alchemical magician) the image is and what it means. The second to the last stanza links the image to "the blaze the planters start" in the sugar fields after the harvest; the planters "burn off the bagasse from the canefields/ after a harvest."

In the final stanza, again Lorde says that "The image is fire." It is, she writes (mixing street language with the supernatural and occult), "the high sign that rules our summer." The fire, the sun, and the comradely sign of friendship among urban young men are linked together. The linking of these elements turns the supernatural warlock of the long central stanza back into the potentially violent city. The image is fire, Lorde continues: "I smell it in the charred breezes blowing over/ your body." The body is the city landscape she had described in the first stanza: "blackening the vague lines/ into defiance across the city." The work of the poem has been to turn those vague lines of defiance into accessible language. The body she smells in the fire is "close/ hard/ essential/ under its cloak of lies." The lies are the fictive devices of an ancient way; the truth is the actual historical experience of purifying destruction.

Forms and Devices

As a dramatic monologue, Audre Lorde's "Summer Oracle" is in the tradition of modern poetry that emphasizes the seemingly natural cadences of spoken language while it participates in the resonant and historically significant language of classical prophecy. As an oracle or prophecy, it is in the tradition of an African-American rhetoric of spirituality and political empowerment.

One striking example of the use of "natural" language to suggest a spiritual realm is that of the "high sign" in the last stanza. At one level, the high sign is a slang expression for the glance or gesture meant to be a warning of impending danger—it is therefore a kind of oracle in itself. In addition, Lorde evokes the elaborate greeting young men give one another in the street or the high sign with which they celebrate an important shared achievement; it suggests friendship and community. Finally, Lorde's use of the phrase points directly to the sun, the transforming life source which is the most immediate and compelling—the highest sign of all. It is, she writes, "the high sign that rules our summer."

The dramatic monologue, as is customary, is addressed to another person, a persona for the community for whom the poem is a prophecy. While she imagines him in the third stanza as wearing on his cloak the magical symbols of the occult, in the last stanza the inherited symbolic world is revealed to be a "cloak of lies."

While Audre Lorde uses few of the elaborate devices associated with traditional poetry, her "Summer Oracle" draws on the power of poetic statement to inspire and awaken. This power is realized by means of the juxtaposition Lorde makes between the extremes of destruction and survival. Linking such emotional extremes is characteristic of the sublime or the power to envision and communicate a sense of greatness to a reader.

Themes and Meanings

"Summer Oracle" is about envisioning the future; it conveys a sense of impending disturbance and political unrest in the ghettoes of the United States, but it also, by the end, suggests the possibility of purification and personal authenticity. The necessary rebirth can only come after the old historical forces have in some way been destroyed. This is made clear in the image of the canefields burning after the harvest—the burning of the crushed sugarcane refuse is a stark analogy to the destruction that the poem forecasts for the city. When the poem begins, the future is seen as shocking, unmapped by hopes and expectations. As the poem progresses, the indistinct sense of the city is replaced by precision, defiance, and the warming of a "cold country" that had been without the "symbols of love."

Lorde is able to look at her city and the people of her city and say to them that she is able to "imagine you into fire." The theme of fire in its many forms (as the sun, as the magical fire that the warlock's fingers draw, as the burning canefields, and finally as the burnt body from whom "charred breezes" blow back to the poet) gives Lorde the multiple visions of fire as destroyer and purifier. Finally the "Summer Oracle" foretells itself and holds within itself the warning and promise of urgent political change.

Sharon Bassett

THE SUN RISING

Author: John Donne (1572-1631)
Type of poem: Lyric
First published: 1633, in *Poems by J. D.: With Elegies on the Authors Death*

The Poem

"The Sun Rising" is a lyric poem divided into three stanzas of ten lines each. Each stanza is further divided into two quatrains, respectively rhyming *abba* and *cddc*, and a couplet rhyming *ee*. The title, "The Sun Rising," suggests an aubade, a song sung by lovers upon parting at morning; John Donne, however, renders a parody of the tender love songs written for such occasions. Parting from his beloved is the last thing the speaker of the poem desires to do. Moreover, the title allows for a physical image of the sun actually getting out of bed, an action that the lovers refuse to follow.

In this poem, Donne uses both personification—figurative use of language in which human qualities or feelings are attributed to nonhuman things—and apostrophe—a figure of speech in which a personification is addressed—when the poem's speaker addresses the sun in all three stanzas. The persona or speaker in this poem is the lover who argues with the sun about the power of love to exist outside time and space.

In the first stanza, the speaker irreverently rebukes the sun, whom he calls a "busy old fool" and a "saucy pedantic wretch" for daring to disturb the lovers as if they were mere "schoolboys" or "sour prentices." Donne's allusion to King James I's passion for early hunting outings (line 7) is often used for dating this poem after 1603, the date of James's ascension to the throne of England. The stanza ends with the lover claiming, in the couplet, that perfect love is not bound to the progression of time.

The second stanza begins with an apparent reversal of tone. The lover seems to flatter the sun when he exclaims, "Thy beams, so reverend, and strong." This statement is undercut and reversed in the next lines, however, by the lover's claims that he can obliterate the sun by merely closing his eyes and that his mistress' eyes can blind even the sun's brilliance. He tells the sun to make its appointed daily journey around the earth and discover that all the wealth and power the world has to offer are contained in the bed where the two lovers are resting. (Writing in the seventeenth century, Donne knew quite well that the sun does not make a daily revolution around the earth but uses the image for the sake of the argument.)

The last stanza continues the outrageous qualities that the lover claims for the love between him and his mistress. The two become all states and all rulers, while "Nothing else is." The speaker then changes his apparent dismissal of the sun in the first stanza and invites the sun to join the lovers in the bedroom, arguing that the duties of the sun to warm the world are fulfilled by warming them. The invitation gathers the force of a mild command in the couplet, making the reversal from the opening stanza complete: "Shine here to us, and thou art everywhere;/ This bed thy center is, these walls, thy sphere."

Forms and Devices

The power of Donne's poetic voice is characterized by his dramatic monologue and intensified by his use of the present tense. His approach in "The Sun Rising" illustrates the immediacy that such a voice creates. His speaker (the lover) and his addressee (the sun) are strongly characterized; the present tense allows the reader to experience a progressive development of the speaker's claims and arguments. The inclusion of such mundane things as curtains and beds and the juxtaposition of schoolboys and kings create a strong scene.

The claims that Donne makes for the exclusiveness of love in "The Sun Rising" are created by his expert manipulation of hyperbole, the trope of exaggeration. In the first stanza, the lover elevates mutual love to dimensions beyond the confines of time, while simultaneously dismissing hours, days, even seasons, as mere "rags of time." In the second stanza, the hyperbolic assertions gather force as the lover piles his exaggerations in quick succession; the mistress' eyes are more brilliant than the sun's beams; both Indias—one is not enough—are contained in her; and the bed sleeps all the world's kings and their wealth.

Having reached the near pinnacle of hyperbolic manipulation in the second stanza, Donne makes his most exuberant but logical leap in hyperbolic argument in the third stanza: "Nothing else is." This affirmation of love independent of the world obliterates anything and anybody but the lovers in their bed and bedroom, which now has attained cosmic dimension as well as cosmic significance.

In conjunction with his manipulation of hyperbole, Donne uses meter and intricate syntactical arrangements to convey the superiority of the love portrayed in "The Sun Rising." He employs an uneven syllable count in his lines by varying his line length from short, pithy lines with four syllables to longer iambic pentameter lines. His manipulations of the syllable count allow Donne to operate with different levels of stress and syntactical arrangement. The terse four-syllable lines create a forceful tension in each stanza.

In the first and second stanzas, these short lines are questions addressed at the sun. In the first stanza, "Why dost thou thus" follows its subject—the sun—but Donne delays its completion by syntactical inversion so that the sun literally has to push through windows and curtains, the intervening adverbial phrases, to find its verb. The lovers are protected not only by the physical presence of windows and the like but also isolated by syntax.

In the second stanza, Donne reverses the syntactical arrangement, starting with the direct object instead of the subject, although the reader does not know that until the short second line is read. Whereas in the first stanza the short line questions the sun's authority, in the second stanza this line denies the sun its authority.

The force of the short line is especially immediate in the third stanza as it embodies the ultimate hyperbolic claim of the separateness of love: "Nothing else is."

The power of carefully chosen syntactical structure in line 1 of the third stanza illustrates the relevance of such syntax to the understanding of the poem and affirms that attention to such matters can assist the reader to a heightened appreciation of the poem. By syntactical placement of "She" at the beginning of the line and "I" at the end, Donne traps the whole world and its power structure between the lovers: "She is all states, and all princes, I."

Themes and Meanings

The theme of love in all its rich variety fascinated Donne, and he expressed this fascination in the range of attitudes and responses to love in his *Songs and Sonnets*. Heir to the Petrarchan code of the abject lover prostrate before his proud and unrelenting mistress, Donne parodies this tradition in poems such as "The Blossom" and "The Funeral." He advocates promiscuity in lighthearted poems such as "The Indifferent" and writes a witty seduction poem in "The Flea." He questions the constancy of men and women in such cynical poems as "Loves Usury" and "Womans Constancy," and he portrays love that is both physical and spiritual in poems such as "The Good-Morrow," "A Valediction: Forbidding Mourning," and "The Ecstasy."

"The Sun Rising," although it does not explicitly blend body and soul, is nevertheless an argument for the grandeur of love that can combine spiritual and sexual love in perfect equality. Donne insists that the sun has no power over perfect love, reasoning that, since the lovers are the world, the sun will fulfill its duties by remaining in the bedroom; he outrageously asserts that "Nothing else is," testifying to the superiority of a love that is "all alike."

The power of hyperbole, the trope chosen by Donne to embody the separateness of love, lies in its forcible straining of the truth and its ability to go beyond truth to express an ideal. Hyperbole, however, can also overshoot its mark and become an empty affectation, undercutting the ideal it is intended to defend. Eminently aware of the dangers inherent in the hyperbole, Donne manages to push each hyperbole in this poem to its limit so that the mistress, the reader, and the sun are convinced of the unsurpassing beauty of the beloved and the sacredness of mutual love.

Another theme found in Donne's love poetry is the juxtaposition of the sacred and the profane, mirroring secular love in divine concepts and expressing spiritual truths by linking them to secular experiences. In "The Sun Rising," the speaker calls the sunbeams "reverend," an adjective that alludes to a level higher than the physical; by analogy, the mistress also takes on more than physical characteristics. The lovers mirror in their mutual love the Incarnation, since in them the world and its material and spiritual values are contained: "All here in one bed lay."

Ultimately, the poem asserts neither that earthly love mirrors heavenly love nor that mutual love that is both physical and spiritual is the only valid perspective on love. The serious portrayal of love in this poem is but part of the rich variety of human experiences that Donne offers readers of his poetry.

Koos Daley

SUN STONE

Author: Octavio Paz (1914-   )
Type of poem: Lyric
First published: 1957, as *Piedra de sol*; *Sun Stone*, 1963

The Poem

The title, *Sun Stone*, refers to the massive calendar stone of the ancient Aztecs. The well-known Aztec calendar measured the synodical period of the planet Venus (the period from one conjunction of the planet Venus with the sun to another). For the ancient Mexicans, Venus was one of the manifestations of the god Quetzalcoatl, the plumed serpent. The calendar begins, as the poem does, at day 4, *Olín* (movement), and ends 584 days (and exactly 584 lines) later at day 4, *Ehécatl* (wind), the conjunction of Venus and the sun: the end of one cycle and the beginning of another. The poem's 584 lines are each composed of eleven syllables (hendecasyllables).

Since the Aztec calendar cycle of fifty-two years always begins with *acatl*, the year of the east, it indicates not only the beginning of the world but also the birth of the sun and the dominance of Quetzalcoatl, who, after he is sacrificed, appears in the east as the morning star. The symbol of the east, then, is one of rebirth and resurrection. The opening (and closing) six lines set the poem's tone by describing the world of nature and its rhythms (life and death, day and night). Into this harmonious world, man, the poem's speaker, and history intrude in the fourth stanza.

Stanzas 4 through 9 are a hymn of praise to the speaker's beloved, in which the woman's physical attributes are described in abstract terms. She is ultimately likened to a rain goddess ("all night you rain, all day/ you open my chest with your fingers of water"). In the concluding stanza of this first hymn, the speaker wanders through the corporeal geography to which he has ascended from his abstractions and returns to the first landscape. Youth, growth, beginnings, dawn, vegetation, and water are all clearly attributes of the east echoed in the poem's opening.

With the stanza beginning at line 67, there is a transition that continues to praise the beloved's body and a parallel continuation of nature imagery. Now, for the first time, nature becomes ominous ("a mountain path/ that ends in an abrupt abyss"). The speaker's shadow, his identity, is shattered, and he tries in vain to recover the fragments.

The next two stanzas focus upon the total disintegration of the speaker's personality. Everything that he sees and touches, everything that he is, evaporates, as does time. In his despair, he declares: "I tread my shadow in search of a moment."

In lines 98 and 99, the speaker continues his search, but with less loneliness and fear. A group of girls is shown leaving school, coming out of "its pink womb," an image suggesting birth. One temporarily unnamed girl is at the center of a litany in the lengthy stanza that follows (lines 109-141). More than representing an individual, however, she becomes a composite of all women.

As the east was the dominant spirit of the introductory section of the poem, the western point of Aztec cosmology is invoked here. The west, known as Cuiatlampa, was the place of women and residence of the goddesses and demigoddesses, including the goddess of childbirth. Octavio Paz uses birth imagery and the nameless girl who represents all women (including Melusine and Persephone) to extend the direction of his Aztec calendar to the west. This section ends, like the section on the east, with a return to the nameless, faceless, and timeless moment (lines 146-152).

Instead of moving to north and south, as might be expected, Paz shifts the main weight of the poem's meaning to the remaining pre-Columbian cardinal (and symbolic) point, the center. This symbolic center in the first half of the poem is evoked through the reduction of the speaker's consciousness to his center, to the awareness of his own effort to understand. This shift to the center is preceded, however, by a disintegration of the perception of the "real" world, involving the speaker's figurative dismemberment: "I pick up my fragments one by one/ and go on, bodiless, searching and groping." The speaker is first led and then destroyed by a feminine figure.

In the stanza headed by line 142, at the quarter point of the poem, an invocation of time occurs that fuses its positive aspects, the goal of the search, with the negative, the impossibility of its attainment. All of time becomes encapsulated into a single moment that the speaker attempts to find, capture, and express.

Time's circularity resumes, after the stanza break between lines 194 and 195, with a further development of its destructive features. The unidentified woman addressed seems to portray the opposite characteristics of the sensual vision of line 41. Instead of being a rescuer from time's forces, she is now the instrument of time's punishment. Addressing her, the speaker says: "and your sharpened words dig out/ my chest and desolate and empty me." The only definable reality is the speaker's awareness of his own awareness: "awareness pierced by an eye/ which sees itself looking at itself until it is annihilated in clarity." The conclusion of the first half of the poem suggests that the speaker has not progressed in his quest, since he continues to be imprisoned by his own awareness — the only successful weapon against time.

In the second half of the poem, the direction of the speaker's experience moves outward rather than inward. Society, rather than the individual psyche, is its main subject. This change is further intensified by the images of violence in the bombing of Madrid. In the midst of this bombardment, a couple seeks security and peace by making love. In this act, they display a process of integration that is in direct contrast with the speaker's earlier disintegration; the couple is united and untouched by time, invulnerable in "a single body and soul."

The experience of love is dominant in the poem's second half; love becomes life's goal. It is the symbolic center that unites the poem's structure. The tone, in contrast to the first half of the poem, is optimistic. Both halves, however, share the speaker's desire to transcend time and reality.

After a catalog of caricatures of professions and types, followed by a long discourse on history that leads to questions about its meaning, it becomes clear that the speaker has reached a philosophical dead end in his search. He abandons a direct treatment of time in the concluding section of the poem and transfers his anguish instead to the meaning of life and the understanding of the individual's place in it. The prayer of the conclusion (beginning with line 533) is anticipated in the summoning of Eloise, Persephone, and Mary (history, mythology, and Christianity) to reveal their true identities so that the speaker may find his.

Ostensibly addressed to a pre-Columbian deity, the prayer is, in its urgency, the most emotionally charged section of the poem. The anguish of the litany stems from the speaker's hope that he (and humankind) may be released from the narrow confines of time. The prayer is granted (lines 574-583), and the speaker enters a paradise, constructed of the intricate water imagery of the poem's final six lines. With the description of the river that is both source and terminus, the poem concludes with an adverb and a colon that promise infinity: "a course of a river that turns, moves on,/ doubles back, and comes full circle,/ forever arriving:"

The colon contributes to the circular structure of the poem by creating the expectation of continuation. If the reader is not aware at first reading that lines 585-590 are repetitions of the first six lines, then the colon dramatically returns him to the beginning.

Forms and Devices

A major feature of *Sun Stone* is its circular structure. The poet achieves this circular structure through his use of language and by drawing upon Mexican tradition, specifically, Aztec mythology. Transcending Mexican history and setting the poem in a universal dimension, time (the poem's theme), like the poem's structure, becomes cyclic. Endings become beginnings, for man and for nature.

The closing of the poem's cycle with line 584, the synodic course of Venus, recalls the connection with the Aztec calendar system. Particularly noteworthy are the five days at the end of the solar year that do not fit into a regular unit and yet somehow must be counted before a new year can begin. In a system otherwise so symmetrical, the Aztecs dreaded these odd days, called *nemontemi*, the "nameless" or "unfortunate" days. Thus, the final five lines of Paz's poem, since they occur outside the final line count as a refrain, draw a comparison with the *nemontemi*.

In Aztec mythology, the world had been destroyed and re-created four times. The entire Aztec cosmology, therefore, was not only elaborately cyclical but also fragile, for the circular movement could be halted at any juncture. Any moment of ending and beginning, of which the concluding lines are a symbol, was regarded with awe and, finally, with a reverence that culminated in the worship of the forces of renewal. This is the same effect achieved by Paz at the end of his poem.

Although the entire Aztec calendar is composed of interlocking cycles, the deity who is most specifically charged with the process of renewal after destruction is Quetzalcoatl. His calendar sign is 4, *Ehécatl* (wind); in his hand, the deity carries the wind jewel, a round section of conch shell with five segments.

The use of Aztec myth at the poem's conclusion to symbolize the forces of destruction and renewal is linked with the intention of the epigraph (a quotation from

the opening lines of the poem "Artémis," by Gérard de Nerval; these lines emphasize the uniqueness of each moment of love and its ever-repeating rhythm, which
returns always renewed—like the planet Venus evoked by Paz), and suggests that
destruction and renewal, like the two halves of the poem that each dominates, are
both separate and identical. The first half of the poem analyzes time and reality
through a process of disintegration; the second half attempts to achieve the same
objective through the opposite process of integration and synthesis. The two halves
of the poem are, therefore, opposite sides of the same reality. The poem's conclusion, which applies to both halves, is that any discernible meaning, whether negative
or positive, must be derived from the process of circularity.

Themes and Meanings

   Sun Stone is essentially a quest or a pilgrimage in which the unnamed speaker
attempts to define his identity. Ostensibly the subject is love, or, more specifically,
the beloved. Transcending the experience of love, however, is the real theme of the
poem: time and its relationship to reality. In describing his own feelings of love and
those of lovers in general, the poem's speaker attempts to describe love in terms of
its transience and permanence, illusion and reality. In the poem, the speaker attacks
the moment and surrounds it in his quest for its permanence—a permanence that he
feels is capable of revealing his true identity to himself.

   Throughout the poem, there are many reminders of time's circularity, which is
both a dilemma and a symbol of disorientation. Whether the present is meaningless
because it is prolonged interminably, or whether events, both personal and historical, lack significance because they are endlessly repeated, the poet's reaction to
time's circularity is summed up in line 498: "each minute is nothing forever." The
first lines of the final stanza express his reaction to the dilemma: "I want to continue,
to go farther, and I cannot:/ the moment plunged into another and another."

   Considered against the backdrop of linear time, which extends itself in measured
units both forward and backward, is the poet's (and the Aztecs') conception of time
as circular. Yet the awareness of the moment that is simultaneously first, last, and
unique brings no resolution, no peace of discovery. On the contrary, it implies to the
poet that there is an ultimate reality, a timeless realm, which he searches for beyond
all other realities, and which is evoked by several experiences of love dramatized in
the second half of the poem. The brief attention that the poet gives to the concept of
the timeless paradise is in inverse relation to its importance as the poem's emotional
goal, which is defined in the penultimate stanza (lines 562-570). Above all other
descriptions of time in the poem, this one holds the most abiding hope of a final
fulfillment.

Genevieve Slomski

SUNDAY MORNING

Author: Wallace Stevens (1879-1955)
Type of poem: Meditation
First published: 1915; revised in *Harmonium*, 1923

The Poem

In its final form, "Sunday Morning" consists of eight self-contained, fifteen-line strophes, written in Wallace Stevens' customary version of blank verse. The speaker's meditation on life, death, and change is presented through a description of a woman who prefers the world of the senses to "The holy hush of ancient sacrifice" associated with religious practice, but who is not really sure that she can be satisfied with temporary delights.

The stage is set with a description of the woman's Sunday morning, when the effects of vibrant colors and relaxation are dissipated by the call of religious services. The poet, however, questions why the woman should be distracted from her enjoyment of life by a religion that is available "Only in silent shadows and in dreams." Rejecting the pallid consolations of spiritual belief, the speaker says that she must find divinity "within herself."

In the third strophe, Stevens evokes Jove as a representative of the inhuman gods of ancient religious belief. Jesus, because he was partly human, was a step forward but not the final stage in the evolution of divinity. Humans should recognize that their own divinity should be enough, since it is the only thing upon which they can finally rely. If they accept that there is nothing beyond this world, they will be able to enjoy the world for what it is: "The sky will be much friendlier then than now// Not this dividing and indifferent blue."

The woman speaks in the fourth and fifth strophes, saying that although she finds contentment in earthly beauty, she still needs "some imperishable bliss." The poet responds that permanence is not only impossible, it is also unnatural and undesirable. The fifth and sixth strophes use vivid imagery to present the major theme that "Death is the mother of beauty" and that impermanence is essential to the human ability to perceive beauty.

The final sections of "Sunday Morning" present images conveying what the poet regards as proper celebrations of the bonds between humans and the natural world. In the last strophe, the woman hears a voice that denies the divinity of Jesus, and the poem ends with the poet's final evocation of the transitory beauties of the world.

Forms and Devices

"Sunday Morning" is composed of self-contained strophes, all of the same length; the order of the final version is different from that of the poem's original form. The basic line in all Stevens' longer poems is a solemn and somewhat heavy blank verse, employing iambic pentameter and making use of echoing sounds rather than end rhyme. In the second strophe, for example, successive lines begin with the words "Passions," "Grievings," "Elations," and "Emotions." At several points in the poem, the verse has a majestic quality and an intensity that are used to emphasize the strength of the poem's message. This is especially the case in the final seven lines of the poem, where deer, the whistling cry of quail, and the sweetness of ripening berries represent the attractions of the natural world.

"Sunday Morning" makes much use of assertions and rhetorical questions that are designed to cast doubt on the validity of traditional religious belief. The poem, however, presents its message primarily through imagery, much of it evoking bright colors, movement, and vivid tastes and smells to provide a contrast to the dimness and insubstantiality of spiritual appeals. Death, as it brings "sure obliteration," is an active and positive force, imaged through verbs such as "strews," "shiver," and "stray impassioned." Passion and other strong emotions are possible only because one knows that life is only temporary. The description of a human ritual in the seventh section makes use of energetic images: "Supple and turbulent," "boisterous," "savage."

On the other hand, in an imagined paradise, there is "no change of death," but only rivers that never reach the sea, ripe fruit that never falls from trees; the images associated with religion and dreams of an afterlife are sinister and lifeless: "haunt of prophecy" and "old chimera of the grave."

Stevens' fondness for obscure words and unusual phrasings is less marked in "Sunday Morning" than in many of his other poems, but it is evident in such words as "chimera" or "mythy," in the opening phrase ("Complacencies of the peignoir"), and in the following lines from the final strophe: "Or old dependency of day and night,/ Or island solitude, unsponsored, free,/ Of that wide water, inescapable." There are few similes in the poem, and most of the metaphors are subtle, such as the use of "measures" in the second section to suggest both musical divisions and ways of measuring.

Stevens, however, makes considerable use of personification, not only by ironically imaging death as an active force, but also by giving being to emotions such as sorrow and passion. In some places, he deliberately uses archaic words and phrases to suggest that religious belief is out of date: "such requital to desire," for example, or the lines "Neither the golden underground, nor isle/ Melodious, where spirits gat them home."

Themes and Meanings

Stevens' lifelong conviction that poetry and poets must take the place of religion and priests to provide form and meaning for human life is implicit in "Sunday Morning," not explicit, as it would become in his later poetry. "Sunday Morning," however, does clear the way for those poems, and it establishes basic themes that Stevens would employ in all of his subsequent work.

The most important of these themes is the idea that human perception of beauty requires the recognition that everything earthly is temporary. Everyone will die, everything will change; permanence must be recognized as an illusion. Christianity,

Judaism, or any religion promising permanence is false because it envisions a paradise that is something like our earth but without the inherent changes in earth's life and circumstance.

This does not mean that religious emotion must be stifled, only that it must find a more appropriate outlet. This new form is presented in the seventh strophe, and it amounts to the worship of nature and the integral connection between humans and the rest of the natural world. The men in this image, dancing in an orgy, celebrate the sun as the natural source of life, present with them, and the tune they chant is composed of the objects in the world around them.

At the time he wrote "Sunday Morning," Stevens had not yet developed fully the idea that all systems of order are necessarily fictions, fulfilling a need all humans have for fictions that will make life seem comprehensible. Since religion, in his view, had failed to provide a meaningful order, poetry would have to do so. This idea would receive extended treatment in works such as *Notes Toward a Supreme Fiction* (1942). While celebrating "chaos," "Sunday Morning" also anticipates the later theme by suggesting that aspects of religion, such as worship and ritual, are important to human existence.

"Sunday Morning" has remained one of Stevens' best-known poems. Written at the beginning of his career as a poet, this poem introduces the themes that would dominate his verse, and it establishes a unique poetic manner. It is most memorable, finally, for its vivid use of color and action imagery and for its romantic evocation of the natural world.

John M. Muste

A SUPERMARKET IN CALIFORNIA

Author: Allen Ginsberg (1926-   )
Type of poem: Narrative
First published: 1956, in *Howl and Other Poems*

The Poem

"A Supermarket in California" is a short poem in free verse, its twelve lines divided into three stanzas. The title suggests a bland setting—not the expected source of a poem. The title and setting prove ironic, however, as Allen Ginsberg demonstrates that for most people in America, exploration goes no further than the local grocery store.

The poem is written in the first person, which is typical of Ginsberg's work; he writes very personally of his visions and experiences in America. Ginsberg is speaking in the first person not only to share his immediate sensuous experiences but also to invoke, by using this perspective, the American poet in whose footsteps he is attempting to walk: Walt Whitman.

In fact, Ginsberg speaks directly to Whitman in the poem's first line as he wearily trudges down the streets of suburban California, "self-conscious looking at the full moon . . . shopping for images." He enters a bright "neon fruit supermarket" (line 2) as if here he might find the same image of America—the diversity and freedom, the limitless, democratic possibilities—that Whitman saw. What he sees in the market, however, is only the multitude of fruit and the families shopping together as if this were the richest experience they could share.

At the end of stanza 1, Ginsberg also spies the twentieth century Spanish poet Federico García Lorca standing by the watermelons. The sighting of García Lorca—a homosexual like Ginsberg and, many suspect, Whitman—creates a smooth transition to stanza 2, where Ginsberg chides Whitman for "eyeing the grocery boys" (line 4). In his mind he hears Whitman asking mundane questions about food prices, about "who killed the pork chops," and if anyone will be his "Angel"—that is, will follow him (line 5). There is no response, but Ginsberg continues following the elder poet past aisles of canned goods, perhaps trailed by the store detective, who has noted Ginsberg's suspicious appearance.

Stanza 2 ends with the poets tasting delicacies along the way but buying nothing. At the beginning of the final stanza, they find themselves with no place to go, since in an hour, when the store closes, they will be given their freedom again. Ginsberg looks to Whitman for advice and direction, and even "touches" Whitman's book (presumably *Leaves of Grass*, 1855) for inspiration.

He gets no response and thus finds himself out on the "solitary streets," with the "lights out in the houses," where he and Whitman will "both be lonely" (line 10). He asks if it is possible that their walk will be a pleasant memory of "the lost America of love" (line 11), meaning the freer, untamed America of Whitman's day, since, as he notes, they will also have to walk past the same blue cars in the same driveways, house after house. The poem ends on a note of despair as Ginsberg asserts that when Whitman's journey ended, he found himself by the mythical waters of Lethe, one of the rivers in Hades. "What America did you have then," he asks Whitman, and since the poem began in the first-person singular and shifted to the plural in stanzas 2 and 3, as if the two are journeying together, he seems to be including himself in this haunting question.

Forms and Devices

What is most noticeable about the form of "A Supermarket in California" is its free verse, which again alludes to Whitman, the founder of the free verse style. Ginsberg even more closely associates himself with Whitman by exploiting the complexity of the structure and rhythm of this form. Whitman's famous self-referential poem "Song of Myself" (1855) is the particular model for Ginsberg, as both poems employ convoluted sentence structures and lines that cannot be contained within the typeset of one line on the typical printed page.

Each line of "A Supermarket in California" "contains multitudes," as Whitman said of himself in "Song of Myself" (line 1326). For example, the first line invokes Whitman himself, sets the poem down on a suburban street in America, describes the speaker as having a "headache," being "self-conscious," and looking at "the full moon," which, though traditionally a sign of lunacy, functions even better here to contrast with the artificial "neon" light of the supermarket in the next line. Outdoor America is easily traversed, an opposite notion to Whitman's idea and to the reality of America in the nineteenth century.

The third line also supports this premise as it speaks of various fruits, families spending time shopping, and finally the homosexual poet García Lorca. By using García Lorca, Ginsberg points to two clear distinctions between the average American and the poets mentioned: the poets' confusion and despair over the loss of the art and beauty of unspoiled America and their sense of alienation at deviating from the sexual norm of America.

Rhythmically, "A Supermarket in California" also matches "Song of Myself" through the use of opening repetition. Each of the first three lines of stanza 2 begins with the first-person-singular pronoun followed by an active verb: "I saw you, Walt Whitman . . . ;/ I heard you asking questions . . . ;/ I wandered in and out." The last line of that stanza, while switching to first-person plural, only varies the same pattern: "we strode down the open corridors." This rhythmic pattern works as well in the last stanza through Ginsberg's questioning of Whitman, similar to Whitman's questioning of his readers in "Song of Myself": "Where are we going . . . ;/ Will we walk all night . . . ;/ Will we stroll dreaming." The repetition of certain patterns serves as an incantation in which Ginsberg tries to break the spell that suburban, homogeneous America has on its citizenry.

Finally, the supermarket is an obvious metaphor for Ginsberg's view of the final product of what Whitman had seen as the great promise of America's vast, unexplored frontier. The age of exploration in nineteenth century America pushed the frontier to the Pacific Ocean. Whitman advocated following America's paths and thereby exploring and finding oneself—one's imaginative and spiritual potential. All Ginsberg has found at the end of the frontier is a neon-lit supermarket full of people who seem to have nowhere else to go or who have lost the drive to explore. Thus, the potential of America has been transformed, or has "progressed" to that of easy shopping.

Themes and Meanings

Ginsberg uses Whitman and his "Song of Myself" as an ironic counterpoint to "A Supermarket in California," though the irony is shaded by Ginsberg's remorse for himself, Whitman, and America. For Ginsberg, America in the twentieth century has reneged on its promise of opportunity, freedom, and liberty. Where Whitman in the nineteenth century found and celebrated diversity in the American people, as he sings in "Song of Myself," Ginsberg finds only homogeneity. Where Whitman saw an endless horizon of land to explore—the pageant of the American landscape—Ginsberg sees only "solitary streets," houses with their lights out, "blue automobiles in driveways," and "the neon fruit supermarket."

Thus the images of America that Ginsberg sees are not the ones he is "shopping for." This town and supermarket exist everywhere in the United States, each market and each town, in their design and emphasis on materialism, trying to keep up with all the others. America's melting pot has become an all too grim reality.

Try as America might to obscure its differences—its variety of people and their desires, ambitions—it cannot hide all of its parts. The very fact that poets such as Whitman, García Lorca, and Ginsberg, who have deviated from the norm sexually as well as artistically, exist testifies to this truth. That Ginsberg still wants to write about America, even in lamentation, indicates the emotional attachment and investment he has made in the country, as well as the force with which he has believed in Whitman's dream. No matter how hard the mainstream tries to homogenize and tame the wild, "barbaric yawp" (as Whitman put it) within us, Ginsberg and others continue to sound it out loud and strong.

In the final stanza, though, he is faced with the troubling question of where to go to find his joy and inspire his innermost being. His remorse for himself, Whitman, and America surfaces in the parenthesis of this stanza when he "touches" Whitman's "book" (*Leaves of Grass*). Instead of being comforted and inspired, as Whitman intends in "Song of Myself" when he tells his readers not to fear taking the journey through America, for he (Whitman) will go with them, Ginsberg can only think of his "absurd" walk through the supermarket, perhaps followed by the store detective who is a symbol of the watchful eye of the nation's conformity. As he leaves Whitman in Hades at the poem's end, asking the "lonely old courage-teacher, what America/ did you have" then, one suspects that ultimately Ginsberg believes that he is the one who is left alone on the shore of "the black waters of Lethe."

Terry Barr

SWEENEY AMONG THE NIGHTINGALES

Author: T. S. Eliot (1888-1965)
Type of poem: Lyric
First published: 1918; collected in *Poems*, 1920

The Poem

"Sweeney Among the Nightingales" is a modernist lyric poem of forty lines, divided into ten quatrains and focusing on Sweeney, a brutish modern man in the company of disreputable women ("nightingales") in a café (also perhaps a brothel) at night. The poem ranks with the finest of T. S. Eliot's early poetry, as the author himself wrote to his brother, Henry, when it was later included in *Poems* (1920): "Some of the new poems, the Sweeney ones, especially 'Among the Nightingales' and 'Burbank' are intensely serious, and I think these two are among the best that I have ever done. But even here I am considered by the ordinary Newspaper critic as a Wit or satirist, and in America I suppose I shall be thought merely disgusting."

"Sweeney Among the Nightingales" is very much a serious commentary on the paltriness and insensitivity of modern humanity by comparison with the tragic grandeur and mighty passion of ancient heroes such as Agamemnon, who headed the Greek conquest of Troy and who returned home to die violently by his own wife's hand. Elements of satire and comedy are present to teach, through muted ridicule, a genuine disgust for the coarseness and coldness of the modern sensibility as personified by Sweeney and the equally detached call girls and owner of the café.

In the title, the nightingales connote prostitutes around Sweeney but also refer to a Greek tale about the transformation of lust into mythic beauty: Philomela, who was ravished and had her tongue cut out by her sister's husband, King Tereus, wove the story of the rape into a tapestry that she sent to her sister, Procne. In revenge, Queen Procne served her own son as a stew for the unsuspecting king to eat. Just as the enraged Tereus was about to kill the fleeing sisters, the pitying gods transmuted Philomela into a lovely swallow, Procne into a beautiful nightingale, and Tereus into an ugly hawk.

The poem's Greek epigraph, from Aeschylus' *Agamemnon* (458 B.C.), "ah, I am struck a deadly blow and deep within," is the first of two cries by King Agamemnon as his wife, Clytemnestra, stabs him to death in his bath while throwing robes over his dying body.

The animality of Sweeney and his tipsy female companions, frolicking distrustfully in a café, is unredeemed by any mythic transformation or tragic elevation. In myth or legend, lust-ridden violence was resolved in mythic beauty (as in the tale of Philomela and Procne) or by divine justice (at the end of Aeschylus' *Oresteia*, 458 B.C.); here, it has degenerated to crude and trifling gestures of estrangement and indifference between the modern sexes. Apelike Sweeney's facial features have a sinfully bestained ("maculate") and bizarre animality that are even uglier than Tereus' transformation into a hideous bird. Unlike the pitiful ebbing of Agamemnon's strength and life from his wife's dagger blows, Sweeney's sprawling posture betrays only a careless eroticism (lines 1-4). Sweeney's sexually inviting sprawl becomes a trap for a woman who falls from his lap to the floor; she falls with absolute indifference (line 11-16).

Sweeney, the modern man, is as benighted as the beclouded, moonlit sky that obscures his vision of great myths surrounding death, the constellations Orion (the hunter) and "the Dog" (the hunter's dog), and the gates of horn in Hades, through which accurate dreams and prophecies ascended to mortals. He stands outside the gates of underworld prophecy, living in a becalmed sterility of "hushed" and "shrunken seas."

There is an absence of connectedness among the café's customers. Sprawling Sweeney, an effete low-life vertebrate, stiffens sexually but musters only enough energy to decline the call girl's "gambit," or sexual overture, because he is distrustful of a conspiracy between two women, one of whom is a degenerate version of the biblical Rachel who apes Clytemnestra's murderous gesture by tearing café fruit (lines 16-28). Instead, Sweeney walks outside and stands apart, looking in with a stupid grin, as the host and another customer converse in indifference and detachment. All these people are estranged, aimless, and oblivious to the great myths of pagan transmutation (the singing nightingales), Christian resurrection (reverenced at the nearby "Convent of the Sacred Heart"), ritual regeneration (ancient sacrificial killings of old priests by their successors in the "bloody wood" of Nemi), and divine justice. All these myths revolve around a pattern of sacrifice and ultimate exaltation sorely missing in a feckless, mundane modernity.

Forms and Devices

The stylistic devices of "Sweeney Among the Nightingales" are typical of Eliot's best early poetry, culminating in *The Waste Land* (1922), and relate to modernist literary conventions that he popularized and developed from Metaphysical and Symbolist traditions of poetry in, respectively, the early seventeenth and late nineteenth centuries.

No simple label describes Eliot's early poetry. He consciously rebelled against what he termed the "dissociation of sensibility" — the supposed breakdown of a fusion of intellect, emotion, and imagination in poetic creation — since John Milton's time and especially under the flabby subjectivity of early Romantic authors. Eliot reacted with a demand for a Metaphysical wit (a sharp conceit or alert poetic consciousness apprehending the many-sidedness of anything), for dense allusiveness (embracing all cultural history as a backdrop for modernity), and for telling irony (contrasting past grandeur and present squalor, ancient myth and modern mediocrity).

Eliot saw in the Metaphysical poets of seventeenth century England a fusion of intellect and feeling and sought to capture this fusion in a conceit such as the image of a disgustingly lax modern Sweeney aping the tragic posture of dying Agamemnon as strength and life ebb from the king's body ("Apeneck Sweeney spreads his knees/ Letting his arms hang down to laugh").

Eliot was drawn also to the ideas of Théophile Gautier (1811-1872), who aspired to a poetry of highly wrought artifice and impersonality, devoted to artistic beauty for its own sake (*l'art pour l'art*) and devoid of bourgeois utilitarian didacticism. Most of these traits can be found in "Sweeney Among the Nightingales," except that Eliot seeks less an aesthetic escapism for beauty's sake and more a classical perspective on the mundane ugliness of modernity.

Coming later, the French Symbolists cultivated an aristocratic impersonality, intense craftsmanship, and a care for precise imagery and suggestiveness in a poem's words as they combine to create new sensations and meanings not communicated by the individual words themselves. The combination of precision, symbolic suggestion, and ironic mockery found in a witty, urbane speaker in the poetry of Jules Laforgue (1860-1887), for example, directly anticipated Eliot's early style.

"Sweeney Among the Nightingales" is a highly crafted work written in chiselled iambic tetrameter quatrains (end-rhyming in the second and fourth lines), containing alliteration and assonance and some very compressed metaphors (such as an implicit comparison of Sweeney to a giraffe, an odd animal stained or "maculate" with sin). There are precise imagery and a compressed suggestiveness of meaning springing from repeated juxtapositions of words and phrases; the juxtapositions lend a descriptive vividness and a mythically rich range of allusion that embrace a broad cross-section of Western cultural experience as a backdrop for Sweeney, the modern swain (and swine), who is a dime-store degradation of the legendary King Agamemnon.

As Eliot wrote in "Tradition and the Individual Talent" (1919), the modern poet must surround his subject matter with a revealing historical sense of past tradition: "[T]he historical sense compels a man to write not merely with his own generation in his bones, but with a feeling that the whole of the literature of Europe from Homer and within it the whole of the literature of his own country has a simultaneous existence and composes a simultaneous order" for the modern chaos of the poet's subject matter. With its Homeric-Aeschylean frame of reference, "Sweeney Among the Nightingales" could have been written with this passage in Eliot's mind.

Themes and Meanings

"Sweeney Among the Nightingales" is about the depraved coldness, callousness, and cowardice of modern life as embodied in Sweeney's uneventful encounter with two call girls in a sleazy café setting. Sweeney's evasion of an assignation is ironically compared to mighty Agamemnon's tragic confrontation with a wife of legendary infamy.

The poem demonstrates Eliot's characteristic method of presenting his meaning through multiple parallels and contrasts. There are complex ironies and analogies generated between the comically inconclusive seduction of Sweeney in a nonheroic present and the tragic but regenerative violence against Agamemnon, mythological Philomela and Procne, and Christ, the crucified redeemer of humankind. In heroic times, lust, betrayal, and violence sprang from passions of love or hate and became embodied in meaningful myths of sacrifice and redemptive transformation. The shabby animality of Sweeney, however, eluding the conspiratorial advances of tipsy call girls in a café-brothel, is unrelieved by any such epic significance, sacrifice, or regeneration.

Despite the multiplicity of mythic allusions in the poem, Eliot's ironic conception of Sweeney (a Celtic surname in keeping with Eliot's condescending view of a slovenly, sensual Irishman) depends principally upon two conflated classical descriptions of Agamemnon in Homer's *Odyssey* (c. 800 B.C.) and Aeschylus' *Agamemnon*. According to the *Odyssey*, Ulysses in his descent to Hades meets Agamemnon, who recounts his slaying at a banquet table: "You have seen many die in single combat or in battle, but never one who died as we did, by the wine bowl and the loaded tables in a hall where the floor flowed with blood. Cassandra's death-shriek rang in my ears as she fell. Clytemnestra slew her over my body. I tried to lift up my hands for her, but they fell back. I was dying then." Eliot modernizes this Homeric account in an ironically mundane fashion by having Sweeney sit at a fruit-filled café table with a futile sprawling gesture of relaxed arms, letting a latter-day Cassandra fall to the floor.

Imposed on the Homeric account is the Aeschylean portrayal of the climactic death scene in *Agamemnon*, in which Cassandra, the captive Trojan prophetess and mistress of Agamemnon, prophesies the king's murder and her own slaying, but to no avail: "Oh for the nightingale's pure song and a fate like hers. With fashion of beating wings the gods clothed her about and a sweet life gave her and without lamentation. But mine is the sheer edge of the tearing dagger" (lines 1146-1149). Cassandra's cry for a different destiny is the inspiration for Eliot's own poem, which is the ironic inversion of the "nightingale's pure song" and is similarly dependent on the Philomela legend for a contrasting mythic perspective on the action at hand.

Aeschylus' Agamemnon is compared to a lion, dies with rich robes thrown over him by his wife, and falls with legs buckling under him, as vengeful Clytemnestra calls him a philandering "plaything of all the golden girls of Ilium" worthy of lying beside his slain mistress Cassandra in bloody death. Eliot's Sweeney is compared to odder animals; he, too, relaxes his body muscles — if not in death, then in an uneasy assignation with the woman who falls off his lap. Another woman harmlessly reenacts Clytemnestra's violent tearing motion, as the "liquid siftings" of Agamemnon's torrential bloodletting "stain the stiff dishonored shroud" (lines 38-40) spread over him in the bath by Clytemnestra.

Thus, classical prototypes provide a rich and pervasive mythic texture for "Sweeney Among the Nightingales," down to the most minute details of Eliot's description of characters, gestures, situations, and setting. Indeed, Sweeney's innocuous café food of "oranges,/ Bananas figs and hothouse grapes" possibly reverberates with ironic overtones of the horrid cannibalistic fare served in the two principal myths underlying the poem. In the Philomela myth, Procne turned her son into a stew for tyrannical Tereus to consume. As part of the Agamemnon legend, the father

Atreus had a brother dine on his own two sons in imitation of the crime of Tantalus, their ultimate ancestor. For Tantalus committed the sin of trying to trick the gods into eating his son and thereby cursed the entire family line down through Agamemnon.

Sweeney's café fruit is a pale counterpart of the sumptuous repast denied Tantalus in Hades in retaliation for the horrible human meal offered the gods. Tantalus is doomed to eternal hunger in Hades by being deprived of "pears, and pomegranates, and apple trees with their bright fruit, and sweet figs, and luxuriant olives above his head" (*Odyssey*, XI: 582-592). Sweeney is one of Eliot's modern antiheroes who parodies classical prototypes for an ironic portrayal of mediocrity and meaninglessness in the present.

Thomas M. Curley

THE TABLES TURNED

Author: William Wordsworth (1770-1850)
Type of poem: Lyric
First published: 1798, in *Lyrical Ballads*

The Poem

"The Tables Turned" is subtitled "An Evening Scene on the Same Subject," indicating that it forms a pair with the poem published immediately ahead of it in *Lyrical Ballads*, "Expostulation and Reply." A reader should understand one to understand the other.

In "Expostulation and Reply," William Wordsworth's friend Matthew, finding the poet sitting on a stone, urges him to quit dreaming and to read those books through which the wisdom of the past sheds essential light on the problems of the present. William replies that while he sits quietly, he feels the force of "Powers" which give his mind a "wise passiveness." By implication, this passiveness is more precious than the knowledge that can be gained by reading.

"The Tables Turned" is a short lyric poem of thirty-two lines arranged in eight stanzas. It takes the form of an address by a speaker (who most readers will agree is Wordsworth himself) to a friend, the Matthew of "Expostulation and Reply." The scene is presumably that of the other poem ("by Esthwaite lake") in England's Lake District; by its subtitle, "An Evening Scene on the Same Subject," one may assume that the events of the poem take place later in the same day.

Wordsworth metaphorically turns the tables on his friend, for this time it is Wordsworth who makes the confrontation. The poet's general argument has not changed: The mind is much better off when it responds to the influences of nature than when it takes on intellectual tasks. The central concern of the poem is to develop this contrast and this argument.

In stanza 1, Wordsworth forcefully yet playfully urges Matthew to stand "Up! up!" lest he "grow double" in the "toil and trouble" of reading. In stanza 2, the poet paints a picture of the glories to be seen in nature as the sun appears above a mountain and gives the "long green fields" their "sweet evening yellow." From stanza 3 on, nature is embodied specifically in the sounds of birdcalls in the woods — the music of the linnet and the "blithe" song of the throstle (or thrush).

Wordsworth is interested in more than simply giving the reader specific images of nature, however; most of the poem is given over to an argument. The "dull and endless strife" of reading books, the preachers' wisdom they contain, and even the "ready wealth" they may bring are not so sweet and wise as a bird's song. The argument becomes more intense in stanzas 7 and 8, where the poet's objections to books widen to include most kinds of knowledge found in books, especially that "barren" knowledge which comes from rational (perhaps scientific) analysis, by which "Our meddling intellect/ Misshapes the beauteous forms of things—/ We murder to dissect."

In contrast, Wordsworth urges Matthew, "Let Nature be your teacher" by responding to bird songs, by deriving "Spontaneous wisdom" from them in a state, not of dull toil, but of "health" and "cheerfulness." The poet states his program for wisdom in stanza 6: "One impulse from a vernal wood/ May teach you more of man,/ Of moral evil and of good,/ Than all the sages can." Because this is so, Wordsworth ends his poem in stanza 8 by calling on his friend to "come forth" from his books with an alert heart ready to receive nature's lessons.

Forms and Devices

"The Tables Turned" contains eight quatrains of a specific kind; they are "ballad stanzas." Such a stanza generally has four lines of alternately eight and six syllables, which rhyme *abab*. Many of the poems published in *Lyrical Ballads* are written in this kind of verse. This was the stanza in which many folk ballads were composed, so to choose to write in it signaled that a poet was departing from the usual poetic form of the eighteenth century, the heroic couplet.

The poem begins playfully. The poet remonstrates with Matthew, calling forth a fanciful image of his friend's growing double over his books with a witty implication that he is behaving like, and perhaps coming to resemble, the witches in William Shakespeare's *Macbeth* (1606), with his "toil and trouble." The next three or four stanzas are also light in mood. The poet continues to use the imperative voice to call upon his friend to come away from books, and he uses most of the poem's vivid visual images in so doing. Most of the poem's few metaphors (bird as preacher, nature as teacher) occur in stanza 4. In each, the amount of semi-serious and abstract assertion increases: from none in stanza 2 to almost all of stanza 5.

In the climax of the poem, stanzas 6 and 7, the reader finds almost no images, no metaphors. The poet is serious, not urgent or playful. Stanza 6 states the positive side of Wordsworth's argument. Its language has a grand and prophetic simplicity; its rhythm is appropriately regular and calmly emphatic. Stanza 7 states the negative: It is more cacophonous, irregular in rhythm, and polysyllabic than stanza 6. Its final line ("We murder to dissect") is the poem's most forceful in meaning and most dramatic in presentation. The poem ends on a somewhat less intense but hopeful note, as it returns to the imperative to call Matthew forth and to define how he will attain the insights the poet has described.

Themes and Meanings

When Wordsworth chose to employ the ballad stanza, he not only broke with the poetic practice of serious English poetry of the past, he also implied that he held new values. If those values were not (at least in this poem) the values of common folk, they were at least quite different from those common to educated persons in the eighteenth century.

Matthew, the representative of older values, has been identified in part with William Taylor, Wordsworth's boyhood schoolmaster. Wordsworth once said that this and the poem that preceded it "arose out of conversation with a friend" (possibly

William Hazlitt) "who was somewhat unreasonably attached to modern books of Moral Philosophy."

It is precisely the kind of ideas about moral philosophy found in books that Wordsworth attacks in this poem. In the all-important sixth stanza, Wordsworth asserts that when a person is affected by a perception of beauty in the natural world in springtime ("an impulse from a vernal wood" — a bird song), that person is made immediately and intuitively sensitive to what is good and what is evil. This kind of moral intuition is more to be trusted than judgments made on the bases of philosophical systems.

The seventh stanza describes what such systems do. They reject what can be learned from the pleasing ("sweet") impulses of nature ("the lore which Nature brings"). Instead, these systems encourage the mind ("Our meddling intellect") to analyze ("dissect") the "beauteous forms of things." This last phrase is somewhat vague; presumably the mind attempts to analyze not only the beautiful impulses from nature but human actions as well. In either case, before the mind can analyze, it must kill: "We murder to dissect." The action of the logical mind destroys what it touches and defeats its own purpose of discovering moral principles.

Wordsworth criticizes how the logical mind operates upon moral questions. Some readers also take the powerful statements in stanza 7 to apply to the analytical mind in all of its operations. Although elsewhere he expresses different opinions, here Wordsworth seems to have much in common with other Romantic poets, who generally valued imaginative understanding much higher than logical and rational thought.

George Soule

TAR

Author: C. K. Williams (1936-   )
Type of poem: Narrative
First published: 1983, in *Tar*

The Poem

"Tar" is a poem divided into three stanzas, set around the poet's own experience of the Three Mile Island nuclear-reactor accident. In March, 1979, this accident threw many people around the nation (and especially people in Pennsylvania, where the poet lived and where the reactor is located) into a state of alarm over the danger of a full-scale nuclear meltdown that would have unleashed a cloud of deadly radioactive gases over a wide area.

As the poem begins, the juxtaposition of the nuclear accident, mentioned in the first line, with the workmen who are mentioned in the second line seems incongruous, and, in fact, it seems to be this incongruity that has attracted C. K. Williams' attention. He talks about wandering out to watch the men at work to distract himself from the news that he spent most of the night watching.

As the poem progresses in the second stanza, as the official denials of danger from the nuclear-reactor accident seem to him more confused and less trustworthy, and as he sees that the work the men do on his roof is "harrowingly dangerous," watching the roofers and their work becomes not so much a way of avoiding thinking about the nuclear accident as a way of confronting it. That is, the dangerous work of reshingling his roof becomes a metaphor for the precariousness of living in the nuclear age.

By the third stanza, the events of this day have convinced him of the inevitability of a disastrous nuclear mishap. "We'd understood," he says, "we were going to perish of all this . . . if not soon, then someday." As the narrator—who is clearly Williams himself—reflects on the whole incident, he tries to understand why these roofers stay so clear in his mind, while the rest of the events have become such a haze to him. Not only did the glitter of the metal they were working with stay in his mind, but the carats of tar that formed in the gutter, "so black they seemed to suck the light out of the air," became for him an appropriately threatening image of the fear he felt that day, and the graffiti— "obscenities and hearts" —that the children in the neighborhood write with these pieces of tar stays in his mind as an expression of the chaos of this experience.

As becomes clear in the first stanza, when Williams discusses watching the news for long hours, the terror of an accident like this happening nearby is amorphous and hard to grip mentally. By the end of the poem, however, he realizes that his memory has found a form for this terror by selecting images of the whole experience, especially the images of the workmen.

Forms and Devices

C. K. Williams is known for a narrative style of poetry that has an organic and almost casual sound to it. A poem such as "Tar" (and most of the poems in the collection of the same name) does not force language into self-consciously "poetic" forms. Instead, it tries to shape a poem out of the rhythms of natural-sounding speech.

The careful reader, however, will not let the casual sound of the language lull him or her into overlooking the careful shaping of the poem. Although true to Williams' style of poetry, the central metaphor, in which he thinks of the Three Mile Island accident in terms of the work that was done on his roof that day, is not presented self-consciously as a metaphor, but rather as a coincidence; this metaphor constitutes the heart of the poem. When the narrator says he never realized how "matter-of-factly and harrowingly dangerous" it is, he is referring literally to the work of tarring and shingling a roof, but there is also a clear figurative level being worked out on which he is referring not only to how dangerous nuclear plants are, specifically, but also to how dangerous life in the nuclear age is.

The things that make the work on the roof particularly dangerous are the decaying materials, the rusty nails that have to be pulled out, the under-roofing that crumbles under the weight of a workman, and the old furnace that is kept burning to heat the tar. The extent to which he sees the crumbling of these fairly simple tools and materials as stand-ins for the nuclear power plant becomes clear when a "dense, malignant smoke shoots up" from the furnace, reminding him of the danger of radioactive gases being released from the nuclear core of the Three Mile Island plant. The furnace is adjusted rather crudely by a workman hitting it with a hammer.

When the poet looks inside the heated tar pot, he sees a "Dantean broth" and compares the tar to the images of hell presented in *Inferno* (c. 1320). The bubbling tar looks bland, almost like licorice, in the crucible in which it is cooked, but when spilled, it "sears, and everything is permeated." Again, the comparison to the "crucible" within the power plant is clear; the water that is used both to cool the nuclear core and to convey the tremendous amount of heat it takes to operate the turbines in the plant is innocuous so long as it is kept contained. If this water were to be spilled as radioactive steam, however, it, like spilled tar, would permeate and contaminate everything around it,

The middle stanza ends when the men go to lunch, leaving the air above the roof "alive with shimmers and mirages." Literally, Williams is referring to the shimmer of heat rising from the hot tar on the roof, but this image also completes the comparison the stanza has been developing by implicitly referring to the cooling tower of the Three Mile Island plant, which, in news reports of the accident, was prominently displayed giving off heat and radioactivity.

Themes and Meanings

Although the themes of the poem are developed throughout, it is in the third stanza especially that they are brought into the forefront. When the poet says that by the afternoon "we'd understood:/ we were going to perish of all this, if not now . . . then someday," it is clear that the image of the battered furnace boiling a "Dantean broth" and spewing "malignant smoke" into the atmosphere has become more than a metaphor for the potentially lethal technology of the Three Mile Island plant. This furnace and the nuclear accident happening not far away are both images for him of the precariousness of life in late twentieth century America.

For a moment, he has a clear and bleak vision of a future generation cursing "our earthly comforts . . . our surfeits and submissions." That is, the demand for earthly comforts will eventually lead to the destruction of the planet when the increasingly complicated technology that has been developed to sustain an American life-style rich with such comforts backfires.

The mention of "the president in his absurd protective booties, looking absolutely unafraid, the fool," is a reference to a tour of the plant that President Jimmy Carter took when the crisis was winding down but was by no means over. Some frequently re-printed photographs of this tour showed Carter wearing no special protective clothing other than some protective footwear, but smiling and looking confident. Within this poem, Williams seems to see the president's confidence as a part of the larger social machinery that is malfunctioning. Rather than facing the danger with an examination of the larger social forces that have led to such a breakdown, the president responded with a display of confidence that Williams clearly thinks was misplaced.

The most vivid image the poet retains from this incident is of the workmen "silvered with glitter from the shingles, clinging like starlings beneath the eaves." Calling a comparison of the workmen to birds "clinging . . . beneath the eaves" the most vivid image of this incident suggests that the relative helplessness of birds who try to find a home in a building they have no real power or control over is, to Williams, a situation akin to the dilemma of residents of twentieth century America who live in a society that is reliant upon technologies that most people can neither understand nor control.

The image with which the poem actually ends, "obscenities and hearts" scribbled with hardened lumps of tar on sidewalks by the children in the neighborhood, has a number of meanings. On a very basic level, this is a reassuring image, in that the lightheartedness of children scrawling graffiti is something of a relief from the heavier images and issues with which the poem has been dealing; even after a crisis such as this, one might read the poem as saying, children will be children. Coming as it does at the end of a poem called "Tar," however, this image of "obscenities and hearts" being scribbled with lumps of tar "so black they seemed to suck the light out of the air" takes on additional meaning. Williams seems to be suggesting that one danger of such a baffling crisis is that such things as scrawled obscenities can seem to be the only possible response, and the very magnitude of the crisis can make any other response seem reduced to the level of unoriginal, quickly scribbled graffiti on the sidewalk. Against the backdrop of these scribblings, the poem itself emerges as an attempt to try to find lasting truths from these images he recalls from a brush with what had threatened to be a national (if not a worldwide) calamity.

Thomas J. Cassidy

TEARS, IDLE TEARS

Author: Alfred, Lord Tennyson (1809-1892)
Type of poem: Lyric
First published: 1847, in *The Princess*

The Poem

Though often printed as a separate poem, "Tears, Idle Tears" is actually part of *The Princess* (1847), a long poem in which Alfred, Lord Tennyson explores questions of feminism and the proper roles of the sexes. In fact, the lyric is not titled at all in the original publication; rather, the first words of the opening line have come to serve as an identifying tag for the poem.

While one need not be familiar with *The Princess* to appreciate "Tears, Idle Tears," some understanding of the dramatic situation in which the lyric is presented may help explain its theme and account for its particular imagery. This lyric is sung by one of the maidens residing at the castle of Princess Ida, an independent young woman who has retreated from society with some of her female colleagues to found a school from which men are excluded. She is pursued there by the Prince, who is in love with her; he infiltrates her castle disguised as a woman. At the moment in *The Princess* when this song is sung, Ida, her friends, and the Prince are relaxing at sunset. Hence, the mood of this lyric, that of sober melancholy, seems appropriate for the setting in which it appears.

Even if one is not familiar with *The Princess*, however, "Tears, Idle Tears" can be read as a powerful statement about the impact of the past. In the poem, the speaker laments the passing of time that has robbed him of the chance to relive cherished experiences. This meditation is brought on by a sudden unexplained welling-up of tears in the speaker's eyes. The cause for the speaker's feeling of sadness cannot be determined, and he never hints directly at what might be the source of his own tears; instead, he tries to explain how he feels by comparing his feelings to a series of events that produce similar emotions in others.

In the middle two stanzas, the speaker focuses his attention on these "days that are no more"—a phrase that serves as a kind of refrain in the final line of each stanza of the poem. He first compares his feelings about bygone times to the experience one has when anticipating the arrival of friends from afar, and then seeing them sail away beyond the horizon as they return to faraway lands. In the third stanza, the speaker likens his emotions to those of a dying man who sees a summer dawn and hears birds piping outside his window. In the final stanza, the speaker compares his feeling for the past to that of "remember'd kisses after death" (line 16)—though it is not clear who has died and who lives on—and to the recollections of one's first love with all its passion and all its regret.

Forms and Devices

One might expect that if a poem's first line speaks of tears, the poem would be about uncontrolled emotion. Perhaps Tennyson is relying on such an initial response to create a certain tension in "Tears, Idle Tears," for there is little sense of wild abandon in these lines. On the contrary, all the formal devices and literary tropes suggest a great sense of emotional restraint.

As he does in most of his compositions, Tennyson relies on several formal devices to convey a note of restraint. The blank verse lines and the extensive use of enjambment create a meditative, conversational atmosphere. Each of the stanzas is linked to the others, however, by a closing phrase: "the days that are no more." This refrain develops in readers a sense of anticipation and fulfillment and establishes a common thread to each of the images described in the stanzas: All are intended to remind the reader of the passing of time and the losses that come with such passing; by implication, the reader is reminded also of the inevitability of death.

Even more than these formal devices, the imagery of "Tears, Idle Tears" focuses the reader's attention on the melancholy calm and the sense of irony that comes with the mature contemplation of life's passing. Each stanza concentrates on a single example that illustrates a sense of loss. In the first stanza, the poet presents an individual looking out at "happy Autumn-fields" (line 4) — certainly a time for bittersweet memories, as autumn traditionally suggests an impending ending — and reflecting, as the seasons change, on times past. This reflection brings these "idle tears" to the eyes.

In the second stanza, the sense of loss is compared to the feelings one has when good friends come to visit and then leave. This is the most complex image in the poem. There is a sense of joy at seeing the "glittering on a sail" (line 6) as the ship bringing the friends tops the horizon; that feeling is balanced with the sadness that sweeps over one when those same friends depart. Of particular interest are the words Tennyson chooses to describe the arrival and departure of the ship: the friends appear to be coming "up from the underworld" (line 7), and when they depart, the ship carrying them seems to sink "below the verge" (line 9). This voyage carries symbolic overtones; it is as if the voyage represents the passage of life itself.

That same image is carried forward and made explicit in the third stanza, where the speaker suggests that his idle tears are like those of the dying man who sees a summer dawn. This individual knows that he will not see many (if any) more, and the melancholy produced by that realization is the source of his tears. Similarly, in the final stanza, the tears are likened to those that well up in people who recall with joy and regret a love affair that has ended with no hope of renewal. The individual who experiences such feelings is living a "Death in Life" (line 20): He is alive, but he knows that a part of him — the part that shared those happy times in the past — is gone forever. The realization of his loss is the cause for what appears to be unexplained melancholy and the source for his "idle tears."

Themes and Meanings

Within the context of *The Princess*, this lyric provides Tennyson with an opportunity to show the immaturity of his heroine, who rebukes the maiden singing the lyric. Recognizing that the song's purpose is to remind the listeners of the sadness that comes from reflecting on the past, the Princess rejects that attitude explicitly and vehemently, saying that "all things serve their time . . . let the past be past." She even calls such reminiscences "fatal to men" and recommends that the company "cram our ears with wool" to avoid hearing such maudlin thoughts. As the long narrative poem progresses, however, the Princess comes to realize that a mature contemplation of the past is an important attribute of sensitive adults.

Viewing the lyric outside the context of the long poem in which it first appeared, readers should see that Tennyson's major theme is the sadness and irony that accompanies such reflection on bygone times. There seems little hope or optimism in these lines; every image suggests the futility and even the incomprehensibility (on an emotional level, if not on an intellectual one) of coping with lost time. It is important to note, however, that no image in the poem suggests that these feelings of sadness result from missed opportunity. Rather, the images convey a sense that they come from the realization that pleasurable experiences of the past may never be enjoyed again. Tennyson told his friend Frederick Locker-Lampson that the poem was motivated by "the yearning that young people occasionally experience for that which seems to have passed away from them forever" (Hallam Tennyson, *Memoir*, 1897). Such a remark is consistent with Tennyson's persistent infatuation with the past, and with his constant recognition that man is not able to relive past times and experiences. Though "Tears, Idle Tears" is not a part of Tennyson's most famous long poem, *In Memoriam* (1850), it shares the same mood as many of the lyrics that make up the poet's elegy to his dear friend Arthur Henry Hallam, who died suddenly in 1833. Tennyson spent almost two decades composing poetry inspired by feelings of loss at the death of Hallam; composed in the mid-1840's after a visit to the region where Hallam is buried, "Tears, Idle Tears" shows the same characteristics of restraint in its presentation of emotion and the same penetrating insight into the nature of loss that the poet expresses so poignantly in his major elegiac work.

Laurence W. Mazzeno

THE TEETH MOTHER NAKED AT LAST

Author: Robert Bly (1926-   )
Type of poem: Meditation
First published: 1970; revised in *Sleepers Joining Hands*, 1973; further revised in *Selected Poems*, 1986

The Poem

"The Teeth Mother Naked at Last" is a long, frequently subjective, meditation on the American involvement in the Vietnam War. It describes the "harm" the war has done to America and to Americans "inwardly." The poem is divided into seven numbered and self-contained sections ranging in length (in the final *Selected Poems* version) from eight to fifty-three lines. Each section is divided into stanzas of uneven lengths. Several sections are further divided into subsections, separated by asterisks, and section 3 contains two paragraphs of prose. One part of section 2 was originally published independently, in quite different form, in *The Nation* (March 25, 1968), and another part of this section originally appeared in Robert Bly's play, *The Satisfaction of Vietnam* (1968).

The title refers to one of the "mothers" that make up the mystical cult of the Great Mother, which first appeared in ancient times. The Teeth or Stone Mother attempts to destroy consciousness and spiritual growth and has come to stand for the destruction of the psyche in Jungian psychology.

The poem begins with airplanes and helicopters ("death-bees") lifting off from the decks of ships and flying over Vietnamese villages to bomb the people huddled in the "vegetable-walled" huts. This massive destruction, without mercy even for innocent children, is seen as the end result of what has happened in the American political system. The voices of soldiers are heard ordering the killing of "anything moving," and the reed huts of the Vietnam villagers are set afire. The war, with its wanton death and destruction, is defended and even rationalized by political and religious leaders and political and religious institutions back home in America. These rationalizations are "lies," however, and these lies "mean that the country wants to die." Things have already gone so far that even objective truths (such as the name of the capital of Wyoming, the number of acres of land in the Everglades, and the time the sun sets on any given day) now can be lied about by the president and the attorney general. This kind of corruption of the facts, in addition to the travesties and literal horrors of the war, are detailed primarily in the first three sections of the poem. "This," readers are told, "is what it's like for a rich country to make war."

The transitional fourth and fifth sections suggest a literal, structural, and thematic turn in the poem. The fifth and shortest section begins with the most pertinent question of the whole poem: "Why are they dying?" Since, as has been seen and shown, there is no rational reason given, nor any answer available, the remaining sections of the poem move beyond the rational, into the mystical or metaphysical realms, in an attempt to deal with the atrocities inherent in war psychologically. In this sense, although the clear focus of the poem remains fixed on the Vietnam War, the poem expands this focus to a treatment of the psychological accoutrements of war in general.

The sixth section of the poem, which describes the burning of innocent children, is the most graphic and the most condemnatory. The speaker finds himself suddenly forced backward through the evolutionary chain, to the consciousness of his "animal brain," which allows for a more emotional and less intellectual way of dealing with existence. Such a place in the psyche is also the place where poetry has its source and, thus, this movement down into the depths of the psyche prepares the reader for the poetic paean of the last two sections of the poem.

At the beginning of the seventh section the speaker says that he wants to sleep without being awakened. In his apocalyptic dream vision, from "waters" deep beneath the surface of self and consciousness, "the Teeth Mother, naked at last," rises up and points to the possibility of both a political and a psychic renewal, one which may vitiate the problems posed both by the war in Vietnam and by war in general.

Forms and Devices

If "The Teeth Mother Naked at Last" is thought of as political satire, it may also be seen to combine elements of several of the traditional kinds of satire. It is a formal satire in that it makes a direct frontal attack on its adversary, naming names. At the same time, Bly combines elements of the two traditional varieties of satire: the Horatian (through his use of informal diction and the long Whitmanesque line) and the Juvenalian (through the gravity and seriousness of the threat posed and the hoped for serious and positive reaction solicited). Further, using another traditional satiric device, Bly approaches his theme indirectly via the third-person point of view — although, significantly (after slipping in and out of the first and third persons) the point of view shifts dramatically to the first person in the short, climactic fifth section, and it keeps to that point of view throughout the rest of the poem. This shift in the point of view, from the third person to the first, forces the theme and meaning of the poem to the immediate moment and puts it in terms that make it definitively personal.

One of the most conspicuous poetic devices in the poem is Bly's vivid, often surprising and startling (if sometimes arbitrary or gratuitous) use of imagery and metaphor. Bly is known for his interest in, and his often obsessional use of, "deep images" — that is, images that combine or fuse disparate or unlikely elements and often attempt to connect the physical world with the psychic or spiritual world. Such images are clearly in evidence throughout this poem and they come to climax at the very end of it in such lines as "Let us drive cars/ up/ the light beams/ of the stars."

Another conspicuous device (which Bly here appropriates for the first time in his work) is the long line, which he discovered in the poetry of Walt Whitman. This long line, and the form his poem takes are, according to Bly himself, most appropriate for "public" and "political" poetry because, as he says in his essay "Whitman's Line as a Public Form," "The subject of political poetry is power, and . . . I felt drawn to a line that handles power . . . directly."

Finally, in a poem of this length, what is perhaps most important is rhythm. As "The Teeth Mother Naked at Last" moves smoothly through its themes and through the nightmares of the landscape of war, there are logical and imaginative "leaps" in the lines, as well as seemingly irrational associations. These "leaps" are intended to suggest and parallel similar leaps and irrational shiftings in the political and social fabric of a society attempting to justify its involvement in war. Such imaginative "bullets" are Bly's own "bombing raid" on warmongers.

Themes and Meanings

The main theme of "The Teeth Mother Naked at Last" is the age-old theme of the terror and the horror wrought by war. This poem reminds one of other powerful antiwar poems, both about the Vietnam War and other, earlier, wars. Now that war involves the prospect of and, indeed, the inevitability of, mass destruction— including the innocent as well as the "guilty"—the issues have become more demanding, just as the terrors have become more terrifying. There is, then, a greater pressure to protest. Bly's poem leads the way.

"The Teeth Mother Naked at Last" is a poem that demands a response and a reaction. In form and theme, in its large and small design, it forces the reader toward making a response, toward a reaction, and toward taking action.

Like many of Bly's shorter antiwar poems in *The Light Around the Body* (1967), "The Teeth Mother Naked at Last" is didactic, propagandistic, and controversial, both in terms of its theme and its "meaning" or significance. It is a political, social, even psychological analysis of the malaise of modern society, which came to a climax in the Vietnam War—a war here seen and described as the latest, the most immediate, and the most terrifying example of man's inhumanity to man. In forcing these issues on the reader, Bly is attempting to awaken readers from the sleeplike state in which they have existed and continue to exist, to awaken them to what they are doing to themselves as well as to others by allowing such things as the Vietnam War to occur, and to motivate them toward taking positive action (life-giving instead of life-taking) to see that such wars never happen again.

In order for this to happen, however, men and women must be able to understand themselves to the depths of their beings; they must be able to acknowledge the Teeth Mother, "naked at last," and they must be able to deal with her in appropriate political and psychological ways. This is what the final lines of Bly's poem imply. Humans must, yes, move outward into space and explore the outer reaches of the universe, but even more important, they must, simultaneously travel through the depths of their own inner psychic "spaces" and make, if necessary, even a martyr's sacrifice for what they find there, for what they must most believe in.

Here, then, is the shock of recognition and realization, the full and final realization of the significance and the power of the "Teeth Mother" who has hidden away in Western culture and in everyone's own individual psychic selves for so long, buried so deeply that only something like the Vietnam War could force her, "naked at last," back into view, demanding to be seen and heard. "The Teeth Mother Naked at Last" is Robert Bly's most important poetic response to the demands forced out into the world by the Teeth Mother.

William V. Davis

THE TENNIS COURT OATH

Author: John Ashbery (1927-   )
Type of poem: Lyric
First published: 1962, in *The Tennis Court Oath*

The Poem

"The Tennis Court Oath" is a poem in free verse, its forty-nine lines divided into six stanzas of varying length. The title has a double suggestiveness, only one aspect of which turns out to be relevant to the actual poem. The Tennis Court Oath was a key event of the French Revolution, an event in which the commoners (or Third Estate), having been locked out of a meeting of the Estates General, gathered in a nearby tennis court and vowed there to stand together until the Constitution could be reformed. John Ashbery's poem in no way retells or even refers to this incident. The title is also that of a famous painting by the French painter Jacques-Louis David, one in which the oath-taking is seen in an extremely heroic light. David never completed the painting, and this irony of heroism combined with incompleteness is very relevant to the methods of this poem, a poem whose first-person speaker remains permanently "incomplete."

The key to enjoying this difficult poem is found in its very first line. The phrase "What had you been thinking about" offers perspectives from which to view the many unfinished sentences and narratives that arise and disappear willy-nilly throughout the piece. The phrase asks a question that can never be completely answered, because one person's thoughts can never be completely transferred to the mind of another; thoughts are unique and finite events. Because it is "thinking" itself that this poem wishes to penetrate, it rightfully proceeds as a stream of consciousness, a flow of partial and only partially comprehensible incidents, images, and assertions.

The first stanza initiates the stream of consciousness with phrases of sinister import, such as "the face studiously bloodied" and "a terrible breath in the way," whose tones are of paradox and obscurity. Someone is not elected, though he or she "won the race." There is a fragmentary journey concealed not only by incompleteness but also by literal "fog and drizzle," and the journey is threatened with failure by a horse's fatigue. No wonder, then, that the stanza ends, "I worry." The promptings of hidden danger and violence and of unreached destinations cannot help but conjure a mood of anxiety—the sort of anxiety which, in other circumstances, might well prompt one to ask a friend or lover (the theme of hopeless love surfaces briefly in line 4), "What had you been thinking?"

Through the ensuing stanzas, the poem gathers dizzying momentum, leading the motifs of danger and journey through many variations. In the second stanza, an insect's head becomes a grotesque mirror that reflects breathing and dancing, while the journey is transformed into both a postal correspondence and a camping trip. Stanzas 3 and 4 bring one to a house in which one is approached (but never reached) by a nameless woman. Then, in the final two stanzas, one is outdoors once again, responding along with "the doctor and Philip" to some indistinct but bloody emergency, perhaps inside the house that had been so briefly entered. In the end, "there [is] no turning back but the end [is] in sight." The stream of consciousness becomes a dream, part of a fevered illness that is past now. True to its nature, the poem does not conclude but rather disappears through a dark hole, inscrutably "glad" to have made its inscrutable journey.

Forms and Devices

Virtually all the elusive but memorable effects of "The Tennis Court Oath" are products of its central technique: its stream-of-consciousness approach. In the modern period, such innovative novelists as James Joyce, William Faulkner, and Virginia Woolf employed this technique as a means of probing beneath the social and dramatic façades of their characters in order to illuminate psychological motives and complexities which might otherwise have passed, as do most thoughts, out of existence unremarked. In novels, stream of consciousness usually has a context within the wider frame of setting and plot. In poetry, however, it appears unframed and so challenges the reader with the suddenness of surprise. Thus, Ashbery's technique has much more in common with the aleatory or "automatic writing" methods of André Breton and other French Surrealist poets of the early twentieth century. Since the poem's title refers, however ironically, to an incident of French history and was indeed composed during Ashbery's ten-year residence in Paris, its use of a characteristically French poetic technique seems entirely appropriate.

The principal effect of aleatory poetry is one of disruption. By rejecting conventional expository techniques, by rejecting even the conventions of syntax and grammar, it forces readers to abandon their usual habits of reading and thinking and so to improvise new ways of understanding that will, of necessity, be unique to each individual poem. Every aleatory poem is a category unto itself, and this absolute originality is a primary aim of the technique. Nothing but "The Tennis Court Oath" teaches one to read "The Tennis Court Oath." It accumulates rather than unfolds, as its fragmentary lines — by not completing their thoughts — trigger new fragments via undisclosed motives of free association and private emotion. Amid these fragments, readers become co-authors of the poem, sorting and combining the fragments according to their own experiences and states of mind. In this way, the poem becomes an event of potentially infinite variety, as opposed to an object to be dutifully comprehended, and this is clearly another aim of the aleatory poet: to win an active instead of a passive readership and so gain a permanent timeliness for the poem.

One may think of "The Tennis Court Oath" as one thinks of a collage. The lines, like newspaper clippings, once removed from an ordinary narrative context, placed alongside other lines similarly removed, and then arranged in an explicitly suprarational sequence, challenge a reader to make the connections which the artist refuses to make on the reader's behalf. The effect is atmospheric rather than thematic, similar to that of a dream whose emotional atmosphere lingers in the mind long after the incidental details of the dream have faded away. Everything in "The Tennis Court Oath" is a potential metaphor, and each image stands willing to allow any reader to use it as a key to his or her interpretation of the dream that is the reading of the poem.

Themes and Meanings

On one level, "The Tennis Court Oath" is a poem about the possibilities of poetry itself. For John Ashbery, the purpose of poetry is not communication in the sense of a message delivered or of an idea expressed. It is, instead, communication as the continuous encounter between ideas and things in language on the page and in language in the mind. In the fragmentary rhetoric of this poem, one can never be certain whether a given word is the object of one verb or the subject of the next. One does not know what to subordinate to what, just as one cannot determine plot from subplot or reality from dream in the inconstant landscape of the poem's progress. For Ashbery, this indeterminacy represents the liberation of poetry from poetic precedent, a chance for the poem to be read only by its own and its readers' own lights. The poem becomes an exemplary act of literary sabotage, a bomb tossed into the anthologies that readers carry in their minds from one work of literature to another.

Yet the theme of "The Tennis Court Oath" resonates beyond the limits of poetry alone. Its stylistic indeterminacy, when applied to its enigmatic journeys, emphasizes the uncertainty of all travel, the intriguing if unsettling reality that not all destinations are reached or even known. As the poem is enriched by incompleteness, so too may the actual journeys of life be enriched by liberation from fixed objectives. Since the only absolutely certain point of arrival is death (a point anticipated by the poem's allusions to violence and melodramatic murder), perhaps it is best to postpone arrival, just as Ashbery's sentence fragments strive to postpone the inevitable, final punctuation mark.

This poem works to revise accepted notions of interpretation as well as those of anticipation. As the ends of things are entrusted to uncertainty, so too are the precise identities of objects and events encountered en route to the ends. This is why the poem moves restlessly back and forth between tones of menace and of slapstick, images of blood and of surreal vistas of candy and pink stripes. Every stanza can be several, utterly contradictory stanzas, depending upon which words a given reader chooses to emphasize. It is the final randomness of such emphasis that calls into doubt the possible accuracy of any interpretation of any circumstance. For Ashbery, experience is too quick and too complex to be contained by interpretation. Language can only pursue reality, never apprehend it. In "The Tennis Court Oath," this pursuit becomes a wild, improvisational dance to the limits of coherent writing.

Donald Revell